MEDIATING MODERNISMS

MODERNIST EXCHANGES

General editors: Ruth B. Phillips

and Nicholas Thomas

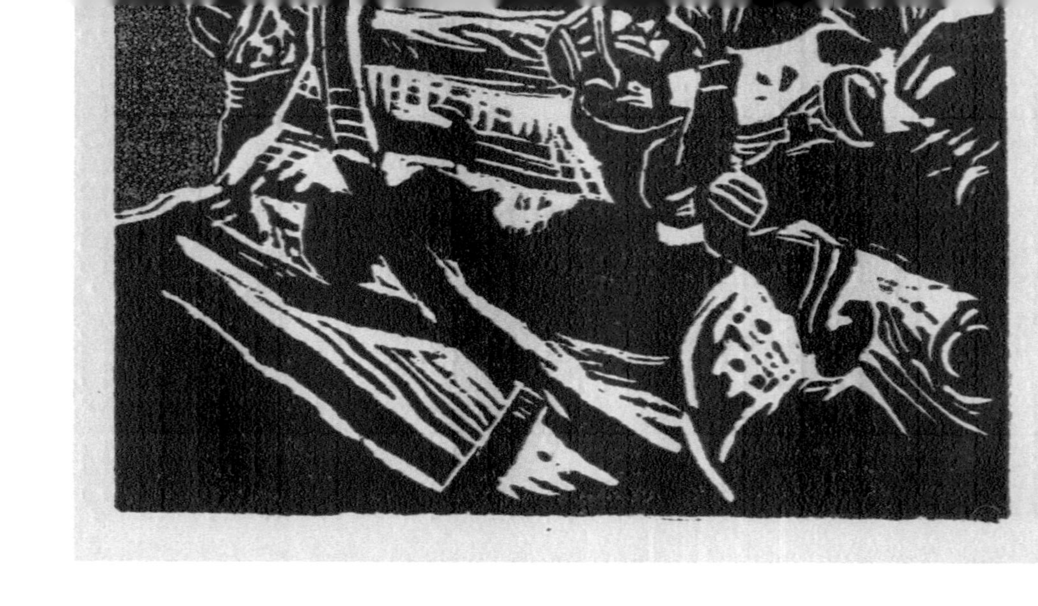

OBJECTS/HISTORIES: CRITICAL PERSPECTIVES ON ART, MATERIAL CULTURE, AND REPRESENTATION

A series edited by Nicholas Thomas

Ruth B. Phillips and Norman Vorano | EDITORS

MEDIATING MODERNISMS

INDIGENOUS ARTISTS, MODERNIST MEDIATORS, GLOBAL NETWORKS

Duke University Press | Durham and London | 2025

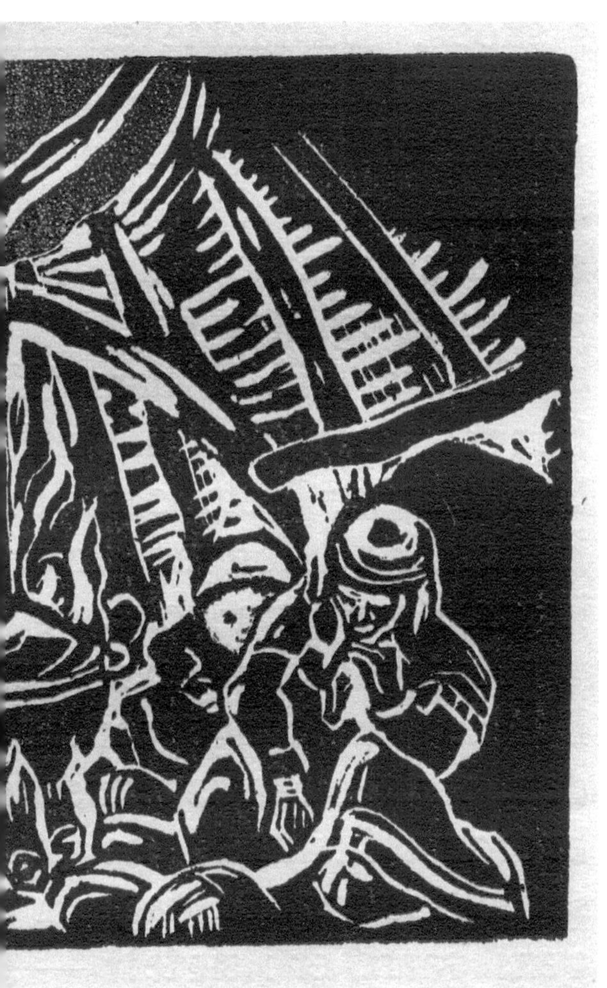

Printed in the United States of America on acid-free paper ∞
Project Editor: Michael Trudeau
Typeset in Minion Pro and Futura by Westchester Publishing Services

Library of Congress Cataloging-in-Publication Data
Names: Phillips, Ruth B. (Ruth Bliss), [date] editor. | Vorano, Norman, [date] editor.
Title: Mediating modernisms : Indigenous artists, modernist mediators, global networks / Ruth B. Phillips and Norman Vorano, editors.
Description: Durham : Duke University Press, 2025. | Series: Objects/histories | Includes bibliographical references and index.
Identifiers: LCCN 2025006813 (print)
LCCN 2025006814 (ebook)
ISBN 9781478032366 (paperback)
ISBN 9781478029007 (hardcover)
ISBN 9781478061212 (ebook)
Subjects: LCSH: Indigenous art—Themes, motives. | Modernism (Art) | Intercultural communication in art. | Influence (Literary, artistic, etc.)
Classification: LCC N6351.2.I53 .M43 2025 (print) | LCC N6351.2.I53 (ebook) | DDC 709.05—dc23/eng/20250228
LC record available at https://lccn.loc.gov/2025006813
LC ebook record available at https://lccn.loc.gov/2025006814

Frontispiece: Emilie Demant Hatt, Untitled, undated. Linoleum block print. Printed at page 47 in E. D. Hatt, *Ved ilden* [By the fire], 1922.

Cover art: Jacques Zigoma, Untitled, 1955. Gouache on vellum, 31 cm × 34.5 cm. Photo courtesy of the Annex Galleries, Santa Rosa, California.

Duke University Press gratefully acknowledges the Department of Art History and Art Conservation, Queen's University at Kingston, Canada, and the Social Science and Humanities Research Council of Canada, which provided funds toward the publication of this book.

CONTENTS

ILLUSTRATIONS

RUTH B. PHILLIPS AND NICHOLAS THOMAS

GENERAL EDITORS' FOREWORD

Within the larger Objects/Histories series, this smaller set of volumes addresses the diverse lives that artistic modernism has had beyond the West during the twentieth century. This book, the second of two volumes, explores the fertile exchanges between local artists and those of European descent, among them radical expatriates, in colonial settings. A symptom of the complexity and heterogeneity of such settings is that some of those local artists are referred to, and refer to themselves, as Indigenous; for others, that term is less appropriate. The focus on Africa, Oceania, and the Americas fills a gap in current scholarship that is a legacy of Western modernism's much-debated primitivism.

In response to the striking absence of these art histories from global narratives, in 2010 we initiated a program of research and discussion that has resulted in these publications. From the outset, the agenda was not simply to pluralize a monolithic Western construct. We take it for granted, as many readers will, that the humanities and social sciences have moved in that direction. Yet this epistemological sea change does not in itself enable any genuine understanding of the diversity of modernist innovation beyond the West, the legacies of modernist primitivism, or the ambivalent exchanges between European cultural brokers and those they stimulated and mentored. Whereas globalization was already a cliché of the international art world by the late twentieth century, the apparent inclusiveness of biennials had in no way been matched by an adequate account of the Native modernisms of the interwar years or those of the fifties and sixties. In part for telling reasons—these artists' notions of self, history, and culture preceded and were somewhat incommensurable with the formations of identity politics that gained ascendancy in the seventies—the art world, and the critical writing around it, has suffered a kind of amnesia regarding these remarkable and formative histories.

Scholars have produced fine studies focused on artists in specific countries and regions, including books previously published in the Objects/Histories series, but the subject also demands a wider, comparative approach, which can reveal both the shared experiences engendered by colonial policies and the specificity of local responses. This set of volumes draws on the work of scholars from Australia, Canada, Aotearoa New Zealand, South Africa, the United Kingdom, the United States, and elsewhere who collectively bring decades of research experience into the remarkable lives of Indigenous artists and their strange and paradoxical dealings with Western mentors and institutions. The heterogeneity of milieux and artists' trajectories, as well as the successes and failures of these artists' work, are vital to the understanding we seek to achieve and convey. One aim is to tell some of their stories. Another is to exemplify, rather than merely declare the need for, a genuinely global art history.

We wish to acknowledge the support of the Sterling and Francine Clark Art Institute, Carleton University, Victoria University, the Museum of Archaeology and Anthropology at the University of Cambridge, and our major sponsor, the Leverhulme Trust. A Leverhulme international network award (2013–14) and the institutions mentioned supported workshops and public conferences at the Clark, in Williamstown, Massachusetts (2011); the National Gallery of Canada, Ottawa (2012); Cambridge (2013 and 2017); the Museum of New Zealand Te Papa Tongarewa, Wellington (2014); Wits University, Johannesburg (2016); and the University of Cape Town (2016). It is a pleasure also to thank Ken Wissoker of Duke University Press for his long-standing and continuing enthusiasm for this project.

RUTH B. PHILLIPS AND NORMAN VORANO

PREFACE

This volume is the second to be produced by the Multiple Modernisms collaboration. In the genealogy of our project, however, the focus on mediation came first and provided the point of departure for the broader project. The book thus complements our first publication, *Mapping Modernisms: Art, Indigeneity, Colonialism*, coedited by Elizabeth Harney and Ruth Phillips, which introduces key issues that arise out of the Indigenous uptake and cocreation of twentieth-century artistic modernism. That volume both frames and extends the case studies presented here.

Mediation is an ever-present issue for scholars who study the modernist arts produced by Indigenous and colonized peoples. To be sure, mediatory processes lie behind the emergence of all artistic forms across time, but for twentieth-century Indigenous arts, such processes were inevitably enmeshed within matrices of post/colonial cultural politics and their related discourses of anthropology, fine art, craft, and tourist art. Mediation haunts accounts that assign primary agency for the emergence of these arts to outsiders who taught, marketed, commissioned, bought, or otherwise promoted the works of Indigenous artists who had previously been assigned to and confined by the category of primitive art. Equally, however, it haunts narratives that credit Indigenous artists as the sole originators of these arts, representing them as unique and autonomous actors.

For us, as editors, as for many of our collaborators, that haunting has been both personal and professional. Each of us encountered the phenomenon of mediation and the miasma of compromised authenticity it generates early in our careers. For Phillips it arose in the 1960s when, as an undergraduate interested in African art, she visited her parents who were working in northern Nigeria. Her mother had recently seen two local exhibitions, one displaying art produced by young Yoruba artists in the workshops organized by Ulli and Georgina Beier at

Oshogbo (see chapter 1, this volume), and the other wooden panels produced with the support of a Ford Foundation program that encouraged Nupe carvers to adapt their tradition of relief carving on wooden doors to a new production of self-standing, marketable panels that could be hung as works of art in expat living rooms. "Are these art forms authentic?" her mother asked. How to answer that question would preoccupy Phillips for decades to come.

For Vorano, the problem of mediation arose from an arresting juxtaposition that struck him as an undergraduate student in the mid-1990s. He had read the recently released autobiography of James Houston, *Confessions of an Igloo Dweller*, before proceeding to the Art Gallery of Ontario to view a large exhibition of Inuit art. The modern gallery's aestheticization of Inuit sculpture, which presented the art within an isolated and atemporal "ethnographic present," obscured the complex networks of influence, interaction, and intervention that were plainly evident throughout Houston's memoir as he recounted his efforts to create the formal market for Inuit art in the 1950s and early 1960s. For Vorano, Houston's activities elicited a complex admixture of admiration, circumspection, and curiosity and raised uneasy but necessary questions about the ethics of intercultural work in Indigenous and colonial contexts. Are intercultural efforts doomed to reinscribe the very imbalances they purport to dismantle, or, in our increasingly globalized world, are such efforts more necessary today than ever before?

Surely, these histories have much to offer to our contemporary moment, in which we celebrate the prominence of global contemporary arts while navigating the revivals of cultural essentialisms, new tribalisms, and ethnic nationalisms. Like many others, we and our contributors have had to negotiate the pull of art historical narratives toward simplistic origin stories for Indigenous modernisms. As the case studies presented in this volume illustrate, the histories of Indigenous modernism have shown themselves to be much more complex, reflecting global networks and dialogic interactions that unfolded through relationships and encounters that were pedagogical, commercial, collegial, friendly, or a combination.

The problem of mediation inspired the launch-gathering organized by Ruth Phillips in 2011 and generously supported by the workshop program of the Clark Art Institute in Williamstown, Massachusetts. The initial group of ten art historians and anthropologists who assembled there on two memorable days in May to discuss "Global Indigenous Modernisms: Primitivism, Artists, Mentors" included many of the contributors to this book as well as other important voices.[1] We are indebted to the Clark Art Institute for providing an ideal venue for our initial discussions and to all the participants for helping us to map out the project as a whole. The design of the book has also greatly benefited from the helpful comments of the anonymous reviewers engaged by Duke University Press. With their encouragement, we have broadened the volume's initial geographical and conceptual scope by including additional chapters that address Australian Aboriginal, Sámi, and Mithila modernisms.

This volume's more specific origin lies in the second of our symposia, held in 2013 at Corpus Christi College, University of Cambridge. We thank both Corpus Christi College and the Museum of Archaeology and Anthropology for their warm hospitality and support of that conference. We are especially indebted to the Leverhulme Trust for the International Network Grant it awarded to Nicholas Thomas that funded the Cambridge meeting and the two that followed in New Zealand and South Africa. The grant also funded the salary of our network facilitator, Georgina Amos, who ably organized the Cambridge conference and coordinated communications and arrangements for the others. The award of a Social Sciences and Humanities Research Council of Canada research grant to this volume's editors supported additional research and the invaluable research assistance of Lisa Truong, without whose patient and efficient help this volume could never have come into being. Queen's University generously provided financial assistance for this publication while in-kind support was provided by Carleton University.

This book has taken far longer to complete than any of us could have foreseen. The global halt imposed by the COVID-19 pandemic was, of course, a huge brake on its completion, but beyond that, several contributors and their close family members have experienced serious health crises that brought about further delays. We cannot sufficiently express our gratitude to them and to our other collaborators — including Duke University Press — for their patience and commitment to seeing the publication through to completion amid so much personal and societal turmoil. We hope and trust that the results more than fulfil their faith in the importance of the project.

Note

1. The Clark participants were Bill Anthes, Peter Brunt, Elizabeth Harney, Sandra Klopper, Ian McLean, Kobena Mercer, Anitra Nettleton, Chika Okeke-Agulu, Ruth Phillips, Jackson Rushing, Nicholas Thomas, Susan Vogel, and Norman Vorano. Michael Ann Holly, Keith Moxey, Griselda Pollock, and other Clark staff and fellows sat in on a number of the discussions and made important comments.

RUTH B. PHILLIPS AND NORMAN VORANO

INTRODUCTION **INDIGENIZING MODERNISM, MODERNIZING PRIMITIVISM**

Mediators and Artists in Twentieth-Century Global Art Worlds

Four Moments of Mediation

The global history of modern art is punctuated by innovative modernisms mediated through the encounters of creative artists from Indigenous and colonized communities with cosmopolitan men and women who conveyed the tenets of artistic modernism into local art worlds. Consider, for a start, four nearly contemporaneous vignettes from the early 1960s:

> ***Maphumulo, KwaZulu-Natal, South Africa*** *The young Swedish artists Peder and Ulla Gowenius, recently married graduates of Stockholm's Konstfack, begin to teach at the Evangelical Lutheran Church mission, later to become the home of the Rorke's Drift Arts and Crafts Centre. In accordance with the missionaries' desire to impart remunerative skills to African students, they focus on "crafts" that can be marketed to tourists and settlers. Azaria Mbatha, one of Peder's first students, is drawn instead to graphic expression and the medium of black and white linoleum prints. His images blend elements of his Christian and Zulu identities but also reference the brutal violence of the apartheid system.*[1] *For Western modernists, Mbatha's prints are reminiscent of German Expressionist woodcuts. Five years later, in 1967, Mbatha's powerful images are among the first works created by a South African artist to be acquired by New York's Museum of Modern Art.*

Red Lake, Ontario, Canada *Nine-thousand miles away, artist and educator Selwyn Dewdney, a graduate of the Ontario College of Art, is pursuing research on Indigenous rock paintings in the northern Ontario mining town of Red Lake. He befriends an Anishinaabe "informant," an aspiring young artist named Norval Morrisseau, and the two begin an active correspondence. In his letters, Dewdney describes modern easel painting techniques and advises Morrisseau on how to sell his paintings in urban galleries. Morrisseau sends him his drawings and transcriptions of Anishinaabe oral traditions and Dewdney sends back his copies of rock paintings no longer known to most Anishinaabeg. Access to this ancestral graphic tradition proves critical to Morrisseau's reinvention of Anishinaabe pictorial representation in a modernist mode and leads to his 1962 breakout exhibit in a Toronto art gallery.*[2] *Morrisseau's paintings, inspired by Anishinaabe stories and spirit beings, are snapped up by cosmopolitan collectors and museums and launch a new art movement. In 2007, he becomes the first First Nations artist to be given a retrospective exhibition at the National Gallery of Canada.*

Ruatoria, Aotearoa New Zealand *Gordon Tovey, a professionally-trained artist and civil servant in Aotearoa New Zealand's education ministry, is devising innovative school art programs that include both traditional Māori arts and modernist European concepts and practices. His teacher-training program attracts a coterie of young Māori students, including Ralph Hotere, Para Matchitt, and Clifford Whiting, who begin to work in modernist modes alongside their employment as art teachers.*[3] *A critical moment comes in 1960 when Tovey invites discussion of the relationship between Māori tradition and modernist innovation at a national hui, or meeting, at Ruatoria. Master traditional carver Pine Taiapa explains the rules of traditional design and advises the young Māori artists: "In tackling anything new, study the old first. Having absorbed it, pick up its best points . . . then launch out." Tovey responds: "I think, from what you've said, that as a very learned Māori . . . you would have no quarrel with a chap with a sensible changing of the symbols." "Correct," says Taiapa, "I'm all with him, all the time."*[4] *Matchitt, Whiting, and other artists respond, speaking to the ways in which the new practices and aesthetics offer opportunities to express their lived experiences as modern Māori. The meeting publicly legitimizes the modern Māori art movement.*

Osogbo, Nigeria *Ulli Beier, a young linguistics professor at the University of Ibadan, and his wife Georgina, a British-trained artist, begin running art workshops for students from the countryside who have had little access to formal art training. The Beiers invite the modernist Guyanese painter Denis Williams to run painting classes that introduce the students to Western materials and techniques derived from dada, surrealism, abstraction, and other European modernist movements foreign to traditional Yoruba modes of visual art production.*[5] *A young performer, Olaniyi Osuntoki, gravitates toward the free-form abstract painting exercises taught by the Beiers and Williams. His paintings re-imagine traditional Yoruba stories and cosmology in colorful, densely patterned compositions and are exhibited to great acclaim in the bustling metropolis of Lagos. Taking the name Twins Seven Seven, the young artist soon rises to prominence through exhibitions in modern and contemporary galleries around the world. Before his death in 2011 he becomes the subject of a book-length study by a renowned specialist in folk art and is appointed a* UNESCO *ambassador for art and peace.*[6]

The mediatory processes and dialogic relationships illustrated by these episodes are the subject of this book. Its chapters document and analyze twentieth-century exchanges between Indigenous artists living in colonial or neocolonial societies and men and women imbued with modernist aesthetics and ideologies who bridged highly diverse spaces of artistic production. These fertile relationships enabled artists to create new fusions of modernism with Indigenous art traditions. In many cases their experiments initiated or advanced innovative artistic movements through which art-world hierarchies and other barriers that prevented the recognition of Indigenous modernisms were broken down. They resulted in new genealogies of the modern and, we argue, fostered the wider institutional and discursive practices that have created the conditions for today's "global contemporary" art world to come into being. Yet despite their importance to Indigenous and world art histories, these critical episodes of mediation and the histories of heterodoxical modernisms to which they gave rise have been poorly documented, silenced, and mythologized. When studied, they have been considered in isolation from each other and, as a result, their shared features and historic interlinkages have stayed beneath the surface of standard narratives of artistic modernism.

It would be impossible in a single volume to survey the many such episodes that mark the twentieth-century history of global modernisms. Rather, this book presents a set of case studies that draw on recent research and, at the same time, represent a larger historical pattern. Their juxtapositions reveal shared ideological and aesthetic dynamics produced at the juncture of modernism, colonialism and postcolonialism and call out for focused scholarly attention. Our comparative framing reveals the structural parallels that link artists' negotiations of the dual duress of colonial educational policies and primitivist definitions of authenticity in different parts of the world. It yields insights into the dynamics of power as constituted and exercised by mediators and artists operating in an art world being rapidly reshaped by decolonizing, nationalist, and globalizing forces. Equally, by placing side-by-side episodes of mediation that occurred in Africa, North America, India, Scandinavia, Brazil, Australia, New Zealand, and the Pacific, we reveal the historical and cultural contingencies that made each iteration distinctive.

The fine-grained explorations of complex interactions and projects of cultural translation presented in this book also instantiate the variety of roles mediators have assumed as teachers, friends, patrons, dealers, advisers, and mentors, allowing us to posit a typology of mediatory roles. A further product of our comparative framing is the identification of networks of circulation that enabled ideas, people, texts, and objects to travel across widely dispersed sites around the world, interconnecting artists, mediators, markets, and institutions. These transnational networks were forged by colonial bureaucracies, individual and collective educational projects, migration, commerce, wars, exile, and travel, as well as by the concomitant flows of artworks, images, and media. These networked circulations of people, objects, and texts set modernism in motion, conveying modernist ideology and its stepchild, modernist primitivism, through an expanded global arena. By excavating little-known histories alongside better-known examples, we offer, then, a multisited exploration that demonstrates the generative potential of modernist ideology in colonial contact zones. These first-generation Indigenous modernists and the mediators with whom they worked laid the groundwork for the epochal shift from twentieth-century colonial matrices of institutional and political power to the global ecumene of today.

Discourses and Politics: Colonial/Postcolonial, Primitive/Indigenous

Each of the case studies is deeply entangled not only in imperial systems and localized experiences of twentieth-century modernity but also in anti-colonial movements and post–World War II geopolitics. Our focus on the twentieth century, and particularly on its middle decades, thus attends not only to the historical origins of many modernist Indigenous movements but also to the period — the Cold War looming in the background — when the formal structures of colonialism were beginning to break down. In this context our use of the term *indigeneity* requires explanation. In different parts of the world the term has been differently imposed, rejected, and embraced in relation to the colonial, postcolonial, and decolonial political dynamics that have played out during the past two centuries.[7] Indigenous identity (with a capital *I*) is claimed today by peoples who remain internally colonized in settler nations across the Americas, Australia, New Zealand, South Asia, Scandinavia, Russia, and elsewhere. In Africa and the independent nations of the Pacific, in contrast, self-identification as *indigenous* or *native* has become anachronistic and can be deemed politically compromised because it references evolutionist theories and colonial racial hierarchies. In East Asia — a regrettable omission in this volume caused by limits of space — *indigenous* is an evolving and highly contested concept and references yet another contrasting set of meanings.[8]

We use *Indigenous* here as a historically contingent construct assigned by colonial regimes during the nineteenth and twentieth centuries. During this historical period, designation as *Indigenous* or *native* carried significations of the primitive, the timeless, and the a-historical and legitimized the imposition of repressive social, political, and educational policies. It created similar barriers to and possibilities for artistic production in colonial societies around the world and stimulated recurrent patterns of relationship between artists and mediators in the geographically and culturally dispersed case studies we examine in this book. The cross-cutting and global applicability of indigeneity thus enables comparisons of shared systemic obstacles that had to be negotiated in order to access modernist art training and art world acceptance. Indigenous arts, we argue, continue to be haunted by these specters, which continue to shape institutional practices in relation to contemporary Indigenous arts and hinder the full recognition of twentieth-century modernisms.[9]

Virtually all the mediators whose activities are documented here were initially drawn to work with Indigenous artists because, as modernists, they were attracted to what they initially saw as survivals of "primitive art" doomed to soon disappear. As numerous scholars have shown, early critical appraisals of these pioneering modernists' work were also filtered through the temporal conventions and geographic hierarchies of midcentury modernist primitivism, preventing full acknowledgment of the artists' originality and contemporaneity while often positioning Indigenous artists as "lagging behind" or emulating their European and American counterparts.[10] The discursive possibilities offered by the category of "primitive art," like those associated with "folk" art, were simultaneously enabling and limiting. Identification with "primitive" or "folk" traditions might be the price of admission to a more cosmopolitan art world, exposure in national and international art magazines and exhibitions, and sales to a global clientele, but it also interposed a reductive and marginalizing lens and presented a key challenge to Indigenous artists drawn to modernism by associating them with the premodern.[11]

During the middle decades of the twentieth century, artists and mediators were thus differently motivated in their appropriations of ancestral traditions. Mediators treasured — at least initially — what they saw as precious remnants of disappearing traditions, while artists might appropriate primitivist discourse to create a space within modern Western art worlds for the affirmation and reinvigoration of ancestral beliefs. Our studies of mediation demonstrate, in other words, that modernist primitivism was not *just* a barrier to the recognition of the Indigenous modernisms but could also serve as a portal to the creation of new artistic amalgams of ancestral traditions and modernist formal innovation. Our studies of this "primitivist perplex" reveal how artists and mediators negotiated these apparent contradictions and, in the process, transformed not only modernism itself but also the preconceptions of mediators who gradually came to understand the new art forms as valid expressions of the artists' own modernity.

High stakes were and are involved in historical and current evaluations of Indigenous artistic modernisms. As the modern artistic productions of Indigenous peoples have come to be recognized as such, the impacts have reverberated well beyond the art world and into the world of politics and policy, preparing the ground for and supporting movements of social and political decolonization. In throwing off the identification of these arts with the "primitive" or the "folk," and affirming them as modern, artists claimed for themselves and their societies an equivalent modernity with colonial (or former colonial) mother countries and compelled a broader recognition of the survival and viability of Indigenous traditions within modernity. In modernism, then, artists and mediators discovered modes of expression whose value was at once personal and political. This point was expressed poignantly during research for this book in an interview with Peder Gowenius, who recounted meeting Paulo Freire, the influential Brazilian theorist of liberation pedagogy, at an educational conference in Africa in the 1970s. Freire described Gowenius's work with Black South African artists as "doing in practice what I have only written about."[12]

The expansive and transformative possibilities of modernism, albeit initially offered through a primitivist appreciation for folk arts, are also explored by Jyotindra Jain in this volume through his discussion of the painter Ganga Devi's development from her rural "folk" heritage of Madhumani mural painting to the intensely personal expression of her experiences of social marginalization, international travel, and ultimately fatal battle with cancer.

Global Paths of Dispersion: Refugee Modernists, Settler Nationalists, and Indigenous Artists

Our mid-twentieth-century focus also brings into relief the central importance to histories of Indigenous modernism of the diasporic movements of key bearers of artistic modernism that was set in motion by the rise of National Socialism in Germany and the global convulsion of World War II. These men and women were not only artists but also teachers, scholars, art dealers, patrons, museologists, and collectors. Anitra Nettleton notes the importance of refugee German Jewish art historian Maria Stein Lessing at the University of Johannesburg in introducing Cecil Skotnes—who would become a key teacher and mentor of Black South African artists in the 1960s—to African art. Other mediators imbued with a love of modernism who had been flung out of Europe and around the globe by World War II include Ulli Beier, introduced in one of our opening vignettes and further discussed by Chika Okeke-Agulu in his chapter. Beier arrived in Nigeria in the 1950s from England where he had found refuge as a youth with his German Jewish family.

The representative nature of these case studies is borne out by the agencies of other refugee artists such as Victor Lowenfeld and Olga Fisch, both of whom were trained in modernism in continental Europe art schools during the prewar period. Lowenfeld, an Austrian Jew who had studied art in Vienna, fled to the United States in 1938 and found a job teaching art to African American students at Hampton University in Virginia. One of his students, John Biggars, would become a leading figure in African American modernism and would, throughout his career, acknowledge the formative impact of Lowenfeld's tutelage and introduction to African art.[13] After his move to the University of Pennsylvania Lowenfeld would come to have a major influence as a theorist of art education designed to encourage children's creativity and mental growth. "The absolute necessity of this freedom of expression," writes Robert Saunders, "had become increasingly important to Lowenfeld as he fled with his family during the pogroms and purges of the Third Reich."[14] Olga Fisch had trained in modernist craft in Hungary and painting in Germany before fleeing to New York and then to Ecuador to escape Nazi persecution. Her primitivist tastes immediately led her to seek out Indigenous Ecuadorian "folk artists" with whom she worked to develop new textile genres that could be marketed through her gallery. One of the first clients for her rugs was the Museum of Modern Art, whose director she had met in New York City. Fisch's work with Indigenous Tigua artists resulted in a new genre of commercially viable paintings made by artists who had previously painted their pictorial scenes on ceremonial drums.[15]

The stories of Lowenfeld and Fisch are paralleled by that of George Swinton, the son of Austrian Jews whose family converted to Christianity soon after his birth and later fled Vienna for Canada after the Nazi Anschluss of 1938. After the war, Swinton studied art at the School of the Montreal Museum of Fine Arts and New York's Art Students League. He became an enthusiastic collector of the new Inuit soapstone carvings during the 1950s after joining the art faculty at the University of Manitoba in Winnipeg, where shipments of the sculptures were sent semiannually by the Hudson Bay Company. For twenty-five years Swinton made annual trips to the Arctic, befriending Inuit artists and writing about their work in widely read books and magazine articles. Although he had initially believed that he was witnessing the last phase of an authentic primitive art tradition, Swinton came gradually to understand and write about it as a fully modern aesthetic expression in the contemporary world, aligned with rapidly modernizing Inuit life ways and political goals.[16]

Unlike Lowenfeld, Fisch, and Swinton, Leonhard Adam was neither a professionally trained artist nor a man of means. He was, rather, a trained ethnologist specializing in law and anthropology who had held prominent positions in Berlin as the editor of a major journal and an associate of Berlin's ethnographic museum. Forced to flee to England after the Nazi purge of Jewish civil servants, Adam was interned as an enemy alien and sent to Australia after the outbreak of war. He remade his career as founder and curator of the University of Melbourne Museum and persuaded an indifferent university administration to create important ethnographic collections.[17] His evolving understanding of the aesthetic sophistication and contemporary authenticity of Australian Aboriginal bark paintings was manifested in his curatorial work for two major exhibitions of "primitive" and Australian art during the 1940s. Adam is, however, best known for making the subject of primitive art accessible to general audiences through the introductory survey he wrote for Penguin Books. First published in 1941, Adam's *Primitive Art* and its subsequent revisions testify to the changes that occurred in his understanding of his topic after he, like

Swinton, found himself living in a settler society with an Indigenous population still viewed through the lens of cultural evolutionist theory and subjected to racist laws and policies.[18]

The patronage role-played by other refugees could be equally influential. Walter Koerner, for example, a member of a Jewish family who collected old master and modernist art, fled Czechoslovakia for Canada in 1938. His impact would manifest itself through major projects of philanthropy and his friendship and support for the pioneering Haida artist Bill Reid. In a brief autobiographical account that prefaced the unpublished catalogue of his collection of historic northwest coast art, he contrasted Europe "as Hitler struck dread in the hearts of millions" to Canada, "a new land of hope." Traveling north in British Columbia to develop his lumber business, he commented that "to me, the endless forests, the gigantic size of the country, and the unknown were most exciting. Understandably, nothing seemed more desirable than to learn and see more of the indigenous people of this new land."[19]

Many other such men and women whose roles are less well known were joined in their mediatory projects by settler and Indigenous artists, teachers, and other intermediaries similarly imbued with modernist tastes and ideologies. In 1957, for example, the Brazilian graphic artist Servulo Esmeraldo adopted an abstract style in his prints after studying in Paris with Johnny Friedlaender, a modernist graphic artist who had fled Eastern Europe in 1937 as a Nazi refugee. By the early 1960s, Esmeraldo invited the Brazilian woodcut book illustrator of mixed African and Portuguese descent Mestre Noza to create a set of images for the Paris publisher Robert Morel. Esmeraldo's encouragement helped transform the woodblock prints made for ephemeral *cordal* booklets into framed "fine art" prints, which were soon featured at the São Paulo Biennial and picked up by commercial art galleries.[20]

In contrast to the refugee cohort, settler mentors were often motivated by additional goals that could include socialist or neoliberal political sympathies, opposition to racism and support for movements of social justice, and desires to forge distinctive national art movements that arose as their societies sought to free themselves from their own colonial and Eurocentric cultural dependencies. In the interwar years, Marsden Hartley and John Sloan in the United States, Margaret Preston in Australia, and Emily Carr in Canada focused attention on Indigenous arts through their quest to create an authentic national iconography. Preston cocurated (with Leonhard Adam) the first exhibition to position Australian Aboriginal bark paintings as admired "primitive art," while Carr mentored George Clutesi, a pioneering Nuu-chah-nulth artist who was developing his own artistic career by combining Western pictorial formats and easel painting with his ancestral northwest coast stylistic traditions and visual iconography. These widely dispersed and varied examples follow patterns of interaction that are modelled by the rigorously researched case studies offered by this volume. They — and no doubt many other still obscure episodes of modernist mediation — await fuller excavation that reveal the processes by which Indigenous modernisms emerged from local traditions in negotiation with Western modernism.

Like modernist primitivism itself, such projects were ridden with unresolved contradictions. Debates over the appropriation of Indigenous imagery by Preston, Carr, and other settler artists are ongoing, while accusations of paternalism striate these and many other mediatory encounters.[21] Yet, viewed within the terms of their own times, the mediatory activities of these artists appear more complex. Hanna Horsberg's chapter discusses an early twentieth-century encounter between Johan Turi, a Sámi man aspiring to represent his culture in text and image, and Emilie Demant Hatt, a young Danish art student who was fascinated by the nomadic life of Sámi reindeer hunters. As T. J. Jackson Lears has argued with regard to early twentieth-century American artists and intellectuals, such responses typify the antimodernity movement sweeping through industrializing and urbanizing Western nations.[22] Yet the relationship Turi and Hatt developed combined elements of friendship and bidirectional mentoring — foreshadowing the later engagements of Carr, Preston, and James Houston with Indigenous peoples and their arts. Friendship, rather than a pedagogical or commercial agenda, was central to the relationship of Zulu sculptor Alson Zuma and white farmer David Fox as discussed by Sandra Klopper in her contribution. Klopper's chapter describes the affinity created by a shared sense of the absurd that nurtured their productive engagement over many years. It also speaks to the value of friendships in contexts where artists have little or no support from educational or commercial institutions. Many settler mediators shared with European refugees and exiles the modernist's admiration for primitive art, and for both, the horrors fomented in Europe by racism during World War II could engender a missionary zeal for disseminating modernism's presumed liberatory and universalist ideology. This is amply demonstrated in the biography of Selwyn Dewdney, whose voice is heard in the document section edited by Ruth Phillips. Well before meeting pioneering Anishinaabe modernist painter Norval Morrisseau, Dewdney had been active in socialist political movements and had resigned his position as a high school art teacher in protest against an anti-Semitic episode at his school. That Morrisseau considered Dewdney as his friend is clearly stated in their voluminous correspondence. This volume offers an expanded critical and historical framework within which to reconsider the activities of Dewdney and other key modernist mediators in ways that cut across their national and media boundaries.

Writing Mediation: Silences and Mystifications

Intercultural negotiations in the art world have become an increasingly active research area since the late twentieth century. Anthropologists of art began to examine touristic production and the advent of a market for Indigenous fine arts as part of their return to the anthropology of art and material culture studies in the 1970s. Nelson Graburn's introductory essay for his pioneering 1976 anthology *Ethnic and Tourist Arts: Cultural Expressions from the Fourth World* offered an initial typology of intercultural modern arts and addressed the impacts of outside buyers and the introduction of Western techniques and materials. He classified the Indigenous modernisms we discuss here as "assimilated [fine] arts," situated them at one end of a spectrum ranging from "functional traditional," "replica commercial," "reintegrated," "souvenir," and "popular" arts, and defined them as "characteristic of extreme culture domination and hence a desire to assimilate."[23] Paula Ben-Amos brought together studies of patron-artist interactions in contemporary African art in a 1980 issue of *African Arts* and investigated underlying social networks and interpersonal relations.[24] Comparing modern Indigenous art forms to pidgin languages, she argued for the value of a linguistic model of creolization in understanding their creative syncretic and creative aspects. James Clifford's analysis of the Western art-culture system in *The Predicament of Culture* (1988) offered a theoretical model for conceptualizing the periodic reclassifications and movements of objects across categories of value; his book has provided a critical point of departure for many authors and remains an important reference point for the histories traced here. Ruth Phillips and Christopher Steiner's 1999 edited volume *Unpacking Culture: Arts and Commodities in Colonial and Postcolonial Worlds* returned to Graburn's global comparative scope and focus on touristic and commercial production, while Fred R. Myers and George E. Marcus's introductory essay and the anthologized essays in their 2005 *The Traffic in Culture: Refiguring Art and Anthropology* explored global flows and exchanges of art forms and the late twentieth-century convergences of contemporary art criticism and anthropological theorizations — central areas of interest to the case studies here.[25]

In their edited volume *New Histories of Art in the Global Postwar Era: Multiple Modernisms*, Flavia Frigeri and Kristian Handberg neatly summarize the proliferation of regional and transgeographic studies of modernist traditions that have created an expanded field of discrepant modernisms around the globe.[26] Close studies of patronage and mediation in the world of modernist Native American painting from the Southwest have been undertaken by J. J. Brody, Bruce Bernstein and W. Jackson Rushing, and Michelle McGeough, among others.[27] Nicholas Thomas's *Possession: Indigenous Art/Colonial Culture* (1999, rev. ed. 2022) considered the cross-appropriations of modern and Indigenous artists in New Zealand, while important monographs and surveys by Myers, Howard Morphy, Ian McLean, and others have included analyses of the critical, commercial, and cross-cultural forces at work in the rise of Australian Aboriginal fine art. For Africa, the connections between artistic modernism and anti-colonial nationalist movements are explored with particular rigor by a number of scholars, including Elizabeth Harney in her study of Senegalese modernism, *In Senghor's Shadow: Art, Politics, and the Avant-Garde in Senegal, 1960–1995*, and Chika Okeke-Agulu in his book on mid-twentieth-century Nigeria, *Postcolonial Modernism: Art and Decolonization in Twentieth Century Nigeria*.[28] Scholarship on Southeast Asia, in particular focusing on the legacy of the Bengal School of Art, has added to the expanding frame of global midcentury modernisms, with R. Siva Kumar's 1997 exhibition and catalog *Santiniketan: The Making of a Contextual Modernism*, Partha Mitter's *The Triumph of Modernism: India's Artists and the Avant-Guard, 1922–1947*, and Sonal Khullar's *Worldly Affiliations: Artistic Practice, National Identity, and Modernism in India, 1930–1990*, offering particularly detailed studies.[29] Indeed, these and other critically important analyses bring into focus the processes of commoditization, colonial power relations, and creative self-invention in transcultural art worlds that have partly inspired the chapters presented in the current volume.[30]

Our current project of decolonization is adding a further level of analysis to the consideration of the profoundly colonial interactions considered here. Revisionist and global scholarly perspectives on hegemonic constructs of the modern and the postcolonial have animated major scholarly journals such as *October* and *Art History* and have produced numerous exhibitions, catalogs, and monographic accounts of key twentieth-century artists who fit this pattern of Indigenous or colonial modernism.[31] The studies in this volume contribute to these discussions by drawing unrecognized and marginalized artistic modernisms into a comparative framework and problematizing the silences and mystifications that obscure the importance of the mediatory figures and processes critical to their emergence.

Without more accurate accounts of both inter- and intra-cultural mediation, issues central to the growing fields of world art history and multiple modernisms will continue to be poorly understood. Perhaps most at issue has been the modernist insistence on a universal linear temporality, which has generated the widespread view that Indigenous and other non-Western modernisms are retardataire copies and imitations of European models. The reframing of constructs of temporality and periodization in the work of Susan Stanford Friedman and others undercuts the central premises of Western artistic modernism's cult of primitive art and its elevation of the avant-garde. In keeping with Friedman's argument that we need to recognize the possibility of "polycentric modernities and modernisms at different points of time and in different locations," the case studies in this book are not organized according to an overarching temporal unfolding but, rather, to demonstrate the equal validity of different global temporalities.[32] Our comparative approach reveals with particular clarity that the timelines of modernism in different locales were contingent on specific histories, themselves often activated by the movements and networks formed by individuals within colonial and neocolonial structures of possibility. They also demonstrate that the new concepts, practices, technologies, and artworks introduced by artists and mediators functioned not as models or templates to be copied but as catalysts. They led not to secondary and imitative replays of European modernism but to reinventions whose hybrid vibrancy has turned modernism in new directions unanticipated by the mediators themselves.

The originality of these reinventions emerges most clearly when the works of Indigenous artists are compared with those made or introduced by the mediators. As already noted, many of these intermediaries were teachers trained as modernists in professional art schools. Mark White's discussion of Sioux painter Oscar Howe's master's studies at the University of Oklahoma makes the originality of the modernist work he produced for his master's degree clear in its careful comparison with the practices of his adviser John O'Neil and other art department faculty. The intense interest of these modernists in "myth and metaphor," White argues, was supported Howe's own research into his ancestral Sioux traditions, which "encouraged him to see his project as parallel to that of other modernists." Although trained in art schools, most of the men and women who became mediators were making their own artwork as an avocation by the time they came to interact with aspiring Indigenous modernists. For the most part, their work was figurative, influenced by the early twentieth-century modernist movements of postimpressionism, cubism, and surrealism and would have been judged retardataire in relation to the avant-gardes of the second half of the twentieth century. As a result, their art has been preserved primarily in the private collections of family and friends and remains largely unpublished, poorly documented, and insufficiently researched. We can presume that for aspiring Indigenous artists, the art made by teacher-mediators would have modeled the modernist movements they favored and influenced the formative phases of their protegee's work. These omissions thus exemplify the archival silences and gaps that inhibit studies not only of mediatory processes but also of Indigenous modernisms more generally. Both for this reason and in light of contemporary revaluations of art history's dominant avant-gardist bias, the artwork of the mediators also now invites a second look.

The problem of the archive is exacerbated by the silences and mystifications that characterize accounts of artist-mediator interactions given in monographic studies, exhibition catalogs, and mediators' autobiographies. Reading across such accounts, the reader is struck by a widely shared rhetoric of "noninterventionist" teaching. This trope appeared early in writing about early twentieth-century Indigenous artists, teachers, and patrons in the southwestern United States. In his *Primitive Art*, for example, Leonhard Adam praised the non-Native mediators in the Southwest because they "wisely refrained from demonstrating to their Indian pupils 'how to do it.' . . . Instead, they strictly confined instruction to the technical side, but left it entirely to their students to choose their own subjects"—a view that is contradicted by later scholars who have systematically examined the roles played by teachers such as Dorothy Dunn at the Santa Fe Indian School or Oscar Jacobson at the University of Oklahoma in fostering the appreciation of their Native American students' work as folk art.[33]

In keeping with his judgement, however, Adam criticized the adoption of Western landscape painting conventions—which he, as a "Sunday painter," used himself—by the acclaimed Australian Aboriginal artist Namatjira and the Hermannsburg school as "irrelevant for the solution of a much deeper, and more important problem, namely the future of *real* Australian aboriginal art and the development of the aborigines' own artistic talent rather than their imitative ability."[34] As many studies in this volume clearly show, assertions of nonintervention belie the complexity of mediatory relationships and suppress the reciprocal influences that impacted not only artists but also mediators. Although the outward denial of influence drew from progressive education theories that asserted self-realization as the primary aim of education, the noninterventionist rhetoric could be harnessed for more specific political ends. Ulli Beier sharply distinguished his art workshops in Osogbo from the more formalized modes of instruction found in the official art academies of Ibadan and Lagos established under the colonial regime that were modeled on British schools. In his widely read book *Contemporary Art in Africa*, Beier recounted the teaching method used by his artist-wife Georgina Beier in the influential workshops she ran between 1961 and 1965: "She has always refused to be called a 'teacher' because what she was aiming at was in fact a working community in which artists stimulate and criticize each other and she always maintained that she gained at least as much as she gave."[35] Beier's acknowledgment of reciprocal influence was exceptional for its time, but his presentation of the workshop as a kind of egalitarian artistic kibbutz and his reticence about his wife's privilege as an educated white European oversimplify the power dynamics at work in these encounters. James Houston, the "discoverer" of modern Inuit art — whose promotion of modern Inuit art is sampled in the document section edited by Norman Vorano — also fits this pattern. One of Houston's first essays about Inuit sculpture, published in the Hudson Bay Company journal *The Beaver* in 1951, made the emphatic claim that "none of these crafts has been *taught* . . . they are age old in the Eskimo culture. The enormously strong creative urge of the Eskimo is found in children."[36] While this might make for effective marketing copy, it obscures the depth, character, and complexity of his relationships with Inuit artists.

The motivations for such disavowals are more complicated than a simple modernist desire to foreground the artist's individual freedom. They are both discourse and market driven. They have reinforced the audience's romantic view of the Indigenous artist as existing in an untainted ethnographic present, making it possible to collapse the modern artistic productions of Indigenous artists into the admired and desired category of "authentic" primitive art. At the same time, they have also allowed both private dealers and government-sponsored marketing agencies to sell the work of Indigenous artists as forms of fine craft and/or as affordable survivals of primitive art. In this context, the art historical omissions around mediatory histories bring into even higher relief the contradictions inherent in modernist primitivism and the politics of authenticity and agency it imposed on Indigenous artists.

On another level, however, the aversion to acknowledging patronage and influence could — and can still — reflect a postcolonial discourse of Indigenous resistance and agency and arise from a concern that awarding too much credit to mediators represents Indigenous artists as passive recipients of colonial teachings and reaffirms colonial power structures. Yet this approach, in our view, simply replaces one set of mythologies with another and further obscures the reciprocal influences and agencies of both the artists and the mediators. As suggested earlier, mediators have tended to be heavily invested in their own self-fashioning, most readily accomplished by writing about the new Indigenous arts and their own involvement in their development. Examples of mediator self-fashioning through memoir abound. Houston, to return to this example, left the Arctic in 1962 after having established the formal marketing structure for Inuit sculpture and prints. A compelling storyteller, he subsequently wrote numerous books of fiction and nonfiction. His recollections of his early efforts to develop Inuit art in the first of his three memoirs, *Confessions of an Igloo Dweller*, echo Leonhard Adam's noninterventionist language. Despite its title, Ulli Beier's *Decolonizing the Mind: The Impact of the University on Culture and Identity in Papua New Guinea, 1971–1974* is as much a memoir of his shift from Africa to Papua New Guinea as a documentation of his organization of the Centre for New Guinea Cultures and its art program at the University of Papua New Guinea. Dewdney, too, documented his personal life's work in *Daylight in the Swamp: Memoirs of Selwyn Dewdney*, a book that glances over his relationship with and influence on Norval Morrisseau during the early 1960s. These and other autobiographies make for captivating reading, but their strategic gaps, uncanny parallels, and glossings over provoke key questions explored in this book.

The mirror image of such omissions and distortions is the allegation that the mediator relationship was inherently controlling or paternalistic. Such an accusation collapses the production of modern Indigenous arts into a narrative of hegemonic Western cultural domination. Accusations of paternalism could, however, be supported by a mediator's own narrative that stresses his or her benevolent mentoring and prescient moments of "discovery." If, then, marketing strategies that silence the role of the mediator have given too little credit to the roles they have historically played, decolonization politics that exaggerate their controlling power have sometimes given too much. Both forms of misrepresentation intervene in the recognition of the authenticity and originality of modern Indigenous arts.

Another important issue obfuscated by the silences and mystifications that surround mediatory relationships is the intersectional nature of power and the different degrees of (in)visibility associated with gender, race, nationality, sexuality, and other components of identity in modernist art worlds. As shown, for example, by Roberto Conduru's chapter in this volume, the Afro-Brazilian sculptor and mediator of modernism Agnaldo Manuel dos Santos found it expedient to strategically deploy different components of his identity in different contexts. In 1957, he actively positioned himself as an "Afro-Brazilian" artist at the Oxumarê Gallery in Bahia, northeast Brazil, but as a "modernist" sculptor at the São Paulo Biennial later that year. Five years later, in 1962, he saw himself as a "Brazilian" folk artist at his exhibition at the Walker Art Center, Minneapolis. His race, artistic lineage, and nationalism were carefully stage-managed as he moved through different circles of patronage, criticism, and support. Such negotiations are powerfully revealing of racist, primitivist, and other discourses that shaped the climate of reception for Indigenous modernisms. In this context, too, mediators' accounts can on occasion be deeply confessional, illuminating the transformations and self-questioning arising from their work with Indigenous artists. When mediators engage in reflexive self-examinations their analyses can transform the ways in which they project themselves and their expertise. In this volume, Peter Brunt discusses the relationship between New Zealand artist Tony Fomison and his close friend Sulu'ape Paulo, master of the traditional Samoan art of *tatau* — or tattooing. After he was tattooed by Paulo in the early 1980s, Fomison began a series of allegorical body paintings that reexamined his personal anxieties as a settler in New Zealand during years when the state was adopting policies that would ostensibly mark its shift from a colonial to a postcolonial nation — a project that demonstrates the transformative impact an Indigenous artist could have on a mediator.

The apparent nervousness that informs most existing accounts of global modernist artistic mediation is, then, rooted in colonial power relations on the one hand and responds to a postcolonial politics of representation on the other. These silences and mystifications remain anomalous in light of the traditional centrality of studies of patronage and influence to art historical study. Through the research presented here we hope to rebalance these accounts. Our contributors bring the lens up close in order to assess the economies of power and agency that had to be negotiated by artists and mediators alike under colonial and neocolonial regimes. At the same time, they acknowledge the creativity and humanity of the actors who were party to these mediations while remaining sensitive to the limitations and possibilities offered by particular historical contexts. They seek to reveal the dialogic nature of mediatory relationships and the ways in which they could profoundly transform mediators' understandings of the projects in which they were engaged, altering the concepts of the primitive and the modern that had initially drawn them to Indigenous artists.[37]

In the remainder of this introduction, we offer a set of analytic tools for the studies that follow by positioning mediators of Indigenous modernisms within broader theorizations of the cultural broker, examining key historical patterns that controlled the global diffusion and reinvention of artistic modernism during the twentieth century and identifying in more detail the roles and modalities of mediatory processes.

The Modernist Mediator as a Cultural Broker

The art-world mediators we discuss here are a subset of the "cultural broker," an intercultural figure who has long preoccupied anthropologists, sociologists, literary scholars, and historians. An early theory of the cultural broker was schematized in sociologist Georg Simmel's "The Significance of Numbers for Social Life" (1908), which emphasized the broker's self-interest in navigating between competing social groups.[38] Simmel argued that the broker—whom he described as "the third" or *tertius gaudens*—was motivated by self-interest, a premise that is both supported and complicated by a number of the case studies in this volume.

Anthropologists turned to the figure of the cultural broker during the 1950s as a means of challenging models of research and representation that viewed cultural groups as isolated and self-contained communities. In studying how the "local community" is conjoined to a much larger world system—a key problematic of this volume—these anthropologists sought new ways to conceptualize what Robert Redfield described in his 1956 book *Peasant Society and Culture* as the "two-way relationship" between "primitive tribal people" and the "towns and cities" that empowered nation states and their institutions.[39] This schematic resonates with the political vectors traced by midcentury mediations of Indigenous and modern traditions through which artists living on the peripheries of Western art worlds produced local styles, regional modernisms, and "national cultures" by adopting elements of global modernism.

As we have noted, many modernist mediators were themselves artists. For the West African painter Demas Nwoko, discussed by Okeke-Agulu in his chapter, aesthetic modernism was a means of challenging the neotraditionalism advocated by British colonialists and creating an artistic subjectivity that expressed a new "national art" for a postcolonial Nigeria. Other examples demonstrate that, even when artists did not adopt modernism to advance their ethno-regional or nationalist ambitions, their art is often taken up by other "nation elites" as affirming unique national cultures. In short, Redfield's model, which considers the cultural broker as a figure who mediates relationships between rural communities and urban nation-elites, is applicable to a fundamental dynamic informing our case studies. It illuminates the role artists played in reworking their "local" traditions for a larger art world associated with metropolitan institutions and global centers of cultural authority and economic power.

Contemporaries of Redfield, such as Eric Wolf and Irving Hallowell, identified key attributes of the cultural broker that continue to resonate in studies of modernist mediation. Tracking the social integration of community-based groups within larger systems and national institutions in colonial Mexico, Wolf identified brokers as colonial entrepreneurs and "marginals" who "stand guard over the crucial junctures or synapses of relationship which connect the local system to the larger whole."[40] Wolf envisioned brokers as "Janus-like" figures who faced in two directions in order to buffer intergroup relations. For Wolf, these brokers were not only situated at the crossroads of conflicting interests but also actively invested in maintaining these conflicts in order to secure their own indispensability.[41] Put another way, the focus on modernist mediators in colonial contexts should be sensitive to the reality that while mediators were interested in creating networks — promoting artists with dealers and audiences — they often took steps to ensure that their own positions within the networks they cocreated were understood as inviolable. Rather than closing the gap between artist and audience, some sought, at critical moments, to ensure the *separation* of artists and audiences to confirm their own authority, whether by policing the boundaries of authenticity, exercising judgments of taste, or by becoming the self-appointed spokespersons for the artists they represented. Some artist-mediators also freely appropriated visual or stylistic elements from Indigenous art traditions in order to shape their own professional identities — Theo Schoon, for example, among Māori in New Zealand or Susanne Wenger among Yoruba in Nigeria. In such cases, mediators of modernism juggled potentially conflicting motivations to "help others" while advancing their own artistic careers.[42]

Cultural brokers typically operate in contact zones where they work to bridge colonial, settler, and Indigenous worlds. Thus, central to previous and contemporary understandings of cultural brokers is their ability to forge links between disparate geographical zones, stations of power, and cultural groups. In the context of artistic modernism, brokers manage the flow of information, the trade in objects, and exchanges of cultural knowledge. For anthropologist Robert Paine, brokers *manipulate* these flows — often, as already noted, by processing information to protect their own mediatory roles.[43] J. J. Brody shows, for example, how mediating figures in the American Southwest manipulated the economic and cultural value of Indigenous artworks at critical junctures in the chain of production, distribution, reception, and commoditization while heightening their own value as "experts." The case studies in this volume instantiate the different ways mediators become invested not only in the peoples and cultures they promote but also in their own self-identification as "experts," "mentors," "teachers," or "dealers" who both create and control access between artists and audiences.

As Aaron Glass argues in his study of the Kwakwaka'wakw artist Mungo Martin, Indigenous artists have also performed the role of broker, often, as in Martin's case, in collaboration with settler mediators such as the University of British Columbia Museum of Anthropology's founders Harry and Audrey Hawthorne.[44] Megan Tamati-Quennell's chapter offers an illuminating discussion of the parallel and near contemporaneous brokering project to which we have already referred. Institutionalized through a school curriculum rather than a museum, it was created by master Māori carver Pine Taiapa and his settler collaborator Gordon Tovey.

Given the long history of cultural brokers in Indigenous and colonial situations, twentieth-century artistic mediators frequently stepped into familiar, if at times ambiguous, roles as cultural intermediaries. As Ian McLean discusses, prior to the arrival of art mediators at the Buku-Larrnggay Mulka art center at Yirrkala, Australia, in the mid-1950s, Yolngu clans had for several generations been using graphic expressions to mediate the new economic and knowledge systems first introduced by missionaries and anthropologists during the nineteenth century. Similarly, after he moved to the Arctic community of Kinngait, or Cape Dorset, in the early 1950s, Houston was appointed not as an "arts administrator" per se but as a civil servant and representative of the Crown charged with vast responsibilities, ranging from justice of the peace and game warden to the administration of social services. Art administrators among the Inuit, much like those at Yirrkala, fit the pattern of a white outsider as a de facto or official colonial representative. Thus, while the discourses around artistic modernism might stress "ruptures" between tradition and modernity, in practice mediators of modernism oftentimes represented a *continuation* of existing social and cultural practices characterized by power relations with outsiders. Una Rey's chapter explores how this pattern has played out in the Western desert art centers of Australia, in large part due to the interactions of manager Geoffrey Bardon with the Aboriginal artists of Papunya Tula. The model he initiated endures, as she writes, "of a federally funded transcultural cooperative, under the auspices of local government councils directed by Indigenous board members and managed by mediators on short-term contracts." As

Margaret Szasz, Arthur Ray, and other historians have shown, such brokering relationships have deep genealogies that are central to the very workings of the project of colonialism itself and share in its ambivalences and contradictions.[45] Our case studies instantiate and interrogate such complexities and the ways that they have shaped the global modernist art world.

Objects and Texts as Mediators

While the study of human mediators provides important perspectives on the globalization of the art world in the mid-twentieth century, it is also important to recognize the agency of material circulations of texts, images, and objects. The efflorescence of art publishing after the Second World War spread ideas about modern and primitive art to all corners of the world. Robert Goldwater's *Primitivism in Modern Painting* (1938), Herbert Read's *The Tenth Muse* (1957), Leonhard Adam's *Primitive Art* (1940), Franz Boas's *Primitive Art* (1927), along with the *Studio* (London), *Arts Magazine* (New York), *Cahiers d'Art* (Paris), and other books, journals, and popular magazines were physically carried by mediators into new and improbable contexts. Joseph and Esther Weinstein brought an art library and an art collection to the Northern Ontario mining town where he practiced medicine and where they became the young Norval Morrisseau's inspirational gateway to global art from prehistory to Picasso. Such circulations of books, journals, and works of art were also mediators, creating a far-flung, imagined community of critics, collectors, middlemen, gallerists, artists, and intellectuals. People and objects together helped to crystalize a globally shared "taste culture" for primitive and modern art, to use Herbert Gans's term, which was frequently associated with ideals of social progress, racial equality, and the refusal of European academic and beaux-arts traditions. They activated artists, curators, and galleries to create their own autochthonous and national iterations of modernism through amalgamation with Indigenous traditions.

Circulations of artworks themselves also exemplify the new art-world geographies within which periphery-periphery networks could begin to compete with the center-periphery models of the imperial age. As noted by Roger Butler, for example, exhibitions and publications of Inuit prints circulating through Australia and Papua New Guinea as early as 1963 were admired by the first Australasian Aboriginal printmakers and gave artists such as Bede Tungutalum direct inspiration to begin creating his own prints, promoted as a modern-primitive art.[46] The document section edited by Nicholas Thomas exemplifies this global circulation as represented by Georgina Beier, who went on from working with artists in Osogbo, Nigeria, to work with Kauage and other Papua New Guinea visual artists in the creation of their modern prints and drawings. The chapters in this book provide further examples of the ways Indigenous artists inspired and influenced each other in the mid-twentieth century while challenging the reductive assumption that artists on the peripheries slavishly emulated the modern styles of New York City, London, or Paris.

Modes of Mediation

As is by now evident, the phrase *modernist mediators* encompasses a range of different roles and functions. Teachers, fellow artists, buyers and patrons, enterprising commercial gallerists, researchers, museum curators, government administrators, and, occasionally, missionaries were, however, at the center. We have grouped the case studies in this volume according to three broadly defined roles played by mediators: teachers and mentors, friends and collaborators, patrons and marketers. These categories, which we discuss in further detail in our brief introductions to each section, are overlapping rather than rigidly bounded. They describe key motivations that brought intermediaries and artists together, but they also intermingled and played out differently according to the institutional matrices through which these relationships primarily operated and the discursive authorities they invoked. Thus, although we placed Nettleton's chapter in the section on teachers and mentors because of the importance of classes given by Cecil Skotnes and others at the Polly Street Art Centre in Johannesburg, the "Amadlozi effect" she describes in the work of black South African artists was equally influenced by the mediations of his close collaborator Egon Guenther whose roles as gallerist and collector are the focus of the third section.

The multiple roles mediators often played could evolve over time, and any of these roles could also become a mentoring relationship. Despite the inherent difficulty of disentangling overlapping roles, each required different kinds of negotiations. The identification of these modalities can also help us discern cross-cultural and transnational patterns in artist-mediator relations and the networks of galleries and commercial collaborations that resulted in creative re-stagings of Indigenous visual traditions. Thus, while the typology that follows is inevitably oversimplified, we argue that it is nevertheless useful to the work of understanding the institutional and discursive contexts and the underlying power relations that framed relations between mediators and artists.

We complement these case studies with four "Archival Explorations" sections. The first, edited by Elizabeth Harney, opens the book by instantiating the complex and overlapping character of modernist mediations in newly independent Senegal, where mediators and artists directly encouraged by Leopold Senghor often played several roles as teachers, patrons, friends, and even dealers. The other three sections complement and make vividly present the three corresponding types of mediatory roles that structure our case studies in more specific ways. In each of these sections, a brief contextualizing discussion is followed by a set of primary documents that further illuminate mediatory processes in different parts of the world. These Archival Explorations serve two important purposes for the volume. First, they make it possible for the voices of artists and mentors to speak directly to readers, and second, they sample a historical record, both published and unpublished, that, for many Indigenous modernists and mediatory figures, remains ephemeral and unorganized. Their inclusion here operates as a kind of teaser, intended to raise awareness of the value — and also the fragility and vulnerability — of an archive that is not only documentary but also still oral, and the urgent needs for preservation if we are to develop its potential to arrive at new understandings of the mediatory processes in which Indigenous modernisms are historically embedded.

Notes

1. See Hobbs and Rankin, "Prints and the Politics of Culture," 160–206; and Gowenius, *The Hungry Red Lion.*

2. See Phillips, "Norval Morrisseau's Entrance"; Robertson, *Norval Morrisseau*; and Ace, "Norval Morrisseau."

3. See, for example, Henderson, *A Blaze of Colour*; Bieringa, *The heART of the Matter*; Christensen, *Cliff Whiting*; and Skinner, *The Carver and the Artist.*

4. Transcribed from Tovey, "Talk by Gordon Tovey, Copy of Tape One."

5. See Okeke-Agulu, "Ulli Beier and the Problem of Postcolonial Modernism," chap. 1, this volume; Beier, *Contemporary Art in Africa*; and Probst, *Osogbo and the Art of Heritage.*

6. Glassie, *Prince Twins Seven-Seven.*

7. On current deployments of "indigeneity," see Cadena and Starn, *Indigenous Experience Today*; Clifford, *Returns*; and Harney and Phillips, "Introduction: Inside Modernity."

8. On Indigenous Taiwanese and Filipino modernisms, see, for example, Flores, "Belatedly and Finally"; and Bernal, "Woven Together."

9. This persistence is illustrated by the installations of African, Pacific Islands, and Native North American art in many European and North American museums — for

example, the Louvre's Pavilion des Sessions and the Musée du quai Branly. See Price, *Paris Primitive.*

10. See, for example, Connelly, *The Sleep of Reason*; Torgovnik, *Gone Primitive*; Errington, *The Death of Authentic Primitive Art*; Price, *Primitive Art in Civilized Places*; Hiller, *The Myth of Primitivism*; Barkan and Bush, *Prehistories of the Future*; and Foster, "The Primitive Unconscious of Modern Art."

11. Goldwater, *Primitivism in Modern Art.* Citation refers to 1967 edition.

12. Personal communication with Norman Vorano, Ruth Phillips, and Alexandra Nahwegahbow, Vaxjo, Sweden, June 25, 2016.

13. See, for example, Holt, "Lowenfeld at Hampton."

14. Saunders, "The Contributions of Viktor Lowenfeld to Art Education."

15. See Colvin, *Arte de Tigua.*

16. Phillips, "Aesthetic Primitivism Revisited," 12; and Phillips, "The Turn of the Primitive."

17. Slogett, "Dr. Leonhard Adam and His Ethnographic Collection at the University of Melbourne."

18. Phillips, "Aesthetic Primitivism Revisited."

19. Preface to the unpublished catalogue of the Koerner collection of Northwest Coast art, compiled by Madeleine Rowan, series 2, Walter C. Koerner Fonds, University of British Columbia Museum of Anthropology Archives.

20. Known also as Inocêncio Medeiros da Costa or Inocêncio da Costa Nick. See, for example, Casimiro, *Mestre Noza.*

21. On settler artists and appropriation, see Thomas, "Indigenous Signs in Colonial Art.; Moray, *Unsettling Encounters*; Mundine, "Aboriginal Landscape 1941," 20; and Scott, *A Strange Mixture.*

22. Lears, *No Place of Grace.*

23. Graburn, "Introduction: The Arts of the Fourth World," 7.

24. Ben-Amos, "Patron-Artist Interactions in Africa," 56–57, 92.

25. See Zitzewitz and Ciotti, "Art and Anthropology."

26. Frigeri and Handberg, "Introduction: Toward a New Understanding of Globalism in Postwar Art."

27. Brody, *Indian Painters and White Patrons*; Brody, *Pueblo Indian Painting*; Bernstein and Rushing, *Modern by Tradition*; McGeough, *Through Their Eyes.*

28. Harney, *In Senghor's Shadow*; Okeke-Agulu, *Postcolonial Modernism.* See also Giorgis, *Modernist Art in Ethiopia*; Gerschultz, *Decorative Arts of the Tunisian École*; and Seggerman, *Modernism on the Nile.*

29. Kumar, *Santiniketan*; Mitter, *The Triumph of Modernism*; Khullar, *Worldly Affiliations.*

30. For helpful theorizations of global modernity relevant to artistic expression, see Mitchell, "The Stage of Modernity"; Friedman, "Periodizing Modernism"; Appadurai,

"Disjuncture and Difference in the Global Cultural Economy"; Chakrabarty, "Provincializing Europe"; Mitter, "Interventions—Decentering Modernism"; O'Brien, introduction to *Modern Art in Africa, Asia and Latin America*; Huyssen, "Geographies of Modernism in a Modernizing World"; Said, "Voyage in and the Emergence of Opposition"; Canclini, *Hybrid Cultures*; and Mercer, *Cosmopolitan Modernisms*.

31. See, for example, Copeland et al., "A Questionnaire on Decolonization"; Grant et al., "Decolonizing Art History"; Gardner, "Whither the Postcolonial?"; Joselit, *Heritage and Debt*; Quijano, "Coloniality and Modernity/Rationality"; Mignolo, "What Does It Mean to Decolonize?"; Mignolo, "Delinking"; Grosfoguel, "Decolonizing Post-Colonial Studies and Paradigms of Political-Economy"; Harutyunyan, "Opting for Decoloniality"; and Watson and Wilder, *The Postcolonial Contemporary*.

32. Friedman, "Periodizing Modernism," 426. See also Friedman, *Planetary Modernisms*.

33. Adam, *Primitive Art*, 212. Adam praised the mediators while at the same time criticizing the "Hermannsburg school" in Australia, which had seen the emergence of Namatjira and other Australian Aboriginal landscape painters who had adopted aspects of Western perspective and naturalistic depiction. See Bernstein and Rushing, *Modern by Tradition*; and Horton and Berlo, "Pueblo Painting in 1932."

34. Adam, *Primitive Art*, 215.

35. Beier, *Contemporary Art in Africa*, 110.

36. Houston, "Eskimo Sculptors," 39. Emphasis in original.

37. Phillips, "Aesthetic Primitivism Revisited."

38. Simmel, "On the Significance of Numbers for Social Life."

39. Redfield, *Peasant Society and Culture*, 23, 25.

40. Wolf, "Aspects of Group Relations," 1075.

41. Wolf, "Aspects of Group Relations," 1076.

42. On Schoon, see Skinner, *Theo Schoon*. On Wenger, see Probst, *Osogbo and the Art of Heritage*; and Beier, *The Return of the Gods*.

43. Paine, "A Theory of Patronage and Brokerage."

44. Glass, "From Cultural Salvage to Brokerage." Also see Hawthorn, *A Labour of Love*.

45. Szasz, *Between Indian and White Worlds*; Ray, *Indians in the Fur Trade*.

46. Butler, *Islands in the Sun*, 9.

Bibliography

Ace, Barry. "Norval Morrisseau: Artist as Shaman." Aboriginal Curatorial Collective. Last modified December 2005. http://www.aboriginalcuratorialcollective.org/research/morriseau.html. Internet Archive. https://web.archive.org/web/20160408013116/http://www.aboriginalcuratorialcollective.org/research/morriseau.html.

Adam, Leonhard. *Primitive Art*. 3rd ed. New York: Penguin, 1954. Originally published 1940.

Appadurai, Arjun. "Disjuncture and Difference in the Global Cultural Economy." In *Modernity at Large: Cultural Dimensions of Globalization*, 27–47. Minneapolis: University of Minnesota Press, 1996.

Barkan, Elazar, and Ronald Bush, eds. *Prehistories of the Future: The Primitivist Project and the Culture of Modernism*. Stanford, CA: Stanford University Press, 1995.

Beier, Ulli. *Contemporary Art in Africa*. London: Frederick A. Praeger, 1968.

Beier, Ulli. *The Return of the Gods: The Sacred Art of Susanne Wenger*. Cambridge: Cambridge University Press, 1975.

Ben-Amos, Paula. "Patron-Artist Interactions in Africa." *African Arts* 13, no. 3 (May 1980): 56–57, 92.

Bernal, Abigail. "Woven Together: Art, Indigeneity, and Community in the Cordillera." In *Asia Pacific Art Papers: Contemporary Contexts, Practices, Ideas*. Queensland Art Gallery / Gallery of Modern Art, 2021. Exhibition catalog. https://apap.qagoma.qld.gov.au/wp-content/uploads/essay-pdfs/essay-802.pdf.

Bernstein, Bruce, and W. Jackson Rushing III. *Modern by Tradition: American Indian Painting in the Studio Style*. Santa Fe: Museum of New Mexico Press, 1995. Exhibition catalog.

Bieringa, Luit, dir. *The heART of the Matter*. Wellington, NZ: BWX Productions, 2016. DVD.

Boaz, Franz. *Primitive Art*. Cambridge, MA: Harvard University Press, 1927.

Brody, J. J. *Indian Painters and White Patrons*. Albuquerque: University of New Mexico Press, 1971.

Brody, J. J. *Pueblo Indian Painting: Tradition and Modernism in New Mexico, 1900–1930*. Santa Fe, NM: School of American Research Press, 1997.

Butler, Roger. *Islands in the Sun: Prints by Indigenous Artists of Australia and the Australasian Region*. Canberra: National Gallery of Australia, 2001. Exhibition catalog.

Cadena, Marisol de la, and Orin Starn, eds. *Indigenous Experience Today*. Oxford: Berg, 2007.

Canclini, Néstor García. *Hybrid Cultures: Strategies for Entering and Leaving Modernity*. Minneapolis: University of Minnesota Press, 1995.

Casimiro, Renato. *Mestre Noza*. Recife: Fundaj, Instituto de Pesquisas Sociais, 2001.

Chakrabarty, Dipesh. "Provincializing Europe: Postcoloniality and the Critique of History." *Cultural Studies* 6, no. 3 (1992): 337–57.

Christensen, Ian. *Cliff Whiting: He Toi Nuku, He Toi Rangi*. Palmerston North, NZ: He Kupenga Hao i te Rea, 2013.

Clifford, James. *Returns: Becoming Indigenous in the Twenty-First Century*. Cambridge, MA: Harvard University Press, 2013.

Colvin, Jean G. *Arte de Tigua: A Reflection of Indigenous Culture in Ecuador*. Quito: Abya Yala, 2004.

Connelly, Frances S. *The Sleep of Reason: Primitivism in Modern European Art and Aesthetics, 1725–1907*. University Park: Pennsylvania State University, 1995.

Copeland, Huey, Hal Foster, David Joselit, and Pamela M. Lee. "A Questionnaire on Decolonization." *October* 174 (Fall 2020): 3–125. https://doi.org/10.1162/octo_a_00410.

Dewdney, Selwyn H., and A. K. Dewdney. *Daylight in the Swamp: Memoirs of Selwyn Dewdney*. Toronto: Dundurn Press, 1997.

Errington, Shelly. *The Death of Authentic Primitive Art and Other Tales of Progress*. Berkeley: University of California Press, 1998.

Flores, Patrick. "Belatedly and Finally: The Early Time of the Indigenous in the Concurrent Contemporary." *Pacific Arts* 22, no. 2 (2022): 183–203. https://doi.org/10.5070/PC222259601.

Foster, Hal. "The Primitive Unconscious of Modern Art, or White Skin Black Masks." In *Recodings: Art, Spectacle, Cultural Politics*, 181–210. Seattle: Bay Press, 1985.

Freidman, Susan Stanford. "Periodizing Modernism: Postcolonial Modernities and the Space/Time Borders of Modernist Studies." *Modernism/Modernity* 13, no. 3 (2006): 425–43.

Friedman, Susan Stanford. *Planetary Modernisms: Provocations on Modernity Across Time*. New York: Columbia University Press, 2015.

Frigeri, Flavia, and Kristian Handberg. "Introduction: Toward a New Understanding of Globalism in Postwar Art." In *New Histories of Art in the Global Postwar Era: Multiple Modernisms*, edited by Flavia Frigeri and Kristian Handberg, 1–11. New York: Routledge, 2021.

Gardner, Anthony. "Whither the Postcolonial?" In *Global Studies: Mapping Contemporary Art and Culture*, edited by Hans Belting, 142–57. Ostfildern: Hatje Cantz, 2011.

Gerschultz, Jessica. *Decorative Arts of the Tunisian École: Fabrications of Modernism, Gender, and Power*. University Park: Pennsylvania State University Press, 2019.

Giorgis, Elisabeth. *Modernist Art in Ethiopia*. Athens: Ohio University Press, 2019.

Glass, Aaron. "From Cultural Salvage to Brokerage: The Mythologization of Mungo Martin and the Emergence of Northwest Coast Art." *Museum Anthropology* 29, no. 1 (March 2006): 20–43.

Glassie, Henry. *Prince Twins Seven-Seven: His Art, His Life in Nigeria, His Exile in America*. Bloomington: Indiana University Press, 2010.

Goldwater, Robert. *Primitivism in Modern Art*. Rev. ed. New York: Knopf, 1967. First published as *Primitivism in Modern Painting*. New York: Harper, 1938.

Gowenius, Peder. *The Hungry Red Lion: Art and Empowerment at Rorke's Drift, Thabana Li Mele and Oodi*. Cape Town: Print Matters, 2022.

Graburn, Nelson H. H. "Introduction: The Arts of the Fourth World." In *Ethnic and Tourist Arts: Cultural Expressions from the Fourth World*, edited by Nelson H. H. Graburn, 1–32. Berkeley: University of California Press, 1976.

Grant, Catherine, and Dorothy Price. "Decolonizing Art History." *Art History* 43, no. 1 (February 2020): 8–66.

Grosfoguel, Ramón. "Decolonizing Post-Colonial Studies and Paradigms of Political-Economy: Transmodernity, Decolonial Thinking, and Global Coloniality." *Transmodernity* 1, no. 1 (2011). https://doi.org/10.5070/T411000004.

Harney, Elizabeth. *In Senghor's Shadow: Art, Politics, and the Avant-Garde in Senegal, 1960–1995*. Durham, NC: Duke University Press, 2004.

Harney, Elizabeth, and Ruth B. Phillips. "Introduction: Inside Modernity: Indigeneity, Coloniality, and Modernism." In *Multiple Modernisms: Art, Indigeneity, Colonialism*, 1–29. Durham, NC: Duke University Press, 2018.

Harutyunyan, Angela. "Opting for Decoloniality: A Politics of Non-Politics." *Art History* 42, no. 5 (November 2019): 996–1000. https://doi.org/10.1111/1467-8365.12475.

Hawthorn, Audrey. *A Labour of Love: The Making of the Museum of Anthropology, UBC: The First Three Decades, 1947–1976*. Vancouver: UBC Museum of Anthropology, 1993.

Henderson, Carol. *A Blaze of Colour: Gordon Tovey, Artist Educator*. Christchurch: Hazard, 1998.

Hiller, Susan, ed. *The Myth of Primitivism: Perspectives on Art*. New York: Routledge, 1991.

Hobbs, Philippa, and Elizabeth Rankin. "Prints and the Politics of Culture." In *Rorke's Drift: Empowering Prints*, 160–206. Cape Town: Double Storey, 2003.

Holt, Ann. "Lowenfeld at Hampton (1939–1946): Empowerment, Resistance, Activism, and Pedagogy." *Studies in Art Education* 54, no. 1 (Fall 2012): 6–20.

Horton, Jessica, and Janet Catherine Berlo. "Pueblo Painting in 1932: Folding Narratives of Native Art into American Art History." In *A Companion to American Art*, edited by John Davis, Jennifer A. Greenhill, and Jason D. LaFountain, 264–80. Malden, MA: Wiley-Blackwell, 2015.

Houston, James. *Confessions of an Igloo Dweller*. Boston: Houghton Mifflin, 1996.

Houston, James. "Eskimo Sculptors." *The Beaver*, no. 282 (June 1951): 34–39.

Huyssen, Andreas. "Geographies of Modernism in a Globalizing World." *New German Critique* 34, no. 1 (Winter 2007): 189–207.

Joselit, David. *Heritage and Debt: Art in Globalization*. Cambridge, MA: MIT Press, 2020.

Khullar, Sonal. *Worldly Affiliations: Artistic Practice, National Identity, and Modernism in India, 1930–1990*. Berkeley: University of California Press, 2015.

Kumar, R. Siva. *Santiniketan: The Making of a Contextual Modernism*. New Delhi: National Gallery of Modern Art, 1997. Exhibition catalog.

Lears, T. J. Jackson. *No Place of Grace: Antimodernism and the Transformation of American Culture, 1880–1920*. Chicago: University of Chicago Press, 1981.

McGeough, Michelle. *Through Their Eyes: Indian Painting in Santa Fe, 1918–1945*. Santa Fe, NM: Wheelwright Museum of the American Indian, 2009.

McLean, Ian. *Rattling Spears: A History of Indigenous Australian Art*. London: Reaktion, 2016.

Mercer, Kobena, ed. *Cosmopolitan Modernisms*. Cambridge, MA: MIT Press, 2005.
Mignolo, Walter. "Delinking: The Rhetoric of Modernity, the Logic of Coloniality and the Grammar of De-coloniality." *Cultural Studies* 21, no. 2–3 (2007): 449–514.
Mignolo, Walter. "What Does It Mean to Decolonize?" In Walter Mignolo and Catherine Walsh, *On Decoloniality*, 105–34. Durham, NC: Duke University Press, 2018.
Mitchell, Timothy. "The Stage of Modernity." In *Questions of Modernity*, edited by Timothy Mitchell, 1–34. Minneapolis: University of Minnesota Press, 2000.
Mitter, Partha. "Interventions — Decentering Modernism: Art History and Avant-Garde Art from the Periphery." *Art Bulletin* 90, no. 4 (2008): 531–48.
Mitter, Partha. *The Triumph of Modernism: India's Artists and the Avant-Garde, 1922–47*. Chicago: University of Chicago Press, 2007.
Moray, Gerta. *Unsettling Encounters: First Nations Imagery in the Art of Emily Carr*. Vancouver: University of British Columbia Press, 2009.
Mundine, Djon. "Aboriginal Landscape 1941." In *Margaret Preston*, edited by Deborah Edwards and Rose Peel. Sydney: Art Gallery of New South Wales, 2005. Exhibition catalog.
O'Brien, Elaine. Introduction to *Modern Art in Africa, Asia, and Latin America: An Introduction to Global Modernisms*, edited by Elaine O'Brien, Everlyn Nicodemus, Melissa Chiu, Benjamin Genocchio, Mary K. Coffey, and Roberto Tejada. Malden, MA: Wiley-Blackwell, 2013.
Okeke-Agulu, Chika. *Postcolonial Modernism: Art and Decolonization in Twentieth-Century Nigeria*. Durham, NC: Duke University Press, 2015.
Paine, Robert. "A Theory of Patronage and Brokerage." In *Patrons and Brokers in the East Arctic*, edited by Robert Paine, 8–21. St. John's: Institute of Social and Economic Research, Memorial University of Newfoundland, 1971.
Phillips, Ruth B. "Aesthetic Primitivism Revisited: The Global Diaspora of 'Primitive Art' and the Rise of Indigenous Modernisms." *Journal of Art Historiography* 12 (2015): 1–25. https://arthistoriography.files.wordpress.com/2015/06/phillips.pdf.
Phillips, Ruth B. "Norval Morrisseau's Entrance: Negotiating Primitivism, Modernism, and Anishinaabe Tradition." In *Norval Morrisseau: Shaman Artist*, edited by Greg Hill, 42–77. Ottawa: National Gallery of Canada, 2006. Exhibition catalog.
Phillips, Ruth B. "The Turn of the Primitive: Modernism, the Stranger, and the Indigenous Artist in Settler Art Histories." In *Exiles, Diasporas, and Strangers*, edited by Kobena Mercer, 46–71. Cambridge, MA: MIT Press, 2008.
Price, Sally. *Paris Primitive: Jacques Chirac's Museum on the Quai Branly*. Chicago: University of Chicago Press, 2007.
Price, Sally. *Primitive Art in Civilized Places*. Chicago: University of Chicago Press, 1989.
Probst, Peter. *Osogbo and the Art of Heritage: Monuments, Deities, and Money*. Bloomington: Indiana University Press, 2011.
Quijano, Aníbal. "Coloniality and Modernity/Rationality." Translated by Sonia Therborn. *Cultural Studies* 21, no. 2–3 (March/May 2007): 168–78.

Ray, Arthur J. *Indians in the Fur Trade: Their Role as Trappers, Hunters, and Middlemen in the Lands Southwest of Hudson Bay, 1660–1870*. Toronto: University of Toronto Press, 1974.

Read, Herbert. *The Tenth Muse: Essays in Criticism*. Freeport, NY: Books for Libraries, 1957.

Redfield, Robert. *Peasant Society and Culture*. Chicago: University of Chicago Press, 1956.

Robertson, Carmen. *Norval Morrisseau: Life and Work*. Toronto: Art Canada Institute, 2016. https://www.aci-iac.ca/art-books/norval-morrisseau.

Rowan, Madeleine. Preface to the unpublished catalogue of the Koerner Collection of Northwest Coast Art. Series 2, Walter C. Koerner Fonds, University of British Columbia Museum of Anthropology Archives, Vancouver, BC.

Said, Edward. "The Voyage in and the Emergence of Opposition." In *Culture and Imperialism*, 239–61. New York: Knopf, 1993.

Saunders, Robert J. "The Contributions of Viktor Lowenfeld to Art Education. Part I: Early Influences on His Thought." *Studies in Art Education* 2, no. 1 (Autumn 1960): 6–15.

Scott, Sasha. *A Strange Mixture: The Art and Politics of Painting Pueblo Indians*. Norman: University of Oklahoma Press, 2015.

Seggerman, Alex Dika. *Modernism on the Nile: Art in Egypt between the Islamic and the Contemporary*. Chapel Hill: University North Carolina Press, 2019.

Simmel, Georg. "On the Significance of Numbers for Social Life." In *The Sociology of Georg Simmel*, edited and translated by Kurt Wolff, 87–95. New York: Free Press, 1950.

Skinner, Damian. *The Carver and the Artist: Māori Art in the Twentieth Century*. Auckland: University of Auckland Press, 2008.

Skinner, Damian. *Theo Schoon: A Biography*. Auckland: Massey University Press, 2018.

Slogett, Robyn. "Dr. Leonhard Adam and His Ethnographic Collection at the University of Melbourne." PhD diss., University of Melbourne, 2009.

Szasz, Margaret. *Between Indian and White Worlds: The Cultural Broker*. Norman: University of Oklahoma Press, 1994.

Thomas, Nicholas. "Indigenous Signs in Colonial Art." In *Possessions: Indigenous Art / Colonial Culture*, 126–63. London: Thames and Hudson, 1999.

Torgovnik, Mariana. *Gone Primitive: Savage Intellects, Modern Lives*. Chicago: University of Chicago Press, 1990.

Tovey, Gordon. "Talk by Gordon Tovey, Copy of Tape One." National Library of New Zealand. Gordon Tovey Archive Sound Recordings, OHLCD-2086. Audiocassette.

Watson, Jini Kim, and Gary Wilder, eds. *The Postcolonial Contemporary: Political Imaginaries for the Global Present*. New York: Fordham University Press, 2018.

Wolf, Eric. "Aspects of Group Relations in a Complex Society: Mexico." *American Anthropologist* 58, no. 6 (December 1956): 1065–78.

Zitzewitz, Karin, and Manuela Ciotti. "Art and Anthropology: Twenty-Five Years of *The Traffic in Culture*." *Journal of Material Culture* 27, no. 1 (2022): 3–9. https://doi.org/10.1177/13591835221074151.

ELIZABETH HARNEY

ARCHIVAL EXPLORATION 1 **A POET AND PAINTER IMAGINE BLACK MODERNISM IN DAKAR**

In 1959, at the Second Black Writers and Artists Congress in Rome, an auspicious meeting took place that would determine the shape of African modernism. Léopold Sédar Senghor, a charismatic thinker and poet who would, the following year, be named Senegal's first president, had arrived in Rome eager to continue the rich exchanges with fellow African and diasporic intellectuals he had begun three years earlier at the first congress, held in Paris, to discuss the nature of a shared Blackness and African contributions to a new postwar humanism. Pierre Lods, a French mathematician, amateur painter, and expatriate living in the Belgian Congo, had joined the Congress to mingle with others invested in the fate of a modern, postwar Africa and its creative practices.

Both Senghor and Lods delivered addresses at the Congress, and after listening to Lods's paper about the establishment of a workshop-studio for local artists in his neighborhood of Poto-Poto, Senghor identified the Frenchman as a potential collaborator in his endeavors to craft a structured art world in Senegal. Though we do not know if they were drawn together first through artistic sensibilities—as poet to painter—we do know that they shared a belief in the innate nature of African creativity and cared deeply about retaining or reviving traditions that had been threatened or weakened by the colonial project.

Influenced by the literary works of African American poets and scholars of the Harlem Renaissance and the revolutionary, at times surrealist, writings of West Indian classmates in Paris, Senghor, along with Martiniquan poet and statesman Aimé Césaire and poet Léon Damas, promoted the notion of

Negritude, a shared "Black soul" that drew its strength from the reclamation or reanimation of pan-African cultural heritage. Negritude was a powerful counter-discourse, brought to life by assertive acts of invention and reconstruction of pan-African images and ideologies that had been denigrated by colonial regimes. As Denis Ekpo writes, Negritude "distinguished itself from other strands of cultural nationalist ideologies by being the only one that took Africa's fate in the colonial opening to modernity as the centerpiece of political thought and manoeuvres."[1]

First as a young writer, then as a statesmen and international figure, Senghor set out to systematically identify the values, social institutions, and epistemologies of "traditional" African cultures to which he believed the Black soul was inextricably linked. But Senghor also repeatedly encouraged acts of appropriation, famously asserting that African artists/thinkers should "assimiler sans être assimilés" (assimilate without being assimilated). Though he declared that "we must drink each day from the gushing springs of rhythm and the image-symbol of love and faith," he also insisted that "a civilization would stagnate and die if it were not vivified by the power of cultural spirit; its style crystallizes into vacant forms, into formulae, if it does not borrow from others."[2]

Senghor was responsible for the founding of the first formal art schools in Senegal. And as head of state, Senghor built an extensive system of governmental arts patronage and penned innumerable speeches, essays, and poems, addressing the importance of culture to the development of his modern nation and its contributions to a revived international order. With the establishment of annual salons, fairs, and international touring exhibitions, Senghor encouraged a new generation of artists to draw from archival sources of the African continent while remaining open to international cultural currents. Ultimately, he saw the arts as instruments of cultural diplomacy and symbols of uplift and hope. As such they were not simply representations of Negritude or nationalist culture (a widely held misreading of the so-called Ecole de Dakar), but rather contributions to a nascent postwar humanism.

Pierre Lods, for his part, was a mathematics teacher and amateur painter who maintained close connections with filmmakers, artists, and writers in France. Unlike other expatriates who founded informal artist workshops and served as mentors or patrons, Lods was not a "coopérant" or a colonial administrator. Instead, he had come to Africa in 1946 as part of Noel Ballif's Ogoué-Congo Mission, an ethnographic and film expedition that studied the Sangha region of northern Congo. When its work finished, Lods had decided to stay. As an experiment in artistic pedagogy and mediation, the Poto-Poto school in Brazzaville had begun by chance, as Lods was fond of reporting: "I shall never forget the joy of Ossali, my servant, when I found him after two days of absence, painting bluebirds on an old survey map of the Ubangi," he recalled: "They were disturbing and droll, those birds, with their form of a throwing-knife; they had a presence equal to that of the finest African masks."[3]

Lods's attitude toward mentoring local talents at Poto-Poto could be compared to similar efforts in other studios set up by expatriates like Romain-Defossés at Elisabethville (also in the Congo), Frank McEwen in Rhodesia, Margaret Trowell in Uganda, and Ulli Beier in Nigeria. All insisted that their methods were to offer little training for fear that it would interfere with native creative genius, yet all provided imported materials and intentionally encouraged references to surrounding traditional sources. All of these workshops rested upon pervasive notions of the primordialism and the primitive nature of African traditional arts.

After their meeting in Rome, Lods would accept an invitation from Senghor to join in the promotion and training of modern visual artists, arriving in Senegal in 1961. In Dakar he was part of one-half of the programming at the École des Beaux-Arts, coleader of Section de Recherches Plastiques Nègres (along with Senegalese painter, tapestry maker, and draughtsman Papa Ibra Tall). The other section of the école, Section Arts Plastiques, was run briefly by Iba Ndiaye and later by a number of French and Italian cooperants who offered the formalist training characteristic of European art schools. When Tall left the art school to direct a tapestry studio, Lods became one of its main teachers. He also ran a salon out of his own home that continued to be frequented by artist friends for many years after the art school's most influential period had passed. Although he retired from the École des Beaux-Arts in 1984, Lods remained active as a colleague and continued hosting a salon until his death in 1988.

Often referred to as the *section libre*, the Section de Recherches Plastiques was a space for research and exchange, for reestablishing and reasserting connections to pan-African and Black Atlantic visual traditions. There have been conflicting reports about the extent of Lods's "teaching," but most suggest a "laissez-faire" approach. Some, like Ibou Diouf (one of the best known of Lods's students in Dakar), insisted that Lods aimed "to preserve something . . . he never denatured the spirit of the artist . . . he wanted to preserve the essence of the African, meaning the essence of a true African."[4] Diatta Seck, in contrast, noted that "Lods used to have me identify one formal element in a painting, a detail, pull it out and use it as the foundation in my next canvas."[5]

Two texts are reproduced here. "Picasso en Nigritie" is an address Senghor gave in 1972 at the opening of a Pablo Picasso exhibition held at the flagship

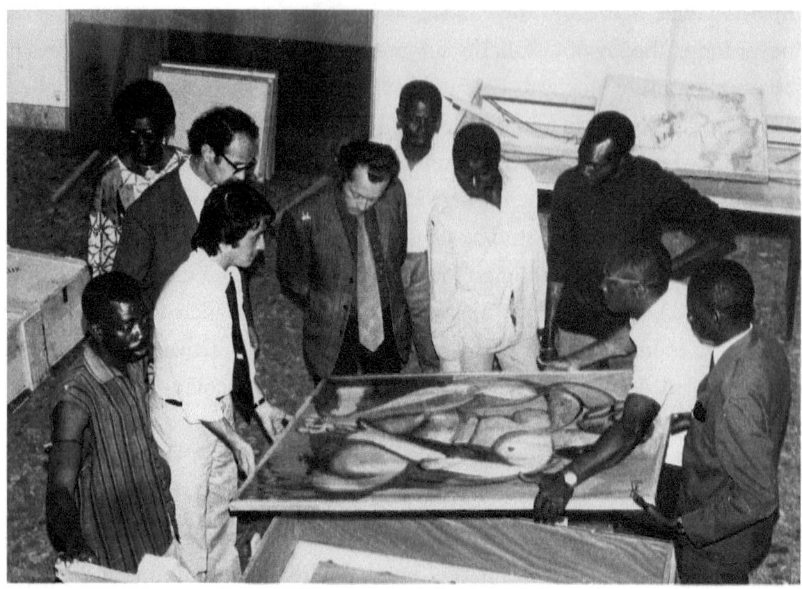

FIGURE AE1.1 L'exposition Picasso, Musée Dynamique, Dakar, May 1972. Fonds Jean-Gérard Bosio (50AP). Archives Musée du quai Branly–Jacques Chirac, Paris.

modern art space built by Senghor's government in Dakar for the Premier Festival Mondial des Arts Nègres (1966). It was one of the few major exhibitions of Picasso's work that has taken place on the continent—the other was held in South Africa in 2006. Its opening also occasioned an accompanying conference, Picasso, art nègre, et civilisation de l'universel, at which the complexities of Indigenous and international currents of modernism were debated.[6] In his address, Senghor co-opted the figure at the heart of the European modernist movement, Pablo Picasso, and used him as a model for École de Dakar artists. It was Picasso's constant innovation and bold adoptions from multiple sources that moved him away from classical European mimetic art toward stylization and abstraction that most impressed Senghor. Senghor also pointed to the painter's ability to combine a respect for his local roots in Andalusia with opportunities to learn and borrow from a diverse array of sources. Senghor thus affirmed this modernist icon not simply as a master but as a fellow artist from whom the president's artists could learn.

This speech is particularly illuminating for the insight it offers into the multilayered questions of artistic inspiration, cross-cultural appropriation, and heritage that lay at the heart of Senghor's vision of a proud, emerging style of

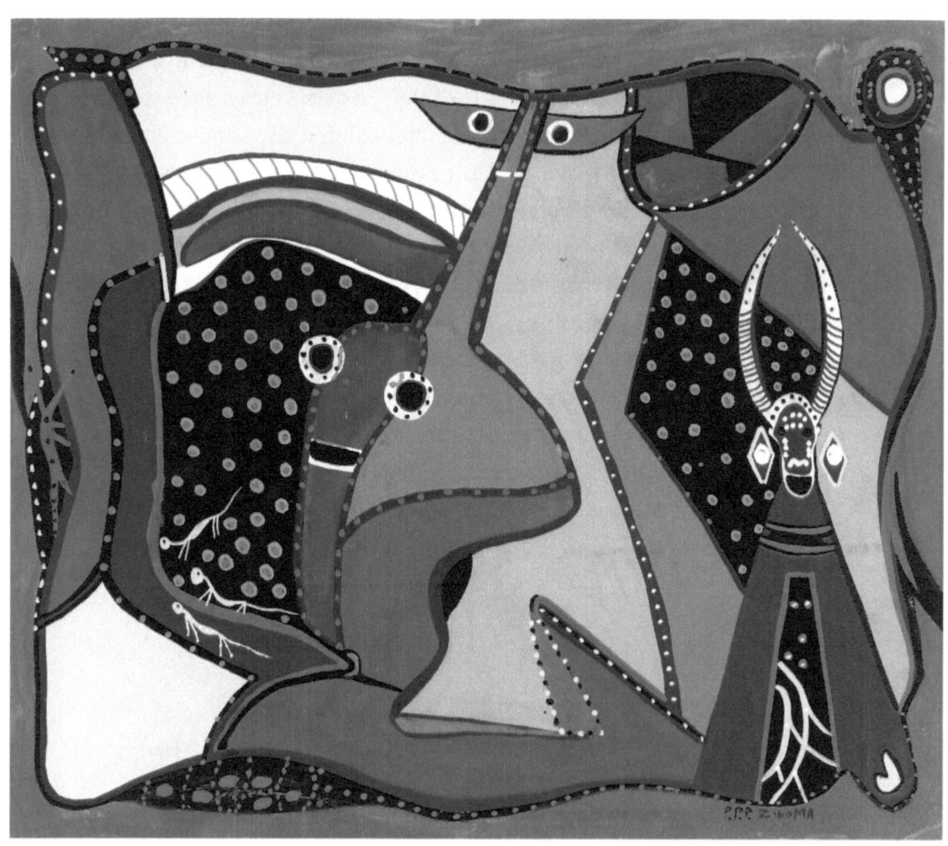

FIGURE AE1.2 Jacques Zigoma, Untitled, 1955. Gouache on vellum, 31 cm × 34.5 cm. Photo courtesy of the Annex Galleries, Santa Rosa, California.

modernism in Dakar — a modernism that drew generously from pan-African material legacies and European cultural traditions to address the needs of a growing nation and its emancipated people. He adopts Picasso as a role model for Senegal's aspiring artists not out of a blind love of French modernism or an unreflective mimicry, as early critics have suggested, but rather as a logical and strategic tool for co-opting and revising narratives of modernist primitivism. It was a way of enabling African artists to claim the right to modernism — a process similar to Alain Locke's calls to Harlem Renaissance artists to lay claim to African forms as European artists had.

The second text reproduced here, "Les peintres de Poto-Poto," is the address Pierre Lods delivered at the 1959 Rome Congress of Black Artists and Writers to an audience that included Léopold Senghor. The French painter describes the moment he decided to commit himself to fostering modernist artists in what was then Elisabethville in the Belgian Congo. It was later published bilingually in a special issue of the Parisian journal *Présence Africaine*—the mouthpiece of anticolonialism and cultural decolonization in the immediate postwar period—which also included entries from African and diasporic writers, painters, politicians, and activists such as Aimé Césaire, Kofi Antubam, and Gerard Sekoto. Part testimony, part manifesto, Lods's contribution details what he calls the "experiment" of his Poto-Poto project, calling it one of an "unlimited number of possible experiments in a population where everyone is an artist." His ambitions for modern African arts aligned nicely with those of Senghor, stating in the conclusion of his address that "world culture, recently revivified by Negro Art, will be digested by Africa and restored to the world with a new dynamic and resplendent countenance," thereby claiming a space, as Senghor had, for African artists to feature in processes of appropriation and re-appropriation that paralleled those of their European counterparts.

THE DOCUMENTS

Document 1: Léopold Sédar Senghor, "Picasso en Nigritie"

INAUGURATION ADDRESS, PICASSO EXHIBITION,
DAKAR, SENEGAL, APRIL 1972

As you are all aware, the human phenomenon we call *civilisation* did not come into existence, nearly five million years ago, with the first stone tools, or even with the first halting attempts at language, but in the Upper Palaeolithic period, with the first work of art: the first fertility statuette. It was for this reason that *Homo faber* was then named *sapiens*, "wise"—in other words, civilised.

Why is this exhibition of the work of Picasso taking place in black Africa, and in Dakar? Before answering, I must take a few words to introduce the exhibition itself. Apart from the sculpture, this exhibition covers all the genres in which the artist worked. There are paintings, original drawings, signed engravings, pottery, tapestries, posters and, last but not least, a collection of thirty books devoted to Picasso or illustrated by him.

Why Picasso *en Nigritie*? The success of an experimental Chagall exhibition last year encouraged us to continue the initiative. So we came up with the idea of organising, from 1973 onwards, an annual Dakar season, in which the visual arts would hold pride of place with an internationally renowned artist as guest of honour. This year, we are giving the idea a trial with Pablo Picasso.

No artist could be more exemplary. The Dakar School regards Picasso as a model whose kinship serves as a firm promise, and whose differentness serves as a powerful encouragement. This is what makes our choice so natural and so strange . . .

To come back to Picasso and the visual arts — and especially to painting, the most intellectual of these arts — the Andalusian artist did, of course, have precursors, if not instructors: Cézanne and Gauguin, Vlaminck and Derain and, last but not least, Matisse, as Jean Laude shows in *Peinture française 1905–14* and *L'Art nègre*. Nevertheless, he was the first, with his *Demoiselles d'Avignon*, to break ruthlessly with classical aesthetics, to go even further than his semantic and syntactic borrowings from negro art to get to the heart of things — in other words, to change not so much his language as his vision, even his *reality*. As he commented one day to one of his critics, "one of the fundamental tenets of Cubism was to displace reality; reality no longer resided in the subject, it was in the painting." And again, "painting is never prose, it is poetry, it is written in verse with visual rhymes."

The Andalusian felt, therefore, that it was necessary to turn away from the concept of art as imitation, and replace it with that of art as invention. It was no longer a case of *re-presenting* nature but of *re-producing* it in the image of God's voice and actions, to create a more humane natural world — an *objet d'art* which conveys, visually, in the same way as a poem does verbally, our idea-sentiments or, more accurately, our sentiment-ideas. This line of enquiry led Picasso to his encounter with negro art, which convinced him he was on the right track. Let us hear what he had to say about his first visit to the Musée de l'Homme in Paris: "I was so depressed that I wanted to leave, there and then. But I forced myself to stay, to examine these masks, all these objects which had been made by men with a sacred, magic purpose in mind, so that they would act as intermediaries between them and the unknown, hostile forces which surrounded them, trying to master their fear in this way by giving it colour and form. *And I then realised that this was the true meaning of painting.* It is not an aesthetic process; it is a type of magic which stands between the hostile universe and us, *a way of seizing power, by giving shape to our fears and our desires.*"[7]

This appears to run counter to the opinion of many critics, who insist on the intellectual nature of Picasso's works. This needs clarification, because the latter has often said that he is an "anti-rational" artist, and that, initially, he has only a vague idea of the object to be created, which appears much like a "controlled" dream, but one dreamed by a sleepwalker. I remember that day in the 1940s when Picasso, accompanying myself and his Andalusian compatriot the painter Pedro Florès, said, "We must remain savages." Again, there is a striking similarity with Arthur Rimbaud who, in *Une Saison en Enfer*, named the Barbarians — not only his Gaulish and Scandinavian ancestors, but also negroes; in short, primitivism — as his source of inspiration and expression: "I went back to the east and original, eternal wisdom." This caused Jean Laude to say to André Salmon, "By choosing primitive artists, he was not ignoring their barbarism. But he logically understood that they had tried to achieve a true representation of being and not the sentimental realisation which, more often than not, we achieved. He wants to present us with a complete representation of people and objects. This was what the barbaric sculptors wanted to do."

This proves, people would argue, that Picasso condemned sentimentality in an artist's work. It probably does. To explain why, I must finish my analysis. Although Picasso often took exception to sentimentality, it was for its lower-middle-class, exaggerated and naive aspects. *Sentiment*, in other words emotion, is something else again, being the trance which buoys up the creator while he is working: the *poet*, to get back to the original meaning of the word. What Picasso condemns in the self-styled "modern" artist is the factual vision that the average European has of people and objects, educated as he is in the mould of western rationalism. The twentieth-century artist, rather than being ruled by the conventional notion which has prevailed in the west for over two thousand years, and by the feelings stirred up by the external natural world which is physical, should instead use them as a dictionary of forms and colours to translate the true response of our inner nature, which is moral. In fact, as Rimbaud wrote, the "fight" is "spiritual." So, using the dictionary of the external natural world as well as that of our dreams, the aim is to compare the two types of "nature," by giving a form or forms to the sentiment-ideas born of our desires, our fears and our joys — in other words, to reveal our inner vision, as well as our striving, by substituting the overall structure of the object that is both felt and thought for an anecdotal and diverting multiplicity of feelings. This is at the root of the so-called "stylisation" of forms and, consequently, of their abstract nature. Once again, it is no longer a matter of aesthetics, of pleasing forms and colours, but of *magic* — a set of procedures, here visual, to tap the cosmic forces and trap them, using analogical but rhythmical images. This was the same problem which Rimbaud had faced earlier, and he had come up with the solution: "I invented the colour of vowels! I regulated the form and movement of each consonant and, using instinctive rhythms, I prided myself on inventing a poetical language, accessible, one of these fine days, to all the senses. I kept the translation back."

This magic — in other words, the new procedures and forms — was sought and found by the Andalusian among his Mediterranean ancestors, going back to the earliest, the Iberians. They obtruded on him, as on any genuine artist. "There's nothing I can do," he had to admit to his critics. "Painting does not choose. Certain forces obtrude on it. And they sometimes come from an inheritance which dates back to a time before animal life. It is extremely mysterious and terribly irritating." As has been stressed, pre- and proto-historic Iberian sculpture had led him to other Mediterranean sculptures dating from around the same period: Etruscan, Aegean and Egyptian. The point is that these pre-Indo-European sculptures had their origin in the same feeling for magic and poetry, and employed the same vocabulary, the same syntax, even the same style. And since black blood had nourished Saharan art, from which early Egyptian art derived, it should come as no surprise that when he discovered negro art Picasso found in it a strong confirmation of his Mediterranean research, particularly as many Spanish historians believe that the prehistoric art of the Levant has African origins.

It is these methods of Picasso's art-magic that we are going to try to summarise, by referring to the conventions of pre-Indo-European arts, and firstly those of negro art, not to mention Rimbaud's poetics. The first of these procedures is synthetic structure, the simultaneous representation of reality in its essence and in its entirety. So, after *Les Demoiselles d'Avignon*, Picasso often depicts his subject — man or god, object or dream — from various angles: full face or from the back, in profile or three-quarter view, from above, from below, from the side, as well as in a fixed state of immobility. The subject is promoted from a changeable individual to the rank of type, of eternal archetype.

If we come down from the philosophical, ontological level to the operational, poetical level of the work, once again we come face to face with the artist who, like the ancient Mediterraneans and black Africans, used analogical images, form-symbols, both to express his inner vision and make it known.

The Mediterraneans and black Africans have bequeathed us a complete "repertory of forms" scorned by European, and especially Graeco-Latin, classicists, who are primarily concerned with detail and imitating nature. Picasso himself highlighted the difference in a graphite drawing, entitled *l'Atelier*.[8] The repertory of forms in question is basically made up of lines and masses or volumes: straight lines, curves and angles, circles, squares and rectangles, spheres, cones and cylinders, etc. *L'Atelier* contains two compositions: you can perceive at first glance the difference between the reclining nude on the easel and the recreated nude on the table, between prosaic description and lyricism. In the composition on the right, the artist has retained only the most significant elements of femininity, while adding other symbolic elements of virility which are not in the easel painting. Over and above the repertory of forms, which were not ignored by the classicists, Picasso's originality resides in having restored their symbolic roles. Everything has its significance in Africa: form and colour, images, of course, but also material, even the fabric used for the picture. However, Picasso's genius went even further, inventing new forms, new groupings, new structures, while giving a new meaning to the same integrated, assimilated and transformed form.

The images are not important in the classical manner, for the story they are telling. The forms, to use the most general term, have a symbolic value achieved only by visual means. This is why Picasso begins by rejecting the devices employed by classical rhetoric: perspective and its space, chiaroscuro and its light and shadow, the model and other devices. He does away with the space by filling it with a "balanced architecture of forms," breaking free of a single focus of light, and giving the objects in the painting a greater degree of reality by dint of their sculptural "corporeity." This is achieved by drawing the forms more boldly, joining together the various parts of the body, the subject or the landscape more distinctly, presenting them like an interplay of geometric masses. Last but not least, blacks and whites are substituted for colours, or are used as values which are more spatial than symbolic.

That was the second set of procedures, relating to vocabulary and syntax. We will now finish with the "figures," which I liken to "visual rhythms." These correspond perhaps more precisely to alliteration, assonance and rhyme in poetry — in other words, to style. As you know, black people reign supreme in the field of rhythm, whether dance or music, sculpture or painting, poetry or drama. Here again, Picasso makes use of Mediterranean and black African rhythmic devices, integrating them, yet transcending them by highlighting the most original. His style is more easily understood if we go back to *L'Atelier* once more. The artist only retains — or adds — significant elements of femininity and virility, but far from using them to form a couple he creates a new being. And he moves us — which is the aim of art, rather than to please — probably less due to the array of symbols than to their rhythmical grouping.

What makes Picasso remarkable is that, once again, he goes as far as possible, to the utmost limits, in the originality of his chosen methods. His use of rhythm is anything but monotonous. It is not a simple repetition of an element, a sound, a word, a visual phrase — in other words, a form. It is a varied repetition: in another place, on another level, in a new light or colour, even taking another form. It is a syncopated rhythm, made up of asymmetrical parallelisms, with the famous "swing," before the term was ever invented. In other words, there is also a rhythm of contrasts and antitheses, of dissonances and "counter-rhymes" — in short, a dynamic, living rhythm, even in the sculptural nature and apparent immobility of the representation.

In conclusion, the great lesson to be learned by us all, but none more than the Africans, from Picasso, is not so much his allusions to non-Indo-European arts, particularly to "negro art," as his rejection of *art as imitation* in favour of *art as invention*. The lesson takes on a deeper meaning if we consider that, to be an inventor of new forms, a creator of beauty yet above all of human emotion, Picasso began by going back to his racial roots, the mix that comes from the Mediterranean, the crossroads of all routes and races, and consequently the home of civilisation.

The Andalusian artist teaches us — Arabo-Berbers and black Africans — that there is naturally no such thing as art without the active assimilation of foreign contributions and, above all, no such thing as original genius which is not rooted in a native land, which is not loyal to its ethnicity. I do not mean its "race," but its national culture.

Reprinted with permission from Clémentine Deliss, ed., *Seven Stories about Modern Art in Africa*, 228–30, 318 (Paris: Flammarion, 1995); exhibition catalog.

Document 2: Pierre Lods, "The Painters of Poto-Poto"

PRÉSENCE AFRICAINE 1, NO. 24–25 (1959): 354–59

The Painters of Poto-Poto, Pierre Lods

This unprecedented century has already overwhelmed us with inconceivable horrors and incurable physical and spiritual wounds, though at the same time with unexpected and grandiose enthusiasms, with unhoped-for satisfactions in the human field such as our Western forefathers cannot have glimpsed, installed as they were in a humanism of the sarcophagus as a result of the study and internal contemplation of dead civilizations which were, as they thought, irreplaceable in their distant prestige.

We have experienced in shame the revelation of the sudden, savage and degrading bestiality of nations reputed to be the most civilized on earth and the proof of the most subtle intelligence and the most refined procedure among peoples charged with the most primitive barbarism.

That will be one of the marks of our time.

"A new romanticism will come; I am not waiting for it, I am forestalling it" said Leon Moussinac as long ago as 1940.

The honest modern man, freed from his complexes, is pursuing, in wonder, the cultural stocktaking of mankind, aided by the ease of travel and the technical means of reproducing image and sound.

There is no joy more moving than to apprehend the reality of one's own epoch and to share in it.

The unforgettable comradeship of the Maquis between representatives of different social categories during the Occupation showed me the vanity of class distinctions, and if I had had any race prejudices they would not have survived the revelations of my stay in Africa.

I shall never forget that night of talk with an old fisherman of the Sangha — our paddle-boat stranded on a sandbank — and his question to the "all-knowing and ingenuous White man."

"Whence comes this road which goes back before my birth and before the birth of my father and before that of my father's father?"

His French was summary and my *lingala* ludicrous, but the intense need to communicate that "mass of things in the air which one would not have missed for anything in the world," as Mezz Mezzrow says, put us into a state of receptivity which made words almost unnecessary to understand what he added from the myths of the tribe to my over-rational explication of the cycle of the waters. An angel passed . . . "Same thing for the water, same thing for man" said the fisherman of the Sangha, thus joining forces with the greatest philosophers, "all is a circle and a sphere."

Thus a new perception of the world was born in me; that night gave me my comprehension of Africa and my participation in its real life.

I was on the road towards my "further education in Poto-Poto."

I shall never forget the joy of Ossali, my servant, when I found him after two days of absence, painting bluebirds on an old survey map of the Ubangi. They were disturbing and droll, those birds, with their form of a throwing-knife; they had a presence equal to that of the finest African masks.

I had never seen anything like them in all African arts, but they were unquestionably Negro by their effective impact and the grandeur and magic which emanated from them.

Next day the same Ossali was painting a vermilion mountain on a black ground, in oil. At the top five red strokes represented a palm, like an open hand; the same thing repeated twice lower down. The brush left a line of black which mingled with the red. In reply to my remarks and advice designed to avoid what I thought a mistake, Ossali answered, "But it is more beautiful like that." And he was right. We had the most beautiful mountain in Africa, crammed with life and death, hallucinating and attractive.

That was my first lesson in *silence* and *respect*, and ever since then that has been one of the principles of my method.

On the following days the little brothers, the cousins and the friends tried. I took all these people home, to my studio-hut in Poto-Poto. Then there was an orgy of talent, an overspill of ideas, an astounding blossoming of inspiration, a paradise of colour, joy and songs. Paper, cardboard, canvas, a sacrificed sheet, floors, walls, windows and doors were covered with gesticulating characters, hunting, dancing, marching, fishing, going to war, of birds, insects, fish and vegetation, masks, bewildering heads, sometimes all these together, but no flowers, none of those arrangements of objects known as "*still life*" (and nothing to lead one to expect them). The whole perhaps clumsy at first, but harmonious in colour, well placed, teeming with invention, as though by miracle, in a word the augury and sign of the imminence of a true painting far from the obsessions of the "Imaginary Museum."

Moved to tears, fascinated, losing my sleep for several nights I dared not say anything for fear of breaking the charm.

At that time, twelve years ago, I was the same age as the young people around me with my old bicycle and my shorts. I was their comrade. We used our first names, and when, some years later, I bought a second-hand car and the telephone was installed in the studio, Ossali said to me "Now you are a boss you will have to wear long trousers."

On the sleepless night when the idea crystallized in me that it was possible to help in the birth of an art, I wandered with my head full of fever in the immense squarely laid out village under the palms of Poto-Poto, whose life was already a complete and fabulous opera. It was absolutely essential to canalize this wealth of painting, to make it blossom, to show it. I constantly think of that year passed in the bush, of the sympathy and welcome which enabled me to take part in the life of the villages everywhere. I noted down a dialect and the subtleties of its grammar. (*A beautiful language is an unconscious and collective masterpiece*, says André Demaison.) I recognized its tonality on the drum, I was amazed to understand certain words and later reproduce them. I was initiated into the *balafon*, into hunting and fishing, and later into ceremonies which were even more fascinating to me. I witnessed dances, story-telling which became plays and ballets which ended by my being unable to distinguish actors from spectators.

One morning a dance chief took me near to the seven secret drums in a thicket behind a village, the ones that you hear but must not see. Another time a fetishist took me to a remote corner of the forest to see the remains of masks and statues hanging up, and rotting away, eaten by ants and damp and which will never be replaced.

You can imagine the infinite sadness of these memories. And since I had nothing to buy or sell, as Roger Erell, the architect of Sainte-Anne du Congo has said, and for my own peace of mind, I promised myself to devote myself to safeguarding this art, at any rate in its living spirit, and to help in its adaptation to the modern life of Africa.

The fortuitous and sudden outburst of the talent of Ossali's companions decided the beginning.

Some friends of mine, Mr. and Mrs. Pepper, who were devoting themselves on their side to the study and recording of African music, introduced me to the Director of Social Affairs. I explained my ideas to him. An intelligent and cultivated man, he understood and approved my plan for a studio-museum, helped me to get it built in local materials, mainly a large steeply pitched roof of dried palms supported on pillars of Palmyra palm, with underneath a verandah and a suite of two rooms. Everything was completed by June 1951.

Meanwhile the painters had dispersed. Ossali disappeared, tempted and culled by a labour tout in Gaboon. I had to sound the recall and try out novices. In a few days the studio was full. The miracle began again and two months afterwards we already had more than a hundred paintings which enabled us to hold our first exhibition at Brazzaville, which was a great event.[9]

And Max-Pol Fouchet was able to say on the occasion of the first Paris exhibition at the *Palmes* Gallery in 1952, "At one blow Africa has come into the hut at the top of her form. Spontaneously, because now she feels herself *free* and *respected.*

"And thus we have art in the state of newborn oxygen. Certainly it did not start from zero; it could not. The African civilizations are expressing themself very strongly here, greatly concerned with *signs.*

"The ornamental themes of the hut in the bush or the forest, those of the tom-tom or the ritual object, surge up, re-created with gouache made in Paris. Happily a style is maintained, that is to say the figure which men give not to life but to the meaning they confer upon life. Thus, these 'savages' run in their first spontaneous movement to the essence of aesthetic truth. They sweep away the ant-hills of error. In face of the immense absurdities of trompe-l'oeil, the optical illusion, which is a much graver illusion of the soul, an illusion of man, they unseal the eye, they cleanse the soul and liberate man."

Charles-Henri Favrod wrote in the *Gazette de Lausanne* in connexion with a similar experiment in Elisabethville, "This Liberty is a liberation. Unhampered images spring from the depths of the ages, from the time of fear and death and they emerge into the times of scorn, which they will end by vanquishing."

Thanks to this prodigious and incredible assembly of spontaneous talents, I was able to make a specific choice and only keep the painters who showed straight away all the natural qualities of *drawing, composition, harmony* and *imagination*, which enabled me to intervene solely to sustain the internal tension of the artists, to encourage them or free them of their doubts, to distribute their material to them and give them the essential indications about the use of colours, brushes and medium, paper or canvas.

The talents of our beginners could have been able to orient themselves towards the different branches of the plastic arts. That was my first project, but we were too soon submerged by all the possibilities of painting and we had to stop there until credits, encouraged by our success enabled us to expand.

For fear of fire, I gave up collecting works of art which were too beautiful in the thatched studio. We postponed the idea of a museum until we could build a lasting one.

To nourish the inspiration of the painters I surrounded them with traditional African objects, with a great variety of plants in the gardens, and I organized festivals. Sometimes we read African legends, proverbs or poems which seemed to me to correspond with the Negro world, or share the same values (Senghor, Césaire, Saint-John Perse, Michaud, Prévert . . .).

It is the *unlimited* number of possible experiments in a population where everyone is an artist, *which mainly* explains the success of the Poto-Poto Studio.

It is a result which would have been impossible if I had had pupils imposed upon me, even gifted ones. We should have had impositions, perhaps excellent classroom work by "scholars in class and not on recreation" (Max-Pol Fouchet).

For them Art and Craft Schools are necessary. We do not wish to enter into competition with them, but to contribute ideas; our collaboration can be effective and beneficial, provided that the teachers do not take umbrage at our anterior success and do not lose their breath in trying to follow the different routes of our researches and our renown.

You must not imagine that it is our ambition to impose an eternal and immutable method. This is only a stage, a witness, one season's harvest of the culture conditioned by the fortuitous circumstances of present day life for young Africans with the possibility always present of a future return to the sources.

On the contrary, our experiment, completed by a similar experiment in all the arts, exhausted if possible, preserved and conserved, we can then hope for the introduction of universal culture into Africa to counterbalance the effect of the machines and the ineluctable bad side of Western civilization, as with a young girl in Poto-Poto, apparently enraptured by the pink and blue images of Church bric-a-brac, to whom I showed, in order to pave the way for her "purification," first Bakwiri and Fan masks and then the finest religious paintings of Raphael.

André Parinaud has written in *Arts*: "Contemporary taste has undergone a prodigious mutation and has enriched itself with all the sensitiveness of the past" and one could add, with all the present sensitiveness of other peoples.

And we can predict with certainty that if Western culture did not begin with Egypt which no-one has yet dared to discuss in public with Cheikh Anta Diop, world culture, recently revivified by Negro Art will be digested by Africa and restored to the world with a new dynamic and resplendent countenance.

Pierre Lods

Bibliography

Max-Pol Fouchet, *Les peuples nus.*

Pierre Paraf, *Rendez-vous africains.*

Alexander Campbell, The Heart of Africa. (*Les deux visages de l'Afrique.*)

Rolf Italiaander, *Von Urwald in de Wuste.*

Charles-Henri Favrod, *Le poids d'Afrique.*

Notes

1. Ekpo, "Speak Negritude but Think and Act French," 228.

2. Senghor, "The Foundations of Africanité or Négritude and Arabité," 44; Senghor, "Le problème de la culture," 96.

3. Lods, "The Painters of Poto-Poto."

4. Ibou Diouf, interview by Joanna Grabski, tape recording, Dakar, September 14, 1998, in Grabski, "The Historical Invention and Contemporary Practice of Modern Senegalese Art."

5. Diatta Seck, interview with Joanna Grabski, tape recording, Dakar, September 15, 1998, in Grabski, "The École des Arts and Exhibitionary Platforms in Postindependence Senegal," 284.

6. Senghor, *Art nègre et civilisation de l'universel.*

7. Author's emphasis.

8. See Jean Leymarie, *Picasso, metamorphoses et unité*, 54.

9. An uninterrupted series of exhibitions followed, first in South Africa in 1953 (Johannesburg, Pretoria, Salisbury, the Cape), in New York in 1955, Hamburg in 1956, Switzerland in August and September 1957, and finally at the Institut Pédagogique National in Paris, in October and November 1957. [PL]

Bibliography

Ekpo, Denis. "Speak Negritude but Think and Act French: The Foundations of Senghor's Political Philosophy." *Third Text* 24, no. 2 (March 2010): 227–39

Grabski, Joanna. "The École des Arts and Exhibitionary Platforms in Postindependence Senegal." In *A Companion to Modern African Art*, edited by Gitti Salami and Monica Blackmun Visonà, 276–93. Malden, MA: Wiley-Blackwell, 2013.

Grabski, Joanna. "The Historical Invention and Contemporary Practice of Modern Senegalese Art: Three Generations of Artists in Dakar." PhD diss., Indiana University, 2001.

Lods, Pierre. "The Painters of Poto-Poto." *Présence Africaine* 1, no. 24–25 (1959).

Senghor, Léopold Sédar. *Art nègre et civilisation de l'universel*. Conference proceedings. Dakar: Les Nouvelles Éditions Africaines, 1975.

Senghor, Léopold Sédar. "Le problème de la culture." In *Liberté I: Négritude et humanisme*. Paris: Editions du Seuil, 1964.

Senghor, Léopold Sédar. "The Foundations of Africanité or Négritude and Arabité." In *Présence Africaine*, translated by Mercer Cook. Paris: Présence Africaine, 1971.

PART I

TEACHERS/MENTORS

Formal and informal educational and training programs were one of the most common means through which artist-mediator relationships were created in the mid-twentieth century. The progressive educational ideals and modernist ideologies espoused by teachers who engaged with Indigenous artists as mediators were often at variance with the conservatism and racism of twentieth-century art worlds and with the assimilationist goals of the vocational/industrial school model that shaped curricula in the schools established for Indigenous peoples by colonial regimes. Settler governments in North America legislated mandatory attendance at schools established to assimilate Indigenous children — boarding and day schools in the United States and church-run residential schools in Canada. Both systems became notorious for their aggressive efforts to extinguish Indigenous languages and cultures, the frequently abusive treatment of the young children who were forced to attend, and their inferior teaching and restricted curricula. Similarly, the schools created for Indigenous students under Australia's Aboriginal Protection Act and the 1953 Bantu Education Act in South Africa offered only vocational training and debarred entry into professional art schools.

The study of teacher-mentors can, however, track the ways that individual progressive educators around the world found to break out of this system and their influence on the emergence of the first modern Indigenous artists in the mid-twentieth century. Several of these teacher-mentors are briefly evoked in the opening pages of this book and are amplified by the case studies in this section. Other equally compelling case studies could be brought forward. In the United States, for example, pioneering Ho-chunk artist and advocate Angel De Cora began teaching art in 1906 at the Carlisle Indian School in Pennsylvania, where she laid an important foundation for the advent of modern Indigenous arts.[1] After successfully fighting for professional training herself, she sought to refashion the curriculum and teaching methods offered to Native American students in boarding schools to better reflect Indigenous values. During the next half-century other isolated examples from residential schools across America introduced modernist principles of art education that emphasized free and creative self-expression, providing temporary respite from the oftentimes punishing conditions of life.

The Alberni Indian Residential School in British Columbia was one of the most notoriously abusive, but even there the lives of the students were brightened by the art classes offered by volunteer teacher Robert Aller, who ran casual studio classes between 1959 and 1966.[2] The Chipewyan-Cree abstract painter Alex Janvier also acknowledges the key role played by the principal of the Blue Quills Indian Residential School at St. Paul, Alberta. He identified Janvier's talents early on and arranged for him to study with German-trained refugee modernist art teacher Carl Altenberg during the 1950s.[3] Janvier eventually went on to receive formal art education at the Alberta College of Art and Design in 1960 and became known as the inventor of a new painterly style that combined Indigenous cosmological references with influences from Klee and Kandinsky. In this volume, Mark White examines similar dynamics in the relationship between the modernist art teacher John O'Neil at the University of Oklahoma and his student Oscar Howe, a young Yanktonai Nakota painter, who challenged the static style he had been taught at the Santa Fe Indian School through his exposure to abstract expressionism, cubism, and surrealism during the 1950s.

In rarer instances, exceptional educators could also succeed in establishing programs that explicitly fostered the development of Indigenous modernisms. The art training offered to public school students in Aotearoa New Zealand, during the mid-twentieth century was perhaps the most notable exception to the repressive pattern. As Megan Tamati-Quennell's chapter describes, Gordon Tovey, a settler artist trained in modernism, was able to introduce an art curriculum into the public schools that promoted both Māori arts and modernism and, critically, collaborated with the eminent Māori traditional carver and teacher Pine Taiapa. Through Taiapa's mentoring, a founding generation of Māori modernists was able to develop an iteration of modernism that could be regarded as continuous with ancestral heritage rather than as a moment of rupture.

The comparative framework this book adopts makes it possible to understand the global networks to which many of these art educators belonged and which remain inadequately researched. One of the surprises that emerged from the Multiple Modernisms project, for example, was the link between Tovey and the inspirational Canadian artist and teacher Arthur Lismer (1885–1969). A member of the Group of Seven, Canada's founding modernists, and a legendary art educator at the Ontario College of Art and the School of the Montreal Museum of Fine Arts, Lismer drew on John Dewey's program of social reformation and the child art education philosophies of Austrian artist and educator Franz Cizek. He saw the untutored child as possessing a universal and inherently creative instinct akin to that of the modern artist. His theoretical premises were also, however, grounded in fallacious tenets of modernist primitivism that conceptually link the child and the non-Western subject. The child, he once said, "*is* primitive man—primitive man who drew animals and feared the dark, believing in good and bad spirits and learned how to use new tools and weapons."[4]

We unequivocally reject such views today and recognize the great harm they have done, but the artistically liberating and culturally affirming programs Lismer inspired around the world need also be assessed in nuanced ways that can better account for the complex relationship between modernist primitivism and the emergence of Indigenous modernisms. During the 1930s and '40s, for example, his modernist teaching and pedagogical beliefs directly influenced art students who studied in the art schools he directed and later became key mediators of pioneering Indigenous artists in Canada—James Houston and George Swinton went on to work with Inuit artists, Anishinaabe painter Norval Morrisseau befriended Selwyn Dewdney and Joseph Weinstein and sought their advice, and Robert Aller, already mentioned, provided a rare artistic outlet for Indigenous residential school students in British Columbia. Less well known is the influence of Lismer's pedagogy, which was disseminated through the global channels of British imperial rule during the 1930s when he made a Commonwealth lecture tour to New Zealand, Australia, and South Africa. Gordon Tovey and his superior, De. Clarence Beeby, Aotearoa New Zealand's director of education, attended Lismer's lecture on "Education through Art" at an academic conference held in Wellington, New Zealand, in 1937. It had a strong and lasting impact on both men and led directly to the creation of the Northern Maori Arts Project in the late 1940s.

In addition to formal schooling, art projects and workshops organized by churches and other private organizations could enable artists to escape colonial regulation and surveillance. The Rorke's Drift project in Natal, South Africa, was created by the Evangelical Lutheran Church of Sweden to provide educational and economic opportunities for Blacks during the early years of

Apartheid. Peder and Ulla Gowenius, trained in Stockholm's socially progressive *Konstfack*, were recruited to begin an arts program and developed a structured curriculum that trained students in the techniques of tapestry weaving, linocut printing, and ceramics, as well as instruction in other applied arts.[5] Graduates of the program formed a founding generation of South African modernists and also taught in the program.

The art workshops organized by Ulli Beier, Susanne Wenger, Denis Williams, and Georgina Beier in Osogbo, Nigeria, throughout the late 1950s and 1960s were supported by the Nigerian playwright and theater director Duro Ladipo and were more informal than the structured classes organized at Rorke's Drift. Characterized as "workshops," they involved multi- and intermedia explorations, including theatrical performances, music, set design, and even literary production. The dominant ethos encouraged artists to discover their individual visions with little direct instruction or guidance. Although scholars have argued that the Osogbo workshops were, in many ways, typical of normative modernist art education, Chika Okeke-Agulu points out in his chapter that a close reading of the interpersonal dynamics within the workshop suggests a new pedagogical space where no single personality dominated, giving rise to "a non-linear flow of artistic influences, and a compelling manifestation of . . . modernist experience in which émigré Europeans, black diaspora, and postcolonial Nigerian artists created a laboratory where local and appropriated forms from diverse artistic genres and disciplines coalesced to produce a thriving, contemporary visual culture."[6]

The dissemination of modernist ideas in schools and workshops almost always had knock-on effects. Anitra Nettleton's chapter instantiates this pattern, as it tracks the mentorships of Black South African artists by European-born art dealer Egon Guenther and settler artist Cecil Skotnes at the Polly Street Recreation Centre in Johannesburg during the 1950s and 1960s. Their tutelage inspired artists such as Sydney Kumalo, Ezrom Legae, and Durant Sihlali who in turn went on to work with younger artists. All negotiated modernism and modernity on their own terms, but, equally, their creative innovations influenced Skotnes's own work, creating a reciprocal movement between "teacher" and "artist" insufficiently recognized in many studies.

Notes

1. Hutchinson, *The Indian Craze.*

2. See Walsh and Robinson, "Alberni Indian Residential School"; and Clements and Walsh, "Something from My Past That I Saw and Recognized."

3. Hill, *Alex Janvier.*

4. Grigor, *Arthur Lismer, Visionary Art Educator*, 325.

5. Gowenius, *The Hungry Red Lion.*

6. Okeke-Agulu, "Rethinking Mbari Mbayo," 157.

Bibliography

Clements, Bradley A., and Andrea N. Walsh. "Something from My Past That I Saw and Recognized: Renewed Efforts in Repatriating and Exhibiting Art from Residential and Day Schools." *Round Up*, no. 274 (Winter 2019): 18–23.

Gowenius, Peder. *The Hungry Red Lion: Art and Empowerment at Rorke's Drift, Thabana Li Mele and Oodi.* Cape Town: Print Matters, 2022.

Grigor, Angela Nairne. *Arthur Lismer, Visionary Art Educator*. Montreal: McGill-Queen's University Press, 2002.

Hill, Greg A., ed. *Alex Janvier*. Ottawa: National Gallery of Canada, 2016. Exhibition catalog.

Hutchinson, Elizabeth. *The Indian Craze: Primitivism, Modernism, and Transculturation in American Art, 1890–1915*. Durham, NC: Duke University Press, 2009.

Okeke-Agulu, Chika. "Rethinking Mbari Mbayo: Osogbo Workshops in the 1960s, Nigeria." In *African Art and Agency in the Workshop*, edited by Sidney L. Kasfir and Till Foerster, 154–79. Bloomington: Indiana University Press, 2013.

Walsh, Andrea N., and Jennifer Claire Robinson. "Alberni Indian Residential School." *There Is Truth Here: Creativity and Resilience in Children's Art from Residential and Indian Day Schools*. Accessed October 7, 2024. https://legacy.uvic.ca/gallery/truth/exhibition/art-work-collections/alberni-indian-residential-school/.

CHIKA OKEKE-AGULU

1 ULLI BEIER AND THE PROBLEM OF POSTCOLONIAL MODERNISM

This chapter considers the work of Ulli Beier who, as curator of the Mbari Artists and Writers Club Gallery, Ibadan, and as art critic for the *Black Orpheus* magazine and other journals promoted the early work of African postcolonial modernists, including Demas Nwoko and Uche Okeke (Nigeria), Ibrahim El Salahi and Mohamed Shibrain (Sudan), Malangatana Ngwenya (Mozambique), and Vincent Kofi (Ghana), among others. With the example of his critical writing on the work of Okeke and Nwoko, I seek to show the simultaneously productive and problematic engagements among African artists and their European supporters at a time both parties differentially imagined the relationship between art, decolonization, and nationalism. Stemming from this, I argue that although Beier understood the task the artists had set for themselves, which was to articulate the artistic conditions of political sovereignty, he also misrecognized the point of the artists' stylistic and discursive engagements with "traditional art" and national culture as a crucial part of articulating their manifold modern subjectivity and artistic vision.

Surprisingly, the crucial role of foundational and early art criticism in shaping the discourse and reception of modernism in Africa has not received its due in the scholarship. A key consequence of this is that our view of the landscape and critical context of the emergence of new art and artists across the continent at mid-century remains partial. As it happens, a good number of critics and commentators writing about modern art at its inception in Nigeria and elsewhere were expatriate art teachers, cultural administrators, and journalists. Though this was a diverse lot, with wide-ranging interests, ambition, and ideological sympathies, they belonged, in my view, to two more or less distinct groups, marked by the extent to which they put their work in the service of the colonial educational and cultural mandate. The first arrived in the wake of the introduction of art teaching in Nigeria during the 1920s and had supported what Tejumola Olaniyan has described as the colonial regime's antipathy to African modernity.[1] Convinced about the African's inability to deal with modernity's complexities, this cohort, exemplified in Nigeria by Kenneth C. Murray (1903–1972), the first official art teacher and later museologist, instead sought to shield their native wards from modernism. The second group consisted of individuals inspired by the antiestablishment work of the European avant-garde and were of the generation that became critical of Western civilization in the wake of the devastations of the Second World War and Nazi genocide. Arriving in Africa in the postwar era, this latter group identified with African political decolonization as well as the literary and artistic modernisms that came in its wake. In some cases, and with a tinge of romanticism, they saw in nonindustrialized Africa an existential antidote to the moral bankruptcy of Europe's soulless modernity.[2] Referring to these "white mentors," Elizabeth Rankin has argued that they were instrumental in the development of what Thomas McEvilley called the "third phase stage in history's identity process." This stage, within which we find the African postcolonial modernists, is that moment when, says McEvilley, "the colonized not only negated the identity of the colonizers, but also redirected their attention to the recovery of their own, perhaps abandoned, certainly altered, identity":[3] "I am concerned here with this type of European, exemplified by Ulli Beier, memorably described by John Thompson as, a border operator—on the border between the European and the local . . . Ulli was able to go back and forth like a smuggler . . . from *avant-garde* European art and *avant-garde* European literature, which at the time were still interested in myth and symbol, to modern and traditional African art and literature."[4] While mentorship does not quite capture Beier's relationships with the artists (and writers) who were part of his literary and artistic circle and networks, he was nevertheless a sympathetic and enthusiastic advocate of their postcolonial modernist enterprise. I am interested here in the productive and mutually affirmative transactions between the European border operator and African artists in a period when both parties saw the end of colonialism as occasion for imagining new modes of artistic and cultural expression. But also, I want to examine moments of conjunction and disjunction, between the ideas and visions of Beier, arguably African modernism's most influential curator and critic, and those of the artists whose work he presented as exemplary of progressive modernism in postcolonial Africa. I wish to show that Beier's framing of the artists' work played a determinative role in its early reception and, more fundamentally, led to the general misrecognition, for a long time, of what constituted this work's value and contribution to African postcolonial modernisms, and in fact its very nature.[5] In making this claim, I must clarify what I mean by *postcolonial modernism*, a term that I introduced in an earlier work but that has since gained currency in the field and in the process has lost its preciseness, its specificity. To clarify, suffice it to say that postcolonial modernism in Africa refers to the work of continental artists who were inspired by the rhetoric and reality of decolonization during the 1950s and 1960s and who called for the renegotiation of their artistic and discursive relationships with colonial European and ancestral African art. This work, drawing on the experimental and formal rigor of the historical modernist avant-garde, prioritized design elements from Africa and thus expressed a politics of form with which the postindependence generation identified.[6] It is the difference in the nature of this politics among the independence generation of artists and their European mentors/allies that informs what I identify here as Beier's misrecognition of what to Okeke and Nwoko constituted the most fundamental aspect and goal of their 1960s work.

Ulli Beier arrived in Nigeria in 1950 as an instructor of English in the Extra-Mural Program at the University College, Ibadan. Born to a Jewish family in Glowitz, Germany (Główczyce, Poland), in 1922, Beier moved with his parents — after the Nazis came to power — to Palestine, where he was interned during the Second World War. There, he earned a bachelor's degree in extramural studies as an external student in the University of London. After the war, he moved to London, completing another degree in phonetics. In 1950 he relocated to Nigeria, having been offered a teaching position in extramural studies at Ibadan, which, like other colonial-era universities in Anglophone Africa, was an affiliate college of the University of London. Introduced to the opera and the visual arts by his father, a medical doctor, Beier was drawn to the primitivist strain of the European avant-garde, particularly the work of the French artist Jean Dubuffet and the German expressionists. Arriving in Nigeria — along with his then-wife, the Austrian modernist artist Susanne Wenger (1915–2009), one of his first art projects was a 1953 painting workshop at a mental home in Abeokuta and an exhibition of the artworks in Lagos. This allowed him the opportunity to rehearse the modernist fascination with the supposedly primary, pure, and authentic art of the mentally ill.[7] Despite that he identified the artists as "Yoruba," as if to suggest that ethnic affiliation determined the painters' aesthetic, that workshop and others that followed in the next decade were indicative of the confluence in Beier's work of the avant-garde's primitivist imaginaries and anti-traditionalism on the one hand and a postcolonial critique of Europe's cultural hegemony on the other. Thus, Beier's writing about this workshop, which presented the painters as products of a unique African culture and as worldly modernists, points to the difficulty of his position as a boundary crosser enmeshed in the contradictions of emic and etic perspectives on African cultural production. This is important to understanding the argument I make in this chapter. I contend that whereas the 1953 workshop revealed the interpretive tension in Beier's early writing on modern art in Nigeria, at the height of his powers in the early 1960s when a new generation of artists came on the scene in Zaria and Lagos, he still did not quite grasp the politics and formal propositions of the artists he ardently promoted.

Beier's participation at the First International Congress of Black Writers and Artists—organized by the Senegalese writer and cultural entrepreneur Alioune Diop at the Sorbonne, Paris, in 1956—fully immersed him in the world of modern African art and literature and catalyzed what would become his lifelong preoccupation with African art and literature. Impressed by the robust debates and presentations by distinguished intellectuals convened at the 1956 congress, Beier also realized that the nascent Anglophone African writing, some of which he encountered in Nigeria, could never match the vitality and sophistication of its francophone counterpart without an Anglophone literary forum comparable to Diop's influential Black literary and cultural journal *Présence Africaine*. Within one year, in collaboration with Janheinz Jahn (1918–1973), the German writer and advocate of Negritude literature, Beier founded *Black Orpheus*, a literary magazine that soon became the prime space for the work of the new generation of Anglophone African and black Diaspora writers and artists. Four years later, he also cofounded the Mbari Artists and Writers Club at Ibadan in partnership with several young African writers, including Wole Soyinka (b. 1935), Chinua Achebe (1930–2013), Eski'a Mphahlele (1919–2008), and the artists Vincent Kofi (1923–1974), Demas Nwoko (b. 1935), and Uche Okeke (1933–2016)—all leading voices in African literary and artistic postcolonial modernism. *Black Orpheus* and the Mbari Club's art gallery thus became the central platforms for Beier's art criticism and his curatorial projects, and with his international network of critics and artists, he turned the journal and gallery into arguably the most important theaters of postcolonial modernism on the African continent during the decade of decolonization.

In a seminal essay in the 1958 issue of *Black Orpheus* on Susanne Wenger's work, Beier outlined the thrust of his future art criticism and the basis of his aesthetic preferences, which in turn shaped the scholarship on this art for many years. According to him, Wenger, who as a painter worked in an expressionist mode and had become a high priestess of the Osun Cult of the Yoruba, exemplified a progressive and radical synthesis of the Negritude ethos and the formal sensibilities of European modernism. Compared to her European contemporaries, including Maya Deren, Placide Tempels, and Pierre Verger, Wenger, according to Beier, went the farthest in penetrating "more deeply into the mysteries of traditional African life." Her work, in its focus on Yoruba religious, folkloric, and ritual subject matter, constituted a visual equivalent of literary Negritude—precisely because of its productive mix of European and African cultural experience and artistic traditions. Though situated within the modernist pursuit of innovative and experimental form, Wenger's work, Beier argues, rejects the aestheticism of Parisian modernism and instead identifies with both the more mystical aspirations of German expressionism and the affirmative, universal humanism of Negritude. Although this type of work—in its thematic preoccupation—is more pertinently the product of a deep encounter with "mysterious" African cultures, it only loosely alludes, if at all, to any specific African—or for that matter modernist European—art form or style.

While Beier did not fully describe his understanding of Negritude as a literary movement, one thing is clear: he was convinced by Jean Paul Sartre's argument about Negritude as a self-affirmative return by the Black victim of European racism to the depths of the Black soul in order to acquire the poetic voice of anti-racist resistance.[8] Just as Sartre's Negritude poet, suspended in the darkling zone between Western civilization and his ancient Black soul, relies on trance-like irrationalities to make lyrically revolutionary work, Beier's ideal modernists forged delirious work from an indirect and illogical melding of European and African influences. However, where for Sartre, Negritude was a necessary utterance by Black poets directed at their own people, Beier saw in Wenger—a white woman—the same orphic impulse at the basis of Sartre's Negritude. In other words, for Beier, Negritude was not a racial phenomenon; as an artistic and ontological condition, it was accessible to Europeans like Wenger who, through sympathetic magic, could make the unlikely journey to the Black soul.[9]

But even as he celebrated Wenger's visual Negritude, Beier notes—and here he sounds as though he is deliberately challenging his artist contemporaries in Nigeria and elsewhere—that it was all but impossible for the new generation of African artists to emulate Wenger's inspiring work simply because their art-school training had all but already destroyed their innate creative originality. Wenger, to him, redeemed and cleansed herself of the dross she might have acquired during her time among the Viennese avant-garde by her deep immersion in the liberatory, mysterious, precognitive world of Yoruba religion and ritual. On the other hand, the modern African artists, unable and unwilling to return to this source and pressed by the imperative to be inauthentically modern, faced a precarious, all but impossible path to true originality. This, in fact, is the core of Beier's criticism of modern African art. Moreover, he was convinced that colonial formal art education subjected African artists to a doctrinaire system that destroyed their individuality and prevented their access to progressive developments in contemporary art, specifically surrealism and expressionism; it also foreclosed for them the possibility of devising a new, appropriate, and unique modernist aesthetic. Though doubtful about the possibility of a robust African modernism that is at once sympathetic to the ideological sympathies of Negritude and liberated from the conservative pseudo-academic realism of the colonial era, he paradoxically seemed eager to prove himself wrong. He did this, I suggest, by searching out young artists who, despite their academic training, made the kind of work that came close to his understanding and vision of African modernism at mid-century.

As we shall see, the work of Beier's preferred artists, as anticipated by his reading of Wenger, would show, especially *unintentionally*, a formal or conceptual amalgamation of modernist avant-garde techniques and the sense of enigma he identifies with the Indigenous art, cultures, and religions of Africa. Such work must at once be formally expressive and intuitive rather than deliberate or mannered, but also suggestive of some indeterminate spirituality, and indirectly evocative of Western modernist and Indigenous African artistic traditions.

Two years after his Wenger article, Beier encountered the work of Uche Okeke and Demas Nwoko, as well as Jimo Akolo and Bruce Onobrakpeya, four young artists who at the time were studying painting at the Nigerian College of Art, Science and Technology, Zaria—Nigeria's first art school, established in 1953. Declaring them the irrefutable stars of the new order, he argued that they avoided both the supposedly rigid academic realism of Aina Onabolu (1882–1963) and Akinola Lasekan (1916–1974) and the naïve realism of the Murray School[10] and achieved what Beier calls "the synthesis between African and European elements of style and thought which they are looking for."[11] Moreover, whereas Ben Enwonwu—at the time Nigeria's best-known and most influential artist—represented the problematic position of the contemporary African artist due to his apparent inability to resolve the oppositional pull of a European modernist aesthetic and the impulse to create an ostensibly African style, the Zaria artists developed a positive synthesis of old and new—European and African elements—as had Wenger. This successful synthesis, Beier argues, makes their work "more genuinely and more authentically 'Nigerian' while it is at the same time far more modern in approach. It is the finest monument to Nigerian Independence we could have wished for."[12]

Given that the Zaria students had independently presented their art as fully aligned with cultural and political decolonization, they agreed with the general direction of Beier's art criticism, motivated by a shared commitment to artistic modernism in postcolonial Africa. Just as Beier was attracted to Negritude's universal humanism forged from the mixture of European and African cultural and artistic traditions, the Zaria students, as members of a group they called the Art Society (1958–61), found in the political Pan-Africanism of Kwame Nkrumah of Ghana, Nnamdi Azikiwe of Nigeria, and the Jamaican-born American resident Marcus Garvey the intellectual and ideological basis for their art. Striking a tone remarkably similar to Beier's, Okeke, in a speech to the Art Society that had the tone of a manifesto, declared: "In our difficult work of building a truly Modern African art to be cherished and appreciated for its own sake. . . . We must fight to free ourselves from mirroring foreign culture. This great work demands will power, originality, and, above all, love for our fatherland. We must have our own school of art independent of European and Oriental schools, but drawing as much as possible from what we consider in our clear judgment to be the cream of these influences, and wedding them to our native art culture."[13] In October of the following year, days after Nigeria had celebrated its political independence on the first of the month, Okeke's address to the Art Society took on an even more assertive tone: "Nigeria needs a virile school of art with new philosophy for the new age—our renaissance period." Recalling his argument the previous year for an experimental fusion of European and African artistic forms and ideas, he noted that the "key word is *synthesis*," and that he was "often tempted to describe it as natural synthesis."[14]

As with Beier's frequent use of the term "synthesis" in describing the necessary work of inventing a modern African aesthetic, the Zaria artists adapted Uche Okeke's "natural synthesis" as their operative principle. It is as though both Beier and the Art Society recognized that each constitutive element of the synthesis—the European or African—by itself could not adequately address or account for the reality of the postcolonial condition, which invariably is a product of diverse Indigenous and foreign, African and European, local and global cultural processes and encounters.

Even so, the Art Society used the idea of synthesis in two distinct ways. First, as a condition, which meant the recognition of the historical reality of postcolonial society as constituted by Indigenous and Western elements, each no less valid or important than the other. And second, as a practice, which assumes the capacity of the artist to be an active, free-willed mediator of culture, cultural formations, and the artistic experience in the newly independent nation. Overall, Beier's art criticism and the manifestos of the Art Society reflected the paradoxical mix of realism and romanticism with which African, Africanist, and Afrophile intellectuals grappled with the challenge of reconciling the imperatives of cultural identity and political destiny of decolonizing and modernizing Africa during the late 1950s.[15]

There is little doubt, I am suggesting, about the mutual investment on the part of Beier and the Art Society in a modernism informed by the assertion of the African artist's freedom to mine the artistic archives of Europe and Africa in order to develop a visual language and subject matter appropriate to the postcolonial experience. Even so—and this is the crux of my argument—Beier's positive and enthusiastic reading of the Zaria artists' work also frequently missed its more salient formal aspects and its conceptual scope, in fact its politics. A close reading of Beier's writings on Okeke and Nwoko reveals their moments of alignment and disconnection but also, quite importantly, points to the fundamental tension between their visions of the modern in postcolonial Africa.

Writing about Okeke in his influential 1968 book *Contemporary Art in Africa*—for many years the only widely circulated survey on modern African art—Beier emphatically noted that "[Okeke] was less interested in adapting certain forms of traditional African art. To him it was of vital importance for the artist to study and understand the *content* of African art."[16] However, to suggest that Okeke's depiction of African (or more specifically Igbo) subject matter reflected a lack of interest in exploring the formal possibilities of specific African art forms and aesthetic paradigms is to ignore or misunderstand the work that defined Okeke's personal style after Zaria. In fact, in his own review of the unprecedented survey exhibition, organized as part of the nationwide celebration of Nigeria's independence in October 1960, Beier argued that the significance of Okeke and Nwoko's work lay in their adoption of the formal qualities of Igbo sculpture into their figural compositions. This idea of insinuating Igbo sculpture, without directly emulating it, Beier noted, made their painting, as noted earlier, more authentically Nigerian. Thus, the question is this: Did Okeke's Zaria-period work shown at the Independence exhibition really demonstrate its stylistic exploration of an Igbo art form while his subsequent work failed to sustain this interest, much less expand on it? To what extent did the artist's post-Zaria work step away, as Beier implies in 1968, from the suppos-

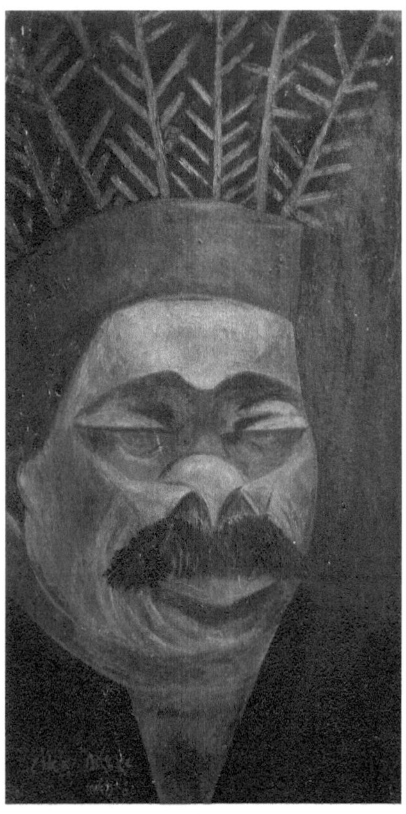

FIGURE 1.1 Uche Okeke, *Egbenuoba*, 1961. Oil on board. Collection of the National Council for Arts and Culture, Abuja. Photo courtesy of the author.

edly rigorous experimentation with specific African art forms already suggested in his 1960 painting, and is that why Beier ignored it?

To be clear, the theory of natural synthesis, espoused at the time Okeke produced the drawings and paintings Beier found so authentically Nigerian and compellingly modern, was only the beginning of what would later be a sustained experiment with the body and mural art form called Uli practiced by Igbo women.[17] Whereas his Zaria-period work (for instance, *Jumaa*, *Egbenuoba*, and *Christ*, all 1961), like that of his colleagues in the Art Society, derived from his adaptation of the expressionist palette of the early-twentieth-century European Fauvists, his figuration revealed a superficial interest in African—though not necessarily Igbo—sculpture.[18] If we consider *Egbenuoba*, to give one example, which depicts a masked figure associated with an Igbo hunters' cult, the face does not so much suggest any known Igbo sculptural style as remind us of the European avant-garde's formal play with the rupturing of representational and formal order inspired by highly stylized African masks (see figure 1.1). In fact, we are hard-pressed to find the bases for the formal connection Beier makes between Igbo sculpture and Okeke's 1960–61 paintings. Yet, that is not the only problem with Beier's argument about Okeke's work.

By 1968 when Beier published his text, Okeke had become a leading contemporary Nigerian artist on account of his traditional Igbo Uli–inspired work, which began with his meticulous examination of the spatial ordering, linear characteristics, and principles of formal abstraction deployed by Igbo Uli artists. While the Art Society manifesto called for work that foregrounded Indigenous aesthetics and formal principles, it was only in 1961, at the very end of his studies in Zaria, that he found the right path to accomplishing that "natural synthesis" mandate. Beginning by observing his own mother's Uli drawings (that he had her make on paper), as well as the murals and body designs by other women in his hometown, Okeke stepped away from European avant-garde-inspired expressionism, focusing instead on the graphic lyricism of Uli drawing. In fact, the radical transformation of his personal style occurred in 1962 and 1963 when he produced his Uli-inspired *Oja Suite* and *Munich Suite* drawings (figure 1.2). These works signaled the emergence of an artistic language rooted in a specific Igbo art form but testifying to his belief in the primacy of formal and experimental rigor that we have come to associate with modernism. Thus, if his late Zaria painting — produced while he was espousing the theory of natural synthesis — belied a tentativeness about his aesthetic relationship with African art, the post-1962 work shows him totally absorbed with exploring its formal possibilities.

Just as Okeke was describing his idea of natural synthesis to his Art Society colleagues, Beier, in an essay on the Indian modernist Francis Newton Souza, proclaimed, "From the ruins of our various traditions in Asia and Africa we are beginning the work of synthesis and reconstruction."[19] Beier also frequently mobilized the term *synthesis* to describe the radical combination of European and African artistic influences in the work of his favorite artists. It seems natural, therefore, that Okeke's Uli-inspired work, informed as it was by the will to combine the rigor of modernist picture making with systematic analyses of an African form in order to develop a distinctly new, yet culturally embedded, artistic style, ought to have been a championed by Beier. This, as I noted earlier, did not happen. Why? One reason may be that while Beier understood synthesis in Hegelian terms — in other words, as a dialectical result (modern African art) that is fundamentally *different* from the thesis (European) and antithesis (African) — Okeke and the Art Society imagined it differently. Synthesis was for them the act of mining and mixing the archives of multiple artistic traditions

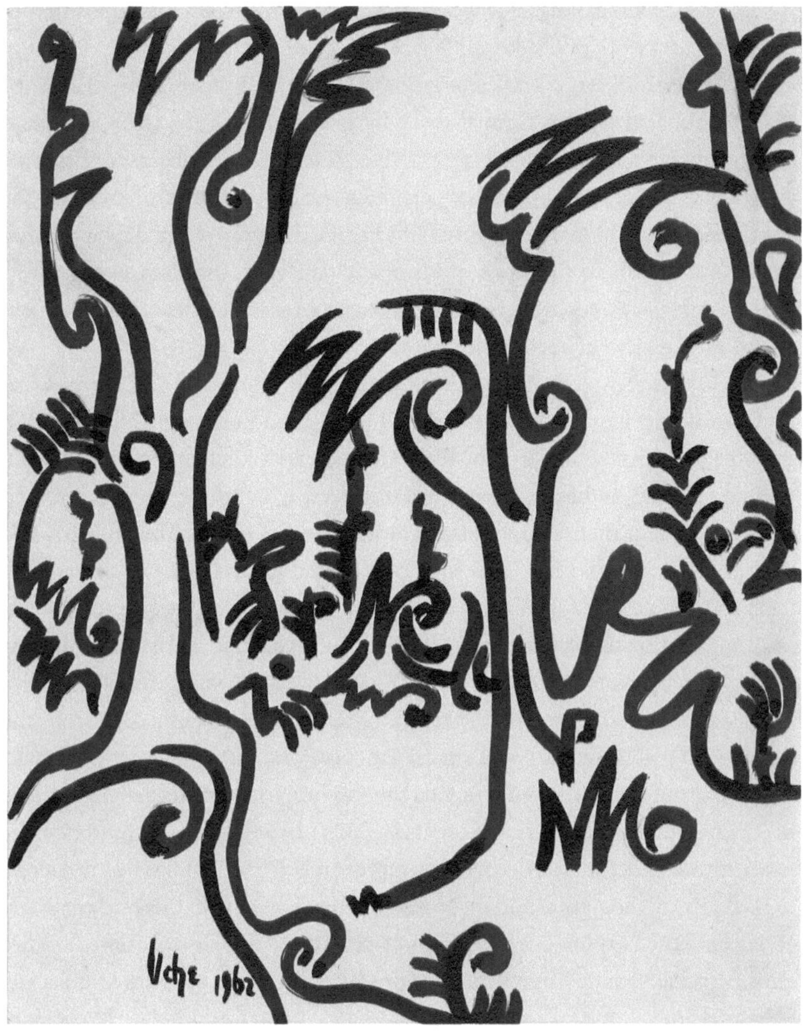

FIGURE 1.2 Uche Okeke, *Savannah Landscape*, 1962. Ink on paper, 10 in. × 8 in. (25.4 cm × 20.3 cm). Collection of the Museum of Modern Art. Gift of Alexandra Herzan from the Collection of Lily Auchincloss (by exchange). Acc. no. 679.2015.

from Europe and Africa in order to reclaim their place within their imagined postcolonial communities. The key difference here is that whereas Beier's synthesis is haunted by the purity and certainties of the thesis-antithesis-synthesis dialectical orders, such that it was important to ascertain and judge any breach of their integrity and distinctiveness, this was of little interest to the Art Society.

In fact, what I am calling Beier's synthesis may help explain his disposition to the post-Zaria work of Okeke and Nwoko.

While Beier all but completely ignored Okeke's Uli-inspired work, he apparently recognized the parallel work by Demas Nwoko as truly and positively transformative, which suggests that Beier was not necessarily against the kind of direct examination of particular African artistic traditions by the continent's postcolonial modernists. Rather, he disapproved of new work that hewed too closely to the work of European artists or appeared to emulate a specific African art form such that it came across as the continuation of an old tradition or a kind of heritage practice.

Like Okeke, Nwoko's Zaria-period painting is reminiscent of the postimpressionist and fauvist composition and palette, and although his figuration gestures to African wooden statuary, it does so in a rather general sense. Even so, there is every indication that Nwoko studied Igbo tutelary figures and had adapted some of their characteristics to his own figuration. This much is evident in his *Adam and Eve* Paris suite of 1962 and in his iconic *Adam and Eve* pair of wood sculptures of the same period (figure 1.3). However, it was not until 1964 when he systematically studied the technique and style of the ancient Nok terracotta sculptures (500 BCE–400 CE) from Northern Nigeria (and to a lesser extent Ife terracotta [twelfth to the fourteenth centuries], from the Southwest) that he developed his most articulate and distinctive personal style. Writing about this work, Beier noted that Nwoko's "clearly African orientation, his deliberate use of traditional forms and his uncompromising attitude have made him one of the first original to emerge in Nigeria."[20] Beier was not alone in recognizing the significance of Nwoko's achievement with this body of work. His friend, the Guyana-born critic and artist Denis Williams, declared, rather enthusiastically, that "Mr. Nwoko has produced work, in my view, immeasurably superior in concept and in sensitivity to the finest examples we know from Nok, and hardly inferior, in the originality of his idiom, to the masterpieces of Ife."[21] For Beier, as for Williams, the formal and material affinities between Nwoko's and Nok terracotta were irrefutable (figure 1.4). Moreover, Nwoko's intentional reprise of and radical departure from the ancient art style—what I have called its quirky, idiosyncratic archaism — exemplified the brand of authentic African modernism Beier's criticism anticipated.[22]

The question at this point is this: How might we explain Beier's contrasting views in 1968 on Okeke and Nwoko when, only a few years earlier, he had suggested that their personal styles and modernist visions were similar? How do we make sense, on the one hand, of his fascination with Nwoko's sculpture

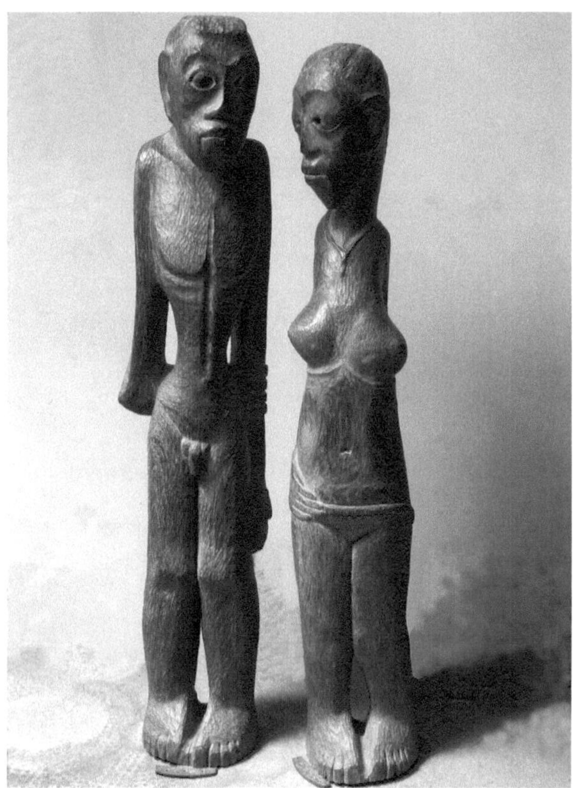

FIGURE 1.3
Demas Nwoko, *Adam and Eve*, 1962–63. Wood. Artist's collection. Copyright Demas Nwoko. Photo courtesy of the author.

that was clearly inspired — both at the level of medium and technique and in terms of formal style — by an ancient Nigerian and African art form and, on the other, his silence on the parallel work Okeke did with Igbo Uli? To be sure, Beier saw Nwoko as the one who most successfully embodied a progressive modernist imagination among the independence generation of Nigerian artists. Beier was also quite enthusiastic about Okeke, but primarily for his folktale drawings (1958–59), which came well before his Uli-inspired drawings and painting. These earlier line drawings, delirious and crisp images of fantastical beings with no obvious formal relationship to any African or European artistic tradition, became, for Beier, exemplary of African modernism ardently advocated.[23] The problem with Okeke's post-natural synthesis Igbo Uli–inspired work, I argue, is precisely that it did not show evidence of the kind of critical distance from traditional African art that Beier wished to see in the work of the postcolonial modernists. In other words, at the level of the visual, Okeke's canonical work smacked too much of an ethnically inflected gesture, a kind

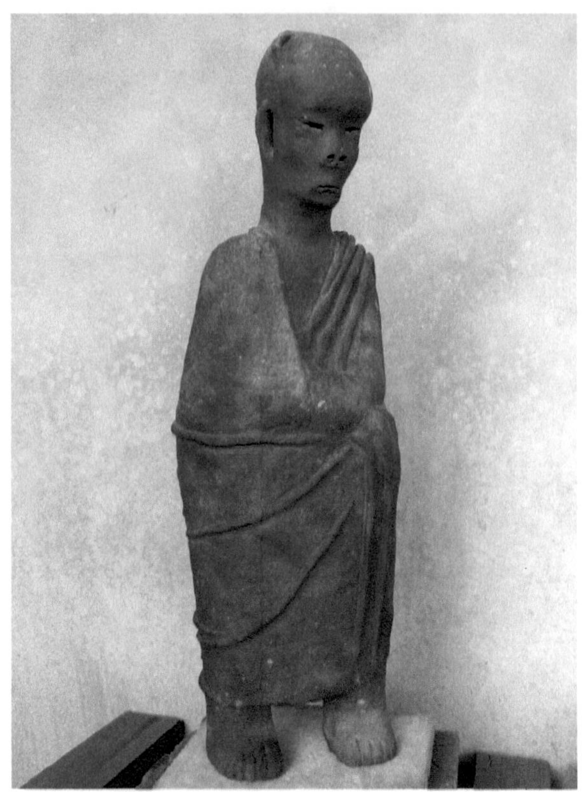

FIGURE 1.4
Demas Nwoko, *Philosopher*, 1965. Terracotta. Collection of the Asele Institute, Nimo. Copyright Demas Nwoko. Photo courtesy of the author.

of visual nationalism that, apparently, limited its potential as a universal statement. What is the basis for this speculation?

Beier's inaugural assertions about Susanne Wenger's work as the ideal model for African modernists were based on two key assumptions. First, her immersion into Yoruba religion, rituals, and social life substantially informed her subject matter and shaped her view of the artist's role as an active player in her community. Second, her development of a personal style owed little or nothing to *any particular* Yoruba or, indeed, any European modernist style, although her mystical expressionism left no one in doubt of her familiarity with both worlds. This might also explain his attraction to the work of artists such as Sudanese Ibrahim El Salahi (b. 1930), who, after training at the Slade, developed a formal style informed by a systematic exploration of Arabic calligraphy, post-cubist abstraction, and diverse African design systems. Whereas Okeke's work singularly focused on Igbo Uli aesthetics, Salahi's shared "formal affinities" with West African masks, folk art designs, and the structural character of the Arabic alphabet. That is, like Wenger, Salahi achieved, according to Beier, a "perfect and successful blending of cultures," and he did this by descending into his African soul from whence came the mystical, complex imagery in which its source elements are at best faint echoes. Another artist who found favor in Beier's criticism is Goan artist F. N. Souza who, with his colleagues in the Progressive Artists Group in 1947, rejected the native revivalism of the Bengal School and the academism of the colonial art schools. In doing so, he developed a personal style that ambiguously drew on both the pictorial tactics of the European avant-garde and Hindu religious figuration and iconography. In other words, Beier's postcolonial modernists had to develop an individual style that simultaneously alludes to and sufficiently transcends any particular Western modernist avant-garde or African Indigenous artistic style. That, it seems to me, was ultimately the problem with the post-Uli work of Okeke, which unlike his Zaria-period work and despite its inventiveness, was too specific in its citation of one African traditional art form (Igbo Uli) and thus failed to establish the kind of aesthetic autonomy he saw in Wenger and Nwoko.

One nagging question remains: How is it that Beier read Nwoko's terracotta sculptures differently given that they were inspired primarily by ancient Nok terracotta? It must be that Beier saw as significant the fact that Nwoko, who like Okeke is an Igbo from southeastern Nigeria, experimented with the Nok corpus, which is associated with a different contemporary Nigerian ethnicity; in other words, the artist could not have been attracted to the ancient art form as a gesture of ethnic nationalism. More pertinent though is that despite its stylistic affinity with Nok, Nwoko's work is also reminiscent of terracotta traditions of ancient Ife and thus sufficiently demonstrates an ambiguous relationship with more than one Nigerian or African artistic heritage to which he could not make a direct ancestral heritage claim. Finally, what I have been suggesting throughout this chapter as the recurring note in Beier's criticism, the need for new work by Africans at mid-century to hold its distance from both European modernism and ancestral African art, cannot be explained simply as a matter of his stylistic-conceptual preferences. Instead, it seems to have been fundamentally motivated by a form of politics—that is, by his anxiety about the intersection of culture and nationalism in decolonizing Africa. While the Art Society proposed natural synthesis as a generative process for a new art in the service of the sovereign nation—as Frantz Fanon demanded, in his contemporaneous essay, the awakening of national cultural consciousness—Beier avoided such co-optation despite being an advocate of cultural decolonization.[24] Might this have anything to do with his own biography? It seems to me that Beier's internment in Palestine during the Second World War, and the widespread anxiety in Europe about the toxic nationalism that fueled the war, informed his rejection of art that appeared sympathetic to forms of cultural nationalism. The artists he wrote about had no such concerns. Indeed, to them nationalism during the independence decade was a good thing, precisely because it propelled the decolonization project and served as the catalyst for the new art that came in its wake.

Why, in the final analysis, does this excursion into Ulli Beier's art criticism during the 1950s and 1960s matter, especially in a volume about modernists and their mediators? To be sure, he was in good measure a promoter, impresario, and an intrepid defender of artists like Nwoko, Okeke, Salahi, and others who became part of the Mbari international network that also included Africa's preeminent modernist writers, poets, and dramatists. Moreover, he might not have been in agreement with these artists and writers on the matter of the political and ideological objective for their work. Yet there was no question that what motivated their tactical alliance was the collective desire to bring forth a new art and critical discourse that matched in tone and substance, the giddy, thrilling experience of African decolonization. In this sense, Beier and the artists constituted a motley group of cotravelers who had, if you will, slightly different ideas about their journey's destination.

Notes

1. Taiwo, *How Colonialism Preempted Modernity in Africa*.

2. V. Y. Mudimbe describes Pierre Romain-Defossés, a Frenchman and founder of the art workshop "Le Hangar" in Lubumbashi, as a "romantic" who was "opposed to what he called 'Western degeneracy,' 'snobism,' and 'folly.'" See Mudimbe, *The Idea of Africa*, 157.

3. See Rankin, "Creating Communities," 55.

4. Quoted in Benson, "'Border Operators,'" 431.

5. Consider, for instance, that Marshall Ward Mount's 1973 book *African Art: The Years since 1920*, one of the most cited modern African survey texts, makes no mention of Okeke and Nwoko's post-Zaria work. Instead, like Beier, it emphasized their early work, before they successfully arrived at the distinctive individual styles anticipated by the theory of natural synthesis they proposed in Zaria. The absence of the artists' most accomplished work—that arguably marked a high point of postcolonial modernism in Nigeria—in these foundational texts of African modernism meant that the subsequent scholarship all ignored this work for decades.

6. Okeke-Agulu, "Politics of Form."

7. See Beier and Beier, *Thirteen Painters from the Mental Home Abeokuta*, n.p. See also Beier, "Two Yoruba Painters."

8. Sartre, *Black Orpheus*. Beier named his magazine after Sartre's text.

9. I am thinking here of the variety of sympathetic magic described by Fraser as based on contagion; intimate contact with Black persons allows the sympathetic magician to will herself into the ordinarily unbreachable space of the Black soul. See Fraser, *The Golden Bough*, 43–55.

10. Murray School refers to the work of the former student Kenneth Crosthwaite Murray, a Briton and first art teacher hired by the colonial government in 1928. Murray rejected academic training for Africans, prescribed instruction in Indigenous craftwork, and condemned modernity's corruption of authentic lifeways of colonized peoples.

11. Beier, *Art in Nigeria, 1960*, 10.

12. Beier, "Contemporary Nigerian Art," 51.

13. See Okeke, "Growth of an Idea," 1.

14. Okeke's emphasis. See Okeke, "Natural Synthesis," 2. For further discussion of Okeke's theory of natural synthesis, see Okeke-Agulu, *Postcolonial Modernism*, 88–99.

15. Okeke-Agulu, *Postcolonial Modernism*, 92.

16. My emphasis. Beier, *Contemporary Art in Africa*, 46.

17. For detailed studies of this art form, see Willis, "Uli Painting and the Igbo World View"; Willis, "A Lexicon of Igbo Uli Motifs."

18. For detailed analysis of these paintings, as well as the Zaria period work by Okeke and his Art Society colleagues, see Okeke-Agulu, *Postcolonial Modernism*, especially chapter 3.

19. Aragbabalu, "Souza," 21.

20. Beier, *Contemporary Art in Africa*, 45.

21. Williams, "A Revival of Terra-Cotta at Ibadan."

22. Okeke-Agulu, *Postcolonial Modernism*, 204.

23. Beier, *Uche Okeke*.

24. Fanon, "On National Culture."

Bibliography

Aragbabalu, Omidiji. "Souza." *Black Orpheus* 7 (1960): 16–21, 49–52.

Beier, S., and H. U. Beier. *Thirteen Painters from the Mental Home Abeokuta: Guide to the Exhibition of Painters at the Exhibition Centre*. N.p., 1953.

Beier, Ulli. *Art in Nigeria, 1960*. Cambridge: Cambridge University Press, 1960.

Beier, Ulli. *Contemporary Art in Africa*. New York: Praeger, 1968.

Beier, Ulli. "Contemporary Nigerian Art." *Nigeria* 68 (1961): 27–57.

Beier, Ulli. "Two Yoruba Painters." *Black Orpheus* 6 (1959): 29–32.

Beier, Ulli, ed. *Uche Okeke: Drawings*. Ibadan: Mbari Publications, 1961.

Benson, Peter. "'Border Operators': Black Orpheus and the Genesis of Modern African Art and Literature." *Research in African Literatures* 14, no. 4 (Winter 1983): 431–73.
Fanon, Frantz. "On National Culture." In *The Wretched of the Earth*, 167–89. New York: Grove Press, 1966.
Fraser, James George. *The Golden Bough*. New York: Macmillan, 1960.
Mudimbe, V. Y. *The Idea of Africa*. Bloomington: Indiana University Press, 1994.
Okeke, Uche. "Growth of an Idea." In *Art in Development—a Nigerian Perspective*. Minneapolis and Nimo, Nigeria: African American Cultural Center / Asele Institute, 1982.
Okeke, Uche. "Natural Synthesis." In *Art in Development—a Nigerian Perspective*. Minneapolis and Nimo, Nigeria: African American Cultural Center / Asele Institute, 1982.
Okeke-Agulu, Chika. "Politics of Form: Uche Okeke's Illustrations for Chinua Achebe's *Things Fall Apart*." In *Chinua Achebe's "Things Fall Apart," 1958–2008*, edited by David Whittaker, 67–86. Amsterdam: Rodopi, 2011.
Okeke-Agulu, Chika. *Postcolonial Modernism: Art and Decolonization in Twentieth-Century Nigeria*. Durham, NC: Duke University Press, 2015.
Rankin, Elizabeth. "Creating Communities: Art Centers and Workshops and Their Influence on the South African Art Scene." In *Visual Century: South African Art in Context, 1907–2007*, vol. 2, *1945–1976*, edited by Lize van Robbroeck, 52–77. Johannesburg: Wits University Press, 2011.
Sartre, Jean-Paul. *Black Orpheus*. Translated by S. W. Allen. Paris: Présence Africaine, 1976.
Taiwo, Olufemi. *How Colonialism Preempted Modernity in Africa*. Bloomington: Indiana University Press, 2010.
Williams, Denis. "A Revival of Terra-Cotta at Ibadan." *Nigeria* 88 (March 1966): 4–13.
Willis, Elizabeth A. "A Lexicon of Igbo Uli Motifs." *Nsukka Journal of the Humanities*, no. 1 (June 1987): 91–120.
Willis, Elizabeth A. "Uli Painting and the Igbo World View." *African Arts* 23, no. 1 (November 1989): 62–67, 104.

ANITRA NETTLETON

2 CHAINS OF MENTORSHIP

The Amadlozi Effect in Johannesburg in the 1960s and 1970s

The deep entanglements of colonialism and modernity complicate any current attempts at dismantling hegemonic Western claims to modernism in the writing of mid-twentieth-century South African art histories. The resultant disentanglement of modernity from colonialist preconceptions of Africans as premodern of necessity involves an examination both of the challenges mounted against such Western claims and of processes of exchange between colonizers and colonized. It is these processes that I excavate in this essay. I focus on how the makers of a particular brand of South African modernism laid claim to an identity they intended to be read as peculiarly African. This claim was most clearly articulated in a 1963–64 exhibition of works by a group of Johannesburg-based artists who called themselves Amadlozi and whose formal and stylistic roots could easily be situated within a modernist framework. I frame their impact as the "Amadlozi effect."

At the core of my argument stands a problem pointed to by Achille Mbembe who suggests, in general terms, that "the possibility of an African modernity was reduced to an endless interrogation of the possibility, for the African subject, of achieving a balance between his/her total identification with 'traditional' (in philosophies of authenticity) African life and his/her merging with and subsequent loss in modernity (in the discourse of alienation)."[1] That there was no question of the modernity of the white artists who showed in the Amadlozi exhibition is clear, throwing the modernity of the single Black participant, by its very exceptionalism, into high relief. The brand-makers of a South African iteration of "African" modern art included artists, their teachers, mentors, gallerists, and art historians, most of whom were white. This search for an African modernity is embedded in the entanglements that intertwined the Amadlozi exhibition's participants and their subsequent involvement in the training they offered young artists in the context of 1960s and 1970s Johannesburg, primarily through or in the ambit of the city's Polly Street Art Centre. I argue further that it is no mere coincidence that the Amadlozi exhibition was staged at the beginning of the commercial and critical success enjoyed by the Black artists trained there.

The Dramatis Personae

Portraits of the five participating South African artists feature prominently on the printed invitation for the preview of an exhibition at the Egon Guenther Gallery in Johannesburg (figure 2.1), which then moved through Fiamma Vigo's Gallery Numero premises in Rome, Florence, Venice, and Milan 1963 and early 1964.[2] They are Cecil Skotnes, Cecily Sash, Sidney Kumalo, Eduardo Villa, and Giuseppe Cattaneo. The name of the exhibition, *Amadlozi*, is an isiZulu term, the plural of *idlozi,* which roughly translates to "spirits of our ancestors." The name was suggested by the only Black participant, Sydney Kumalo, and was thereafter invoked by the exhibition's organizers, Johannesburg gallerists Egon Guenther and Vittorio Meneghelli, to conjure an African identity sufficiently generic to encompass the work of the culturally diverse and polyglot group of artists Guenther had taken into his stable. The lettering of the title, *Amadlozi*, artfully oriented along the vertical axis on upper right side of the printed invitation, announces its intention to make "Africanness" a central motif for the group exhibition, even though only one of the five portraits reveals a person immediately identifiable as African according to the classificatory scheme of skin color or "race." I use this term with full awareness of both its problematic character, eloquently critiqued by Paul Gilroy, and its ubiquitous use in the ways South Africans have interacted with each other over the past five hundred years. Race remained the major discriminatory criterion for identification and critique when Black African artists moved into prominent positions in the modern art world of the 1960s and beyond.[3]

Guenther organized the five artists as a collective specifically for this one exhibition, and the original members of Amadlozi did not form an artists' group beyond the show's run. Yet, this disparate group did have further links, one of which was its ties to his coorganizer, prominent Johannesburg dealer and collector Vittorio Meneghelli. If Guenther and Meneghelli are counted as agents

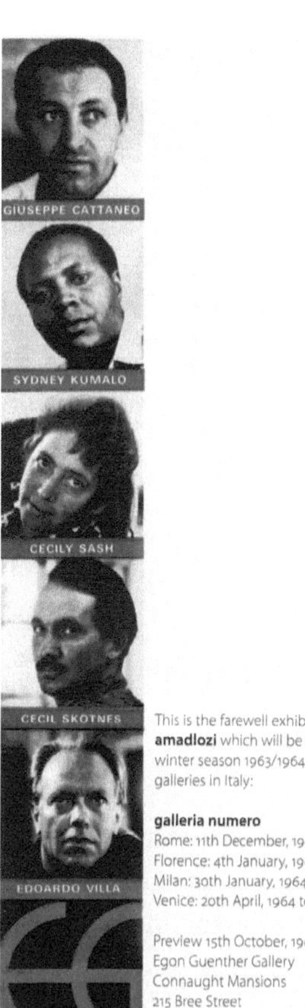

FIGURE 2.1 Invitation to the preview of the *Amadlozi* exhibition, 1963. Collection of the author.

and mediators in the framing, development, and final display of the *Amadlozi* exhibition — and much more beyond — we find ourselves with a complement of seven dramatis personae in the unfolding of the "Amadlozi effect" in the history of South African art. That "effect" was created through an insistence on a particular kind of formal, often still figurative abstraction and stylization in which an "African" essence was distilled. As will become evident, this modernist conceptual and formal framework, premised on notions of universal readability, was the one promoted most stringently by tutors at the Polly Street Art Centre in the 1950s and early 1960s. It was also that in which most of the artists who exhibited with Guenther and Meneghelli worked. Further, all the original artists of the *Amadlozi* exhibition (except possibly Cecily Sash) took on mentoring roles at some time in their careers. Many concentrated on helping young Black artists who had no access to other spaces of training and development.

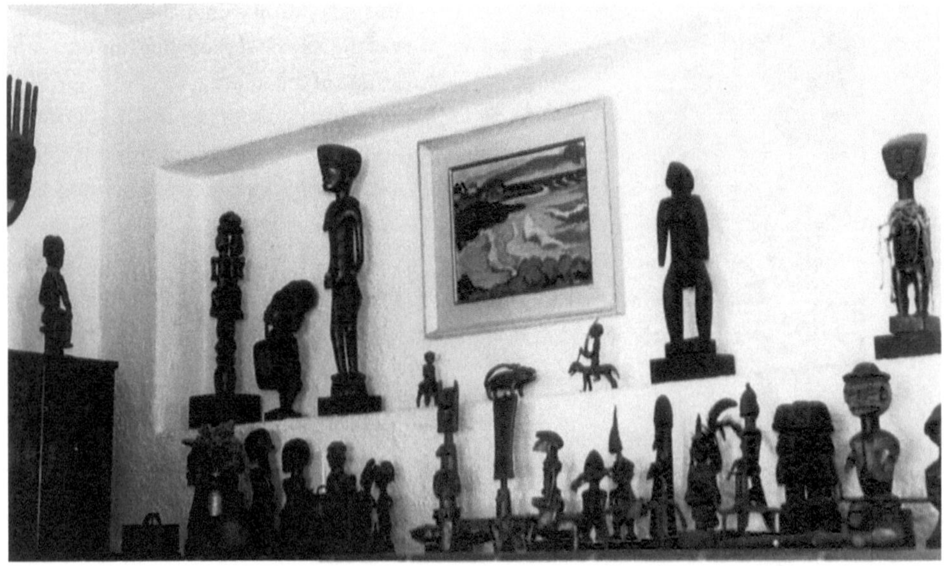

FIGURE 2.2 Part of the Guenther family collection in the 1960s.

Of the seven players brought together in the *Amadlozi* exhibition, only three were actually born in South Africa: Skotnes was the son of a Norwegian father and Canadian mother, immigrant missionaries living in the Eastern Cape; Sash, the only woman in the group, was the daughter of settler Jewish parents living in Delmas, a small town east of Johannesburg; and Kumalo, born and living in Soweto, was the son of isiZulu-speaking parents from Natal and, as noted, the only Black African artist included. The four others were immigrants, artists, and entrepreneurs who had left Europe after World War II.

Egon Guenther and his wife Hanneh emigrated from Germany in 1953 and settled permanently in Johannesburg, where Guenther opened his downtown art gallery in 1957. Guenther had run an art gallery in Mannheim, Germany, and had assembled a collection that included both "traditional" African and modern European art. He sold his African art in Germany to fund his immigration to South Africa but began to make a new collection as soon as he had settled in Johannesburg (figure 2.2). Guenther's story has been told many times, and my telling here is based on my interviews with him between 1973 and 2014, the year before his death.[4]

Vittorio Meneghelli and his wife Paolina left Italy in 1950 and settled in Johannesburg where they started a manufacturing business. They also maintained a strong interest in the visual arts that first publicly manifested in 1968 with the opening of their Totem Gallery. Like Guenther, Meneghelli had previously assembled a modern art collection in Venice, Italy, where he kept a home throughout his life and also started a new collection in Johannesburg.[5] The Meneghelli family collection of African art was made largely through his own travels in Africa from the early 1960s onward.[6] Guenther and Meneghelli were thus linked by their appreciation of historical African art and twentieth-century European modernism.

All the white artists involved in the *Amadlozi* exhibition moved in the same circles as Guenther and Meneghelli and had educational backgrounds that enabled them to work within this twentieth-century modernist context, whose history and manner of operating they understood. Among the five original Amadlozi artists, the four of European extraction all had some formal postsecondary training as professional artists. Edoardo Villa was captured while serving in the Italian army in North Africa during World War II, was interned as a prisoner of war in the Zonderwater camp in South Africa, and remained in South Africa as a settler after his release in 1947. Giuseppe Cattaneo came to South Africa from Milan in 1954 to work in the mines and settled in Johannesburg, teaching at the Fine Arts Department of the University of the Witwatersrand for some time during the 1960s and 1970s. Both Villa and Cattaneo had received professional art training and been exposed to late modernist trends in Italy before they came to South Africa — Villa in Bergamo and Cattaneo in Milan.[7] Cattaneo studied first at Milan's Castello and later at the Brera Academy with Aldo Carpi and Marino Marini. According to Nel, Villa studied sculpture at the Scuola d'Arte Andrea Fantoni in Bergamo under the sculptors Minotti, Lodi, and Barbieri but later became interested in cubism and, through it and his friendship with Guenther and Meneghelli, African sculpture.[8]

Kumalo was the only artist in the original Amadlozi group who had no academic training. He, like all other Black South African artists in these years, was denied access to fine arts training at university or technical school by the policy of separate development, commonly known as apartheid, introduced by the National Party after its electoral victory in the 1948 election.[9] With the implementation of the 1959 Separate Universities Act, Black students were barred from attending universities designated as "white," including the English-language universities that had up to that point allowed Black students access. Fine art training, such as that offered at the University of the Witwatersrand, where Skotnes had studied, and the Art School of the Witwatersrand Technikon, where Sash did her diploma training, remained closed to Black students until the founding of the fine art departments at Black universities such as Fort Hare (1973).[10] Along with a number of other Black artists who were to become professionals, Kumalo received art training at the Adult Education Centre at Number 1 Polly Street in downtown Johannesburg at workshops run by Cecil Skotnes, with the assistance of other white artists.[11] Processes of learning at the Polly Street Art Centre were different from the formal art education offered at the universities and art schools, and the cultural and economic backgrounds of most of the trainees at the center were also worlds apart from those of both the instructors and other mentors such as Egon Guenther.

The history of Polly Street Art Centre has been researched by David Koloane, Elizabeth Rankin, and Elza Miles.[12] Sipho Mdanda has further investigated the teaching methods employed by some of the instructors there.[13] I summarize this work briefly here, in order to pick out individuals and mechanisms of mentorship and mediation from the example of Polly Street as represented in these and other narratives. According to Miles, the Art Centre started life as the Bantu Men's Social Centre but in 1949 became a center for non-European adult education, run by a council that was linked to the Institute for Race Relations—and not the city council as reported elsewhere.[14] The center continued all its functions through the 1950s but was moved to the Jubilee Centre on Eloff Street in 1960 and, soon thereafter, when that location was closed, it moved to the Mofolo section of Soweto. Polly Street Art Centre produced a number of artists who went on to claim major places within the history of Black modernisms, and a rough distinction that can be drawn between the work of two groups of artists neatly illustrates the place of the Polly Street/Amadlozi nexus. In the first group I place Sydney Kumalo, Ezrom Legae (early work), Ben Arnold, Louis Maqhubela, Lucky Sibiya, and Durant Sihlali (later work), all of whom at some time worked with the formalist figurative abstraction that characterizes the Amadlozi effect. In the second group are artists such as Durant Sihlali (early work), Ephraim Ngatane, and David Mogano, who followed the expressive and figurative styles of the earlier generation and have often been grouped as "township" artists. Sitting somewhere on the cusp between these two is Dumile Feni whose sculptural works are more formalist than his very expressive two-dimensional works, although all are resolutely figurative.

Mentorship and Teaching

In tracing the interactions of Polly Street artists, it is important to draw a distinction between mentorship and teaching. If teaching involves passing on knowledge, imparting technical expertise, enabling critical thinking, and developing an individual voice, it generally happens in a situation of asymmetrical power relations. The teacher is set up in a position of one who "knows." The artists who taught at Polly Street Art Centre were initially appointed as *instructors*, a term that clearly suggests such power dynamics. Elza Miles names seven of these early appointees and discusses the input of some, although not in any great depth, largely because the archive is so scanty.[15] However, it is also clear from her survey that there was initially a concentration on watercolor painting, often of landscape, and almost always of rural scenes and figure studies. Students were discouraged from copying from magazines and were encouraged instead to draw or paint from life. Although Alpheus Kubeka stands out in Miles's narrative as an artist who sculpted, the instructors at Polly Street appear to have been mostly concerned with two-dimensional media and craft, and there does not appear to have been any impetus to teach sculptural techniques until 1952.[16]

Miles discusses the attitudes of some of the founders of the art classes at the Adult Education Centre. One expressed reluctance to exert too much influence on the students; a second, Eleanor Lorimer, wanted to expose students to images of a range of artworks that might "rid urban natives of the tendency to imitate magazine advertisements, the type of pictures with which they are most accustomed";[17] and a third claimed that Africans were generally not concerned with color but concentrated on line. None of them seems to have taken a view, common in much later commentary on Kumalo, that Black artists, as Africans, had an innate ability and affinity for sculptural form.[18] Rankin discusses such attitudes among white educators toward an earlier generation of Black artists, suggesting that the "sense of purpose and commitment that drove black artists to pursue an unlikely career in the face of daunting odds" needs greater recognition.[19]

It appears that some of the teaching took place via demonstrations of technique. Fred Schimmel, one of the earliest teachers at the center, engaged with students individually as they drew or painted in class, discussing their work as he went.[20] As pointed out by Rankin, this manner of instruction is one that was common in most art schools — the studio was sometimes set up with a still-life or a life model at the center and students arranged themselves around whatever the subject was with their easels or "donkeys," drawing or painting what they saw.[21] The emphasis on observation of things in "real life" had been part of the training of Western artists from the first academies to the present and has remained in the public imagination throughout the West as a popular, maybe even populist, expectation of "art." Furthermore, it is important to stress that in the South African context, where the only art taught in schools to Black learners was drawing, realistic portrayal in both photographic and painted or sculpted manifestations was constituted by Western-style education as a part of modernity and differed from "traditional" modes of visual representation where they existed.[22] These approaches to art education were also far removed from the European modernist forms that had filtered into South Africa over the previous thirty years.

From the 1920s on there were many professional artists in the wider South African context who had developed modernist forms of expression that rejected naturalism and direct observation.[23] These painters were often vilified in the press for their audacity.[24] Yet observation of nature and its translation into artworks as drawing and painting formed the bedrock of the teaching at Polly Street in the early years, possibly modified by Schimmel's "more intuitive" approach.[25] Under Skotnes, however, the emphasis on drawing from life rather than copying other images did not automatically mean that the kind of direct observation espoused by some artists in documenting their surroundings would be accepted by Polly Street tutors. Miles and Koloane both recount Sihlali's inability to come to terms with Skotnes's approach while Rankin states that most of the past students of the center she interviewed remembered "working predominantly from imagination, following their own ideas."[26] As reported by Koloane, the perception among the "graduates" of Polly Street that Skotnes did not impart what he had learned at art school to the students there thus appears to have had some foundation.[27]

Differentiating Modernity and Modernisms: Schimmel and Skotnes

Fred Schimmel served as a volunteer teacher at Polly Street from 1949 to 1958 and made a valuable contribution to the careers of many Black artists, although its extent has not been fully acknowledged.[28] To understand something of Schimmel's approach, it helps to have an idea of his own work. Although a retrospective exhibition organized at SMAC Gallery in 2008 to mark Schimmel's eightieth birthday contained more than one hundred works, only one work from the 1950s was featured in the online catalogue.[29] This painting draws on abstract expressionist modes of working in which an intuitive freedom and deep involvement with the materials and movement are visible in its gestural brushwork. It is thus very far removed from the more controlled formalism of his 1960s landscape-oriented abstract works where harder edges formed clearly defined and representational shapes.[30] While Schimmel, working with what might therefore be described as evocative abstraction, does not appear to have looked for a particularly African expression and was thus not included in the *Amadlozi* exhibitions, his work was exhibited at the Guenther Gallery in 1964. While this would indicate that his work fell within the parameters of Guenther's strict notions of what constituted "good" art, Schimmel appears to have felt that his approach to art making was incompatible with Skotnes's. He therefore stopped teaching at Polly Street in about 1957, even though he told Miles that he and Skotnes had shared "the same kind of taste."[31]

This taste, which was central to the development of professional artists at the time, seems to have been for modernist, stylized, and expressive forms, especially after the appointment of Skotnes as the person in charge in 1952. Skotnes had served in the South African forces in the Second World War, spending time in Italy after demobilization and then registering for a fine arts degree at the University of the Witwatersrand, Johannesburg. There he received formal academic training in painting, drawing, and printmaking, as well as art history. His own artwork was strongly influenced by the woodcuts of the German expressionists and the African art forms he encountered through his friendship with Guenther, and later Meneghelli. After Skotnes was introduced to Ronald Scharpf's woodcuts by Guenther, he developed a highly individual mode of working in which the woodcut block itself became the artwork (figure 2.3). Using highly stylized forms, Skotnes developed a figurative approach that drew on iconography from African traditions and ways of life. He initially used a very limited color range but increasingly made images on a very large scale, often as commissions for murals.[32]

Skotnes's approach to teaching was, by some accounts, more formalist than Schimmel's.[33] Like Gideon Uys, an earlier teacher at Polly Street, Skotnes had given demonstrations of watercolor painting and he looked for serious commitment in those whom he would mentor rather than teach.[34] Conceptually, Skotnes divided participants in the classes at Polly Street into two groups: those in whom he saw the potential for careers as professional artists and those he saw as leisure-time artists. As Miles suggests, some of his choices in this process were surprising and subsequently proven wrong, yet they explain both his preferences and his preparedness to help artists make their own careers.[35]

Skotnes admitted later that he had at first expected that his Black protégés at Polly Street would have some innate African sensibility but later abandoned this notion and adopted instead the free-art, nonhierarchical forms of art education that were current in many European arts institutions in the 1950s and after.[36] In contrast, however, the artists who were most strongly promoted by

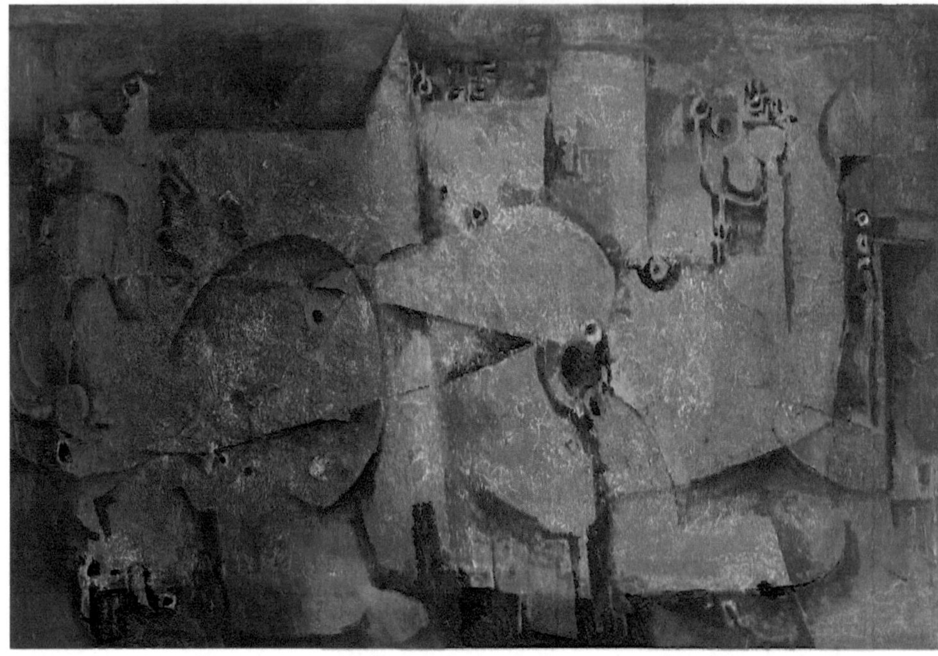

FIGURE 2.3 Cecil Skotnes, *The Legend*, 1962. Oil on board, 91.10 mm × 131.5 mm. Wits Art Museum, Johannesburg.

Guenther and to a lesser extent by other gallerists such as Fernand Haenggi at Gallery 101, Meneghelli at the Totem Gallery, and Linda Givon at the Goodman Gallery were expected to be both African and modern and to have achieved a kind of synthesis in their works that nevertheless did not relinquish the "tribal."[37]

One of the most significant innovations that Skotnes made at Polly Street was the introduction of sculpture using clay.[38] The significance of this move is somewhat underplayed in the literature but is extremely important in the development of the kind of modernist formalism that Kumalo, Legae, and others were to adopt in the 1960s and beyond. Pottery had been offered as a part-time leisure activity at the center before Skotnes's arrival and appears to have continued into the 1960s.[39] Serious attention to sculptural techniques and materials, so essential to the practice of artists such as Kumalo, Legae, and Arnold, was effected, with some help from Villa. Villa's role was particularly important in relation to Kumalo, who worked at Villa's studio twice a week for some three years (1958–1960). Here Kumalo was introduced to a range of technical possibilities

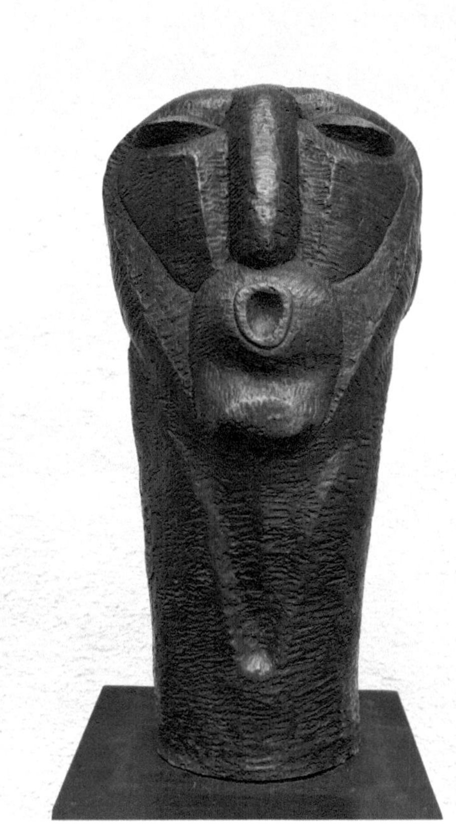

FIGURE 2.4
Sydney Kumalo, *Head (Portrait of Egon Guenther)*, 1965. Bronze, 59 cm × 30 cm × 35 cm. Private collection, Johannesburg.

for making and casting sculptures, and he assisted Villa in a number of projects. That there was a good deal of mutual influence between the two was inevitable and is evident in a shared modernist formal aesthetic. This interchange is suggested, but not documented, through a comparison of sculpted heads executed by both Villa and Kumalo (and by Legae), between 1964 and 1967, in which there is a shared interest in and emulation of conceptual abstractions of the human head found in historical African sculptural forms (figure 2.4).[40]

Making Artists Professional

In 1960, in order to create a professional training for artists at Polly Street Art Centre, Skotnes isolated for promotion a core group of Black artists from the center called the "New Polly Street Group" that included Ben Arnold,

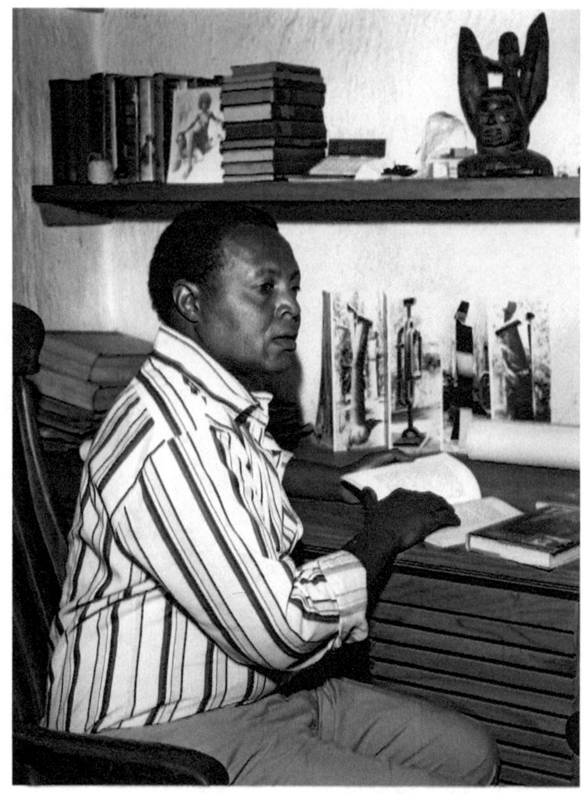

FIGURE 2.5
Sydney Kumalo in his study, with images of sculptures by Villa on the desk and a Yoruba Gelede mask on the shelf above his head. Photo courtesy of Neil Dundas. Goodman Gallery, Johannesburg.

Sidney Buys, John Hlatywayo, Tosby Keipedele, Sydney Kumalo, and George Makganjane.[41] Of these only Arnold and Kumalo would make a very strong impression on the arts landscape over the next twenty years, with Kumalo being the one who really excelled. Miles documents commissions Skotnes procured for various artists he had placed in the core group and the ways in which he referred each to other mentors for advice and technical support.[42] In this way Skotnes initiated the relatively well-known relationship between Kumalo and Villa, a relationship that was extended to Legae via Kumalo at a later stage (figure 2.5). Skotnes drew on the expertise of other artists and entrepreneurs in helping his current and former students. Giuseppe Cattaneo was consulted on one occasion by Louis Maqhubela but did not otherwise play an active part in the processes of mentorship.[43] Skotnes appears to have matched mentors who shared a particular late modernist formation to work with aspiring artists who would benefit from their advice. His criteria excluded many Polly Street artists such as Sihlali, with whose insistence on the documentary importance of naturalistic images of township life Skotnes did not agree.[44] As a result, Sihlali's mentoring relationships were more complex.[45] Skotnes introduced him to Sidney Goldblatt (1919–1979), a South African–born landscape painter who had trained in Paris and worked in a relatively abstract mode. He opened his studio to students between 1955 and 1958, during which years Sihlali worked there. Because Sihlali was not included in Skotnes's core group of professional artists, he continued to produce township scenes — with a definite political agenda — as his main stock in trade.[46]

Notable among the other exclusions from Skotnes's 1960 New Polly Street Group were Moses Tladi, Ephraim Ngatane, Louis Maqhubela, and Winston Saoli.[47] Along with Sihlali, these artists did go on to take up strong positions in the South African art world. All were working in a basically naturalistic mode, concentrating on generalized township scenes. Although many of them were featured in one of the first collective exhibitions of Polly Street artists, their importance was not central to Skotnes's particular program.[48] It may be that Skotnes's choice was governed to some extent by the constancy of the artists' attendance at classes over more than two years and not solely by their individual aesthetic commitments. Of the professional group, Arnold (studied 1957/58–1965), Hlatywato (studied 1954–1960), and Kumalo (studied 1952–1957) would, by 1960, have qualified as "African" and modernist according to Skotnes's and Guenther's criteria. Sihlali (studied 1953–1957) was no longer attending classes by that time and Maqhubela (studied 1957 and 1959) was by then working largely as an independent artist.[49]

Skotnes's identification of these individuals as potentially "serious" artists was arguably influenced by his interactions with Guenther, whose aesthetic ideas helped inform Skotnes's decisions. His division of these Black artists into groups was guided by a modernist polemic, favoring those who espoused a formalism and a degree of abstraction and rejecting those who favored a modernity characterized by naturalistic and realistic representation. Rankin has suggested that the work of the sculptors displayed a greater individualism than that of the painters, but a serious scrutiny of works by painters as diverse as Mogano (figure 2.6), Ngatane, and Sihlali reveals equally individualistic approaches.[50] The differences between the works of the two groups lie in the degrees of their departure from the naturalistic and of their expressive manipulation of line, form, color, and material. They converge most in their general, if sometimes tenuous, adherence to the figurative.

In 1960, when the Polly Street Art Centre was relocated to the Jubilee Centre on Eloff Street, Skotnes was still in charge but Kumalo, who had been appointed

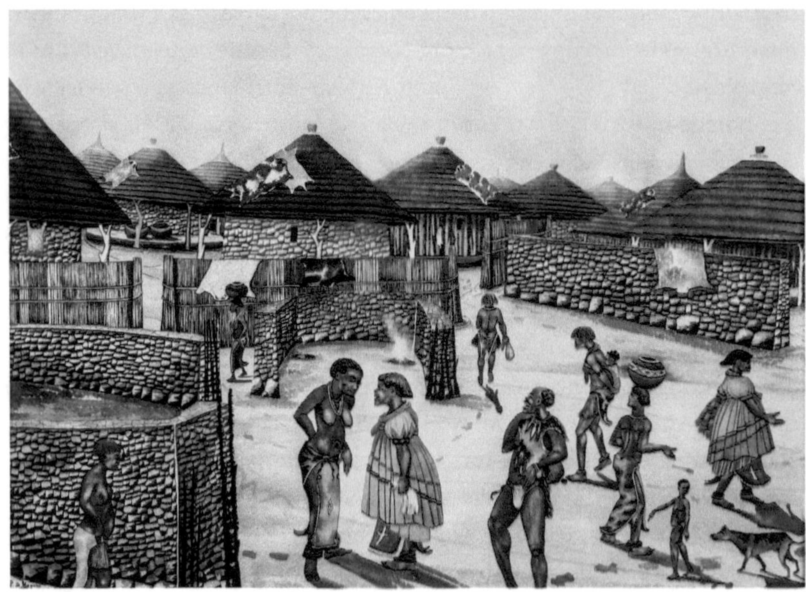

FIGURE 2.6 David Phaswane Mogano, *Untitled (Rural Scene)*, 1972. Watercolor on paper, 50.5 cm × 71 cm. Standard Bank African Art Collection, Wits Art Museum.

as an instructor at the center in 1959, was training artists who came to classes, including, significantly, Legae. By this time the particular modernist-expressionist stylistic imprint favored by Skotnes and Guenther was to be found in the work of Kumalo and other sculptors taking instruction at Jubilee Centre. From 1960 onward, Skotnes's energies were divided between running the center, teaching, and negotiating with mentors and gallerists for his most promising students.

Links in the Mentorship Chain: African Art as Catalyst

The formal contexts of teaching at places such as Polly Street Art Centre and Rorke's Drift Arts and Crafts Centre in Natal fostered interactions among instructors and learners and friendships between artists, which make it relatively easy to trace chains of mentorship. But tracing other subtler relationships is more precarious. Miles and Harmsen have discussed the importance of Skotnes's meeting and subsequent friendship with Guenther, seeing it as central to the narrative of his and others' developments as artists.[51] Guenther's interest in German expressionism and its aftermath led him to show Skotnes works by Barlach, Scharpf, and others, and these influences steered Skotnes in new stylistic and material directions. The authors also acknowledge the importance of Skotnes's training at the University of the Witwatersrand, especially his interaction there with Dr. Maria Stein-Lessing. Stein-Lessing was an art historian and a refugee from Nazi Germany who was fascinated with African material culture and art.[52] Skotnes's interest in these traditions initiated through these two intermediaries was further enhanced by his growing friendship with Meneghelli.[53]

As with all narratives grounded in the memories of individuals, there is some disagreement in assessing the importance of these relationships to the resultant artistic praxes that developed in Polly Street and beyond. While there can be little doubt that Guenther's intervention in introducing Skotnes to the German expressionist tradition of woodcuts via Scharpf's work, and to other printmaking techniques, had a profound effect on his use of materials and possibly on his development of formal approaches, the impact of African art sources is less certain. Guenther often stated that he expected the work of the artists he included in his gallery's stable to reflect the ethos of their place and time.[54] The place he constructed was a generalized Africa, defined through specific genera of environments, flora, and fauna. He was never very clear in interviews about the role of "traditional" African cultures in this construction of place and ethos, but he made a very clear distinction between (historical) African art and contemporary South African art.

"African art" as a category included, in Guenther's estimation, only historical examples of what he deemed "traditional" art, most of which, in accordance with the modernist canon, came from West and Central Africa. The accepted African works possessed an "authenticity" constituted by their putative lack of European influence. Many Western collectors still cling to these now debunked ideas of authenticity, and Guenther was, at heart, a collector.[55] His collection of African art has been held up as immensely influential in the development of the formalist abstraction of artists such as Kumalo and Legae, as well as Skotnes and Villa, but it also included works by artists such as Barlach, Cattaneo, Hannes Harrs, and Georgina Ormiston.[56] In all of these he saw the "specter" of an African inspiration, which consisted of spirit and ethos rather than copying. It was this quality he looked for in his artists' works and found markedly in Legae's sculptures.

Although Miles, following Susanne van Rensburg, identifies direct quotations from African forms and particular traits of figural representation in mural and ceiling paintings executed for churches by Skotnes and Kumalo, or by Kumalo and other Black students, she plays down the direct influence of African art in the work of these artists.[57] She picks up a skein similar to Guenther's, suggesting that Skotnes introduced the students at Polly Street to stylistic impulses similar to those of classical African art by looking at modernists who had learned from African art.[58] In this telling, Polly Street artists would have been reacting to a translation of African visual idioms into modernist forms rather than to ancestral African works. Maqhubela, however, had a different perspective on the problem of influence. In an interview with Martin, he pointed to the near-impossibility under apartheid of Black South African artists' learning about historical African art except through the same "white immigrants" who offered such knowledge to white South African artists.[59] Maqhubela himself was most likely introduced to African art by Skotnes and Kumalo, rather than through contact with Guenther's collection.

In interviews, Guenther recalled Kumalo, Legae, and Arnold congregating in his home gallery in Linksfield, Johannesburg, to critique new works. There is little doubt that in this venue these artists were encouraged to consult his collection of West and Central African art, most consisting of wood sculptures.[60] That these pieces had relevance for the artists is clear from the works they produced in response, especially in their sculptures of the 1960s. Yet Skotnes also introduced genres of African art other than the purely sculptural to his students. His interaction with Stein-Lessing during his student years would have introduced him to the aesthetic qualities, if not the fine art status, of the South African beadwork and pottery she both collected and sold in her shop, L'Afrique.[61] In his turn, Skotnes organized an exhibition in 1963 for his students that included pieces of South African beadwork, borrowed from Hanneh Guenther and Rosemairie Hurwitz. While it is not clear that beadwork per se had any impact on artists in Polly Street, the mural painting traditions of Black South Africa, often closely tied to beadwork in pattern and color, were to manifest themselves in the work of both Sihlali and Maqhubela in later years.[62] This was not, however, the kind of Africa that appealed to the mentors considered here. It could be argued that Guenther's African "art" was strongly gendered as "masculine," in line with the Western gendering of the art/craft divide, everywhere that African "art" collections had been assembled.

The Africa at the center of Guenther's imagination was seen through the lens of modernism, and, it appears, this vision was shared by Skotnes. Both espoused the generalized and allegedly universalized abstractions of German expressionism and cubism that were indebted to the nonnaturalistic traditions defined as "primitive art." Kumalo later made a small collection of African art objects himself, as did Skotnes and Villa, and all did so through Meneghelli.

To summarize, then, all the artists who contributed to the *Amadlozi* exhibition were to some extent indebted to African forms and had passed this on to their students.[63] While there is discussion about the point at which such African influence is first visible in the work of the Black artists at the Polly Street and Jubilee Centre, the debates tend to center on details such as elongated necks, small legs, or general proportions.[64] The artists' use of African forms and subjects is, however, not really reducible to such questions because it disregards Indigenous African iconographic elements and approaches to materials that were to surface ever more strongly in the works of the Black artists in the ensuing decades.

The End of One Chain

Kumalo resigned from Polly Street Art Centre in 1964 and Skotnes in 1965, and their places were taken by Bill Hart and Legae at the Jubilee Centre on Eloff Street. These men continued in the tradition of their precursors, although during those years the center was used by professional artists to execute commissions as well as to instruct students in still-life drawing and painting. Still-life arrangements apparently also included pieces of African material culture—pots, wooden utensils, calabashes, and the like[65]—and Legae's life drawing classes were also remembered by many artists who achieved considerable success. They were continued by Dan Rakgoathe when he took over from Legae in 1969.[66]

The Jubilee Centre was forced to close in 1969 by the enforcement of the Group Areas Act of 1957, which allowed Black people into the city center during the day as workers but banned them by night. This meant that in its old location the center would be unavailable to those who were accustomed to attending classes after work, and it was moved to Mofolo Park, close to the center of Soweto, the township whose residents it was intended to serve.[67] A new building was erected for the center with a series of mosaics designed by Maqhubela on the exterior. Teaching at the center continued under Hart till 1976 and into the 1980s under Rakgoathe, although the latter was frustrated by the fact that its programs were largely aimed at school children whose attendance at afternoon classes was erratic.[68]

Egon Guenther closed his gallery in 1967, a year after Linda Givon (then Goodman) opened Goodman Gallery in Hyde Park.[69] Many of the artists who had been represented by Guenther moved to Goodman Gallery, which continued to champion them throughout the apartheid years, often with a political agenda allied to growing opposition to the apartheid state. In 1985 Givon revived the Amadlozi name for an exhibition that included Kumalo, Villa, and

Skotnes from the original artists' group and added Legae.[70] The consequence of this shift was that sculptors took precedence in the group, although Legae's lyrical drawings accompanied Skotnes's colored woodcut panels on the walls.

An Envoi

The *Amadlozi* exhibition also ushered in a new chain of mentorship, much wider than that which had originated in Polly Street, with Black South African artists who had trained at Polly Street now playing key roles. Following his success as an independent artist, Kumalo was able to build himself a home in Soweto that included three different studios. Vincent Baloyi, a sculptor and painter employed at the Wits School of Arts and a graduate of the Rorke's Drift Art Centre in the mid-1970s, remembers how, as a schoolboy in the late 1960s and early 1970s, he would hang around Kumalo's studios.[71] He describes his own determination, in the face of Kumalo's reluctance, to learn about his art, returning time after time until Kumalo allowed him to sit and watch or work with some leftover materials. From there he graduated to assisting Kumalo in setting up exhibitions at Goodman Gallery, visiting Villa and accompanying him to the bronze foundry in Pretoria. From these experiences Baloyi moved to study at Rorke's Drift and became a teacher at the Funda Community College in Soweto and later a technical assistant in printmaking at the Wits School of Arts. This example demonstrates the ways in which the chain of mentorship wound its way through successive generations and well into the postapartheid era.

This chapter has centered on the ways in which approaches to modernism were mediated, developed, and transformed by a small group of Johannesburg-based artists who found themselves embroiled in the racialized politics and cultural milieus of apartheid South Africa. It is notable that both Black and white artists in the ambit of the Amadlozi group and Polly Street Art Centre all turned to definitions of themselves as in some sense African, often through recourse to African historical art sources. That this referencing happened differently for each artist accords well with modernist assumptions of individual subjectivities working within universalist and essentialist modes of expression. Within the closed circle of Polly Street Art Centre and the Amadlozi group, the imbalance of power between mostly white mentors and Black mentees is inescapably visible in the ways in which Skotnes and Guenther sorted aspiring Black artists into groups, some of whom they regarded as having more "professional" potential than others. These "others," however, often offered a strong resistance to mediation of their modernism, taking on the modes of naturalistic representation and documentation as a modern form and concentrating on social issues. In contrast, the mentor's preferred professionals were those who, through recourse to African sources and European modernist interpretations of those sources, not only fitted well into the universalist modes of modernism but exemplified what I have called the Amadlozi effect.

Notes

1. Mbembe, *On the Postcolony*, 16.

2. Meneghelli, *La mia vita, la mia collezione*, 83; Harmsen, "Artist Resolute," 21; Doepel, *Giuseppe Cattaneo Retrospective*, 13.

3. Gilroy, *Between Camps*. On the intersections of race and critical arts, see van Robbroeck, "Race and Art in Apartheid South Africa."

4. See Miles, *Polly Street*; Nel, "Interview with Egon Guenther"; Rankin, "Teaching and Learning"; Nettleton, "Making a Market."

5. I interviewed Meneghelli several times over a long period.

6. Meneghelli, *La mia vita*.

7. Nel, Burroughs, and von Maltitz, *Villa at 90*, 7.

8. Nel, "Edoardo Villa," 122; Villa, *Edoardo Villa*.

9. Nettleton, "Shaking Off the Shackles."

10. Harmsen, "Artist Resolute"; Thorne, *Cecily Sash*; Rankin, "Lonely Roads."

11. See Miles, *Polly Street*, 16.

12. Koloane, "Moments in Art"; Rankin, "Teaching and Learning"; Rankin, "Lonely Roads"; Miles, *Polly Street*, 16.

13. Mdanda, "Developing a Methodology."

14. Miles, *Polly Street*, 18–20.

15. Miles, *Polly Street*, 17–20.

16. Rankin, "Teaching and Learning"; and Miles, *Polly Street*, 17–20. See also Mdanda, "Developing a Methodology"; Rankin, "Creating Communities."

17. Lorimer cited in Miles, *Polly Street*, 17.

18. Nettleton, ". . . In What Degree."

19. Rankin, "Lonely Roads," 93.

20. Rankin, "Teaching and Learning"; Miles, *Polly Street*.

21. Rankin, "Teaching and Learning."

22. Nettleton, ". . . In What Degree"; essays in Davison, *Art and Ambiguity*.

23. Berman, *Art and Artists of South Africa*. See also Harmsen, "Artist Resolute."

24. Hillebrand, "White Artists in Context."

25. Miles, *Polly Street*, 36.

26. Miles, *Polly Street*; Koloane, "Polly Street Art Scene"; Rankin, "Teaching and Learning," 70.

27. Koloane, "Polly Street Art Scene."

28. Schmidt, "Fred Schimmel"; Sack, *The Neglected Tradition*; Miles, *Polly Street*.

29. "Fred Schimmel at 80."

30. Schmidt, "Fred Schimmel"; Koloane, "Moments in Art"; Oliphant, *Kagiso Pat Mautloa*, 38–43; Koloane, "Collective Exchange and the Politics of Space, 1976–1995"; and Savage, *Making Art in Africa 1960–2010*.

31. Miles, *Polly Street*, 36.

32. See various essays in Harmsen, *Cecil Skotnes*.

33. Miles, *Polly Street*, cites this as Schimmel's own assessment.

34. Nettleton, "Modernism, Primitivism and the Search for Modernity."

35. Miles, *Polly Street*, 80.

36. Ulla Lind, personal communication with author; Grossert, "Art Education and Zulu Crafts."

37. Nettleton, "Primitivism in South African Art"; van Robbroeck, "Race and Art."

38. Miles, *Polly Street*, 45.

39. Miles, *Polly Street*, 47.

40. Nel and Burroughs, "Edoardo Villa."

41. Miles, *Polly Street*, 80

42. Miles's account in *Polly Street* is heavily dependent on van Rensburg, "Sydney Kumalo en Ander Bantoekunstenaars van Transvaal."

43. Rankin, "Lonely Roads"; Miles, *Polly Street*; Martin, "Louis Khehla Maqhubela."

44. Durant Sihlali, personal communication with author, 1989. See also Koloane, "Polly Street Art Scene"; Miles, *Polly Street*.

45. See Miles and Sihlali, *Durant Sihlali*, 17; Peffer, *Art and the End of Apartheid*. Sihlali also worked in the studio of Carlo(s) Sdoya (1914–1996), the "Da Vinci School of Fine Art." See Vincent Art Gallery, "Sdoya, Carlo."

46. Koloane, "Polly Street Art Scene"; Miles, *Polly Street*.

47. Miles, *Polly Street*.

48. *Exhibition of Non-European Paintings and Sculptures*. See Miles, *Polly Street*, 79–80.

49. Miles, *Polly Street*; Martin, "Louis Kehla Maqhubela."

50. Rankin, "Teaching and Learning."

51. Miles, *Polly Street*; Harmsen, "Artist Resolute."

52. Girshick, "Maria Stein-Lessing."

53. See Nettleton, "Making a Market."

54. Egon Guenther, interviews with author from mid-1970s to 2015.

55. See Kasfir, "African Art and Authenticity"; Shiner, "'Primitive Fakes,' 'Tourist Art,' and the Ideology of Authenticity."

56. Leibhammer, "A Fragmented Picture."

57. Miles, *Polly Street*; van Rensburg, "Sydney Kumalo."

58. Miles, *Polly Street*.

59. Martin, "Louis Khehla Maqhubela."

60. Nel, "Interview with Egon Guenther."

61. Girshik, "Maria Stein-Lessing."

62. Miles, "Durant Sihlali"; and Durant Sihlali, "Re-claiming the Significance of Murals."

63. See Nettleton, "Primitivism in South African Art."

64. Miles, *Polly Street*.

65. Miles, *Polly Street*.

66. Miles, *Polly Street*; Langhan, *The Unfolding Man*.

67. Langhan, *The Unfolding Man*.

68. Rankin, "Teaching and Learning"; Langhan, *The Unfolding Man*.

69. Williamson, "Linda Givon"; Pollack, "Art/Architecture."

70. See *Important South African and International Art*. Lots 141–74 came from Harry Lits's collection but included only the artists who constituted Linda Givon's reconfigured *amadlozi*.

71. Vincent Baloyi, personal communication with author, December 2016, at the offices of the Wits Art Museum.

Bibliography

Berman, Esmé. *Art and Artists of South Africa: An Illustrated Biographical Dictionary and Historical Survey of Painters, Sculptors and Graphic Artists since 1875*. Rev. ed. Cape Town: Balkema, 1983.

Davison, Patricia, ed. *Art and Ambiguity: Perspectives on the Brenthurst Collection of Southern African Art*. Johannesburg: Johannesburg Art Gallery, 1991. Exhibition catalog.

Doepel, Rory. *Giuseppe Cattaneo Retrospective*. Johannesburg: University of the Witwatersrand, Gertrude Posel Gallery, 1981.

Exhibition of Non-European Paintings and Sculptures. Johannesburg: Queens Hall Art Gallery, 1960. Exhibition catalog.

"Fred Schimmel at 80: A Retrospective Exhibition, 27 November 2008–15 January 2009." SMAC Art Gallery. Accessed October 8, 2024. https://web.archive.org/web/20141021082228/http://www.smacgallery.com/exhibition/fred-schimmel-at-80-a-retrospective-exhibition-27-november-2008-15-january-2009/#.

Gilroy, Paul. *Between Camps: Race, Identity and Nationalism at the End of the Colour Line*. London: Allen Lane, 2000.

Girshick, Paula. "Maria Stein-Lessing: Setting the Stage for African Art." In *L'Afrique: A Tribute to Maria Stein-Lessing and Leopold Spiegel*, edited by Natalie Knight, 37–44. Johannesburg: David Krut, 2009.

Grossert, Jack. "Art Education and Zulu Crafts." PhD diss., University of Stellenbosch, 1968.

Harmsen, Frieda. "Artist Resolute." In *Cecil Skotnes*, edited by Frieda Harmsen, 11–63. Cape Town: South African National Gallery, 1996.

Harmsen, Frieda, ed. *Cecil Skotnes*. Cape Town: South African National Gallery, 1996.

Hillebrand, Melanie. "White Artists in Context." In *Visual Century: South African Art in Context, 1907–2007*, vol. 1, *1907–1948*, edited by Jillian Carman, 134–55. Johannesburg: Wits University Press, 2011.

Important South African and International Art Including the Harry Lits Collection of Works by the Amadlozi Group, 10 November 2014. Johannesburg: Strauss and Co., 2014. Auction catalog.

Koloane, David. "Collective Exchange and the Politics of Space, 1976–1995." In *Sam Nhlengethwa*, 41–64. Johannesburg: Goodman Gallery Editions, 2006.

Koloane, David. "Moments in Art: A Story from South Africa." In *Seven Stories about Modern Art in Africa*, edited by Clémentine Deliss, 143–57. London: Whitechapel, 1995.

Koloane, David. "The Polly Street Art Scene." In *African Art in Southern Africa: From Tradition to Township*, edited by Anitra Nettleton and David Hammond-Tooke, 211–19. Johannesburg: AD Donker, 1989.

Langhan, Donvé. *The Unfolding Man: The Life and Art of Dan Rakgoathe*. Cape Town: David Phillip, 2000.

Leibhammer, Nessa. "A Fragmented Picture: The Collections of Maria Stein-Lessing and Leopold Spiegel." In *L'Afrique: A Tribute to Maria Stein-Lessing and Leopold Spiegel*, edited by Natalie Knight, 47–66. Johannesburg: David Krut, 2009.

Littlefield Kasfir, Sidney. "African Art and Authenticity: A Text with a Shadow." *African Arts* 25, no. 2 (April 1992): 40–53.

Martin, Marilyn. "Louis Khehla Maqhubela—a Vigil of Departure." In *A Vigil of Departure: Louis Khehla Maqhubela: A Retrospective 1960–2010*, edited by Marilyn Martin, 7–23. Johannesburg: Standard Bank Gallery, 2010. Exhibition catalog.

Mbembe, Achille. *On the Postcolony*. Johannesburg: Wits University Press, 2015.

Mdanda, Sipho. "Developing a Methodology for Understanding Artistic Mentorship in Apartheid South Africa: The Case of the Polly Street Art Centre." Master's thesis, University of the Witwatersrand, 2018.

Meneghelli, Vittorio. *La mia vita, la mia collezione: Memorie e pezzi selezionati dalla collezione di Vittorio Meneghelli* [My life, my collection: Memoir and selected pieces from the collection of Vittorio Meneghelli]. Johannesburg: Totem-Meneghelli Gallery, 2007.

Miles, Elza. "Durant Sihlali: Recorder of Memories and Lived Lives." In *Durant Sihlali: Mural Retrospective, Les Murales, 1960–1994*, by Elza Miles and Durant Sihlali, 5–11. Soweto: Alliance Française, 1994. Exhibition catalog.

Miles, Elza. *Polly Street: The Story of an Art Centre*. Johannesburg: Ampersand Foundation, 2004.

Miles, Elza, and Durant Sihlali. *Durant Sihlali: Mural Retrospective, Les Murales, 1960–1994*. Soweto: Alliance Française, 1994. Exhibition catalog.

Nel, Karel. "Edoardo Villa: Creating an African Presence." In *Villa at 90: His Life, Work, and Influence*, edited by Karel Nel, 122. Johannesburg: Jonathan Ball and Shelf Publishing, 2005.

Nel, Karel. "Interview with Egon Guenther." In *African Art from the Egon Guenther Family Collection: Auction in New York, 18 November 2000*. New York: Sotheby's, 2000.

Nel, Karel, and Elizabeth Burroughs. "Edoardo Villa: The Impact of Steel." In *Re/Discovery and Memory: The Works of Kumalo, Legae, Nitegeka and Villa*, edited by Elizabeth Burroughs and Karel Nel, 73–75. Cape Town: Norval Foundation, 2018.

Nel, Karel, Elizabeth Burroughs, and Amalie von Maltitz. *Villa at 90: His Life, Work, and Influence*. Johannesburg: Jonathan Ball and Shelf Publishing, 2005.

Nettleton, Anitra. ". . . In What Degree They Are Possessed of Ornamental Taste: A History of the Writing on Black Art in South Africa." In *African Art in Southern Africa: From Tradition to Township*, edited by Anitra Nettleton and David Hammond-Tooke, 22–29. Johannesburg: AD Donker, 1989.

Nettleton, Anitra. "Making a Market for African Art in Johannesburg in the 1960s." In *The Challenge of the Object: 33rd Congress of the International Committee of the History of Art*, by G. Ulrich Grossmann, 753–55. Part 2. Nuremberg: Germanisches Nationalmuseum, 2013.

Nettleton, Anitra. "Modernism, Primitivism and the Search for Modernity: A 20th Century Quandary for Black South African Artists." *Revue Multitudes: Histoires Afropolitaines de l'art*, nos. 53–54 (Autumn 2013): 13–19. https://www.lepeuplequimanque.org/histoires-afropolitaines-multitudes-53-54.html.

Nettleton, Anitra. "Primitivism in South African Art." In *Visual Century: South African Art in Context*, vol. 2, *1945–1976*, edited by Lize van Robbroeck, 140–63. Johannesburg: Wits University Press, 2011.

Nettleton, Anitra. "Shaking Off the Shackles: From Apartheid to African Renaissance in Art History Syllabi." In *Compression vs. Expression: Containing and Explaining the World's Art*, edited by John Onians, 39–53. Williamstown, MA: Sterling and Francine Clark Art Institute.

Oliphant, Andries Walter. *Kagiso Pat Mautloa*. Johannesburg: David Krut, 2003.

Peffer, John. *Art and the End of Apartheid*. Minneapolis: University of Minnesota Press, 2009.

Pollack, Barbara. "Art/Architecture: When South Africa Joined the World and the Art World." *New York Times*, March 9, 2003. http://www.nytimes.com/2003/03/09/arts/art-architecture-when-south-africa-joined-the-world-and-the-art-world.html.

Rankin, Elizabeth. "Creating Communities: Arts Centres and Workshops and Their Influence on the South African Art Scene." In *Visual Century: South African Art in*

Context, 1907–2007, vol. 2, *1945–1976*, edited by Lize van Robbroeck, 52–77. Johannesburg: Wits University Press, 2011.

Rankin, Elizabeth. "Lonely Roads: Formative Episodes in the Development of Black Artists in Early Twentieth-Century South Africa." In *Visual Century: South African Art in Context, 1907–2007*, vol. 1, *1970–1948*, edited by Jillian Carman, 92–113. Johannesburg: Wits University Press, 2011.

Rankin, Elizabeth. "Teaching and Learning: Skotnes at Polly Street." In *Cecil Skotnes*, edited by Frieda Harmsen, 65–81. Cape Town: South African National Gallery, 1996.

Sack, Steven. *The Neglected Tradition: Towards a New History of South African Art (1930–1988)*. Johannesburg: Johannesburg Art Gallery, 1988. Exhibition catalog.

Savage, Polly, ed. *Making Art in Africa 1960–2010*. Farnham, UK: Lund Humphries, 2014.

Schmidt, Leon. "Fred Schimmel: An Introduction to His Work." *South African Journal of Art History* 8, no. 11 (1993): 68–79.

Shiner, L. E. "'Primitive Fakes,' 'Tourist Art,' and the Ideology of Authenticity." *Journal of Aesthetics and Art Criticism* 52, no. 2 (1994): 225–34.

Sihlali, Durant. "Re-claiming the Significance of Murals." In *Durant Sihlali: Mural Retrospective, Les Murales, 1960–1994*, by Elza Miles and Durant Sihlali, 12–15. Soweto: Alliance Française, 1994. Exhibition catalog.

Thorne, Victor, *Cecily Sash: Working Years*. Powys: Studio Sash, 1999.

van Rensburg, Susanne Jansen. "Sydney Kumalo en Ander Bantoekunstenaars van Transvaal." Master's thesis, University of Pretoria, 1970.

van Robbroeck, Lize. "Race and Art in Apartheid South Africa." In *Visual Century: South African Art in Context, 1907–2007*, vol. 2, *1945–1976*, edited by Lize van Robbroeck, 79–97. Johannesburg: Wits University Press, 2011.

Villa, Edoardo. *Edoardo Villa: Sculpture*. Johannesburg: United Book Distributors, 1980.

Vincent Art Gallery. "Sdoya, Carlo." Accessed January 10, 2017. https://www.vincentartgallery.co.za/artists/sdoya-carlo/.

Williamson, Sue. "Linda Givon." *Artthrob*, no. 28 (December 1999). http://artthrob.co.za/99dec/artbio.html.

MARK ANDREW WHITE

3 ADAPTING MODERNISM

Oscar Howe, Siouan Traditions, and the Promise of Unlimited Creative Exploration

By the time the Dakota painter Oscar Howe enrolled at the University of Oklahoma (OU) in 1952, he had been a practicing artist for nearly fifteen years and had already served as artist-in-residence at Dakota Wesleyan University. During his brief time at OU, Howe began the development of a new style, by which he departed significantly from the representational tendencies of the Santa Fe Indian School Studio, where he had studied in the 1930s.[1] He derided the so-called Studio Style and the majority of Native painting of his time as "formalized, stylized and symbolized" and advocated in favor of an innovative Indian art informed by but not beholden to the Euro-American modernist values of originality, individuality, and creativity.[2]

The School of Art at OU had fostered the careers of prominent Native artists such as Acee Blue Eagle, Woodrow Wilson "Woody" Crumbo, and W. Richard "Dick" West, providing an environment that was unquestionably sympathetic, yet Howe also sought a program that provided the necessary context for modernist experimentation. Although Howe looked principally to the historic traditions of Siouan quillwork and hide painting for inspiration and presumably could have initiated his project on his own, the modernist abstraction he encountered in the work of his thesis advisers, especially that of surrealist John O'Neil and Mexican muralist Emilio Amero, helped to shape his thought. Similarly, the collection of the OU Museum of Art, which included recent works by modernists such as Ralston Crawford, Stuart Davis, Adolph Gottlieb, and George L. K. Morris provided Howe with various aesthetic possibilities from which he might borrow. Howe's project was not unlike that of the surrealists and abstract expressionists, who sought new expression among the traditional forms of non-Western cultures, yet Howe differed fundamentally in looking to his own cultural past. Howe struck a complicated relationship with modernity, adopting and valuing the trappings of modernism, such as individualism and innovation, while disclaiming any direct stylistic influence from the history of modernism, despite compelling evidence otherwise. He developed this new style in six paintings produced for his MFA thesis, "An Exhibition of Original Paintings in Tempera," and, in the process, pursued a project of aesthetic reinvention and revitalization by adapting historic techniques and aesthetic principles to produce something fundamentally new. By choosing to engage in a dialogue with Euro-American abstraction, Howe created an innovative style that largely rejected his training at the studio in favor of a stylistic hybrid that could straddle perceived boundaries between mid-century modernism and traditional Siouan aesthetics.

Howe's project of reinvention required a repudiation of his training at the Santa Fe Indian School Studio. He dismissed the studio technique as overly formulaic, fostering a uniformity of style that diminished tribal differences. Students painted from their respective cultural backgrounds but worked in an illustrative technique whether they were "Navajo, Hopi, Apache, Sioux, Kiowa, Cheyenne or what."[3] Howe recalled that during his studies between 1933 and 1938 he received little to no instruction and was discouraged from doing research — although he rebelled against the strictures of the studio by undertaking research in collections around Santa Fe.[4]

He depended largely on his knowledge of Siouan aesthetics and the associated symbolism, gained through youthful tutelage under his grandmother, Shell Face. His *Sioux Warrior at Charge* (1936) draws from a Sioux heraldic tradition that includes hide paintings and ledger drawings, though Howe's stylistic approach demonstrates a refinement of draftsmanship and a concern for composition cultivated by the culture of the studio. The subtle geometry of Howe's depiction recalls that of the traditional hide paintings he had been studying in museums.

Howe continued to investigate older forms of representation in the 1940s. His interests may have been encouraged by former OU professor Oscar Brousse Jacobson, who commissioned Howe to illustrate the portfolio *North American Indian Costumes* in 1947.[5] Jacobson and his wife Jeanne d'Ucel completed much of the research prior to the commission by combing through a variety of sources, from archives and ethnographic treatises to works of art by George Catlin and others. Howe lived in Norman, Oklahoma, for part of the year in 1947 to complete final illustrations for the portfolio, which was eventually published as a limited edition in pochoir by C. Szwedzicki in 1952. The portfolio allowed Howe to study patterns and details of dress from numerous tribes over the course of three centuries, and he may have found particular interest in the items of dress he illustrated in *Dakota Woman, 1880* and *Oglala Sioux Chief (Formal), 1885*, both of which include multiple examples of beadwork and hide painting. D'Ucel recalled that Howe "didn't know very much the subject or other Indians," though Jacobson must have been interested in more than the artist's technical facility.[6] Whether or not d'Ucel's recollection is accurate, the detailed drawing of patterns and compositions Howe completed for the portfolio must have encouraged him to consider the aesthetic tradition of Siouan design as a new source of inspiration.[7]

While living in Norman, Howe may also have had the opportunity for additional research. Jacobson probably directed him to Hartley Burr Alexander's pochoir portfolio *Sioux Indian Painting*, also published by C. Szwedzicki in 1938 and available in OU's library collections. Alexander, who was a professor of philosophy at the University of Nebraska and a scholar of Native American religion, chose heraldic imagery for the portfolio, depending not only on hides from museum collections, such as the Peabody Museum of Archaeology and Ethnology at Harvard University, but also on his own extensive collection of ledger drawings, especially those of Amos Bad Heart Bull. Howe also might have read Carrie A. Lyford's 1940 study *Quill and Beadwork of the Western Sioux*, published through the US Department of the Interior. Lyford reproduced numerous designs in the book with the purpose of educating younger generations and creating a revival of traditional arts among the Sioux, and Howe might have considered himself a part of that audience. He would lament later that "so much information of Sioux designs has been lost . . . unlike Indians of the Southwest, the Sioux were nomadic. Their art was applied on clothing and implements. When these were worn out, they were thrown away and the art was lost."[8]

Preservation and renewal of cultural traditions must have been on Howe's mind when he accepted a residency at Dakota Wesleyan University in the fall of 1947 while also completing his bachelor of fine arts degree. His tutelage under his grandmother had provided him with an understanding of aesthetic traditions, and Howe, seemingly in response, explored the passage of knowledge from one generation to the next through pictorial means in a handful of works painted during his residency. His painting *Dakota Teaching* (1951) acts as a form of aesthetic recovery through its complicated iconography, which offers a sampling of the varied stylistic and symbolic traditions of the Dakota. The elder in the foreground discusses the significance of the eagle feather while a boy studies a bone flute. A lesson concerning each of the objects arrayed across the front of the hide will presumably follow, but the inclusion of quillwork and hide painting is particularly notable, given that both would shape the direction of his future investigations. The designs on the elder's robe and each of the moccasins indicate Howe's attention to his visual heritage, a source he looked to not so much for established patterns but for aesthetic inspiration.

Given his interest in the transferal and recovery of pictorial and symbolic traditions, it is little surprise that Howe pursued a thesis that looked to the past for inspiration and for a basis for pictorial invention. Howe would explore the symbolic value of style, technique, and form in his master's thesis at OU, which he began in the fall of 1952. He would argue for greater individuality, as an alternative to what he considered the stultifying tendencies of most Native American painting, and insist that "Aboriginal art," as he called it, "embodied unlimited exploration in all phases of creative expression, having been affiliated with nature and man."[9] While aboriginal art did have formal patterns that limited creative expression to some degree, Howe's concern for experimentation would lead him to adapt those patterns and create new forms from Siouan traditions.

OU's School of Art provided an ideal environment for the development of Howe's new style. It boasted a distinguished roster of Native alumni, including the early Kiowa artists, Acee Blue Eagle, and Woody Crumbo. More importantly, Chief Terry Saul and Dick West had received MFA degrees in the years immediately preceding Howe's enrollment, and both had created theses that departed dramatically from the dominant tendencies among contemporary Native painters.

Like Howe, West had also engaged in the study of historic styles and forms as part of his thesis research and sought some common ground between Cheyenne traditions and modernist abstraction. Their time at OU did not overlap, but Howe may have been encouraged to read the thesis of his peer. West, too, had disparaged "traditional" Indian painting as "hackneyed" and argued, "Since there is little possibility of growth in this style of painting, the Indian artist must inevitably turn in the direction of more contemporary two- or three-dimensional studies."[10] West's thesis bridged Native mythologies and traditional forms with modernist styles such as cubism and surrealism, and he even went so far as to paint his own version of Pablo Picasso's *Les Demoiselles d'Avignon* (1907), substituting Cherokee Booger Dance masks for those of African and Oceanic derivation.[11]

West and Howe shared many of the same faculty on their respective thesis committees. At the time, OU's School of Art had a relatively young faculty committed to modernist experimentation that would have encouraged Howe's inclination to invent new forms. The postwar climate at OU's School of Art paralleled that of other progressive art programs, at least to some degree. Oscar Jacobson had retired from teaching in 1945 and from university service in 1950, and the department had become decidedly modernist under the leadership of John O'Neil, who served as Howe's major professor and thesis adviser. O'Neil later recalled that the period from 1947 through the 1950s was one of "robust health" in which the "energy that fueled the New York School reached even the mid-America places."[12]

O'Neil's style at the time may be best characterized as abstract surrealism, and he looked to medieval traditions as a source for modernist abstraction.[13] O'Neil's stylistic and thematic concerns in the early 1950s are exemplified by *Never-Where* (1950) (figure 3.1), which depicts a fantastic sanctuary of vaguely Gothic origin that, given its cryptic title, exists neither in time nor space. Filled with asymmetrical arches, listing piers, and abstract decorations, the painting borrows from various medieval traditions such as mosaic, stained glass, and cloisonné. Jerry Bywaters, artist, critic, and director of the Dallas Museum of Fine Arts, acknowledged this pedigree of O'Neil's style and suggested that *Never-Where* and other paintings of the period provided a space suitable for imaginative reverie: "The conception of each painting is as bold as an early mosaic, as glowing as a stained glass window, and as organic as a motor, a vegetable, or a geode . . . Each painting is built on a three-dimensional framework as rigid as steel with spaces and planes of vibrant color forming a thoroughly satisfying 'structure' to be inhabited by man's imagination."[14] Bywaters found analogies between O'Neil's style and various elements from the built and natural environment, yet *Never-Where* is also detached from that common frame of experience, providing a figurative and literal space for visionary activity. Bywaters stopped short of associating O'Neil with a broad modernist interest in medieval art; however, the inferences to mosaics and stained glass in *Never-Where* compares in this respect to the work of Lyonel Feininger, Georges Rouault, and the American painter Abraham Rattner.

For Howe, O'Neil's example likely demonstrated how historic traditions could be a source for modernist experimentation, whether or not O'Neil himself considered his quotation of Northern European decorative arts an homage to his heritage. Howe may have taken the same lesson from another member of his committee, former Mexican muralist Emilio Amero, who looked to an

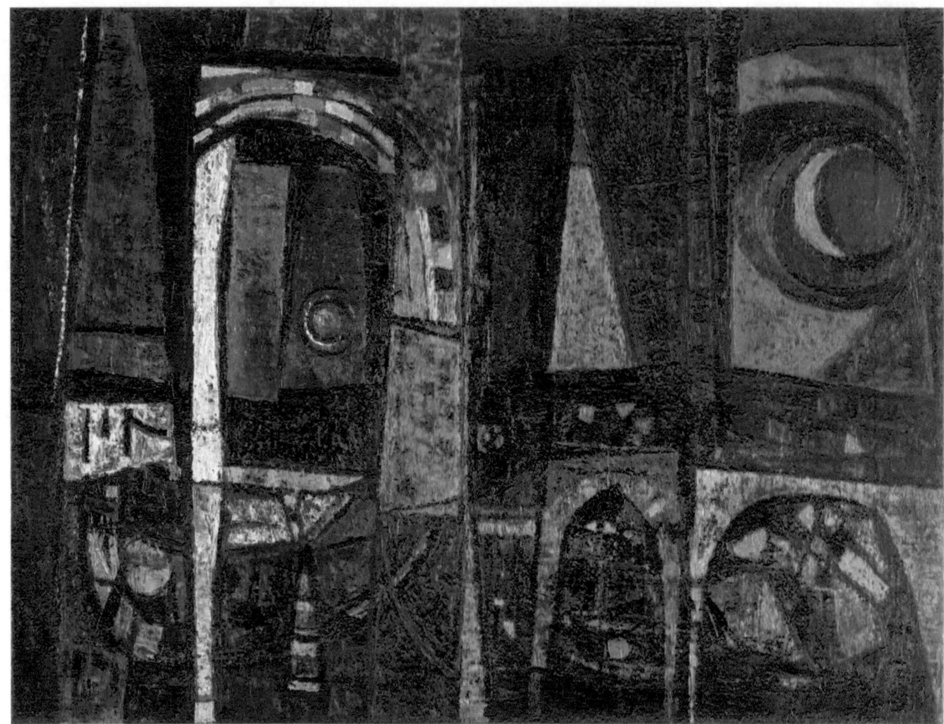

FIGURE 3.1 John O'Neil, *Never-Where*, 1950. Oil on canvas, 18 in. × 24 in. Image courtesy of Joseph Mills. Oklahoma City Museum of Art. Gift of S. Deborah Haines.

Olmec and Mayan past for inspiration. Amero had worked closely with Jean Charlot in 1922–23, who encouraged an interest in the pre-Columbian cultures. Those influences joined with surrealist tendencies in Amero's work in the 1940s and led to paintings such as *The Game*, with its cryptic and vaguely pre-Columbian women positioned against a ruin of unknown provenance.[15]

Neither O'Neil nor Amero exerted direct influence on Howe's work or expressed public opinion on the thesis, though Howe thanked the former for his advice and criticism.[16] Despite the regrettable lack of recorded criticism, visual evidence indicates that both instructors shaped Howe's thoughts. O'Neil's compartmentalization of form in *Never-Where* and other paintings of the period is echoed in many of Howe's more abstract thesis paintings such as *Riders* and *Kini (The Resurrection)*, and the uncanny atmosphere of Amero's *The Game* is similar to the environment of Howe's *The Mourners*.

O'Neil and Amero also may have directed him to important examples of modernist abstraction in the collection of the OU Museum of Art, as both were affiliated directly with management and exhibition of the permanent collection. A series of important acquisitions in the early 1940s brought a number of Works Progress Administration paintings and prints to OU as well as thirty-six contemporary paintings from the US State Department exhibition *Advancing American Art*.[17] *Advancing American Art* was organized by the State Department in 1946 as a form of cultural diplomacy. Fears of Communist influence abroad prompted the State Department to use contemporary art as an illustration of the intellectual and expressive freedom afforded by American democracy, and to this end, the exhibition included conservative trends as well as some of the most innovative work being done in the country. After the exhibition premiered at the Metropolitan Museum of Art in October 1946, *Advancing American Art* toured Paris, Czechoslovakia, Cuba, and Haiti. Ironically, the exhibition became political theater in 1947, when conservative members of Congress learned that not only had the State Department purchased the paintings with government money but some of the artists included had Communist sympathies. The exhibition was recalled by secretary of state George Marshall that spring, and the entire collection was eventually reclassified as war assets and publicly auctioned in 1948, with OU securing thirty-six paintings. When OU's portion of the show arrived in September 1948, it was exhibited immediately, and portions of the collection were displayed over the next several years.

Howe had the opportunity to examine multiple works from the acquisition, but he seems to have derived demonstrable inspiration from two works by Adolph Gottlieb, *The Couple* and *Night Passage*, both of which date from 1946. These paintings with their enigmatic, compartmentalized imagery derived from a complicated stylistic pedigree that included surrealism, Incan and Mayan pictographs, and neoplasticism filtered through the paintings of Uruguayan Joaquín Torres-García.[18] Howe may have found Gottlieb's use of pictographic forms attractive, considering his recent exploration of historic Siouan forms in *Dakota Teaching* and similar paintings, but the latter's partitioned composition would have a visible impact on the thesis.

The collections also offered examples of the linear and planar aesthetic of American cubism and precisionism by artists such as Ralston Crawford, Stuart Davis, and George L. K. Morris. Howe would later refute the claim of John R. Milton and others that cubism had influenced the artist's stylistic evolution, but a direct experience with the paintings of Crawford, Davis, and Morris likely encouraged him to find modernist sensibilities in the aesthetic heritage of hide painting and quillwork.[19] Their planar investigation of pictorial space and the suggestion of the third and even fourth dimension through the investigation of multiple perspectives led Howe to break with the two-dimensionality of hide painting and the emphasis on horizontal, vertical, and straight lines in quillwork. Diagonals and curved lines as well as a more complicated investigation of space played an active part in this new style. Whether these artists influenced Howe directly is debatable, but the complex network of lines, points, and planar geometry in his thesis paintings have an iconic presence equivalent in many respects to the work to which he was exposed at OU. His thesis would straddle the boundaries between his aesthetic heritage and European modernism, a stylistic hybrid difficult to parse. Dorothy Dunn, Howe's former instructor at the studio, recognized both the hybridity and adaptability of this new approach in 1957 by noting that "most of Howe's compositions would be at home in any contemporary show; yet were it possible for the artist's great-grandfathers, Bone Necklace and White Bear, to see them, they could at once recognize each motif and symbol of the rites, the dancers, warriors, and other tribal figures." She concluded that in Howe's paintings "the art of the old chieftains' day appears modern."[20]

Although Howe had been researching Siouan aesthetic tradition for over a decade, the combined influences of his faculty advisers and the museum collections galvanized his thought as he began the six paintings that would comprise his thesis. He relied on subjects from a pre-reservation past but with a decided tendency toward ceremony, spirituality, and mythology. These themes would not have been unusual in Howe's oeuvre but had acquired new significance among American artists at mid-century. Myth and metaphor were central concerns to both the surrealists and the New York School, especially for artists such as Adolph Gottlieb, Barnett Newman, Jackson Pollock, and Mark Rothko. Informed by the thought of Sigmund Freud, Carl Jung, Otto Rank, and Joseph Campbell, the surrealists and the New York School believed that myth provided insights into the archetypes of the individual psyche and connected the individual to the broader fabric of society. Joseph Campbell argued in his influential book *The Hero with a Thousand Faces* (1949) that

> the tribal ceremonies of birth, initiation, marriage, burial, installation, and so forth, serve to translate the individual's life-crises and life-deeds into classic, impersonal forms. They disclose him to himself, not as this

> personality or that, but as the warrior, the bride, the widow, the priest, the chieftain; at the same time rehearsing for the rest of the community the old lesson of the archetypal stages. All participate in the ceremonial according to rank and function. The whole society becomes visible to itself as an imperishable living unit. Generations of individuals pass, like anonymous cells from a living body; but the sustaining, timeless form remains.[21]

Archetypal, mythic forms give metaphysical substance through ritual to the natural processes of life, death, regeneration, and renewal and create a continuity between generations, comparable in Campbell's analogy to a living organism. Campbell's thought, as well as that of Jung, led artists to the exploration of myth, ritual, and natural cycles, all of which gave some insight into the human condition, the history of civilization, and even the anxiety of the postwar world.[22] Given Campbell's interest in tribal rituals, it is little surprise that artists of the period began appropriating ritualistic and totemistic forms from Native American cultures.[23] Howe never expressed his thoughts on the topic of cultural appropriation but looked to his own rich heritage for viable forms and subjects.

Nevertheless, this cultural climate likely nurtured Howe's existing interests and encouraged him to see his project as parallel to that of other modernists. As Bill Anthes has argued, Howe "saw himself as very much like the European modernists in the sense that he also sought to transcend the limitation of tradition," and he allowed himself to adopt the language and thought of modernism without breaking with his aesthetic and cultural legacy.[24] Howe defined his thesis project as painting "with direct imagination in close association with the subconscious," resulting in "a statement of conception rather than perception." Hesitant to ally himself too closely with the irrationality of the unconscious mind, he embraced the subconscious and imagination as vehicles for experimentation, an approach that emphasized individuality over the collective thought usually accorded tribal peoples. Howe acknowledged the "psychological use of catharsis as a means to realize individuality" as intrinsic to his new approach.[25] *Catharsis* was a loaded term in 1953 and was commonly used to discuss abstract expressionism, especially after Sam Hunter described Jackson Pollock's paintings as "cathartic" in 1949.[26] Howe's desire for originality and individuality through cathartic expression allied him further with mainstream modernism.

Even though Howe clearly found some value in modernism, he maintained ties to Siouan traditions or approximations thereof, whenever possible. He preferred to use casein and watercolor instead of oil paint for his experiment,

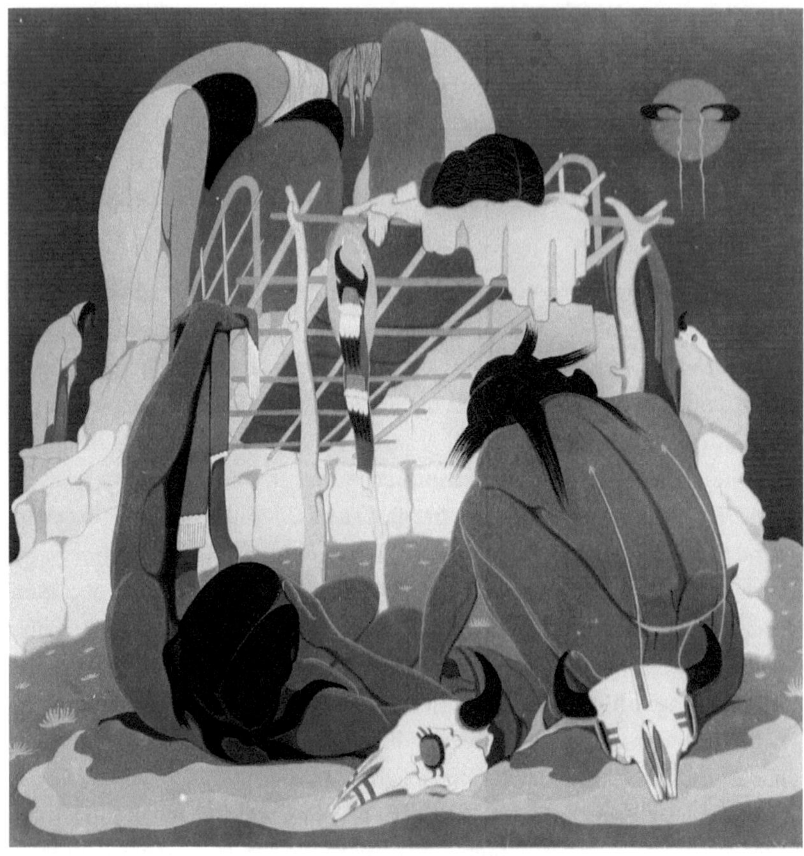

FIGURE 3.2 Oscar Howe, *The Mourners*, c. 1953. Tempera on paper, 18 in. × 18 in. University Galleries, University of South Dakota. Courtesy of the Oscar Howe Family.

not only because of his familiarity with the former media but also because of their physical similarity to the paints used by his ancestors. The fluidity of his media also enabled him to emphasize straight lines and avoid the textural complexity common to oil. Similarly, he chose Fabriano paper for its tooth and texture, which compared to that of the hides used by earlier generations.[27]

Each of the thesis paintings departs in varying degrees from the style Howe practiced following his training at the studio but also demonstrates how his interpretation of tradition could be used to create something distinctly modern. The first painting in his thesis, *The Mourners* (figure 3.2), acknowledged Howe's debt to the studio through the use of fairly representational, flattened forms while also departing from his earlier style through the inclusion of a background, depicted in dramatic perspective. In his description of the painting, Howe emphasized the humility of the mourners, clad in frayed clothing, and the importance of self-sacrifice, practiced by the two men in the foreground who have attached bison skulls to their backs by inserting thongs behind the skin and muscle. Mortification of the body fosters greater communion with the spirit in this respect, and Howe's representation of the mourning ritual infers the ongoing relationship between both the deceased and the living. As he noted, "A buffalo symbol (symbol for life) denotes spirit life as apart from the physical and affirms an old Indian belief that the spirit of the dead remains near the living."[28] By tilting the planes and creating an unnatural recession, techniques likely adapted from surrealism, Howe creates an interstitial space between the physical and the spiritual, made manifest by the depicted ritual. Howe's first thesis painting, though a nod aesthetically to his past training, embodies Campbell's perspective on Native rituals as archetypal manifestations of "life-crises." Whether Howe knew or considered Campbell's arguments when painting *The Mourners* is less important than how the painting would have been perceived by those sympathetic to modernist thought in 1953. The OU faculty and contemporary American artists and critics likely would have understood the painting as conversant in issues of artistic and philosophical relevance.

The Mourners serves as a transition between Howe's established style and his new approach, evident in the next painting of his thesis, *Council* (figure 3.3). He continued his compositional experiments using the shape of the crescent moon to cradle his forms and diminish distinctions with the surrounding space. Those distinctions are lessened further by his use of lines and angles that create homogeneity, suggestive of "close harmony with nature," a quality he desired in his work.[29] Howe explained that "the Indian was in close harmony with nature; his philosophy, religion and physical existence evolved from it. He made use of his environment, from a simple relationship with nature, to a highly complex one; so nature became an integral part of the Indian's life." While Howe's comments are unsurprising in the context of Native art and culture, it should be noted that many of the abstract expressionists considered their relationship to nature harmonious. Hans Hofmann, for instance, considered nature "the source of all inspiration," a philosophy he imparted to many of the modernists he taught, and vitalism — a belief in an animating force that distinguishes organic from inorganic matter — held sway among many of the abstract expressionists.[30] Vitalism led them to seek in their works

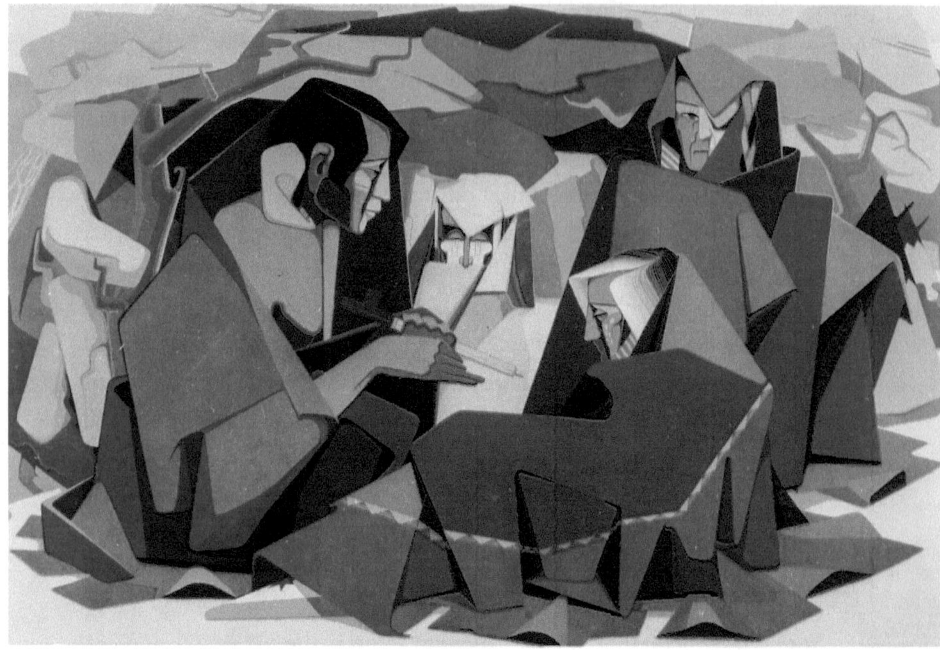

FIGURE 3.3 Oscar Howe, *Council*, c. 1953. Tempera on paper. Location unknown. Courtesy of the Oscar Howe Family.

a formal representation of both the vital energies permeating life and their relationship to those forces. Howe's emphasis on harmony as central to Siouan cosmology would have struck a familiar chord among modernists of the era.

However, a harmonious relationship with nature is not the only reason Howe explored the dissolution of form and space in *Council* and the subsequent painting featured in his thesis, *Riders* (figure 3.4). The latter features a bewildering compositional mass of Sioux warriors and their mounts, who are engaged in combat with an unpictured foe. The outcome seems bleak, with the fallen rider in the foreground and a rearing horse in the upper left possibly struck by a projectile. For Howe, the painting depicted "the Indian's struggle in a white man's world. . . . The art principles constitute both the Indian and the white man's philosophy of [a]esthetics," which suggests conflict with the US military but also serves as a broader metaphor for the challenges of acculturation, assimilation, and bigotry. To this end, he may have been alluding to his own struggle to work within the context of modernism while reinvigorating waning aesthetic traditions. Questions about the role of cubism in his new work

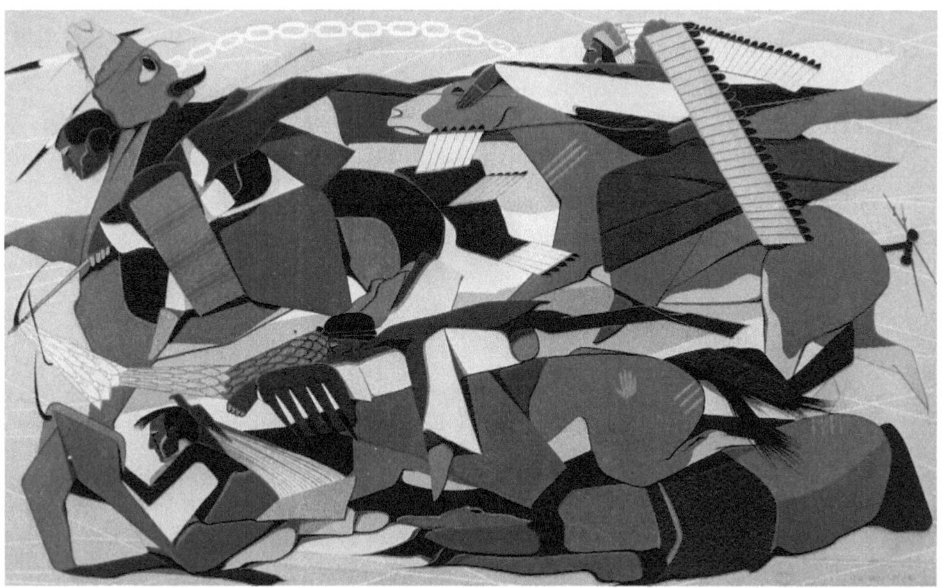

FIGURE 3.4 Oscar Howe, *Riders*, c. 1953. Tempera on paper. Location unknown. Courtesy of the Oscar Howe Family.

might have arisen during his study at OU and, although it would be disingenuous to believe that the examples of cubist art in the OU collections had no influence on the Dakota artist, Howe later cited the source of his style as the Siouan concept of *tahokmu* or the spider web. Although he did not discuss the influence of tahokmu publicly until the late 1960s, it clearly shaped his thesis experiments and provided a foundation for the overt linearity of his style.

Tahokmu manifests most clearly in Howe's work with the numerous intersections of acute angles and the overall geometric flavor of his mature style. Whereas it provided a basis for his new style, one rooted in traditional design and mythology, he used it largely as a point of departure. He looked to another traditional and related practice, *owa*, as the primary vehicle for experimentation and catharsis. Owa uses points or groups of points as the framework for design. During the placement of the points, Howe worked as an automatist, relying heavily on the subconscious as he then began to connect the points with a series of lines. The result has a pictorial uniformity akin to the spiderweb with its delicate tracery, and the fluid, spontaneous nature of his process prompted Dunn to compare him to both Martha Graham and Alexander Calder, modernist parallels to his improvisational approach.[31]

Howe later explained that owa was used principally in nineteenth-century hide painting techniques, but his adaptation allowed for creative exploration akin to the mature work and aesthetic thought of Wassily Kandinsky, exemplified in his 1926 book *Point and Line to Plane*.[32] Both owa and tahokmu are evident in *Riders* and *Council* through the sectioning of the masses into geometric and biomorphic sections, composed by moving from point to line to plane.

In considering the spiritual implications of his technique and how it might allow for "unlimited exploration," it was natural for Howe to look to the myth of the Double Woman in his next thesis painting. Howe organized the *Dance of the Double Woman* (figure 3.5) around the circle, which he associated with unity and the belief "that the spiritual, psychological and physical aspects of nature in unison should complete the life cycle."[33] The totality of the life cycle is implied by Double Woman's duality as the personification of creative and destructive forces. Howe represented Double Woman as two figures, though Dakota myth generally considers her a single entity with two faces, beautiful and terrible. Howe related that her beauty could lure men into the wilderness, only to leave them lost or unconscious. For the artist, this suggested a moral lesson that "a man should have perfect control over his emotions, even in the presence of sheer beauty."[34] Yet Double Woman also inspired great creativity in those who dreamed of her. Howe's painting depicts a man evoking Double Woman after such dreams, and she simultaneously touches his head, inspiring thought and creativity while also inscribing a pictograph on a stone. Howe noted that Double Woman was the author "of strange carvings on rocks which foretold of future events," clearly associating pictorial creativity with prophetic power.

Oddly, although the painting acknowledges tacitly the importance Howe accorded the mythological and spiritual inspiration for his experiments, Howe neglected to mention in his thesis that Double Woman is most clearly associated among the Sioux with the invention of quillwork, a primary inspiration for his own experiments.[35] Despite the role Double Woman and the invention of quillwork undoubtedly played in the genesis of Howe's new style, his new aesthetic approach is largely inconsistent with either hide painting or quillwork, both of which value clear delineation. Howe's individualistic use of tahokmu and owa in suppressing distinctions between form and space and in extending the creative act to every edge of the picture plane may have given his paintings a distinctly modern appearance, but it also expressed his conceptual ambition to demonstrate the close affiliation between the Sioux and nature.

In other thesis paintings such as *Kini (Resurrection)* (figure 3.6) and *Three Women* (figure 3.7), Howe marshaled a complex of points and lines resulting

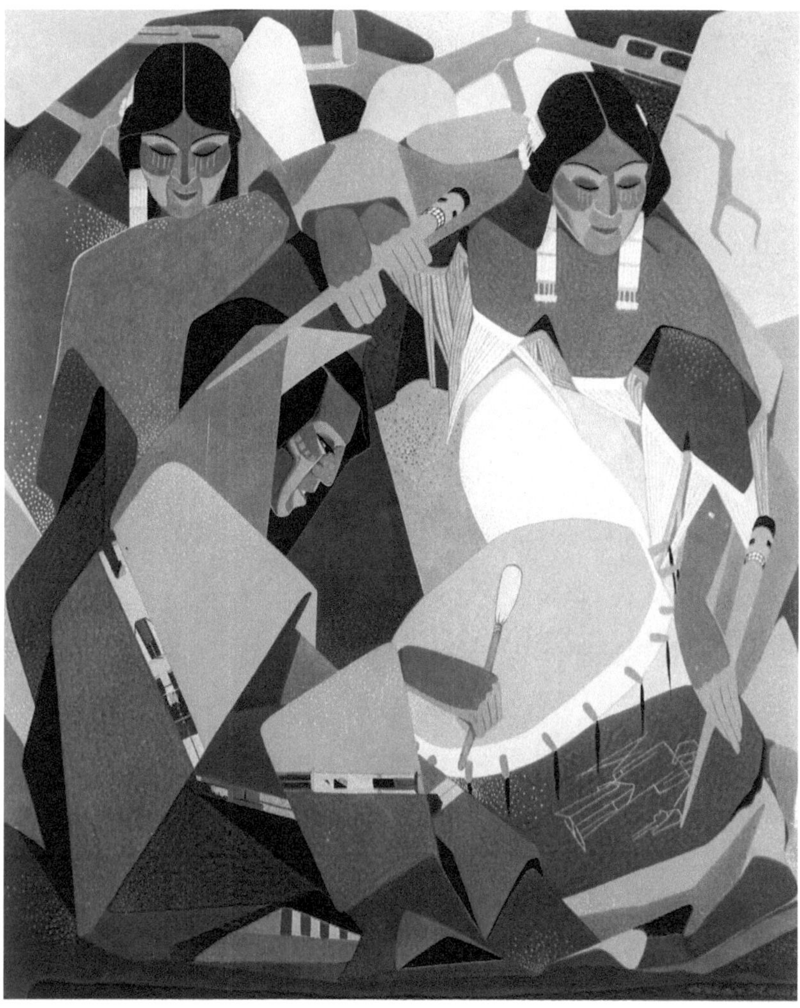

FIGURE 3.5 Oscar Howe, *Dance of the Double Woman*, c. 1953. Tempera on paper. Dakota Discovery Museum, Dakota Wesleyan University, Mitchell, South Dakota. Courtesy of the Oscar Howe Family.

in an overtly planar approach to form, yet it also created an optical three-dimensionality consistent with the flatness of the picture plane. Howe encapsulated the process in his explanation of *Kini*: "From straight lines patterns evolve, the patterns which, though painted flat, still give a feeling of form or roundness."[36] The projection and recession of the planes in *Kini* creates a sense of form and space while also adding some visual confusion to the

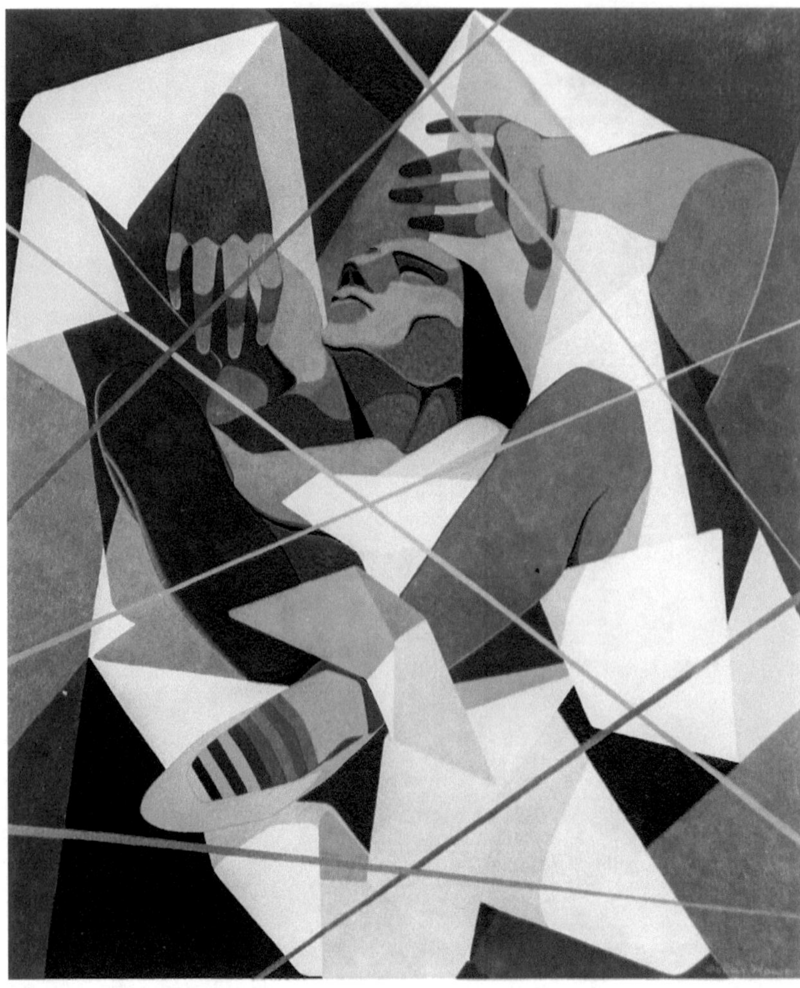

FIGURE 3.6 Oscar Howe, *Kini (Resurrection)*, c. 1953. Tempera on paper. Dakota Discovery Museum, Dakota Wesleyan University, Mitchell, South Dakota. Courtesy of the Oscar Howe Family.

scene. The body of the deceased, his burial shroud, and the surrounding space mingle to such a degree that it requires careful study at times to separate the individual components.

Throughout the thesis, Howe continually used compositional devices and symbols to represent interconnectedness and often through the lens of religion. He remarked in his thesis that "between nature and man lies religion," and, in the case of *Kini*, superimposed the figure against the sky to suggest oneness with

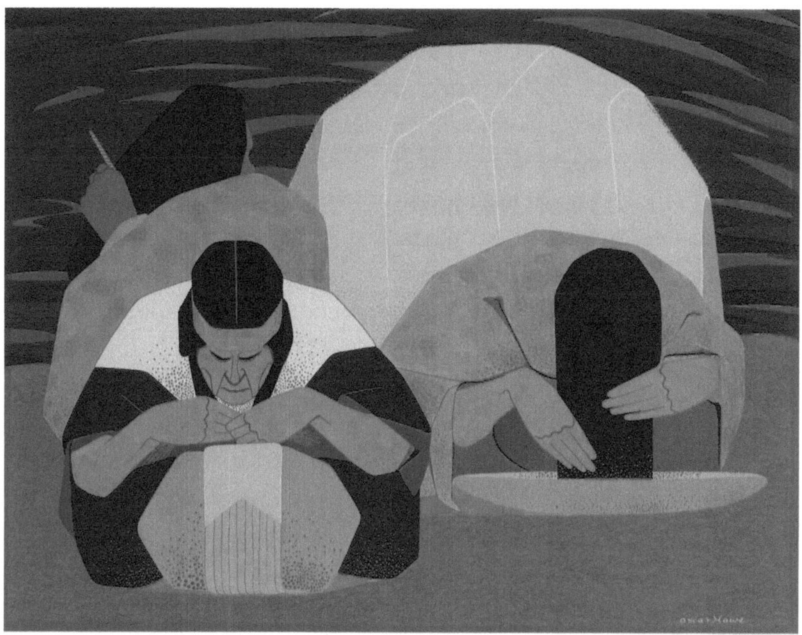

FIGURE 3.7 Oscar Howe, *Three Women*, c. 1953. Tempera on paper. Fred Jones Jr. Museum of Art, the University of Oklahoma, Norman. MFA Thesis selection, School of Art, 1953. Courtesy of the Oscar Howe Estate.

nature and the Great Spirit.[37] In *Three Women*, Howe evoked a "cosmic order" through the use of the crescent, which he had also used in *Council*. The crescent can represent both the moon and the hemispheric sky in Siouan belief, and both the curvature of the women and the nearby hut echo that of the sky to express "man's integration into the pattern of nature."[38]

Howe was hardly the first to utilize symbolic forms in Native American painting to express religious beliefs, but his integration of these forms into the compositional framework breaks with the conventions of his education at the studio. He was likely aware that archetypal forms were used similarly in the 1950s by his instructors at OU as well as by members of the New York School like Adolph Gottlieb with the purpose of returning to a more natural state of being, especially in the anxiety of the postwar period. Whereas the New York School mined the symbols and forms of various non-Western cultures for inspiration, Howe needed to look only to his own heritage to find an acceptable aesthetic language for expressing the desire for oneness with nature and the cosmos.

The adaptation of traditional symbols and techniques provided Howe with a new stylistic approach and a clear break with the legacy of the studio. Although hide painting and quillwork survived to some degree among the Sioux into the 1950s, Howe's interest was the reinvention of traditional techniques to suit the purposes of modern painting. Howe thought as a modernist, looking back to the aboriginal techniques such as tahokmu and owa, to create an aesthetic rooted in tradition yet fundamentally new and experimental, with a result that could hang comfortably next to mainstream modernism.

This is one of the reasons that Howe found himself in conflict with the jury of the Philbrook Art Center's 13th Annual Contemporary American Indian Painting Exhibition in 1958. His new style resisted easy characterization and lived somewhat comfortably at the preconceived boundaries between American Indian painting and mainstream modernism. The Philbrook had already purchased a strikingly modern painting by Howe for its Native American painting collection, *Dance of the Heyoka* (1954), but the jury rejected his *Umine Wacipi—War and Peace Dance* (1958) as "a fine painting—but not Indian."[39] The artist responded harshly, not only emphasizing the Indian roots of his painting but also arguing for greater creative freedom in Native art: "Are we to be held back forever with one phase of Indian painting, with no right for individualism, dictated to as the Indian always has been, put on reservations and treated like a child, and only the White Man knows what is best for him?"[40] Howe equated the constraints of conventional Native painting with both political paternalism and a lack of individuality and challenged the jurors' perceptions of what was possible.

Howe's thesis had set him on a path that would shape the remainder of his career and make him one of the most influential Native American artists working at mid-century. Looking to the traditional forms of hide painting and quillwork, he created a style that was distinctively his own and yet still beholden to his cultural heritage. Siouan cosmology with its archetypal forms and harmonious relationship with nature paralleled similar values esteemed by the abstract expressionists and other American modernists of the period and provided Howe a means of entering a broader conversation without sacrificing his patrimony. In that respect, Howe discovered a means of keeping Siouan aesthetics alive but without strict adherence to older forms of representation, effectively revitalizing waning traditions. His example offered future Native artists a path toward artistic independence but with a healthy respect for their respective histories.

Notes

1. The Santa Fe Indian School was established in 1890 as a boarding school for Native American children across the southwestern United States. Although the primary intent of the curriculum was assimilation into the socioeconomic framework of the United States, the Studio School opened on campus in 1932 under instructor Dorothy Dunn to encourage students to develop their artistic skills and express aspects of their cultural heritage.

2. Howe, "An Exhibition of Original Painting in Tempera," 1.

3. Oscar Howe, interview, July 12, 1977, American Indian Research Project, no. 1044, 10, Institute of American Indian Studies, University of South Dakota. The so-called Studio Style is characterized by naturalistic forms without shading and a general lack of background and perspective. Dunn considered this style, loosely derived from hide painting, petroglyphs, kiva paintings, and pottery, to be the most feasible approach for her instruction at the studio. For a thorough discussion of the program and Dunn's pedagogy, see Bernstein and Rushing, *Modern by Tradition.*

4. Anthes, *Native Moderns*, 156. Also see "Grandmother's Finger Painting First Instruction of SD Artist," *Mitchell (South Dakota) Daily Republic*, December 14, 1951, Oscar Howe Collection, Archives and Special Collections, University of South Dakota.

5. Jacobson stepped down as director of the School of Art at the end of the 1945–46 academic year but remained director of the Museum of Art. He retired from OU in 1950 with the title Research Professor of Art Emeritus.

6. Jeanne d'Ucel, *Memoir and Biographical Writings*, 39, 1962, box 4, folder 5, Oscar B. Jacobson Collection, Oklahoma Historical Society, Oklahoma City.

7. A file of tracings likely produced by Jacobson and his wife Sophie Jeanne Brousse (who wrote under the nom de plume Jeanne d'Ucel), housed in the collection of the Fred Jones Jr. Museum of Art, demonstrate that they based much of their research for *North American Indian Costumes* on historic imagery by the likes of Catlin and Karl Bodmer as well as photographic imagery. Howe presumably used this file for the paintings he created for the portfolio. For further information on the portfolio, see Berlo, *The Szwedzicki Portfolios.*

8. Lyford, *Quill and Beadwork of the Western Sioux*. Lyford was the associate supervisor of Indian education for the Bureau of Indian Affairs' Division of Education. Howe, quoted in Wagner, "Oscar Howe: Indian Artist." Also see Anthes, *Native Moderns*, 162.

9. Howe, "An Exhibition of Original Painting in Tempera," 2.

10. West, "Six American Indian Motifs," 1.

11. For further information on West's thesis and his investigation of modernist forms, see White, "A Modernist Moment."

12. Olkinetzky, "John O'Neil." 6.

13. O'Neil was included in Frederick Sweet's and Katherine Kuh's influential 1947 exhibition at the Art Institute of Chicago, *58th Annual Exhibition of American Paintings and Sculpture: Abstract and Surrealist American Art.*

14. Bywaters, "John O'Neil." *Never-Where* is illustrated in the article.

15. Fernández, "Emilio Amero."

16. Howe, "An Exhibition of Original Painting in Tempera," iii.

17. During the 1950s, the OU Museum of Art was managed by the School of Art, with a director chosen from the faculty. Both Oscar Jacobson and faculty member William Harold Smith were also involved in convincing the university administration to acquire examples from *Advancing American Art.* For a history of *Advancing American Art*, see Ausfeld and Mecklenburg, *Advancing American Art*; Littleton and Sykes, *Advancing American Art*; and Harper, Manoguerra, and White, *Art Interrupted.* For a discussion of its favorable reception at OU, see "OU Purchases 'Condemned' Art."

18. Gottlieb's pictographic works derive from a complex array of influences, including African, Oceanic, Native American, and pre-Columbian art. For a further discussion of the influence from the Americas, see Rushing, *Native American Art and the New York Avant-Garde*, 161–68; Braun, *Pre-Columbian Art and the Post-Columbian World*, 40–46.

19. Howe disclaimed any influence from Cubism in a letter to Bea Medicine, quoted in Medicine, "Oscar Howe and the Sioux (Mazuha Hokshina — Trader Boy)," 15.

20. Dunn, "Oscar Howe," 170.

21. Campbell, *The Hero with a Thousand Faces*, 383. The University of Oklahoma library first acquired a copy of *The Hero with a Thousand Faces* in June 1949, but it is unknown whether Howe read it. Artist John Graham also had a strong influence on the perception that Pollock and other abstract expressionists had of Native American art. He identified Native Americans, along with other non-Western cultures, as "primitive," a term that currently has pejorative connotations but one that he intended as laudatory. He opined that "primitive races and primitive genius have readier access to their unconscious mind than so-called civilized people. It should be understood that the unconscious mind is the creative factor and the source and the storehouse of power and of all knowledge, past and future." Graham, "Primitive Art and Picasso," 237.

22. Polcari, *Abstract Expressionism and the Modern Experience*, 34. See also Sandler, *The Triumph of American Painting*, chap. 4.

23. The primary source on American modernism and its fascination with Native American art remains Rushing, *Native American Art and the New York Avant-Garde.* Anthes also discusses Barnett Newman's role in the appeal and appropriation of Native art; Anthes, *Native Moderns*, 59–88.

24. Anthes, *Native Moderns*, 167.

25. Howe, "An Exhibition of Original Painting in Tempera," 1.

26. Hunter, "Among the New Shows," 9.

27. Anthes, *Native Moderns*, 162.

28. Howe, "An Exhibition of Original Painting in Tempera," 3.

29. Howe, "An Exhibition of Original Painting in Tempera," 5.

30. Howe, "An Exhibition of Original Painting in Tempera," 2. Hans Hofmann quoted from excerpts of his teaching reproduced in Chipp, *Theories of Modern Art*, 536. On the subject of vitalism in abstract expressionism, see Polcari, *Abstract Expressionism*, 52–53.

31. Howe described his approach as similar to a trance in Oscar Howe and Vincent Price, "Oscar Howe: Sioux Artist," directed by Joan McConnell (Pierre: Sanford Gray and South Dakota Indian Arts Council, 1973); Howe, "Theories and Beliefs," 70. Howe specifically defines *owa* as "writing with a point-to-point movement, always esthetic or kinesthetic. The form or form arrangements are guided by one groupal point to another groupal point, etc. For economy of time and space and clarity of meanings, simple but effective esthetic movements are used in objectifying ideas." For a full discussion of Howe's technique, see Anthes, *Native Moderns*, 162–67; White, "Oscar Howe and the Transformation of Native American Art," 171.

32. Wassily Kandinsky's *Point and Line to Plane* was republished in English in 1947 by the Solomon R. Guggenheim Foundation for the Museum of Non-Objective Painting.

33. Howe, "An Exhibition of Original Painting in Tempera," 10.

34. Howe, "An Exhibition of Original Painting in Tempera," 10.

35. For further information on Double Woman, see Walker, *Lakota Myth*; Powers, *Oglala Religion*; Hyman, *Dakota Women's Work*. For a further discussion of Double Woman and creativity, see Berlo, "Dreaming of Double Woman." It has frequently been noted that a man who dreams of Double Woman often becomes a *wintke*, who adopts traits, mannerisms, and clothing generally considered feminine. James H. Howard noted that anyone who dreamed of Double Woman, whether man or woman, was often granted exceptional creativity; Howard, *The Canadian Sioux*, 107.

36. Howe, "An Exhibition of Original Painting in Tempera," 12.

37. Howe, "An Exhibition of Original Painting in Tempera," 12.

38. Howe, "An Exhibition of Original Painting in Tempera," 15.

39. The statement of the jurors, Alice Marriot, Dr. William S. Price, and Jesse Davis, is quoted in Dockstader, "The Revolt of Trader Boy," 47. Howe's reaction to the letter and its ramification for Native American art and art history is discussed in Anthes, *Native Moderns*; White, "Oscar Howe and the Transformation of Native American Art."

40. Howe quoted in King, "The Preëminence of Oscar Howe," 19.

Bibliography

Anthes, Bill. *Native Moderns: American Indian Painting, 1940–1960*. Durham, NC: Duke University Press, 2006.

Ausfeld, Margaret Lynne, and Virginia Mecklenburg. *Advancing American Art: Politics and Aesthetics in the US State Department Exhibition, 1946–48*. Montgomery, AL: Montgomery Museum of Fine Art, 1984.

Berlo, Janet Catherine. "Dreaming of Double Woman: The Ambivalent Role of the Female Artist in North American Indian Myth." *American Indian Quarterly* 17, no. 1 (Winter 1993): 31–43.

Berlo, Janet Catherine. *The Szwedzicki Portfolios: Native American Fine Art and American Visual Culture 1917–1952*. Cincinnati: University of Cincinnati Libraries, 2008. http://digitalprojects.libraries.uc.edu/szwedzicki/01000000.pdf.

Bernstein, Bruce, and W. Jackson Rushing III. *Modern by Tradition: American Indian Painting in the Studio Style*. Santa Fe: Museum of New Mexico Press, 1995. Exhibition catalog.

Braun, Barbara. *Pre-Columbian Art and the Post-Columbian World: Ancient American Sources of Modern Art*. New York: Harry N. Abrams, 1993.

Bywaters, Jerry. "John O'Neil." *Art in America* 43, no. 1 (February 1955): 56–57.

Campbell, Joseph. *The Hero with a Thousand Faces*. 2nd ed. Princeton, NJ: Princeton University Press, 1968.

Chipp, Herschel B., ed. *Theories of Modern Art: A Source Book by Artists and Critics*. Berkeley: University of California Press, 1968.

Dockstader, Frederick J. "The Revolt of Trader Boy: Oscar Howe and Indian Art." *American Indian Art Magazine* 8, no. 3 (Summer 1983): 42–51.

Dockstader, Frederick J., ed. *Oscar Howe: A Retrospective Exhibition; Catalogue Raisonné*. Tulsa, OK: Thomas Gilcrease Museum Association, 1982.

D'Ucel, Jeanne (Sophie Jeanne Brousse). "Memoir and Biographical Writing." 1962. Oscar B. Jacobson Collection, Oklahoma Historical Society, Oklahoma City.

Dunn, Dorothy. "Oscar Howe: Sioux Artist." *El Palacio* 64, nos. 5–6 (May/June 1957): 168–73.

Fernández, Horacio. "Emilio Amero." In *Mexicana: Fotografía Moderna en México, 1923–1940*, edited by Horacio Fernández and Salvador Albinana. Valencia, Spain: IVAM Centre Julio Gonzalez, 1998.

Fernández, Horacio, and Salvador Albinana. *Mexicana: Fotografía Moderna en México, 1923–1940*. Valencia: IVAM Centre Julio Gonzalez, 1998.

Graham, John. "Primitive Art and Picasso." *Magazine of Art* 30, no. 4 (April 1937): 236–39, 260.

"Grandmother's Finger Painting First Instruction of SD Artist." *Mitchell (South Dakota) Daily Republic*, December 14, 1951. Oscar Howe Collection, Archives and Special Collections, University of South Dakota.

Harper, Dennis, Paul Manoguerra, and Mark Andrew White. *Art Interrupted: Advancing American Art and the Politics of Cultural Diplomacy*. Athens: Georgia Museum of Art, 2012.

Howard, James H. *The Canadian Sioux*. Lincoln: University of Nebraska Press, 1984.

Howe, Oscar. "An Exhibition of Original Painting in Tempera." MFA thesis, University of Oklahoma, 1953.

Howe, Oscar. Interview. American Indian Research Project, no. 1044. Institute of American Indian Studies, University of South Dakota, July 12, 1977.

Howe, Oscar. "Theories and Beliefs." *South Dakota Review* 7, no. 2 (Summer 1969): 69–79.

Howe, Oscar, and Vincent Price. *Oscar Howe: Sioux Artist*. Directed by Joan McConnell. Pierre: Sanford Gray and South Dakota Indian Arts Council, 1973.

Hunter, Sam. "Among the New Shows." *New York Times*, January 30, 1949.

Hyman, Colette A. *Dakota Women's Work: Creativity, Culture, and Exile*. St. Paul: Minnesota Historical Society Press, 2012.

King, Jeanne Snodgrass. "The Preëminence of Oscar Howe." In *Oscar Howe: A Retrospective Exhibition; Catalogue Raisonné*, edited by Frederick J. Dockstader, 17–19. Tulsa, OK: Thomas Gilcrease Museum Association, 1982. Exhibition catalog.

Littleton, Taylor, and Maltby Sykes. *Advancing American Art: Painting, Politics, and Cultural Confrontation at Mid-Century*. Tuscaloosa: University of Alabama Press, 1989.

Lyford, Carrie A. *Quill and Beadwork of the Western Sioux*. Washington, DC: United States Department of Interior, Bureau of Indian Affairs, 1940.

Medicine, Bea. "Oscar Howe and the Sioux (Mazuha Hokshina—Trader Boy)." In *Oscar Howe: A Retrospective Exhibition; Catalogue Raisonné*, edited by Frederick J. Dockstader, 15–16. Tulsa, OK: Thomas Gilcrease Museum Association, 1982. Exhibition catalog.

Native American Artists Resource Collection, Heard Museum, Phoenix, Arizona.

Olkinetzky, Sam. "John O'Neil: An Appreciation." *Cross Currents* 11, no. 1 (January/February 1998): 6.

Oscar Howe Collection, Archives and Special Collections, University of South Dakota.

"OU Purchases 'Condemned' Art." *Sooner Magazine* 20, no. 12 (August 1948): 15.

Polcari, Stephen. *Abstract Expressionism and the Modern Experience*. Cambridge: Cambridge University Press, 1991.

Powers, William K. *Oglala Religion*. Lincoln: University of Nebraska Press, 1977.

Rushing, W. Jackson, III. *Native American Art and the New York Avant-Garde*. Austin: University of Texas Press, 1995.

Sandler, Irving. *The Triumph of American Painting*. New York: Harper and Row, 1976.

Walker, James R. *Lakota Myth*. Edited by Elaine A. Jahner. Lincoln: University of Nebraska Press, 1983.

West, Walter Richard. "Six American Indian Motifs Adapted to Contemporary Pictorial Principles." MFA thesis, University of Oklahoma, 1950.

White, Mark Andrew. "A Modernist Moment: Native Art and Surrealism at the University of Oklahoma." *Journal of Surrealism and the Americas* 7, no. 1 (2013): 52–70.

White, Mark Andrew. "Oscar Howe and the Transformation of Native American Art." *American Indian Art Magazine* 23, no. 1 (Winter 1997): 36–43.

MEGAN TAMATI-QUENNELL

4 *KA PŪ TE RUHA, KA HAO TE RANGATAHI*: THE QUIET REVOLUTION

Māori Modernism, Gordon Tovey, Pineamine Taiapa, and Other Motivators of Change

Māori modernism has been defined as a new Māori art, as an alternate or as its own form of modernism. It was developed by a small group of pioneering Māori artists working in New Zealand between the 1930s and the mid-1970s. Primarily painters, sculptors, and printmakers but also including photography, ceramics, and architecture, these artists intentionally distanced themselves from customary Māori art forms such as *whakairo* (Māori carving) and *mahi raranga* (Māori weaving) and explored the styles and techniques of international modern art. They created art that combined Māori ideas, cultural philosophies, and sometimes Māori visual forms with European and American modernism and drew inspiration from international modern artists, including Pablo Picasso, Constantin Brancusi, Barbara Hepworth, Jean Arp, Kazmir Malevich, Ad Reinhart, Alice Aycock, and Mary Miss, to name only a few.

As Damian Skinner has written, modernism provided Māori artists with a means "to negotiate the contemporary world in which they lived." Their work, he said, "aspired to be as good as, as modernist as, the best contemporary art being made in Aotearoa [New Zealand] during the period."[1] Avant-garde in their approach, the Māori modernists were focused neither on customary Māori art nor on reinterpreting "classical" Māori art for the modern age. Their art was not intended to replace *whakairo* (Māori carving) or *mahi raranga* (Māori weaving), nor was it intended to supersede the significance of the *whare whakairo* (the carved and decorated meeting houses), some of the largest forms of Māori visual art in the New Zealand landscape. Modern Māori art was instead designed for the art gallery and for a contemporary art audience.

Highly Individual

There was no set way of being a Māori modernist; no criteria, fixed techniques or stylistic affinities that needed to be adhered to. Writing during the formative years of Māori modernism, artist and Māori scholar Katerina Mataira stressed that modern Māori art was highly individual. She said, "The artist follows his personal vision and relies on the uncertain market of those art lovers who are pleased by it. Pākehā [non-Māori] firms will sometimes commission a work; Māori communities hardly ever."[2] The late Māori art historian Jonathan Mane-Wheoki proposed that although there was no uniform aesthetic style that the Māori modernists conformed to, many were drawn to European and American art such as "[modernist] primitivism and abstraction" in which they discovered similarities to customary Māori art.[3]

The subject matter the Māori modernists worked with was also diverse. Their work did not need to be overtly Māori or to make reference to customary Māori art or culture to be considered Māori modernism. Māori painter Georgina Kirby, for example, undertook private tuition from French-born New Zealand artist Louise Henderson and painted female nudes in Western fine art style. Sculptor Matt Pine was described as "one of the most advanced abstract formalist New Zealand sculptors of the time," and Ramai Hayward (Rongomaitara Te Miha) trained as a photographer before becoming the first Māori filmmaker in the 1940s.[4] The only shared approach of the Māori modernists, much like the contemporary Māori artists of today, was a commitment to contemporary art and their respective mediums. Defining themselves artistically as "modernists first" they saw their work as part of the contemporary art of the period and as sharing many of the same concerns as their non-Māori contemporaries (figure 4.1).[5]

As Skinner has also observed, "Much Māori modernist sculpture features blank smooth surfaces, perhaps smoothed or given texture, but never elaborately carved." Although not all whakairo or Māori carving was elaborately carved (tribal variation and the introduction of steel tools defined some whakairo with intensely detailed surfaces while others did not), Skinner saw the smooth surface of many of the modernist sculptures as "a key marker of difference, to customary forms of Māori art."[6]

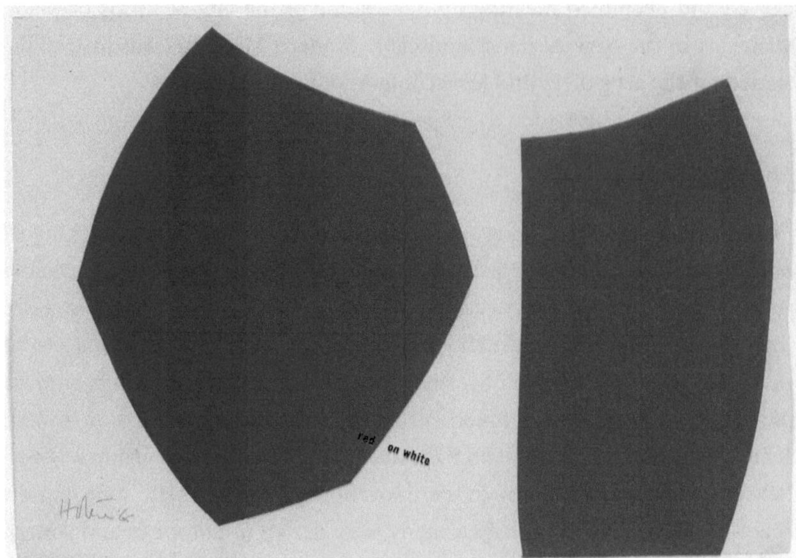

FIGURE 4.1 Ralph Hotere, *Red on white*, 1965. Acrylic on paper, 56 cm × 38.4 cm. © Reproduced courtesy of Ralph Hotere. By permission of the Hotere Foundation Trust. Museum of New Zealand, Te Papa Tongarewa, 2006-0024-6.

The artists engaged with Māori modernism during the mid-twentieth century are now recognized as the founders of what is defined as the contemporary Māori art movement, and their art and ethos as precursors to the contemporary Māori art we now celebrate. But how did Māori modernism come about? What facilitated that break with Māori convention and enabled the creation of a "new art" drawn from Māori and Western art sources? And who and what were intermediaries that assisted in this change? Academic Conal McCarthy has pointed to the importance of the broader sociocultural context. In the 1960s, gaps suddenly opened up. The decade saw pioneering breakthroughs: the first novel, play, and book of poetry in English by Māori writers as well as forays into popular music, television, architecture, and other fields. Dynamic new art forms, pioneered by a generation of Māori artists living in the cities, represented an enthusiastic embrace of modernity and modern art and a break with what was referred to as "museum art."[7] This chapter seeks further answers by looking at how Māori modernism was negotiated by the Māori artists of this period and what impetuses enabled Māori modernism to advance and flourish.

The New Net Goes Fishing

The *whakatauki* or Māori proverb *Ka pū te ruha, ka hao te rangatahi*, used as the chapter title, is a metaphor for Māori modernism. It translates into English as "The old net is laid aside, the new net goes fishing" but can be interpreted conceptually as "enabling generational change." Enabling generational change is a concept that emphasizes that key catalysts for the development of Māori modernism were driven from inside the culture and by the artists themselves. Although Māori modernism was initially rejected by Māori communities, the "new art" was eventually accepted as new Māori expression by Māori elders and leaders even though within the culture at the time it was perhaps still not fully understood. Two significant architects of the development of Māori modernism were, unquestionably, visionary art educator Gordon Tovey and Ngati Porou *Tohunga whakairo* (master carver) Pineamine Taiapa. Both came together within the groundbreaking arts program Tovey established within the Department of Education. They can be credited with creating the milieu for Māori modernism and for setting a lot in motion for the Māori modernists.

Ka pū te ruha, ka hao te rangatahi was first used as an analogy for Māori modernism in 1969 by contemporary Māori artist Selwyn Muru. The proverb appeared in the catalog *The Work of Māori Artists* created for the exhibition of the same name, the first contemporary Māori art exhibition to be held in a public art gallery. Muru coordinated *The Work of Māori Artists* for the New Zealand Māori Council as part of a larger cultural event designed by the council to support *rangatahi* (Māori young people) and recognize their achievements. The council negotiated to have the show installed at the National Art Gallery in Wellington and elsewhere in the capital; however, its showing at the National Art Gallery was a disaster. Rather than being the first successful public art gallery exhibition of contemporary Māori art, *The Work of Māori Artists* instead became an embarrassing episode in the history of contemporary Māori art, one clearly driven by racist attitudes and bias. The National Art Gallery staff were overbearing and vetted the works for the exhibition, reducing the original seventy works submitted for the show to twenty. Muru, as the curator, was sidelined and left out of the decision-making processes. The display of the works was also restricted, Muru said, to "a little space in the corners of the corridors."[8] The twenty participating artists whose work remained in the exhibition were instructed by letter on expected etiquette and how they were to behave at the art gallery and at the opening.

The bias inherent in the views of the Pākehā art world about Māori and Māori art in the 1960s are reflected in a statement made by the director of the National Art Gallery, Stewart MacLennan, in 1966. MacLennan said; "It is true that the Māoris had evolved a form or architecture in which wood carving, plaited flax and reeds, and painted rafter patterns were distinctive enrichments. These and Māori cave paintings have been studied and appreciated both by Māori and by Pākehā. But their meaning and purpose is of the past and they linger on in practice only as traditional crafts. Their motifs have been used effectively in decorative schemes but their original purpose and significance have vanished and, with them, the creative impulse. No Māori artist of stature has yet arrived."[9]

The Māori modernists in *The Work of Māori Artists* wanted to be seen as modern artists and equal to their non-Māori contemporaries (figure 4.2). The National Art Gallery's handling of *The Work of Māori Artists* exhibition and the Māori artists in it, however, worked oppositely and was indicative of the divide between the aspirations of the Māori modernists and the prejudices of the period from mainstream New Zealand art institutions about Māori and Māori art. As Muru commented, "The artists present [at the National Art Gallery], far from being accepted by the art establishment, received the distinct impression that Māori art and Māori people were not welcome."[10]

Māori modernism, as McCarthy has noted, emerged from the dynamic of Māori urbanization as Māori populations moved from *iwi* (tribal) and often rural homelands to New Zealand's urban centers, towns, and cities and from the cultural changes that ensued following those shifts. Māori urbanization intensified after the Second World War, with many Māori who participated in the war having gained a greater exposure to metropolitan lifestyles from time overseas as soldiers. A significant stimulus in this movement was the search for employment and what Mane-Wheoki described as an "increased interest and desire to engage more fully in the monetary economy of western industrial capitalism."[11] He further explains, "In 1936 only 3% of Māori lived in urban areas. At the time of the 1940 centennial [that commemorated the signing of the Treaty of Waitangi] more than 90% of Māori still lived in or close to their ancestral lands. . . . By 1945 19% were living in urban areas. After the war ended, the tempo of migration from the countryside into the towns and cities began to accelerate so that by 1971 the figure of Māori urban dwellers stood at 65%. . . . The first generation of artists was part of this diaspora."[12]

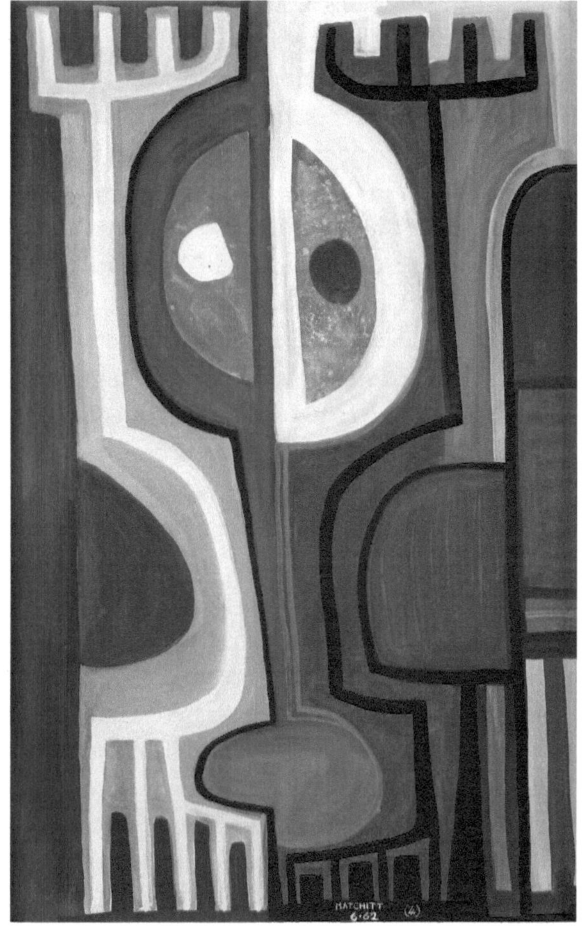

FIGURE 4.2
Paratene Matchitt, *Whiti te ra*, 1962. Gouache on board, 67.5 cm × 43 cm. Museum of New Zealand, Te Papa Tongarewa, 2003-0019-1. Purchased 2003.

Gordon Tovey and the Māori Arts and Crafts Advisers

Many of the first-generation contemporary Māori artists, those who became Māori modernists, were employed by the Department of Education as specialist Māori art and craft advisers under the direction of charismatic educationalist Gordon Tovey (1901–74). Tovey was the national supervisor of arts and crafts between 1946 and 1966. His appointment as the supervisor was controversial because of his lack of qualifications in education. Rather, Tovey brought to the position his vision as an artist, practical experience as a lecturer and teacher, and a proven aptitude for working with children.

In 1941, while working as an art lecturer at Dunedin's Teachers College, Tovey came to the attention of Cecil Beeby. Often described as the "father" or "architect" of New Zealand's modern educational system, Beeby was egalitarian in his views. He believed that every person, irrespective of their circumstances, had a right to a free education best suited to them and their academic ability. Over three decades, from the 1940s to the 1960s, Beeby introduced radical reforms to New Zealand education. Tovey was taken on to implement these new ideas and proposed the idea of teaching Māori art and craft in the context of Beeby's education reforms. Tovey was given "a symbolic open cheque to work in and with Māori communities."[13] His development of a bicultural arts education strategy for all New Zealanders is attributed to Tovey's first real contact with Māori culture in 1947 when he traveled to the East Coast to assess "how new developments in children's art education could be applied to Māori children."[14] There, Tovey recognized the significance of Māori art and saw its long-term potential for New Zealand art education. Skinner points to the connection between Tovey's ideas, children's art, Māori art, and modernist primitivism: "Tovey, in a common primitivist conjunction, responded to Māori art as a source of creative art that was intuitive and fecund."[15] In this context, senior Māori artist and Māori art and craft adviser Paratene Matchitt has commented that "Tovey wanted the expressive qualities of the artist and the child to meet. He invited his artists to play with art as children do. He wanted children's art to be accepted, enjoyed and understood as seriously as one might the finest 'old master' work. Tovey wanted everyone to turn their hand at everything, he wanted no one stuck in the middle of a medium. Art was plural. Everyone in, have a go; wear it; be it."[16]

Tovey's recognition of the vitality of Māori art and the Indigenous Māori culture, combined with Beeby's egalitarian approach to education, ensured there was a new approach to New Zealand art education. The fusion saw Tovey design the country's first bicultural arts education program: "He ensured New Zealand Teachers and children were aware of and were participating in their bicultural heritage for the first time."[17] His program, which merged his personal beliefs about cultural transformation and education's ability to advance race relations in New Zealand, also created the environment for the development of Māori modernism. Tovey handpicked the Māori art teachers who were drawn into the Education Department art and craft advisory service and encouraged them to connect, as Māori, with some of the most progressive art and education ideas of the period. They served as art and craft specialists alongside non-Māori art specialist contemporaries also selected by Tovey. Through this work, Tovey revolutionized art teaching in New Zealand. His influence is de-

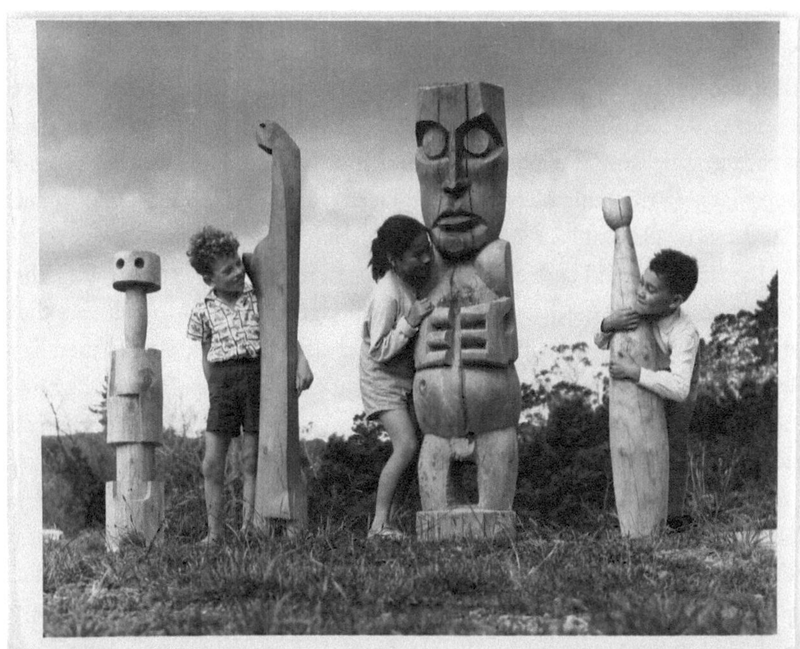

FIGURE 4.3 Ans Westra, Maori — Arts and Crafts, Arnold Wilson sculptures, 1965. Museum of New Zealand, Te Papa Tongarewa, O.010533/02. Purchased 1993 with the New Zealand Lottery Grants Board funds.

scribed as inspiring "a national network of specialists who transformed drab schools into environments ablaze with life and colour."[18] Senior Māori artist Arnold Wilson (nicknamed the godfather of contemporary Māori art by Māori art and craft adviser Sandy Adsett) has said, "Gordon made us feel we had a special talent, a special contribution to make. We just had to focus on where that talent came from" (figure 4.3).[19]

The Founders of Māori Modernism

To list the Māori art advisers employed by Tovey in the art advisory service is to recount the names of many of the founding generation of Māori modernists: Selwyn Wilson was recruited in 1948; Fred Graham and John Bevan Ford in 1951; Ralph Hotere in 1952; Katerina Mataira and Cath Brown in 1953; Mere Kururangi in 1954; Muru Walters in 1955; Cliff Whiting, Paratene Matchitt, and Marilynn Webb in 1957; Clive Arlidge in 1959; Sandy Adsett in 1960; and Mihiata Retimana in 1962. The roles they played as specialist Māori art and craft advisers were essential in introducing Māori arts into New Zealand schools in the early 1960s. Through their work as Māori art and craft advisers, they ensured that aspects of customary Māori art, including *whakairo* (Māori carving), *mahi raranga* (Māori weaving), *kōwhaiwhai* (painted scroll designs), *waiata* (song), *kapa haka* (action songs), *poi* (a rhythmic Māori performing art), and *whai* (Māori string games), had a central place in New Zealand's mainstream classrooms.

The Māori art and craft advisers, however, were not only art educators, they were also practicing artists and were encouraged by Tovey to cultivate their own research and art practice as part of their advisory work. Rather than having to undertake three-year training at an academic art school, Tovey's "philosophy of self-discovery and inherent creativity" ensured the Māori art and craft advisers were given time, were resourced with art equipment and art materials, and were supported to become artists as well as accomplished teachers.[20] As Skinner writes, "Tovey's scheme placed these Māori modernist artists right in the centre of the major support system for modernist art. . . . Tovey, in other words, was interested in creating artists as well as advisers, believing one to be linked to the other."[21] An artist like Ralph Hotere, for example, who Tovey recognized as being exceptionally gifted artistically, was given time away from his job as an art and craft adviser so that he could paint and other members of the department were co-opted to fill in for him: "Gordon took me to the office, but only he and I knew it was really my studio. . . . For me, Tovey made it possible."[22]

Artist and Māori art and craft specialist Marilyn Webb underlined Tovey's philosophy:

> Apart from developing our personal interest areas in education we were also encouraged to engage in our chosen art practice. Creative work time out did not necessarily need to end in exhibitions but always involved discourse with the rest of one's colleagues, which I found rewarding as I emerged as an artist — avenues were in place, through protectionism, if one needed to upskill. I took unpaid leave to travel and investigate graphic developments in Europe. There were no art boundaries — many advisers were multi-skilled while some became very eclectic. We worked across a huge creative range of expressive areas.[23]

"For me it's quite simple," senior Māori artist and Māori art and craft adviser Fred Graham has said, "Gordon was the catalyst, a visionary and an innovator. Without him I would not have become an artist."[24]

Māori writer Harry Dansey noted the dual role of the Māori art and craft advisers in his newspaper review of the *Festival of Māori Arts*, held at St Paul's Methodist Hall in Hamilton, in August 1966. Organized by artist Paratene Matchitt, the festival, which followed on from the first Māori arts festival held three years earlier, in 1963 — the Ngaruawahia Centennial, First Māori Festival of the Arts — included customary Māori art forms alongside displays of contemporary painting and sculpture. "Nearly all the exhibitors make art their primary activity and are engaged in it daily," wrote Dansey, "painting, carving, pottery, etching, casting and sketching. And teaching. That is perhaps the most significant aspect. These young men and women are nearly all employed as art advisers to the Education Department."[25]

Other Māori artists working outside the art advisory scheme were also developing modernist art modes and creating individual expressions of Māori art from as early as the 1930s through to the early 1970s. They include Ramai Hayward (Rongomaitara Te Miha), who as well as being a photographer and having her own photography studio was an illustrator and set designer and went on to become a filmmaker; Pauline Yearbury, who was the first Māori art student to graduate from Auckland University's Elam School of Fine Arts in 1946; and Selwyn Wilson, who graduated from Elam in 1952 as a painter, then later specialized in ceramics and studied at the Central School of Art in London. Arnold Wilson was another Māori modernist artist. He graduated in sculpture from the Elam School of Fine Arts in 1954. There was Selwyn Muru, Buck Nin, and Freda Rankin, the first Māori woman to gain a fine arts degree in 1955 at Ilam, Canterbury University in Christchurch. Also Georgina Kirby, Buster Black (also known as Buster or John Piheama), Mere Harrison (now Lodge), and Matt Pine, who went to both Ilam in Christchurch and Elam in Auckland, and later also studied at the Central School of Art in London and took his lead from American minimalist sculptors such as Donald Judd and Sol Le Witt, land artist Robert Smithson, and Japanese and Māori architecture. These artists, together with the "Tovey/Taiapa artists," became the vanguard of contemporary Māori art in New Zealand: "From the commonalities of their culture, insights, experiences and ambitions and the meeting point of mātauranga Māori (Māori knowledge) and mātauranga Pākehā (settler knowledge) in their lives and work," wrote Mane-Wheoki, "the contemporary Māori art movement was born."[26]

Marilynn Webb believed that without Tovey's art advisory scheme, the connection between Māori and European art forms would not be as it is. John Bevan Ford echoed Webb's sentiments: "At the same time as Gordon committed us to our Māori heritage he also committed us to our international heritage. In the recognition of our roots we discovered the common chord of all humanity. We got the backing of our own people and knew we were in a partnership, Māori and Pākehā; yet when we were at our most nationalistic we became international."[27]

A further dimension of the specialist arts advisory program, developed by Tovey, took book form. In 1961 the Department of Education published and issued to all schools in New Zealand *The Arts of the Māori*, a publication created by Tovey with an advisory committee that included Marewa McConnell, Maud Issacs, Mere Kururangi, Sidney (Hirini Moko) Mead, Whare Issacs, Pineamine Taiapa, and Murray Gilbert. It also featured drawings by Taiapa and Mead and photographs by John Bevan Ford, Donald Campbell, and Peter Campbell.[28] The book was designed as a complement to the courses and work the Māori art and craft advisers were undertaking in schools to support teachers. The publication also represented the many years of work Tovey had given to Māori art and craft training within the Education Department and was one of two books he hoped to release.

"'The Arts of the Māori'" wrote Tovey, "was a book mainly for European children—it stressed the breadth and essence of Māori activities." The second corresponding volume, in the spirit of biculturalism titled *The Arts of the Pākehā*, was planned and proposed to encourage "better understanding in Māori children of Pākehā children": "We had in mind a second book which would primarily be for Māori children. . . . The two books were supposed to dovetail like that in the schools, so the Māori isn't teaching the Pākehā everything and the Pākehā isn't teaching the Māori everything."[29]

Tovey's matching book—*The Arts of the Pākehā*—was never published. *The Arts of the Māori*, however, was followed by a series of supplementary illustrated booklets focused on particular Māori art forms in greater detail and available for teachers. The booklets covered the fields of *whakairo* (Māori carving), *raranga* (Māori weaving), *kete* (basket) and *whariki* (mat) making, *tukutuku* (woven meeting house panels), *whai* (Māori string games), ceremonial costume, *kapa haka* (Māori action songs), *haka* (performance), single long *poi* (a Māori performing art), and *waiata* (Māori song). They were put together by Māori art advisers relating to the subject focused on and the art advisers' expertise. *The Arts of the Māori* instructional booklet for *Carving*, for example, was prepared by Para (Paratene) Matchitt, Muru Walters, and Clifford (Cliff) Whiting.[30] The *Kete Making* booklet was put together by Catherine (Cath) Brown, and the booklet on *The Single Long Poi* was by Mere Kururangi.[31]

Artist and art adviser Katerina Mataira wrote a review of *The Arts of the Māori* book in 1962 for *Te Ao Hou*, the journal of the Department of Māori Af-

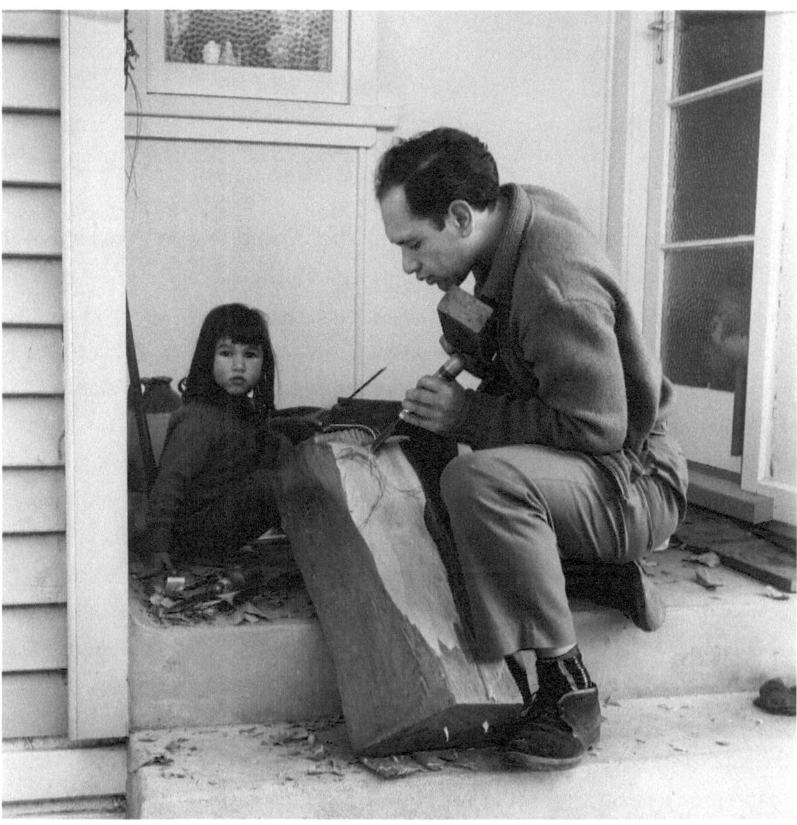

FIGURE 4.4 Ans Westra, Para Matchitt with his daughter at home, 1963. Museum of New Zealand, Te Papa Tongarewa, O.042839. Purchased 2014.

fairs designed to be a meeting place or "a Marae on paper for Māori people."[32] Mataira saw *The Arts of the Māori* as the first promotion by the Education Department of the work she and her colleagues had been undertaking for several years through the teaching of Māori art and craft in schools. She also saw its release as an acknowledgment of the value of Māori art to society and the means by which the understanding between the cultures could be bridged. Mataira perceived its distribution to all New Zealand schools as giving support to the maintenance, development, and growth of Māori art (figure 4.4). "To the Māori," she wrote, "it means a renewal of hope that part of his cultural heritage will remain with him, and perhaps even flourish."[33] Mataira's review both affirmed the importance of Tovey's work and predicted the advance of Māori modernism. In her review she astutely asked, "Will Mr. Tovey be the forerunner of an era of intense and extensive creativeness in the fields of Māori art, resulting in the development of fresh and inspiring works which more closely resemble our life today?"[34]

Pineamine Taiapa *and Māori Modernism*

Māori endorsement of Māori modernism can be said to have come about in March 1960 as part of a week-long in-service training course for select specialist art and craft advisers. Described as a "turning point" by Tovey's daughter Carol Henderson in her writing about her father and his work, the course had been a ten-year vision for Tovey. It took place in Ruatoria, a predominantly Māori community on the East Coast of the North Island. Focused on customary Māori arts, the course introduced Ngati Porou (East Coast tribe) *Tohunga whakairo* (master carver) Pineamine Taiapa (1901–72) to the Māori art and craft advisers and Tovey's art advisory scheme. Taiapa became an important associate for Tovey and a principal influence for the specialist Māori art advisers. Taiapa, as a Tohunga whakairo, was firmly anchored in the concepts and lore of customary Māori art. His significance in the history of Māori modernism has often been overshadowed by the work Tovey is credited with, as a progressive and imaginative educationalist, but Taiapa was unquestionably integral to the success of Tovey's bicultural art education program and the development of Māori modernism. Māori educator Keri Kaa described the meeting of the "firebrand" Taiapa and the erudite Tovey as a "meeting of Titans," with their pairing creating profound results in art education in New Zealand and in the evolution and the development of contemporary Māori art.[35] The Māori modernists who advanced through Tovey's art scheme were for a long time referred to as the "Tovey Generation," a name coined by Mane-Wheoki. The name was related to the confluence of the advisers' roles as both Māori art educators and as leading contemporary Māori artists. The Tovey Generation have more recently and more accurately become known as the "Tovey/Taiapa Generation." The name change not only recognizes Tovey's influence, it acknowledges Taiapa's leadership, guidance, and the cultural gravitas he lent to Tovey's art education program and also highlights the role he played in the new ground the Māori modernists were forging with their work. Both Tovey and Taiapa were vital intermediaries in the development of Māori modernism.

Taiapa was connected to the first Māori renaissance of the twentieth century, known as the "Ngata revival" led by Māori politician, statesman, and scholar Sir Apirana Ngata. Ngata had developed a strategy for the support and continuation of Māori art through meeting-house building. He established a Māori school of customary arts in Rotorua in 1927 and was the driving force behind the construction of whare whakairo, carved and decorated meeting houses, throughout the country. Taiapa had been one of the first students of Ngata's Rotorua school and went on to be recognized as one of the greatest Māori carvers, renowned, among other things, for the fine finish of his whakairo or carving work. A prolific carver, he worked on over a hundred meeting houses during his lifetime. The houses he worked on included the *whare rūnanga* at Waitangi, completed in 1940 to commemorate the centennial anniversary of the signing of the Treaty of Waitangi, the founding document of New Zealand. Whiting emphasized the significance of the whare whakairo to the continuity of both Māori culture and Māori art. Whiting wrote, "The carved and decorated meeting house is an expression of the identity of the people who own the house. The decoration is placed according to the cosmology of the meeting house. This cosmology has continued from the past into the present day."[36] The whare whakairo was an art form Whiting championed throughout his life, through the conservation work on meeting houses he undertook with the New Zealand Historic Places Trust and the building of new meeting houses with Māori communities such as Takahanga Marae in Kaikoura in the South Island of New Zealand.

During the weeklong course at Ruatoria, the attending art and craft specialists, made up of Māori art and craft advisers and some of their Pākehā counterparts, were able to study under Taiapa and other Māori cultural experts. The guest instructors brought into the Ruatoria project included Arnold Reedy, who alongside Taiapa, taught the histories of Māori art and East Coast specific styles and forms; Marewa McConnell was co-opted to teach *poi* (a Māori performing art); Mere Kururangi, one of the Māori art advisers, was responsible for *kapa haka*, including *waiata-a-ringa* (Māori action songs); Ami Tuhaka and Maude Isaacs, experts in *mahi raranga*, or Māori weaving, imparted their skills; and George Reedy, also from the east coast, trained the art specialists in *haka* (Māori dance performance).

Māori Authorization

Tovey knew that the knowledge and skills of customary Māori art were governed by the Māori concepts of *tapu* and *noa*. Tapu and noa are Māori cultural concepts that impose prohibitions. *Tapu* has numerous meanings but can be best interpreted as "spiritual restriction." *Noa* is opposite to tapu and can be defined as being free from the extension of tapu or being "without restriction."

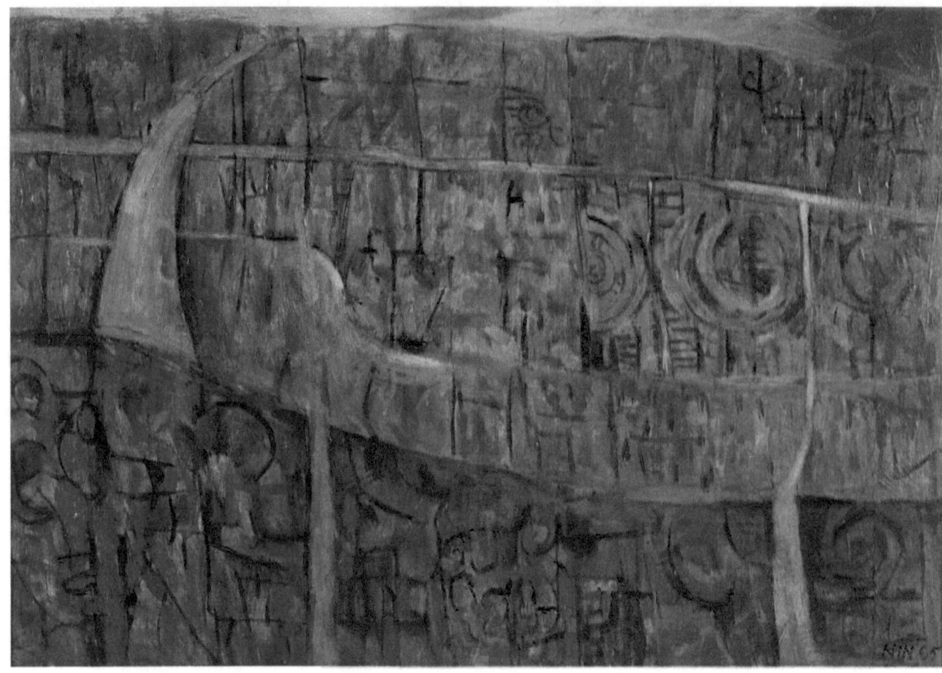

FIGURE 4.5 Buck Nin, *Canoe Prow*, 1965. Oil on board, 81.3 cm × 55.8 cm. Museum of New Zealand, Te Papa Tongarewa, 2000-0022-2. Purchased 2000 with New Zealand Lottery Grants Board funds.

Going into the Ruatoria course, Tovey understood he needed the endorsement of experts like Taiapa and other Māori elders for the work the Māori art advisers were undertaking. Their approval would support the lifting of any tapu or restrictions for the teaching of Māori art and craft in schools to children and would give the advisers freedom, as artists, to innovate and to formulate their own ideas about Māori art and the blending of modern and Indigenous Māori forms. For example, as Whiting has explained, "A major difference between carving and painting figures is that, unlike painting, which produces no residue, a carved figure has a residue of chips that could be fitted back together to make a negative form of the ancestor. It is imperative to know the *karakia* (prayer) to deal with that residue. The fact that painting does not create a dangerous negative form gives painting a new freedom that allows the artist to experiment with new forms" (figure 4.5).[37]

Taiapa was of central importance to the Ruatoria course and the larger milieu of Māori modernism. As Skinner has emphasized, "The point was not just the transmission of information from experts such as Pine but a larger authorization for Tovey's project — its educational, social and artistic agendas."[38] From Tovey's perspective, Taiapa's backing was gained during an address Taiapa gave at the beginning of the weeklong course. He talked about the art forms featured in the Ruatoria Memorial Hall and the modifications that had been made to both the materials and in the designs. He concluded, "The final point I want to make here is that even though the patterns used are traditional, the Māori artist, through the variations I mentioned is allowed personal liberty to express himself creatively."[39] Tovey took Taiapa's words as vindication that change within Māori art was possible and as confirmation that Taiapa recognized innovation, artistic originality, and personal creativity as significant features within Māori art, hallmarks, as Tovey saw it, of the work of the Māori art and craft advisers as Māori modernists.

Tovey ensured Taiapa's continued involvement in his art advisory scheme after the Ruatoria *hui* by hiring him part time as a specialist in the "technical growth and historical background of Māori arts."[40] He saw Taiapa's acceptance of the role created for him as a further endorsement of the bicultural art advisory program he had developed. Although a catalyst for change, being non-Māori, Tovey was not able to negotiate or give Māori authority to the Māori modernist artists involved in his program or endorse from a Māori perspective the new Māori art they developed. That vital authority first came through Taiapa, whose mandate ensured that the alternate modernism the artists created was a Māori modernism.

A Break with Tradition

A key aspect of the Māori modernists' ethos was the desire to break with tradition and to innovate rather than repeat customary patterns and forms. The Māori modernists were interested in exploring what Selwyn Muru termed "the creative avenues leading from Māori art."[41] In an interview published in the Māori affairs journal *Te Ao Hou* in 1961, artist and Māori art and craft adviser Muru Walters called contemporary whakairo (contemporary Māori carving) a "museum art." He felt the carving of the present day "had not yet bridged the gap between, old and the new," and was disappointed that some of the carvers seemed content to continually repeat customary forms without considering how they applied to "modern conditions and times."[42] Arnold Wilson was similar in his criticism and has famously called contemporary Māori carving "wall paper," with the inference that contemporary whakairo had become to be about the surface design and decoration but the innovation and the original deep meaning, through repetition of standardized forms, was missing. Wilson's views about customary Māori art at that time are summed up in the following way: "Reviving so-called Māori arts and crafts is a dead loss."[43]

Ngata's establishment of a template for Māori art, particularly carving and meeting-house design, was established in the 1920s and '30s to maintain Māori art and retain it as a "living art." He too could see Māori art was being eroded culturally and was becoming a "museum art." His strategies for Māori art were intended to reverse that trend. For his part, Matchitt believed the changes being made to Māori art by the Māori modernists were not "a matter for regret" as long as the adaptations were undertaken for the right reasons, that the Māori artists remained true to their "growing self," and were reflections of the "inner development" of Māori people.[44]

The journey of the Māori modernists, Ford has said, "was an uneasy one." Support from Māori communities was not easily won. The elders, he said, "feared that the culture would be trampled on by the introduction of non-traditional modes of expression."[45] The early work of the Māori modernists was misunderstood and often maligned. Taiapa's brother, Hone, also a Tohunga whakairo (master carver) and another of the principal carvers at Rotorua carving school for many years, for example, described the new forms being created by the Māori modernists as "a prostitution of Māori art." The mainstream reinforced Māori apprehension about modern Māori art. In an article written for the *New Zealand Listener* in 1967 about the "new art" being created by the Māori modernists was, for Māori, they wrote, "as much of an anathema as a Hepworth bronze was to some Pākehā" at one stage.[46]

Taiapa, involved directly with the Māori modernists through his work with Tovey, expressed his initial disapproval of his students' art practice. Whiting and Matchitt both spoke of friction between them and Taiapa related to their work. Matchitt recollected an occasion where there was tension about his and Ford's work:

> John and I were involved in an exhibition in Hamilton a number of years ago now, where we exhibited with some traditional pieces. Pine came up to open the show, he was in a hell of a state. Anyway, it eventually turned out that he actually didn't like our work, he was going to come and tell me off. "After all these bloody years, of me teaching about our history and so on, and then you turn around and do this bloody rubbish!" That's almost word for word what he said. And then he went away and thought

about it before the opening of this exhibition, and he came out. "I came down here to blow these boys up." But he thought about it a bit more and he said, "The world is full of art, and there is room in it for everyone."[47]

Similarly Whiting recalled Taiapa's initial reticence toward the work he was creating: "Pine Taiapa was a very powerful force. He was used as a tutor for specialist teachers and was also a great storyteller, with an absolute involvement in the arts of the meeting house. When I started to do murals, Pine thought they were not so powerful, but eventually he realized how times were changing and accepted murals as a valid expression of Māori art."[48]

Bridging the Gap

An event that attempted to bridge the gap between the Māori community and modern Māori art was the first Māori Artists and Writers Society conference or *hui* (Māori gathering) to be held. The hui took place over four days at the beginning of June in 1973 in Te Kaha, in the Bay of Plenty, on the East Coast of the North Island of New Zealand. Instigated by leading Māori poet Hone Tuwhare and facilitated by Matchitt, who later became the long-standing chairman of Nga Puna Waihanga, it was held on Matchitt's home marae of Te Kahanui-a tiki, with the support of Matchitt's father, Hubert, who was the marae chairman. Originally proposed by Tuwhare as a gathering for the Māori writers, many of whom were writing and publishing novels, poems, and plays in English, the conference evolved to include the Māori modernist artists who were also working in new ways as painters, sculptors, photographers, and in other forms. It also included other Māori artists involved in music, dance, and theater, and Māori intellectuals and thinkers. Defined as "an act of self-assertion,"[49] the hui was established with the aim of building a support network for the Māori artists and new art forms that were being created. Over two hundred people attended the hui, including visual artists Ralph Hotere, Buck Nin, Selwyn Muru, Paratene Matchitt, and Kura Rewiri (now Te Waru-Rewiri); photographer John Miller; writer Witi Ihimaera; actor Sonny Waru; and many others. Topics covered in the gathering included dialogue about the position of the Māori artist in New Zealand society, Māori peoples' relationship to the new art being made, and the need for communication about the art and artists to the Māori community. They also discussed "the dilemma of the Māori artist in expressing Māori concepts within a Pākehā medium."[50] A further dialogue considered the role of the marae as a site for creativity. Ford named the artists and writers at the hui as “pioneers of a new consciousness” and further summarized the event and participants in the following way: “[As] single warriors in a battle for new creative direction who came together to support each other at a time of cultural insecurity.”[51] Ford believed the Māori modernists had started a revolution that was attempting to retain the underlying aesthetic of customary Māori art, and that was focused on regaining the innovation within Māori art and the revival of the “Māori creative genius.” “The Māori artist of yesterday,” he said, “created within the constraints of a single culture. Now the Māori artist operates within a multiplicity of cultures.”[52]

As well as representing the burgeoning of new forms of Māori art across a number of disciplines, the Māori Artists and Writers Society hui of 1973 also signaled a new phase in the evolution of Māori art; the establishment of a Māori art organization directed by the Māori artists themselves. The Māori Artists and Writers Society created a conceptual shift for the Māori modernist artists. They became part of a focused collective, their work was legitimized in Māori terms, and although perhaps still not completely understood, it was more accepted by the Māori community. The intentional distance they had placed between themselves and customary Māori art in order to negotiate change was collapsed, and there was a conscious return to the marae that they had separated their work from. The hui was the starting point for the reintegration of Māori modernism within a Māori paradigm and the reconnecting of Māori modernism with the Māori art that had existed before the Ngata revival (figure 4.6).

A small group of Māori artists in the 1930s through to the early 1970s started a quiet revolution. Pioneers in the development of Māori modernism, they instigated an intense creative exploration of international modern art and created new and dynamic forms that combined European and American modernism with Māori philosophies, ideas, and sometimes Māori forms. The movement evolved from a complex set of artistic and cultural conditions, including immense changes to Māori society through Māori urbanization, a profound and progressive bicultural arts education program many of the artists were part of, and the influence of two key mediators: visionary educationalist Gordon Tovey and Tohunga whakairo Pineamine Taiapa. Other catalysts included the determination of the artists themselves, their passage away from an art that they increasingly saw as having lost its validity and without innovation, and their commitment to modern and contemporary art. Resolute and courageous, the Māori modernists overcame the deliberate exclusion of their work and practice as First Nations artists from mainstream art galleries, the challenges of being accepted as “modern” by the galleries and the critics, and

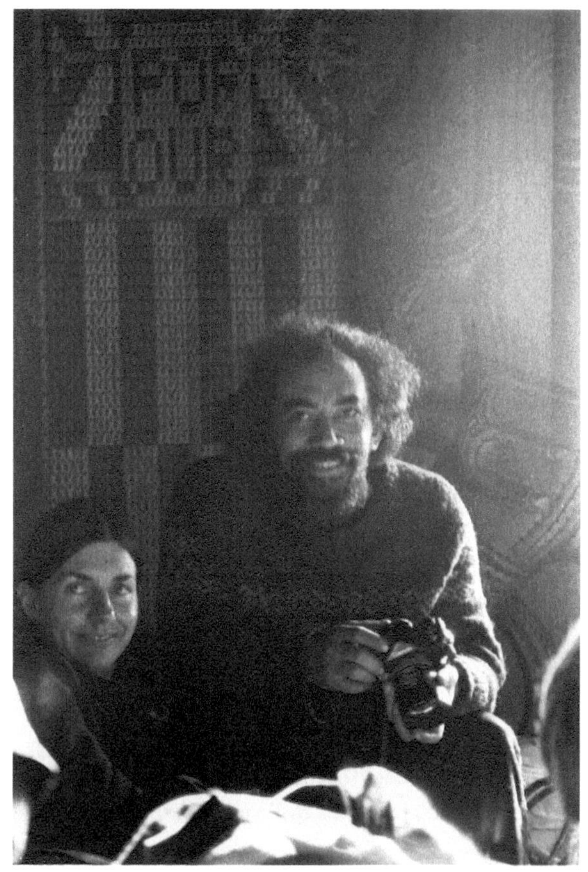

FIGURE 4.6 John Miller, *Tukaki wharenui, Te Kaha-nui-a-tiki marae, Te Kaha.* Marilynn Webb (*left*), Ralph Hotere (*right*), June 1973. Courtesy of John Miller.

having their practice misunderstood and rejected by the Māori community. Māori modernism was a movement of critical negotiation, a purposefully staged difference to what had gone before. Individual, unapologetic, made for the art gallery and to be as good as the best contemporary art of the period, Māori modernism developed from the merging of customary and modernist styles, materials, and concepts and using modern techniques.

Notes

Note: Ka pū te ruha, ka hao te rangatahi = The old net is laid aside, the new net goes fishing.

1. Skinner, "Modern Trends," 80. Aotearoa is the Māori name for New Zealand.
2. Mataira, "Modern Trends in Māori Art Forms," 205.

3. Mane-Wheoki, “Notes towards a History of Contemporary Maori Art.”

4. Mane-Wheoki, “Class of ’66.”

5. Skinner, “Modern Trends,” 80.

6. Skinner, “Modern Trends,” 123.

7. Conal McCarthy, “‘A New Net Goes Fishing’: Contemporary Māori Art,” in McCarthy, *Exhibiting Māori*, 124.

8. Selwyn Muru, quoted in McCarthy, *Exhibiting Māori*, 129.

9. Maclennan, “Survey, Trends, and Influences, 1938 to Present.”

10. Selwyn Muru, quoted in McCarthy, “‘A New Net Goes Fishing,’” 129.

11. Mane-Wheoki, “Te Tai Tokerau,” 104.

12. Mane-Wheoki, “Te Tai Tokerau,” 104.

13. Mason, *Turuki Turuki! Paneke Paneke!*, 18.

14. Skinner, “Modern Trends,” 81.

15. Skinner, “Modern Trends,” 81.

16. Paratene Matchitt, quoted in “Ruatoria: Turning Point,” in Henderson, *A Blaze of Colour*, 173.

17. Henderson, “Tovey, Arthur Gordon.”

18. Henderson, “Tovey, Arthur Gordon.”

19. Arnold Wilson, quoted in “A Revolution Underway,” in Henderson, *A Blaze of Colour*, 139.

20. Smith, “Gordon Tovey, the Māori Art Advisors and the Development of Contemporary Māori Art,” 19.

21. Skinner, “Modern Trends,” 83.

22. Ralph Hotere, quoted in “Expanded Responsibilities,” in Henderson, *A Blaze of Colour*, 142.

23. Marilynn Webb, quoted in Lonie and Webb, *Marilynn Webb*, 25.

24. Fred Graham, quoted in Henderson, *A Blaze of Colour*, 173.

25. Harry Dansey, “Māori Artists Make Mark as Professionals,” *Auckland Star*, September 3, 1966.

26. Mane-Wheoki, “Te Tai Tokerau,” 108.

27. John Bevan Ford, quoted in Henderson, “Ruatoria,” 169.

28. New Zealand Department of Education, *The Arts of the Maori*.

29. New Zealand Department of Education, *The Arts of the Maori*.

30. Matchitt, Walters, and Whiting, *Carving*.

31. Brown, *Kete Making*; Kururangi, *Single Long Poi*.

32. *Te Ao Hou* or *The New World* (1952–1975) published some of the earliest work of the Māori modernist artists and Māori writers of the period.

33. Mataira, “The Arts of the Māori,” 30.

34. Mataira, “The Arts of the Māori,” 30.

35. Keri Kaa, quoted in Henderson, “Ruatoria,” 169.

36. Whiting, foreword, vii.
37. Whiting, foreword, vii.
38. Skinner, "Modern Trends," 82.
39. Henderson, "Ruatoria," 167.
40. Henderson, "Ruatoria," 167.
41. Selwyn Muru, quoted in Skinner, *The Carver and the Artist*, 117.
42. Muru Walters in "Muru Walters," 28.
43. Arnold Wilson, quoted in Skinner, *The Carver and the Artist*, 12.
44. Paratene Matchitt, quoted in Skinner, *The Carver and the Artist*, 117.
45. Ford, "Introduction," 9.
46. A. S. F., "Modern Art and the Māori," *New Zealand Listener*, May 5, 1967, 6–7.
47. Matchitt, quoted in Skinner, *The Carver and the Artist*, 83–84.
48. Whiting, foreword, vii.
49. Ford, "Introduction," 9.
50. Ihimaera, "Conference at Te Kaha," 24.
51. Ford, "Introduction," 9.
52. Ford, "Introduction," 9.

Bibliography

Brown, Catherine. *Kete Making: The Arts of the Maori Instruction Booklet*. Wellington, NZ: Art and Craft Branch, Department of Education, 1975.

Ford, John Bevan. "Introduction." In *Māori Artists of the South Pacific*, by Katarina Mataira, 9. Auckland: New Zealand Māori Artists and Writers Society, 1984.

Henderson, Carol. *A Blaze of Colour: Gordon Tovey, Artist Educator*. Christchurch: Hazard Press, 1998.

Henderson, Carol. "Tovey, Arthur Gordon." *Dictionary of New Zealand Biography*. Accessed July 25, 2020. https://teara.govt.nz/en/biographies/5t17/tovey-arthur-gordon.

Ihimaera, Witi. "Conference at Te Kaha." *Te Ao Hou* 74 (November 1973): 24.

Kururangi, Mere. *Single Long Poi: The Arts of the Maori Instruction Booklet*. Wellington, NZ: Art and Craft Branch, Department of Education, 1972.

Lonie, Bridie, and Marilynn Webb. *Marilynn Webb: Prints and Pastels*. Dunedin: University of Otago Press, 2003.

Maclennan. Stewart Bell. "Survey, Trends, and Influences, 1938 to Present." In *An Encyclopaedia of New Zealand*, edited by A. H. McLintock. Accessed July 25, 2020. http://www.TeAra.govt.nz/en/1966/art-in-new-zealand/page-2.

Mane-Wheoki, Jonathan. "Class of '66." *Off the Wall* 1 (March 2013). https://collections.tepapa.govt.nz/topic/4130.

Mane-Wheoki, Jonathan. "Notes towards a History of Contemporary Maori Art." In *Three Contemporary Maori Artists*. Christchurch: Christchurch City Council, 1990.

Mane-Wheoki, Jonathan. "Te Tai Tokerau and the Contemporary Māori Art Movement." In *Te Puna: Maori Art from Te Tai Tokerau Northland*, edited by Deidre Brown and Ngarino Ellis, 103–21. Auckland: Reed, 2008.

Mason, Ngahiraka. *Turuki Turuki! Paneke Paneke! When Māori Art Became Contemporary.* Auckland: Auckland Art Gallery, 2008.

Mataira, Katarina [Katerina]. "The Arts of the Māori: A Review." *Te Ao Hou* 68 (March 1962): 30.

Mataira, Katarina [Katerina]. "Modern Trends in Māori Art Forms." In *The Māori People in the Nineteen-Sixties: A Symposium*, edited by Erik Schwimmer, 205–16. Auckland: Blackwood and Janet Paul, 1968.

Matchitt, Para, Puru Walters, and Cliff Whiting. *Carving: The Arts of the Maori Instruction Booklet.* Wellington: Art and Craft Branch, Department of Education, 1978.

McCarthy, Conal. *Exhibiting Māori: A History of Colonial Cultures of Display.* Wellington: Te Papa Press, 2007.

"Muru Walters." *Te Ao Hou* 35 (June 1961): 28–29.

New Zealand Department of Education. *The Arts of the Maori.* Wellington: R. E. Owen, Government Printer, 1961.

Skinner, Damian. *The Carver and the Artist: Māori Art in the Twentieth Century.* Auckland: Auckland University Press, 2008.

Skinner, Damian. "Modern Trends in Māori Art Forms, Māori Modernism, 1950–1970." In *The Carver and the Artist: Māori Art in the Twentieth Century*, 79–126. Auckland: Auckland University Press, 2008.

Smith, Jill. "Gordon Tovey, the Māori Art Advisors and the Development of Contemporary Māori Art." In *The Modern World Part Two: Design in New Zealand 1917–1970*, 12–23. Auckland: UNITEC School of Design, 1996. Conference proceedings.

Whiting, Cliff. Foreword to *Painted Histories: Early Maori Figurative Painting*, by Roger Neich, vii–x. Auckland: Auckland University Press, 1994.

NICHOLAS THOMAS

ARCHIVAL EXPLORATION 2 "THE FIRST CONTEMPORARY PICTURES IN NEW GUINEA"

Georgina Beier and Melanesian Modernism

Melanesian modernist art was made by Melanesian artists, but a German British expatriate couple who arrived in Papua New Guinea from Europe via Nigeria in 1966 created the conditions for its existence. Ulli Beier (1922–2011) was born in Germany to a Jewish family and had been brought up in Palestine but went on to study in London and moved in 1950 to Nigeria to lecture in English. He soon began writing about Yoruba literature, art, and society, and while his first wife, Susanne Wenger (1915–2009), supported and collaborated with local artists, he launched journals, famously including *Black Orpheus*.[1] Together with Wole Soyinka, Chinua Achebe, and others, he also founded the Mbari Artists and Writers Club, which subsequently generated a foundationally important exhibition program, featuring leading artists from elsewhere in Africa as well as Nigeria. Beier and Wenger divorced in 1966 and Ulli subsequently married Georgina Beier (1938–2021), who was born in London and studied briefly at Kingston Art School before dropping out because she felt the "academic" atmosphere would impede her own personal and creative development.

In a retrospective reflection on the Oshogbo school, the artist Twins Seven Seven described Ulli and Georgina as "unique," each "a kind of missionary" bearing not the Bible but "brushes in one hand and a bag of knowledge in the other."[2] It could be added that they were missionaries for decolonization and most especially a culture of decolonization. Though well aware of anthropology and interested in the validation of local tradition, customary art, and oral literature, the couple were supportive above all of modern writing, theater, and art and of the work of then-young practitioners energized by changing times. While modernism inevitably valorizes the "new," the new in this context was associated with liberation and a sense that what would now be distinctive and different would come from nations such as Nigeria and Papua New Guinea.

The Beiers did much more than encourage individuals. In an informal and low-key way, they created art worlds: by mounting exhibitions, encouraging friends and associates to mount them elsewhere, and similarly nudging colleagues and acquaintances to buy work on behalf of friends and university academic departments in Australia, Britain, and elsewhere. Georgina Beier was moreover well aware that art could not flourish without critical writing that spread the word and provided potential audiences and patrons with ways of seeing and valuing new and initially unfamiliar images. As in Nigeria, she and Ulli launched journals that published both creative writing and commentary on culture and decolonization in Papua New Guinea, including *Kovave: A Journal of New Guinea Literature* (1969–75) and *Gigibori: A Magazine of Papua New Guinea Cultures* (1974–79). The former was published by Jacaranda Press in Brisbane, Australia — an independent publisher run by Brian Clouston, a friend of Ulli's, which also brought out the first Papua New Guinean novel *The Crocodile* (1970) by Vincent Eri. One of the last issues of *Kovave* was a special issue dedicated to visual art, called *Modern Images from Niugini* (the Tok Pisin [pidgin] name for the country was sometimes preferred at the time); most issues of it and *Gigibori*, which was produced in Port Moresby itself, featured black and white reproductions of drawings or prints by Akis, Mathias Kauage, and Serwai Kepo (figure AE2.1).

Two texts are reproduced here. The first exemplifies Georgina Beier's framing of the work emerging at the end of the 1960s. It was written for one of the very first exhibitions mounted outside Papua New Guinea, at the Aladdin Gallery in Sydney, which had been established in Sydney's eastern suburbs in the mid-1960s by Margaret and Thomas Bolster. Margaret was originally from New Zealand, while Thomas had moved to Australia from the United States after having been denounced as a Communist. The couple were interested in contemporary Australian art and "folk art" and craft from Asia and the Pacific; the Aladdin was said to be the first gallery in Australia to exhibit such work from Asia. There appear to be no extant photographs of the exhibition, which

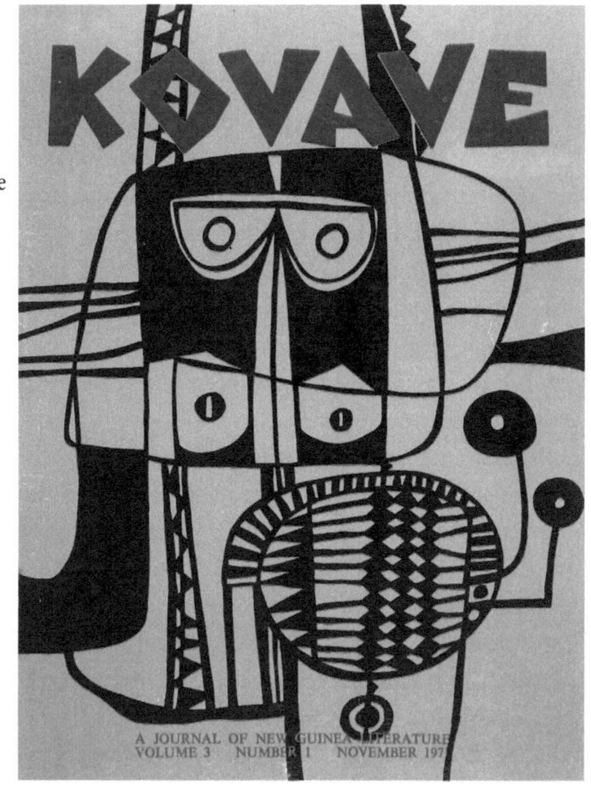

FIGURE AE2.1
Kovave 3, no. 1 (1971). One of the publications launched by Ulli and Georgina Beier, which featured creative writing, commentary, and visual art. This cover, and others, was designed by Georgina Beier.

evidently drew together a group of early Kauage drawings (or possibly prints), work by inmates at the Laloki mental hospital, who notably included Tiabe, and some "paintings from Yule Island." While Georgina had mentored both the Laloki artists and Kauage, the Yule Island work arose from the teaching of a Catholic nurse, Sister Joseph Mary. The women artists, who probably included Mary Afaisa, Rose Apau, and Marie Taita Aihi, created work based on the women's tattoos of the Papuan Gulf area. There appears to have been an Australian government plan to produce silkscreen prints based on their works, which never went ahead; Marie Taita Aihi did work individually with Georgina in Port Moresby on textiles and a few prints, but women would otherwise be marginal to the Papua New Guinean modern art of the 1960s and 1970s.

Georgina's observations are terse, direct, and categorical. She was clear that the colonial impact had changed culture irreversibly; therefore, traditional tribal arts were sustained only in "debased" forms. Ulli also wrote dismissively of tourist art. Neither would have had much time for the case that Nelson

Graburn made in the mid-1970s for a sympathetic reassessment of tourist and souvenir arts. Georgina was still more censorious when it came to the conventional art teaching offered through the education system. The Melanesian artists she celebrated were essentially self-taught and were distinguished by their personal and original vision of colonial modernity. For Beier, Tiabe's recognition, tempered by humor, of the "machine torture" constitutive of the white man's world is both apt and lucid.

Few among the first cohort of modern Melanesian artists articulated their vision and motivations other than through their art or wrote in English. Akis, for example, was either not given opportunities to describe his work and his practice or was reluctant to do so. Hence it is enormously important that Georgina Beier did record a set of Kauage's "stories," edited from conversations over 1979–80 in Tok Pisin. Mathias Kauage (c. 1944–2003), a Chimbu man from the Papua New Guinea Highlands was the most prominent of the first generation of modern artists from the country.[3] Inspired by the work of his contemporary Akis, he formed a close relationship with the Beiers and went on to paint and produce beaten metal panels as well as many prints during periods with the Beiers in Sydney and Bayreuth in the 1980s and 1990s. His work was acquired from the 1970s onward by institutions such as the Australian Museum and the Ethnologisches Museum, Berlin, keen to update ethnographic collections with contemporary work; he famously met Queen Elizabeth II at the time she opened the Museum of Modern Art, Glasgow, and she subsequently featured in a number of his paintings. The "stories" are fascinating for their revelation of Kauage's sense of self and tradition, his aesthetics, and his attitude toward the work of the artist (figure AE2.2).

Note on the Texts

"Contemporary Art from New Guinea at the Aladdin Gallery" was a roneoed document produced by the gallery for exhibition patrons. This copy was among archive materials donated to the Museum of Archaeology and Anthropology, Cambridge, by Professor Marilyn Strathern. The complete leaflet is published here.

Kauage's Stories was produced in an edition limited to twenty-five copies by Migila House (i.e., the Annandale residence of Ulli and Georgina Beier, Sydney). Eight of twenty-three sections are reproduced here.

Typographic errors have been corrected. [GB] at the end of some notes below indicates that the note is Georgina Beier's.

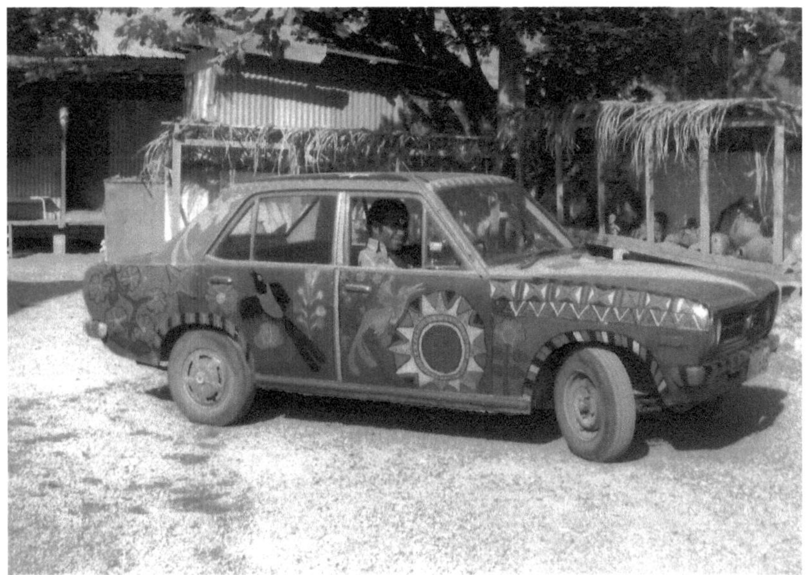

FIGURE AE2.2 Mathias Kauage in his hand-painted car at Village Arts, an artefact outlet sponsored by the National Cultural Council, at Six Mile, Port Moresby, in 1977. Photo by, and courtesy of, Mary-Clare Adam.

THE DOCUMENTS

Document 1: Contemporary Art from New Guinea at the Aladdin Gallery, Sydney, September 1969

NOTES BY GEORGINA BEIER

Kauwagi

Kauwagi's first drawings were brought to me by a Highland friend. They were pitiful attempts to create realism. Some were obviously copied from some schoolbook. In spite of this unpromising beginning, I asked to see more. A pile of equally pathetic drawings was produced a week later, but here and there a creature of his own imagination appeared in a corner of a sheet, drawn in minute scale, as if to hide his first real initiative. Kauwagi is a huge man, a giant among his people. His size embarrasses him and his attempts to diminish it make him awkward and clumsy. It seemed that he would never have the confidence to reveal his own personal imagery. It was only when he had really convinced himself that I was not interested in his derivative work that he suddenly began to draw on his own rich store of imagination.

The first series of drawings that one can truly call his own were insects, which he claimed to be accurate representations of insects in the New Guinea Highlands. He was at that stage still too inhibited and shy to admit that they were his own creations.

He worked on a series of horses and riders, which reminded one of circus bareback riders where horses are gaily decorated. They were inspired by horses he had seen at the mission station in Kundiawa. But soon his imagination utterly transfigured the memory: riders were floating in the air above the horses; horses' bodies were built up of an intricate pattern of faces.

Kauwagi then started on his romantic period. Boys flirting with girls. All the figures were naked of clothes and naked of sex. In spite of the desexed figures, there was no difficulty in determining girl or boy. When he later drew breasts on the girls, he simultaneously gave them shorts or panties or just a band of pattern. The boys and girls never touch. The eternal theme was "Me laik holdim hand bilong meri—meri no laik."[4] The figures had a liquid, floating quality. Kauwagi, the giant, wanted to fly, as all the boys and girls were flying. But boy never succeeded in winning girl.

The courting sequence over, Kauwagi began to draw lonely but more mature figures of men and women accompanied by animal fantasies. Women with fish. Men fighting dragon-like creatures. Men riding birds. Women carrying stars on their heads. Birds making nests.

His women began to wear their band of pattern with an empty patch in the vital area. Immediately after this came a series of magnificent mothers. Big, powerful, all mother women, like goddesses. They still have grace, but it is a majestic grace. The mothers are not floating or flying: they are statuesque protectors.

A book of Kauwagi's drawings is being published by the Centre for New Culture at the University of Papua and New Guinea and will be available toward the end of the year.[5]

Five Artists from Laloki Hospital

This small collection of prints was made by "primitive" tribesmen from remote mountain areas of New Guinea. Two of them have had less contact with the Western world than most people in this country. Yet surprisingly, their work does not appear particularly exotic and some of it astonishes by its modern twentieth-century vision.

Sukoro and Hope are artists who draw on memories of their tradition. When they were young the great artistic traditions of the Papuan gulf and the Sepik River were still alive. But they grew up to witness the sudden capitulation of their culture. Hope's work is related to *Hohao* and *Hevehe* designs of Arehava, in the Papuan gulf. He can remember the ancient motives but also creates new ones and produces endless varieties of design. His work is infinitely more varied than the tradition that inspired it. Hohao and Hevehe designs were never intentionally varied but were faithfully reproduced generation after generation. Hape is free from such rigid discipline and free to invent. Sukoro's work is barely reminiscent of his Sepik origin. His use of pattern and a sense of formalism are perhaps the only indications of his cultural background.

Kupialdo is an artist whose intense love of color and whose simplicity of design may be inspired by the art of face painting in his native Mendi. Mathias is primarily a graphic artist. His work has a great deal of charm, particularly in his *Angel and the Tortoise*. In *Masks* he shows a great appreciation of the fluidity of line. In *Black Fish* this illiterate artist sees lettering as pattern. He designs a background of letters and it works without seeming contrived.

Tiabe is the most remarkable of those five artists. He comes from an inaccessible area of the Southern Highlands. There are no roads near his village. He has no intimate experience of the white man's world. But the little he has observed has an intense effect on his imagination. He has seen cars and ambulances at the hospital in Port Moresby where he is recuperating from a long illness. He has seen planes pass over his village. He is fascinated by the white man's machine world. He is far from romantic about it nor is he confused by it. He views it as a cruel and violent world. His pictures are almost a vision of machine torture, but his sophisticated humor gives them a lightness and vivacity that contrasts with the sinister subject matter. Tiabe's use of color is direct, economical, and pure. He knows no hesitation or uncertainty; he has very firm ideas about what the new world is like. Tiabe is an uncanny and brilliant observer whose work is refreshingly modern.

None of these prints would have been made if not for the fact that the five artists were reconvalescents in Laloki Hospital outside Port Moresby. There they were given materials and encouraged to paint, but they were not "taught" or influenced in any way. Being hospital patients they had none of the responsibilities of everyday living. They had time on their hands. Back at home they could find no motivation for making pictures. There, artistic expression is only meaningful in a religious context.

Circumstances have so far prevented the development of contemporary art in a country that has produced some of the greatest tribal art forms in the world. On the one hand some of the traditional talent has been channeled into a debased form of tourist art. On the other hand the younger generation has been subjected to some of the worst conceivable art teaching in the primary schools of this country. This has produced a new, sickly convention of feeble palm tree, sunset, and village-scene art that is eagerly sponsored and even bought by the suburban white colonials in New Guinea. It is no exaggeration to say that these five patients, thrown together by tragic circumstance in a Moresby Hospital, have produced the first contemporary pictures in New Guinea.

Paintings from Yule Island

Sister Joseph Mary, a nurse and midwife at Yule Island Mission, started to do some art teaching merely because there was no one else at the time to do it.[6] She has no background in art — not even an amateur knowledge. Nevertheless she has had both the sensitivity and the modesty to make a success of it.

She encouraged her students to look at their own culture for inspiration. The girls must have viewed their traditional sculpture with unritualistic eyes, knowing little of its symbolism and cultural significance. They saw pattern and imagery, which they transformed into personal expression. They abandoned the conventional earth colors making full use of the most brilliant colors available. The traditional image, which played an important part in initial inspiration, becomes completely transposed.

Sister Joseph Mary makes no attempt to obtain from her students copies of traditional carvings — sad mistake made by many art teachers in the territory. Instead she uses traditional motives to stimulate fresh ideas in the student rather than impose on them the images of Western art, which must surely be alien to a student who is not sophisticated enough to appreciate purely in abstract terms.

The most important quality in a teacher of creative arts is the ability to recognize freshness and originality — to encourage and help develop a new idea without imposing the teacher's own personality. However brilliant a teacher may be in his own work, if his students mirror his imagery, he is a bad and conceited teacher. Therefore, it is possible, but rare, that a person who knows little of the art world can have the right approach, relying solely on instinct and sensitivity and the *students' own ideas*.

What Sister Joseph Mary is achieving at Yule Island is of particular significance in Papua and New Guinea, where the teaching of art is particularly bad, if not offensive.

Document 2: From Kauage's Stories

FROM CONVERSATIONS WITH GEORGINA BEIER, DECEMBER 1979 TO JANUARY 1980

Growing Up

When Sebastian [Beier] was four years or five years old, he was running to my house. He watched me work.

When we were four years old, we watch our papa breaking firewood, big branches. Okay, we take small axe or knife, we know how to cut the small branches. Now papa get up and talks "All of you, look out for your hands and legs. The knife is sharp!"

We watch our papas, we are behind them. They sharpen their axes. We take our half axes and sit down nearby to sharpen them. We try it. It's like school. Papa does the big work, we do the little work.

Sometimes our papa goes walkabout to a faraway place. Then we are behind our mamas. Mama digs out some sweet potatoes, we get some banana leaves and carry them to the house. We make a little fire. Mama is making mumu.[7] Alright, we help with the stones. She throws them into the fire to get hot. We bring water to make the steam. The mumu is cooking. Then we eat.

When we are eight or nine years old, we try to build a house. All of us boys make a house-man for ourselves. We know how to cut the wood. We get the pitpit,[8] we weave the mats. We know how to make mats. Our people have taught us. We go to the bush, we cut the bamboo. We weave our mats, our beds. This is a man's work. It belongs to us.

We are five or six boys, no girls. Girls stay with their mamas.

Some of us sleep. I make a fire in the middle. Some of us eat. Some put the food in a bamboo basket. That's where it stays. If we are hungry at night, we stir up the fire and eat. If we are not hungry, we sleep until morning time. Then we eat.

When we are small, we go to the bush to eat tree seeds. We've got them—like peanuts. But peanuts are small, ours are big. There are all kinds of tree seeds. We find birds. We find mushrooms: some are blue, some yellow, some white. Black ones we don't eat. We throw them out. Only some black ones we can eat. Some are like a big plate, some round, some are very small.

We kill the birds and carry them to our house. Man! We cook them. Some of them we share with our sisters and mamas.

When mama and papa have no work, when they are not working in the garden, when they are not making fences, that's the time we go around in the bush. When they are working, we help them.

That was before, not now. Now we buy rice, tin fish, saucepan, plate: all kinds of things we buy from the white masters. We have lost the wooden mumu drum: very few of us still have it. The mumu cooked in the ground, yes we still have it. The wooden mumu, it's gone. Now they cut up a big petrol drum to make mumu. But I don't like it. It's not good.

Before we had no saucepans. Cold water was our tea. Now we have all kinds of things belonging to the whites. We have lost the things belonging to our ancestors. It's finished. Very few old men still have it. I would like to hold on to the ways of the ancestors, but I don't know them. They knew a lot! I only know how to make pictures, that's all. I would like to make something that belonged to them, something true. But I don't know it. When I was six or seven years old, I watched the men working. Now I am big, and it's a long time since I saw them working for the ancestors. Some of them are working these things—but it's only for money, that's all. It's like this: the masters want to buy, they ask for something belonging to the ancestors. "Ah, I have it!" they say. Then they work it and sell it quickly. They don't live with it any more.

The Patrol Officer and the Shoot

Now when we had finished looking at the plane, we went back to my uncle's house—my mothers' brothers place.[9] I said to him "Look Uncle, you gave me money. I bought trousers for myself, a shirt, and soap for me to wash." He talked to me. "Okay, it's alright, you look well dressed. Now with marbles, you play and play for another boy to take them, and you lose the money for nothing. It's alright, you keep your trousers and shirt and soap. Now you want to go to your place, or do you want to stay here?" I sweet-talk him. "Ahhh, Mama up in the mountain gave me a little money, but I feel lazy. I can stay with you." I stayed one moon or something.

At this time the government patrol officers were walking about, saying they wanted to get our names. I was small I didn't understand about names and books.

When I was bigger, we went to line up. First time and second time nothing happened. The third time we lined up at this officer's house in our place he stood up and said to us "It's no good, if later you get a big sickness and die. Okay! I'm going to give you something, so you don't get sick later."

Now all the small ones lined up, but I was a big-head boy. I ran away from the line-up and tried to hide. A policeman grabbed hold of me and slapped my face. I crouched on the ground and pretended to cry. When he took hold of my hand, I bit him through his sock and into the meat of his leg. 'Uuuuuuuuuuuuuuuuuuuuuggggggggghhhhhh," That's the noise he made. My people and the Luluai pleaded for me.[10] They said, "This child, we don't like him, he's too much of a big-head, but let him go and later he can get his shoot."

When my people had finished talking, I thought that everybody wanted to fight me. I went and sat down behind the officer. I looked at all of them. I thought. It's no good if they fight me just because I bit the leg of a police officer. I went on looking. So they are not going to fight me. Then the time came to give all of this shoot. The officer says "Hey, bighead boy." That's how he talked. I didn't talk back to him. I pulled a face. I am thinking "Okay, now I am afraid of this shoot, but I am strong enough now." Then the officer said "Later we'll take you to court for biting a policeman."

I ran away forever to my own place. I went the water way, not the bridge way. We have a big water. It's our Chimbu water. I swam underneath, until I came home to my little place.

School Days

People ask me "Did you go to school?" I went to school in my place. Not much of it. Maybe six months, that's all. When I went to school, we were writing numbers, tens and times.

Now I was strong on a little school mate. She was my little girlfriend. Okay, now this young girl, not *too* young, didn't know how to write. She said "Kauage, you write for me." I wrote some tens and times for her, I wrote her name. Now one by one we go to the teacher. I want to give my paper to the teacher, but he didn't call out for me and I was in the middle of the line. Then he said "You come." He called out for me and the girl to come together. Okay, now I gave him my writing. He finished looking at it. Then the girl gave him hers. "So on the first day of school you know how to write? Kauage, you wrote this and gave it to this friend of yours. You two sit down."

Okay, we sat down. We sat down a long time. All the others finished writing. They all go to play outside at sweeping and cutting grass. We stayed inside this school house. We stayed on and on. Four o'clock finished. All the children came back inside.

"Alright, later you look at more of this." He took hold of a very big bible — a big book. He fight my head! My head was truly broken. I feel my head is broken, and he fights me again with this big book. My ear is in pain. One kind of insect knows how to cry and cry in the night. My ear cried out in the same way. I want to really fight this man. I stood up straight and talk to him "I've had enough of school. Now you can't come and get me from my village. If you come and get me, I will give you my spear. You can't come for me and take me from my house. It's forbidden. I don't like school."

I say to everybody "Okay, I finished." I talked to the girl "You finish too! Never mind about more school in this place. They fight too much. It's no good!"

I never went back again.

Marriage

Susanna became a woman.

I came to sit down with her, but she didn't become my friend. She talked to me crossly. "Ehh, you sit down with me here for a long time—two or three hours. You hurry up now and go outside."

This was the time for all the boys to make friends with a girl and sit down together. I sat down with another girl and Susanna got up and cried out "Ehh, two hours you have been with that girl friend of yours. Leave her and go away!" That's what she said.

Now I got up and said to her "Ugh, I'm not your friend. I don't belong to you. You threw me out! I'm staying with this girl."

I was cross with her. Very cross.

In 1968 I came down to Port Moresby. In 1969 I work with you [Georgina]. In 1970 I go on leave to the mountains. Susanna was in Banz.[11] I went to talk to her. She was now a big woman. She pulled a face at me. I am thinking—is she still cross with me?

More than a week went by. On a Friday she called out to me "Hey, you come to my place for the carry leg ceremony and bring some others with you, when you come!"

I went with three brothers to this house to find three girls. We were all thinking about sitting down to carry leg and sing. We went inside. Ah! There were lots of young men there, fifteen something, all singing. We joined them. Some boys sang out to me "Hey, you come and stay with this girl here!" Now I thought it would be another girl, but no, it was Susanna. Everybody said "You go and sit with her!" But I said "I'm tired of her, I don't like to." But I did. I said to her "You're a bigheaded girl."

"Ahh! When was I bigheaded? When I was little, you were a bighead boy. That time, when I was staying at your sister's home on the mountain."

I said "Yes it's true."

"Then you went to Moresby and now you come back. Okay."

Now I had married Maria before, but she became troublesome. So I sent her away. She stayed with me for one year. When I was in Moresby, I heard the stories. She was the friend of plenty of men. So I told my mama to send her away. She got up at six in the morning to work in the garden and came back at six o'clock at night. Then a boy came to steal her. He carried her away and married her.

I was away for two years, that's why she ran away looking for another man.

Bilas

This bird, we call it Kurark. Its feathers are yellow, blue, green and red. Okay, another bird is black. A big, black cockatoo. He is black and red. He has no yellow. He has the same name as me — Kauage.

Now when we want to shoot this Kauage, we go to the big bush, when plenty of flowers have come up on the trees. These cockatoos fly to that place to eat the flowers; then they fly off to another place. They fly between the mountains.

Sometimes we steal them with a stick. Some of them die straight away. Some of them have a broken leg or hand or wing, we take them. Sometimes we stalk them with a long spear of Jingi wood.

When they die we take a razor — before we used a bamboo knife — then we cut him with a razor and take out his bones. The bone stays in the wings, but we take out all the flesh. We collect leaves from the bush and stuff them inside. We have a bamboo stick and thread it through. This bamboo we sharpen like a spear. Then we line up his colour, his wings, on the ground. They dry in the sun. In the evening we pass them over the fire. We put them in the sun and over the fire every day, for two, three, weeks, something. It's no good if it stinks.

Okay, then we pack them in a suitcase. First, we make a mat from a leaf, we call it Karoka. We take it and work it into a mat. When it is finished, we gather all our decorations: arm bands, bilums, feathers, cuscus-laplaps — all our finery — and we pack it inside, mixed up with the good leaf of a tree. We roll up the mat and fasten it with bamboo rope. This is the same as a suitcase.

When the white fellows came, we changed our ways. We hang it up in the house over the fire and there it stays, getting black. Insects like to eat the feathers, but when the big heat comes up, they go away. They can't go inside, they go away. "Ahh, I can't go near the fire, it's not good to die!" That's what they think. And they run away, outside.

When you see that black, dirty mat in the house, you will think "Ah, what kind of something stays inside?" Now, when the time for dressing and decorating comes up, we open it and you will see many different kinds of birds.

In Moresby I don't dress up. Just a little bit, at Christmas time. When we dance and sing.

We don't sing every day, we stay in shirt and trousers. But when the time comes to decorate, all the men change, they belong to the spirit time. We look at them, are his decorations no good, or is he a winner? That's what we are thinking.

Here too, in Sydney, I decorate and I change. But most of the time I am nothing. At home it's the same, now.

But the girls like a well decorated man, whose head carries plenty of feathers.

The Marks of Our Ancestors

When I was five or six years old I didn't know our ancient marks very well. I watched them working bilums, arm bands, the skins of trees, spears, bows and arrows, combs — they put our marks on everything: they marked the strong bamboo too, with our ancient designs. I watched them.

But when I was seven years old, I saw them destroy everything. The Catholic Father talked to them "All of you, burn these things belonging to your ancestors — it is the way of Satan. They will stop you growing into something good." Everything with our marks was burned, cooked, or thrown into the river. But some of them, did the father take them? What did he do with them? I'm not sure. The church is Satan. It is a liar.

All this happened when I was seven, not very big, but I was working hard at looking. Later, when I was grown up, I looked around but there was nothing. No bilums made with cuscus fur, no: only the simple bilum for carrying food, that we still had. Everybody is lazy now about making bows and arrows. But we haven't lost the bamboo flute.

When we kill a pig we play the flutes and we still know how to make new ones. We play the flute and plenty of men will hear it. They will say "Oh, that line is working for their Christmas." That's what they think. And other lines too will be working for their Christmas feast, and killing pigs and playing the flutes.

This cloth you have from our place, the one they weave from orchid stems, we don't make it anymore. In Chuave they still make it, but they don't use it anymore. They sell it for money to white people.

Before, the mamas and papas taught their children — but no more. It is finished. Now, when they dress up, they mix bird feathers with cloth and other things belonging to white people.

Later, our children will lose everything. They cannot hold on to it. They will say "Ah, that is rubbish."

I like the old ways, but I do not hold on to them. I stay in Moresby. I go home to Kundiawa, I come back to Moresby.[12] I can't work in my place. They talk too much. If I want to work, someone comes to talk. Then another one comes, and another one again. When I am a long way off in Moresby, then it's alright. I can work.

Art and Artists

I went to Adelaide. I looked at paintings in museums, in galleries. I went around looking. I look at this one, then another one: on this picture there is a man walking about, there's bits of grass here and there, that's all. They don't make many lines. They take the brush and throw on the paint, they don't make any designs. They get a lot of money, some are $6,000, some are $8,000 or something. I look at one of them — a boat with sails. They don't work at the space, their work is like a fraud: in the middle there was lots of space and nothing on it, it's not filled up.

They don't put on any writing, there's not much story, just a little bit. Two or three words, that's all. I don't understand that. An artist who can't think of a story, it's like stealing money.

Some of them work something good, but many of them are false, truly false.

In New Guinea my boy Chris also wants to be an artist.[13] I've talked to him many times. He makes pictures, but he follows the fashion of the whites, he makes his pictures look real. I say "Alright, but put some of the marks that belong to you and me. Don't make them look like nothing."

Chris was born in our place in Chimbu. When he was four, I bought him down to Moresby. I had left him with his mama, but then she went off and left him. I was sorry, so I carried him away to be with me.

I put him to school, when he reached Grade Five, they threw him out. I said. Okay, I'll teach him to be an artist. For five years I taught him. When he was nineteen, I sent him to the art school.

Sometimes he makes a drawing and puts down the marks that belong to us. Sometimes he makes something real, that's all. Later he decorates it with our marks.

This year he graduates. He wants to be an artist now. He can't be the same as me. Our marks belong to the past, to our papas and their papas.

Then it was good. Everybody knew and understood our marks. They knew the fashion of our ancestors.

My Life

My life is work. It's the same as thinking.

Sometimes I have a good time. I have my own time. I sit down and work. Sometimes plenty men come to my house and I can't work.

Sometimes I am lazy about work. Tired of working. Okay, I go round for two weeks or three weeks being lazy. Then I work again.

Sometimes I am sitting down doing nothing, then plenty masta, missus come. They say "We want to give you a contract. Can you make a picture? How many days?" That's what they ask, and I say "I don't know if four or five days is enough. Maybe two weeks or something, before I finish it altogether. When I finish it, I will bring it to you people." They say to me "How much? How much?" Then I say to all of them "You people pay me. If you don't give me paper money, I won't work. You won't get nothing." Then I am holding their money, I have it, and I am working.

I work for three, four days and I take it to their house. Sometimes I just make pictures. I carry them around, the people look, they buy them.

Sometimes I open the radio. I hear them talking. Ah, some white travellers have come from Australia. Some have come by plane, Air Niugini or Qantas. Some have come by ship. They stay at the Travelodge or Islander Hotel. Okay, I carry my pictures and go. They buy them quickly from me. Sometimes they buy all, sometimes they don't buy many.

Sometimes I ring the government office. I say to them "Oh, I want to bring some paintings and drawings to you. "Okay, what time will you come?" I say "Ah, I will come at ten o'clock or eleven o'clock, something." They say "We drink tea at ten o'clock. Eleven o'clock is okay. Twelve o'clock we go for lunch.

I take my pictures and they are waiting for me. Plenty of masta, missus are waiting to see my pictures. That's how they are. They look and they buy. Some Papua New Guinea girls too, but they are married to whites. Unmarried girls, they don't buy, but they would like to. Some black men, who have plenty of money, they buy my pictures. But they are not too many. The white people, yes, they buy plenty.

Now one masta he asks me, he asks, "Who is your masta?" I say ["]There is no masta. I am me. I am the masta. I work. My life belongs to me and I stay in my own house."

Notes

1. See Okeke-Agulu's chapter, this volume.

2. Beier, *Thirty Years of Osogbo Art.*

3. For discussion of his practice, see Thomas, "'Artist of PNG.'" Other works relevant to understanding Melanesian modernism include Beier, *Decolonising the Mind*; Eastburn, *Papua New Guinea Prints*; and McDougall, *No. 1 Neighbour.*

4. Tok Pisin: "I want to hold the girl's hand; she doesn't like it."

5. No book was published at this time, though Kauage's drawings did appear in *Kovave* and otherwise.

6. For an excellent discussion of these women and Sister Joseph Mary's role, see Conroy, "Textiles from the Sea of Islands."

7. Mumu is a steam oven. A hole is dug in the ground and lined with banana leaves. Hot stones are placed inside with food and a little water. It is covered with banana leaves and earth and allowed to steam. In Chimbu country they introduced an alternative method: they made mumu in a wooden drum. [GB]

8. Pitpit: a type of wild sugar cane (saccharum spontaneum) with edible fruit, resembling an unripe ear of maize. Its stems are used for fences and walls. [GB]

9. Shoot: a pidgin word for "injection." [GB]

10. Luluai: a village head, appointed by the Colonial Government. The office of Luluai was abolished with the advent of elected local government councils. [GB]

11. A settlement about fifty kilometers west of the Highlands center of Goroka.

12. A market town with an airstrip about thirty kilometers west of Goroka.

13. "My boy" refers here not to the artist's son but to an unrelated Chimbu man whom Kauage mentored. However, other members of Kauage's family, including Elizabeth, Andrew, and John Kauage became artists, producing work very much in Mathias's style.

Bibliography

Beier, Ulli. *Decolonising the Mind: The Impact of the University on Culture and Identity in Papua New Guinea, 1971–1974*. Canberra: Pandanus, 2005.

Beier, Ulli. *Thirty Years of Osogbo Art*. Bayreuth: Iwalewa, 2001.

Conroy, Diana Wood. "Textiles from the Sea of Islands: Sacred Heart Nuns and Craft Advisers in Papua New Guinea and Australia." In *Postcolonial Past and Present:*

Negotiating Literary and Cultural Geographies, edited by Anne Collett and Leigh Dale, 3–29. Leiden: Brill/Rodopi, 2019.

Eastburn, Melanie. *Papua New Guinea Prints*. Canberra: National Gallery of Australia, 2006.

McDougall, Ruth. *No. 1 Neighbour: Art in Papua New Guinea 1966–2016*. Brisbane: Queensland Art Gallery / Gallery of Modern Art, 2016. Exhibition catalog.

Thomas, Nicholas. "'Artist of PNG': Mathias Kauage and Melanesian Modernism." In *Mapping Modernisms: Art, Indigeneity, Colonialism*, edited by Elizabeth Harney and Ruth B. Phillips, 163–86. Durham, NC: Duke University Press, 2018.

PART II

FRIENDS/COLLABORATORS

Mid-twentieth-century mediators and artists were often brought together by highly disruptive historical forces over which they had little control—war, forced exile, the assimilationist programs of colonial institutions. In this context it is all the more noteworthy that many artist-mediator relationships that blossomed in often harrowing circumstances were not only deeply affective but provided a mutual sense of satisfaction and opportunities for two-way collaborations, reflective self-explorations, and self-inventions across cultural, ethnic, and political lines. These types of relationships, though deeply entangled in colonial and postcolonial politics, could transcend the prescriptive roles and boundaries inherent to more transactional or instrumental forms of colonial subjectivity. Moreover, these deep relationships often operated under their own logics and took on lives of their own: in some cases, they could burn intensely for brief periods before the winds of change separated the artist and mediator while in other cases they could smolder for many decades and provide intellectual nourishment for both participants over their lifetimes.

In entitling the section that offers instances of these types of relationships "Friends/Collaborators," we are aware that we have chosen terms that are at once unassumingly benign but also laden with possibilities and complexities that defy easy categorization. The two terms offer differently inflected ways to denote the character of voluntary relationships that were cocreated and sustained within the matrix of colonial modernism while also implicating broader discourses concerning human needs, politics, aesthetics, and ethics. The case studies in this section support the premise that mutually transformative friendships and collaborative relationships between artists and intermediaries must be an important dimension of our historical reckoning with the patterns of mediatory interactions, even though acknowledging the complexity of these relationships can upend received assumptions about power and authority in colonial modernisms. Here we push back against what we see as the moral complacency in historically revisionist accounts of colonial modernity in which Indigenous artists are too often seen as unwitting victims of the appropriative machinations of exploitative intermediaries. The friendships and collaborative relationships described in this section reveal the agency not only of the mediators but also, critically, of the artists.

The reasons why artists and mediators came together may be explained by a myriad of external social facts; why they *stayed* together may have owed more to personal facets of their personalities. As Sandra Klopper's essay shows, artist Alson Zuma and his artistic mentor (and employer) David Fox occupied very different societal rungs in South African life, and yet the lifelong friendship they developed was able to thrive in large part because they shared a particular sense of humor and appreciation for the absurd. Other chapters in this section explore the myriad ways artists, through the force of their personalities, were able to share their curiosity about aesthetic modernism and were willing to step outside proscribed social expectations in order to cultivate friendships that opened professional and social doors during a period when those doors would not normally have been open to them.

We are aware that the term *friendship* carries much baggage in the Western philosophical tradition, and we are also acutely conscious of the problematic nature of assuming *friendship*, in a Western sense, to be a universal category. Although anthropological interest in friendship was curiously muted through much of the twentieth century, particularly in contrast to sociological and philosophical inquiries, cross-cultural friendship has attracted greater interest from anthropologists in recent decades.[1] Our use of the word explicitly calls to mind key discussions in the anthropology of friendship concerning the moral needs of humans, local ideas of personhood and kinship, reciprocity, and the social power of relationships outside clan or community. Although the essays in this section do not take for granted that clear conceptual or lexical equivalents of friendship exist across cultures, they do demonstrate that distinctive, apparently voluntary relationships involving mutual trust, open-endedness, and empathy, among other shared attributes, emerged and were differently negotiated within a multiplicity of cultural scripts.

The fact that the bulk of the examples in this section — and indeed the entire volume — involve male artists and male intermediaries also suggests that intercultural friendships that cross-gender boundaries have been rare and bring particular challenges. This lends credence to the anthropologist James Carrier's observation that "the modern notion of friendship, with its stress on involuntary sentiment unclouded by calculation or interest, is particularly congenial to those in certain socio-economic situations."[2] Hanna Horsberg Hansen's chapter in this section, which examines the friendship between the Sámi storyteller Johan Turi and the Danish artist and ethnologist Emilie Demant Hatt, may be the exception that proves the rule. Hansen's nuanced accounting of the societal expectations and boundaries that Turi and Hatt faced in early twentieth-century Scandinavia suggests the relational and situational nature of privilege and power, since both "occupied positions of relative disempowerment within their larger social worlds — Hatt as a woman in a patriarchal society and Turi as a Sámi in a racialized one." As complex as they may be, it is important to keep the social realities of gender, kin, clan, and ethnicity in mind as we think through the ways in which the discourses of artistic modernism, with their implicit views of individualism, selfhood, and attitude toward "tradition," served as a catalyst to bring diverse constellations of peoples together under the guise of friendship.

Friendship, of course, is also a dimension of collegial and collaborative relationships. As suggested above, artists and mediators were often drawn together because of their shared interest in modernism whose humanistic themes and rhetoric of aesthetic universalism, emphasis upon the individual, and cosmopolitanism clearly appealed to both Indigenous and non-Indigenous parties to the relationship, though often for different reasons. Artists and mediators shared books, magazines, ideas, and gossip; they allowed each other a limited passage into and through their respective worlds; and they nurtured and encouraged each other's dreams and aspirations, as friends often do.

It is also important to stress that modernism was disseminated and negotiated as much or more *among* Indigenous artists as between the Indigenous artist and the outsider mediator. In the latter case, however — and even during the waning days of colonial regimes and the neocolonial aftermath — the dimension of friendship provided social and personal connections that often clashed with expectations of class, race, gender, and nationality. For mediators, friendships could shatter the lens of primitivism that had initially led them to appreciate the possibilities of Indigenous and non-Western art, overturning socially ingrained ideas of race and culture. As such, friendships could precipitate a reciprocal shift in the perception of the "other," particularly as these relationships evolved over time.

In light of the social pressures and expectations that circumscribe friendships, it is understandable that the intimacy and intensity of the relationships described in this volume vary dramatically from one case to the other. Moreover, given the paucity of historical records and, more generally, the difficulty inherent in documenting the private lives of artists, efforts to discern the degree of intimacy and other important details concerning artists' relationships to mediators can often lead to frustrating dead ends. For these and other reasons, Peter Brunt's chapter, which looks at the relationship between the Pākehā New Zealand painter Tony Fomison and the Sāmoan tattooist Sulu'ape Paulo II, offers an especially fascinating test case. Their friendship was clearly mutually transformative, resulting in Fomison becoming one of first non-Sāmoans to be tattooed with a full pe'a outside Samoa and providing Paulo with a "watershed client" who anticipated the globalized, boundary-crossing character of his future tattoo practice. What adds to the remarkable and revealing nature of this case is the self-conscious reflexivity with which Pākehā photographer Mark Adams—a close friend of Fomison—captured intimate details of their relationship on film. The act of witnessing these friendships in Adams's photographs evokes what Jacques Derrida described in *The Politics of Friendship* as the mutual recognition of the self in the other and the concomitant recognition of the separation of the self and the other, both of which exists in tension in close friendships. Just as Derrida recognized "the question of friendship *as the* question of the political," we, too, recognize friendships as having the power to create conditions for a new politics. As such, relationships between artists and mediators in Indigenous and colonial contexts had not only aesthetic but also a profoundly political potency.[3]

Notes

1. See especially Bell and Coleman, *The Anthropology of Friendship*; and Desai and Killick, *The Ways of Friendship*.
2. Carrier, "People Who Can Be Friends," 35–36.
3. Derrida, *The Politics of Friendship*, 27.

Bibliography

Bell, Sandra, and Simon Coleman, eds. *The Anthropology of Friendship*. Oxford: Berg, 1999.

Carrier, James G. "People Who Can Be Friends: Selves and Social Relationships." In *The Anthropology of Friendship*, edited by Sandra Bell and Simon Coleman, 21–38. Oxford: Berg, 1999.

Desai, Amit, and Evan Killick, eds. *The Ways of Friendship: Anthropological Perspectives*. Oxford: Berghahn, 2010.

Derrida, Jacques. *The Politics of Friendship*. New York: Verso, 2006.

HANNA HORSBERG HANSEN

5 MODERN FRIENDSHIP AND COLLABORATION IN SÁPMI AND DENMARK

Johan Turi and Emilie Demant Hatt

Johan Turi (1854–1936) and Emilie Demant (1873–1958) met in northern Sweden in 1904 on an iron-ore train traveling between the Swedish–Norwegian border and Lake Torneträsk.[1] If this was a novel, the ore train could have been invented as a chronotope of northern Swedish modernity, yet they did actually meet in this way. The railway between Kiruna in inland northern Sweden and the coastal town of Narvik in northern Norway functioned as a key part of the infrastructure for the mining company in Kiruna, enabling it to extract and export iron ore found in the area. The opening of the railway in 1903 had paved the way for new modes of economic exploitation in this part of Sápmi, the traditional territories of the Sámi, the Indigenous people of northern Scandinavia and Russia.

Turi, a native of the region, was a Sámi reindeer herder, hunter, and storyteller who dreamed of writing a book that would tell others about his people's way of life and worldview. Emilie Demant Hatt was a middle-class Danish traveler and trained artist in search of an opportunity to spend a year living with Sámi nomads. Despite their different backgrounds, both Turi and Hatt occupied positions of relative disempowerment within their larger social worlds—Hatt as a woman in a patriarchal society and Turi as a Sámi in a racialized one. From these different positions, they forged a friendship and a collaboration that crossed conventional social boundaries. Their relationship, as I will argue, exemplifies philosopher Marshall Berman's theorization of modern environments and experiences as cutting across not only social, geographic, and ethnic boundaries but also those of class and nationality.[2] In this chapter I explore the complementary needs that brought Turi and Hatt together — his to be able to tell the world about his people and hers to be accepted within the Sámi community. Their collaboration led to the publication, in 1910, of the landmark book *Muitalus Samid birra = En bog om Lappernes liv* (An account of the Sámi). The book is bilingual with Sámi text by Turi, followed by Demant Hatt's translation into Danish.[3] In contrast to the inequalities of power that informed early twentieth-century relationships between teachers, mentors, and researchers and their Indigenous students and informants, the relationship between Hatt and Turi was characterized by more evenly balanced exchanges. Their dependence on each other led to the development of mutual understanding and a lifelong friendship that were exceptional in their time.

Anthropologist Kristin Kuutma argues that Hatt's modest standing within her own society allowed her to establish a relationship of equality between herself and Turi on several levels and, most importantly, to create an ethnography using a collaborative method that was well ahead of its time. In the context of the patriarchal and gendered world of the turn of the last century, Hatt was boldly independent.[4] Danish women did not even have the right to vote until 1915, yet she was able to break away from the constraints imposed on women and engage in her solitary travels. However, she was not the only white woman at the time to travel alone to distant places. There are several examples from other parts of the world of middle-class women traveling to distant places where they could challenge and escape established constructions of male and female spheres.[5] As a middle-aged, unmarried Sámi man, Turi also had to overcome constraints and barriers. His mother tongue was the dialect of Sámi spoken in Guovdageaidnu, where he was born; he also spoke Finnish quite well, the lingua franca for people in the Karesuando-Jukkasjärvi area, but neither Swedish nor Norwegian.[6]

According to conventional racist ideology of the time, the Sámi were considered only as objects for anthropological studies. Turi defied that conception by making himself and the Sámi the subject of ethnography.[7] Thus, he was a modern man taking advantage of the new conditions created by modernity for dialogue on the past, the present, and the future, as described by Berman, who defines modernity as any attempt by men and women to become subjects as well as objects for modernization and to take hold of the modern world and make themselves at home in it.[8]

By the middle of the nineteenth century, itinerant reindeer herders often practiced "homeschooling" for their children, at least for acquiring basic reading skills for Bible study. Turi was literate indeed and carried a strong belief in the power of the written word, which inspired his desire to communicate on an equal basis with members of the dominant culture by using their own medium. As Kuutma observes, no ordinary man would have taken up a task so inconsistent with the general expectations of the Sámi at this time.[9]

The encounter between Turi and Hatt had a lifelong impact on each, influencing the course of their artistic work, although in different ways. Through close readings of selected visual artworks, I explore the dynamic triangulation created by the association of the deterritorialized Western artist, the colonized and dispossessed Indigenous artist, and the modernist European ideology of artistic primitivism described by art historian Ruth B. Phillips in North American contexts.[10] The same dynamic pattern, I argue, is recognizable in the collaboration between Turi and Hatt at the beginning of their cooperation, but ultimately the collaboration was energizing in excess of the fixed pattern.

The Double-Edged Sword

A third person must be introduced to explore the collaboration between Turi and Hatt—Hjalmar Lundbohm (1855–1926), the Swedish managing director of the mining company Luossavaara-Kiirunavaara Aktiebolag (LKAB) in Kiruna. He displayed a large collection of art in his house in Kiruna. The paintings were mostly genre scenes and depictions of different Swedish landscapes whose plein air process was influenced by French impressionism.[11]

Lundbohm personified the diverse impacts of modernity in Sápmi during these years, which can be thought of as a double-edged sword aimed at Sámi culture. On one level, his work in mining represented Swedish colonial power at its worst, destroying Sámi habitat to exploit the land for economic profit. On another, his recognition of the need to document Sámi culture represented the modern desire to preserve aspects of a nonmodern society as a reservoir of authenticity within modernity.[12]

Wealthy from royalties on mining claims, Lundbohm supported a variety of artists and writers and was openhanded with his Sámi friends. He was familiar with Turi's wish to recount his people's life and supported Turi's and Demant Hatt's collaboration, both morally and financially. One result of this joint venture was the publication of *Muitalus* as the inaugural work in the series *Lapperna och deras land: Skildringar och studier utgifna av Hjalmar Lundbohm* (The Lapps and their land: Descriptions and studies published by Hjalmar Lundbohm).[13] It was followed by Demant Hatt's 1913 *Med lapperne i højfjeldet* (With the Lapps in the high mountains).[14] Lundbohm also published her second book, *Ved ilden* (By the fire) in 1922.[15]

Lundbohm's patronage had different and contradictory impacts. While his financial and moral support of the *Muitalus* project was critical and positive, the need for a book providing a Sámi perspective on Sámi life and culture had been created by that same economic exploitation and the marginalization and threat of cultural extinction it entailed. In retrospect, as Demant Hatt said in a 1940 speech at the Nordiska museet in Stockholm, the book was a plea from the heart of Lapland for the right to live.[16]

Muitalus — *a Collaboration*

When Turi and Demant first met on the iron-ore train, they had no common language. Hatt returned to Denmark where she studied the Sámi language with Professor Vilhelm Thomsen and followed his lectures at the University of Copenhagen.[17] Turi, meanwhile, arranged with his brother Aslak and his reindeer herding family for her to stay with them and their *siida* when she returned to Sápmi in June 1907.[18] Demant remained with Turi's relatives until April 1908, when she joined the family of Anna and Jounas Rasti and traveled with them during the spring migration from Närva, south of Karesuando, to Tromsø across the Norwegian border.[19] In the fall of 1908 she returned to Kiruna from Tromsø and spent six to eight weeks with Turi in a cabin on Lake Torneträsk. During these weeks, the text, and probably also the illustrations for *Muitalus*, took shape. Demant then brought the text back to Denmark, where she translated and edited it.[20] Published in 1910, this was the first secular book written in the Sámi language by a Sámi.

Turi's text was prefaced by two forewords, one by Lundbohm and the other by Demant, and by an essay concerning language by the cotranslator Vilhelm Thomsen. Demant also contributed explanatory captions for the fourteen illustrations Turi supplied, which were reproduced in a separate publication that took the form of a large-format atlas.

Since its publication, the first edition of *Muitalus* has been translated into many languages and republished in Sámi. A substantial academic discourse has arisen around the book, whose text has been canonized as the beginning of modern vernacular Sámi literature.[21] The important role Demant Hatt played in supporting writing, editing, translating, and publishing it is well documented.[22] Yet, despite the book's status, Turi's illustrations in the atlas and his later visual artworks have received little attention from art historians and other scholars.[23]

We know from the correspondence between Demant Hatt and Lundbohm that the illustrations were part of the plan for the book from the beginning.[24] Neither, however, considered them to be of artistic value. Demant mentions the drawings in her foreword and emphasizes that Turi created them on his own—although she adds that this clarification is unnecessary—presumably because this would be clear from his style. At this early point in the collaboration, she saw Turi's drawings within an evolutionist context as primitive—a product of his "naïve need to visualize what he was describing in the text."[25]

A new edition of the book in Sámi (2010), Norwegian (2011), and English (2012) was brought out to celebrate the one-hundredth anniversary of the first publication, and it incorporates the illustrations that had originally appeared in the separate atlas. The editors also added other drawings by Turi and seven of his watercolors and gouaches to demonstrate further facets of Turi's artistic production and the media in which he worked.[26] The original forewords by Lundbohm and Demant have been replaced by one written by the Sámi literary scholar Harald Gaski and an afterword by the translator, American folklorist and Sámi scholar Thomas A. DuBois. The captions Demant wrote for Turi's illustrations are omitted from the new edition.

These alterations give the book a new academic framing and recontextualize the original illustrations. In place of the original goals of anthropological enlightenment and didactic utility, the new framing has the effect of canonizing Turi's text and images within Sámi cultural history. By demonstrating further sides of Turi's artistic practice, however, it also invites a reinterpretation of his visual work and a new exploration of the relationship between Turi and Hatt that focuses on their collaboration as artists rather than as salvage anthropologists.

Johan Turi: Drawings of the Seen and the Unseen

In the atlas accompanying the 1910 edition of *Muitalus*, Turi's line drawings are printed in large format, 50 centimeters by 30 centimeters.[27] By labeling the book in which they are reproduced an "atlas," they are given a very different meaning from that conveyed by the manner of their inclusion within the newest edition. As book illustrations, the drawings are much reduced in size, limiting the viewer's ability to see all their rich details. The term *atlas*, furthermore, associates them with geographical visualizations of territories and universes and other scientific representations of medical and anthropological knowledge. An atlas, in other words, aims to tell the literal truth by visualizing it.

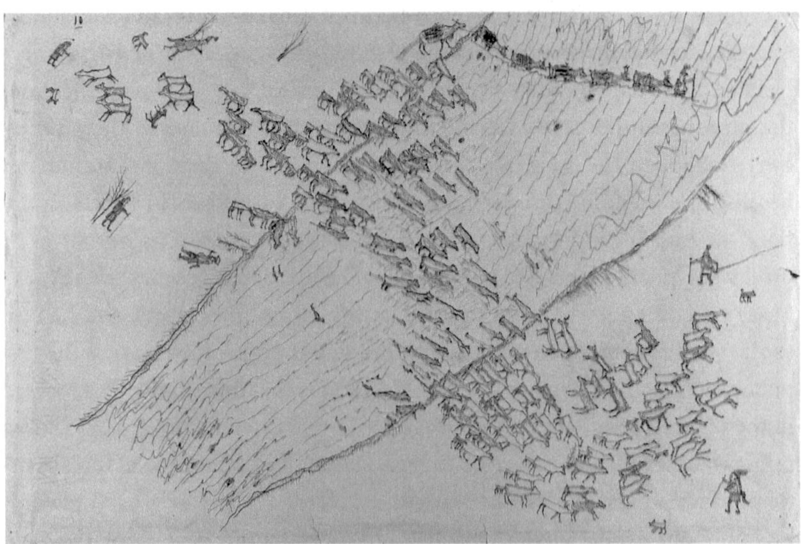

FIGURE 5.1 Johan Turi, *Siidaen krysser en elv om våren* [The siida crossing a river in spring], 1910. Line drawing from *Muittalus samid birra: Atlas med 14 tavler* [An account of the Sami: Atlas with 14 drawings]. Tav. x. © Nordiska museet, Stockholm, L.A. 874 nr. 7.

An example of one such visualized universe is drawing number 10, which, according to Demant's caption, depicts the *siida* crossing a river in spring (figure 5.1). The river flows diagonally from the upper right to the lower left corner. The herd of reindeer cows and calves is depicted as a pack moving through the picture diagonally from the upper left side to the lower right side. Humans and dogs surround the herd on both sides. On the upper right side there are a caravan of six geldings linked together with ropes and led by a man carrying a stick in his hand. The last reindeer in the caravan drags the poles used for the *lávvo* (tent), and Turi has shown its hesitation to enter the cold river by clearly depicting the animal's raised head and the tightened rope connecting it to the reindeer in front. The spot where the caravan fords the river is wider than the place where the rest of the herd is crossing further down. In her caption, Demant explains that this is a deliberate choice because the wider stretch of the river is shallower and slower. Turi illustrates the difference in depth by making visible some of the stones in the river. Fording rivers was, of course, critical to spring migrations, and the importance of keeping equipment dry was a good reason to cross, as depicted in the drawing. Turi describes how it was done in his text and discusses accidents that could occur during crossings.[28]

Demant identifies the two men receiving the herd on the other side of the river as Torne Lapps because of the style of their hats while another man on the far side of the river can be identified as coming from Guovdageaidnu because of the different square shape of his hat.[29] Hat styles and the absence of knives hanging from their belts also identify two of the people as women. Turi's narrative unfolds in a Sámi universe revealed from multiple angles of vision, and his manipulation of perspective is another strategy for conveying detailed Indigenous knowledge. The site is seen from a bird's-eye view while the animals and humans are viewed from a perspective parallel to the spectator.

Turi was a storyteller, and he used his visual tools to convey narratives with great precision. His care with details is one such tool: every animal, person, tree, river, or stone in the drawing is there to tell a part of the story. Sámi language — characterized by a rich verbal terminology for reindeer and other phenomena — is another tool. A two-year-old reindeer male, for example, is called by a specific name, *varit*, and this kind of lexical specificity is expressed in the drawings. One can thus read the details in the drawings as translations from language to visual representation in some cases.

In illustration number 10 there are at least two narratives: one about the herd and herders, another about the caravan carrying the equipment. These two events do not necessarily happen simultaneously, but because they occur in the same place, the stories can be told simultaneously. According to Gaski, this multitemporality demonstrates Turi's intentions as a sophisticated artist who adhered to his own imagistic code. This code surpasses the limitations of literal representation. His drawings in *Muitalus* "see" and narrate the site rather than the people. They depict both what is seen and what is unseen — there is more than meets the eye.[30]

Assemblages for Tourists

After the book and atlas were published Turi had a moment of fame and was admired for both his text and his drawings. Lundbohm provided him with a cottage in the small village of Lattilahti (Latteluokta) near Torneträsk, where he began living in 1910.[31] The Swedish government gave him a royal gold medal and a stipend, but little income came with the fame.

Presumably inspired by his new fame and by the influences of the Western artistic genres he had encountered through Lundbohm and Hatt, Turi began to make drawings and watercolor paintings for purchase. To simplify the drawing process, he developed an innovative "assemblage" technique involving templates of reindeer bodies of different sizes. According to the Swedish ethnographer Ernst Manker (1893–1972), this invention was inspired by stamps he had seen on Hjalmar Lundbohm's desk and was a labor-saving strategy.[32] However, each of Turi's stamps for animals and humans, trees, and numbers was detailed with highly specific features.

Turi's 1933 watercolor painting of his dwelling place with the inscription "Lattilahti, Torneträsk" exemplifies his assemblage technique (figure 5.2). It represents a landscape dominated by three dark summits against a bright sky. The grass, woodlands, and pastures in the foreground are painted with broad brush strokes in dominant colors of yellow and green, and the landscape is depicted from a central perspective point that creates the illusion of three-dimensionality. The trees, people, and animals are added with stamps to create the narrative. We see a reindeer attacked by a predator while other reindeers flee from the threat and people standing on the outskirts, watching the dramatic incident. The stamped figures are rendered with black paint, making them appear to be on top of the painted surface rather than contained within the perspective of the painted landscape. As in the drawings Turi made for the atlas, the site provides the context for the narrative. What is different is the new tool Turi applies — the central perspective point. We know from the price marked on this painting — "10 kr" or ten Swedish kroners — that the picture was made for sale. The price was determined by the number of reindeer Turi had included — the more reindeer, the higher the price. One drawing named *Renhjord* (reindeer herd) found its way into Lundbohm's collection.[33]

Painting the Personal

As noted, to more fully represent Turi's artistic achievement, the new edition of *Muitalus* includes some of the stamp-printed assemblages as well as several paintings, such as a self-portrait, that appear to go beyond the purely commercial to convey more personal subjects.[34] The most interesting of these paintings is reproduced both as an inside illustration and on the book's dust jacket (figure 5.3). It is a small undated painting on cardboard showing two anthropomorphic heads and a small pack contained within a larger shape resembling the

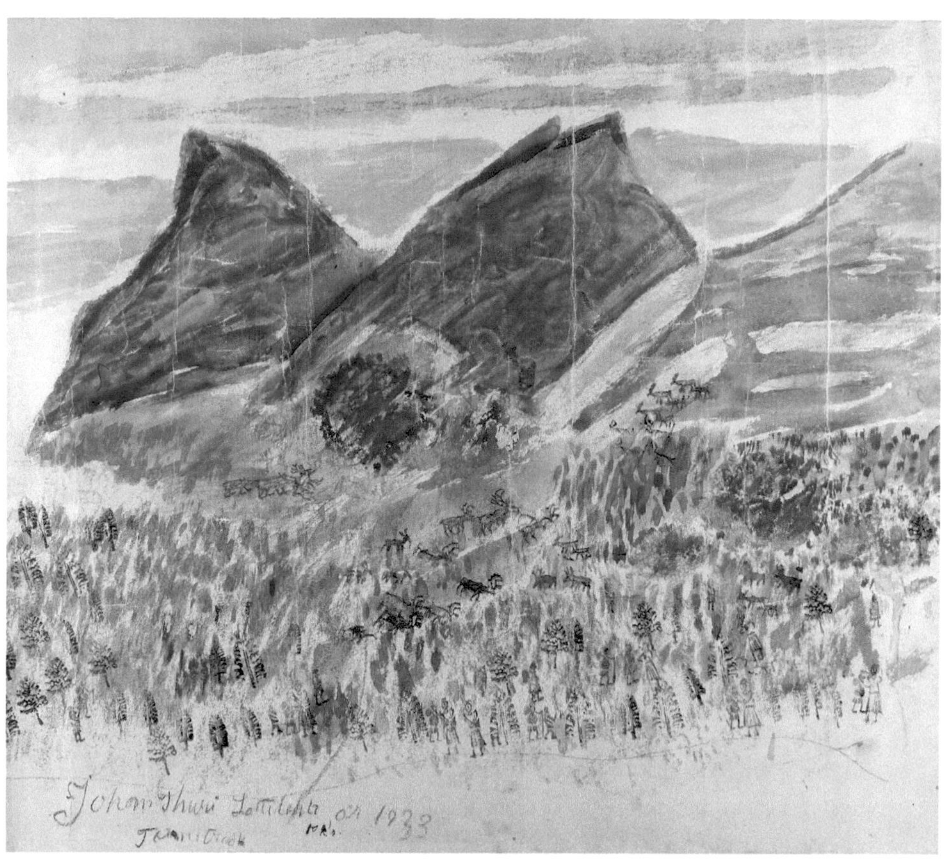

FIGURE 5.2 Johan Turi, *Torne lappmark. Jukkasjärvi socken. Talma lappby* [Torne Lapp district, Jukkasjärvi parish, Talma siida], 1933. Watercolor (and gouache?), crayon, pencil, and stamps on paper. © Nordiska museet, Stockholm, L.A. 659. nr. 8.

front of a boat or sledge — it cannot be conclusively identified because its rear end is unfinished. No further background is shown apart from some turquoise stains on the cardboard. While the smaller head is normally proportioned, the big round eyes, long triangular nose, and lack of a mouth on the larger head recall the African masks that were then inspiring European modernists.

While there is no clear indication of bodies, both heads wear hats and long shawls that cover neck and shoulders. Turi's descriptive precision is evident in the rendering of these garments, which are so detailed that we can see the grid of woven threads in the shawls and the decorations on the hats. According

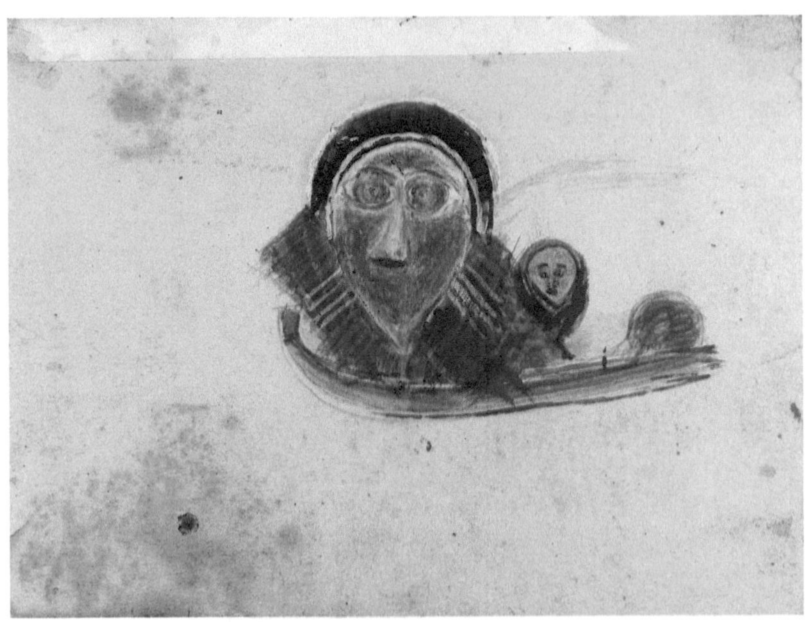

FIGURE 5.3 Johan Turi, Untitled, undated. Gouache and pencil on cardboard. © Nordiska museet, Stockholm, L.A. 659 nr. 5.

to the Sámi artist Britta Marakatt-Labba (b. 1951), the style of the hats signifies young, unmarried women from the Jukkasjärvi district. The lack of an obvious narrative raises the questions: Who are they and why did Turi paint them? There have been several interpretations of this image as a mother and child on a sledge, as supernatural *ulda*, as a *stállu* with his wife popping out of his *gákti* (Sámi tunic), or as the Virgin Mary with her son Jesus.[35] The formal features of this image, with its large, almost abstract mask-like faces, the undefined shape of the sledge or boat, the possibility of a concealed narrative opens up, I would argue, still further possible interpretations. In 1911, Turi went to Copenhagen to visit Hatt. As his hostess, Hatt may have taken him to the National Museum of Art, where he could have viewed the whole gamut of historic art. In 1911 modernist art had not yet made its way into Copenhagen's art galleries and collections — something that would occur a few years later.[36] Perhaps she also took him to the National Museum and ethnographic collections where he could see examples of masks and other "primitive" artifacts from the European colonies, objects that were inspiring European modernist artists during those years.[37] The painting might, for example, be an artistic experiment stimulated by Turi's exposure to what he saw during this visit.[38] If

Turi saw masks or other artifacts in the museum in Copenhagen, perhaps this inspired him as well as it inspired other artists?

In other paintings such as the self-portrait, Turi's depictions of the human body — like those of many untrained adults — were rendered unnaturalistically, with disproportionately large heads and shortened extremities. Yet the strange proportions, oversized head, facial features, and absence of bodies in Turi's picture of the two beings cannot be explained so simply. He does not appear to be attempting naturalistic description, despite the details in the shawls and hats, but rather an artistic expression of a personal experience. The generalized shape of the boat or sledge may signify the two beings as traveling, for in traditional Sámi drum iconography, boats and sledges signified the voyages of the *noaidi* (Shamanic practitioner) between the three different worlds, as well as the transitions of birth and death. The detailing of hats is, furthermore, certainly intentional for, as we know from Turi's drawings, he had a large repertoire of hats, each of which carried specific significations of geographical origin, gender, and age. Turi, finally, never married, but he had three daughters with two different women: his eldest, born in 1877, was Kristina Annesdotter Sara, her sister Inger Katarina Annesdotter Sara was born 1887, and the youngest, Sara Nutti, in 1891.[39] Turi's relationships with his daughters are not mentioned by scholars, but we can nevertheless speculate that the painting might portray two of the sisters traveling in and out of his consciousness and dreams.

Writing about Turi's oeuvre also evidences, however, the more general problems of attempts to categorize Indigenous arts using a Eurocentric, genealogical, evolutionist approach. His visual art resists the Western classification system and creates its own. Turi was a self-taught artist with a strong will to tell stories. To read these stories, it is necessary to leave behind the Western classification system and strive to see the tools he used to create his own visual universe based in his language and knowledge, as well as his encounters with Western art and artists and personal experiences of the modern world.

According to the conventional race hierarchies of Turi's time, the Sámi were valued primarily as objects of anthropological study.[40] Berman defines modernity in terms of attempts by men and women to become the subjects as well as the objects of modernization — to take hold of the modern world and make themselves at home in it.[41] In these terms Turi defied the conventional view of the Sámi by making himself an ethnographic subject — taking advantage of the new conditions created by modernity to establish his own dialogue with his peoples' past, present, and future. Turi's book and his later visual art exemplify this attempt. If I am correct that the mask-like faces he painted were influenced by the same "primitive" artifacts as modernist artists were at the time, his subject position as an artist is even more convincing.

In 1928 Demant Hatt convinced Danish art critic Poul Uttenreiter (1886–1956) to submit a selection of Turi's artworks to the selection committee of Copenhagen's "Den Frie" (the Free Exhibition). This was an association of Danish artists founded after the model of *Salon des Refusés* in Paris.[42] The jury accepted seventeen of his color drawings for display at the fall exhibition under the auspices of the association, with such titles as *A Herd of Reindeer Up on a Dangerous Bridge* and *Two Lapp Girls*. A copy of the printed atlas was also on display, probably contributed by Demant.[43] As Turi had included her in his life and culture, she, it would seem, wanted to include him as an artist in hers. Art reviewers, however, failed to accord Turi recognition either as an artist or as a modern subject. They referred to him as the "Mountain Lapp" and his works as "childlike and unschooled."[44] The modernist European ideology of artistic primitivism and premodern authenticity echo clearly in this critical reception, although here in reference to a man who was regarded as interesting, if also primitive.

Emilie Demant Hatt

Emilie Demant Hatt's grounding in visual art differed greatly from Turi's. In 1897 she had attended drawing classes in Copenhagen with the painters and feminists Emilie Mundt and Marie Laplau. The following year she was accepted as a student at Copenhagen's Royal Academy of Arts and studied there until 1901 and again from 1905 to 1906, as well as studying privately in Berlin. In 1903 she exhibited for the first time in the prestigious spring exhibition at Charlottenborg in Copenhagen. She thus brought to her collaboration with Turi a solid training in the tradition of Western art.

The drawings and paintings Emilie Demant made during her student years are technically accomplished and employ a naturalistic style to represent subjects deemed suitable for a female artist at that time — portraits, interiors, and landscapes. Although her participation in the spring exhibition evidences the positive reception of her work, she later described herself as having worked in an old-fashioned manner and as achieving little public success — a common experience for female artists at the turn of the last century.[45] Yet Demant Hatt did differ in other ways from most of her contemporary female colleagues; unusually, she continued to paint even after her marriage to Gudmund Hatt (1884–1960) in 1911 and participated in exhibitions throughout her life.[46]

The Ethnographer and Photographer

Hatt returned to Sápmi several times after her trip in 1907–8, both on her own and together with her husband. The two books she published under Lundbohm's auspices gave visual expression to her experiences in different media. The first book, *Med lapperne i højfjeldet* (With the Lapps in the high mountains), appeared in 1913. It provides her account of her year among the Sámi and is illustrated with her own photographs as well as some photographs by Borg Mesch (1869–1956).[47]

Hatt's text is a personal narrative of her experiences with different Sámi families, and her photographs depict the daily life of the reindeer herders.[48] Hatt's photographs relate to a change in anthropological studies that took place from the end of the nineteenth century. At that time fieldwork was becoming a central methodology for anthropology, while photography was being recognized as a vital tool in the transmission of data. This new approach, fostered by the American anthropologist Franz Boas and others, required that anthropologists should live among the people they described and urged the value of photography as a crucial mediator.[49] Later scholars have regarded Hatt's book as an unconventional ethnographic travelogue and acknowledge her as an accomplished, if amateur, female ethnographer.[50]

She traveled together with her husband on several fieldwork expeditions and study trips around the world, spending 1914 and 1915 in North America. In New York City, while attending seminars at Columbia University, she learned that Franz Boas knew of the work she had done with Turi.[51] International recognition for her pioneering work thus came early from anthropologists, although artistic recognition came later.

The Illustrator

Demant Hatt's second book, *Ved ilden* (By the fire), published in 1922, is a short collection of Sámi tales and stories she had heard and recorded during her travels in Sápmi and is illustrated by her own linoleum block prints. In the foreword she explains that all the stories are told by the fire and notes that the illustrations may be difficult to understand for someone unfamiliar with Sámi dress and lifestyle.[52] One illustration, for example, shows how a Sámi boy tricks a *stállu* into falling off a cliff in order to steal a bag of money from him (figure 5.4). The two people are dressed in Sámi clothes, but while the smaller person is obviously a human being, the larger has a strange and

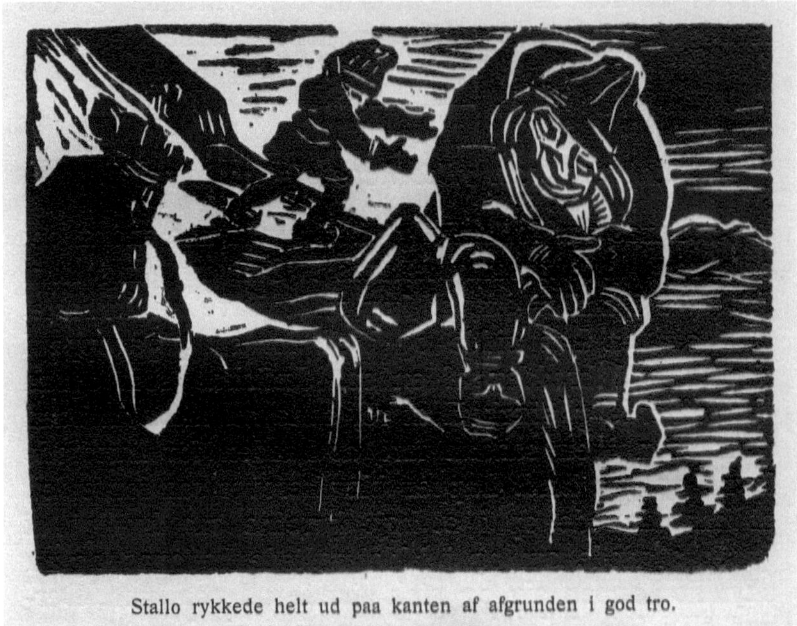

FIGURE 5.4 Emilie Demant Hatt, Untitled, undated. Linoleum block print. Caption: "Stallo rykkede helt ud paa kanten af afgrunden i god tro" [Stallo moved to the edge of the abyss in good faith]. Printed at page 58 in E. D. Hatt, *Ved ilden* [By the fire], 1922.

frightening humanoid face. The landscape is suggested by the low horizon on the right and the dark sky above.

A Sámi version of Cinderella is illustrated by an interior from a *goahti* (a Sámi house type) (figure 5.5). There is an arch constructed of birch trees and a large opening for the smoke from the fire. Food is being prepared in a big pot hanging over the fire. A boy looks down through the smoke hole. Very active contrasting graphic patterns of crosshatching, parallel, and curving lines describe the interior while pointillist dots indicate the sky. In this scene all the characters are human, captured during a crucial moment in the story.

In *Ved ilden*, Demant Hatt's rhetorical stance has become that of the subjective and interpretive artist, in contrast to the position of neutral "participant observer" she had previously adopted to make her notes, sketches, and photographs. The tales and stories place great emphasis on how the existing material world is influenced by and interact with an immaterial world.

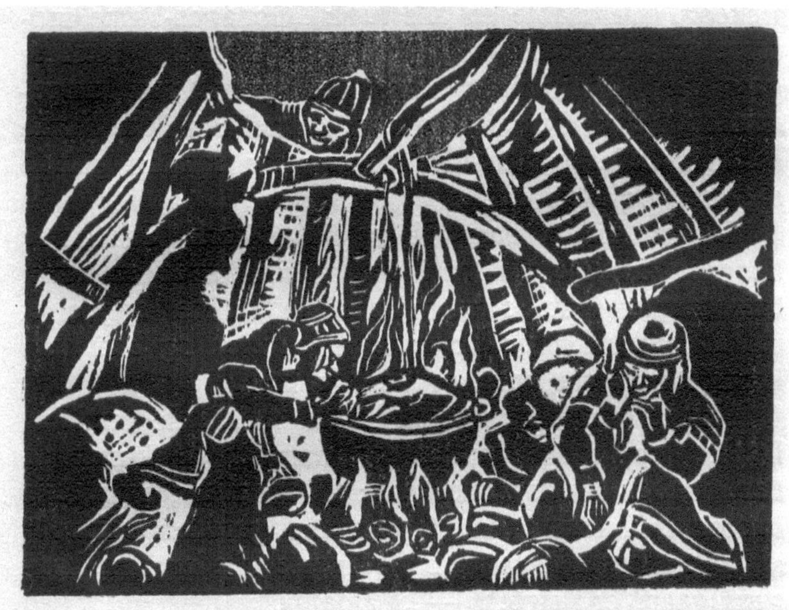

FIGURE 5.5 Emilie Demant Hatt, Untitled, undated. Linoleum block print. Printed at page 47 in E. D. Hatt, *Ved ilden* [By the fire], 1922.

If Demant Hatt's early work was old fashioned, the illustrations in *Ved ilden* have become more modernist. She plays with perspective, as in her representation of the interior of the *goahti,* and she exaggerates the facial expressions, rendering humans and nonhumans alike as existing in the real world. The artist illustrates not only what she had seen but also what she had heard and imagined. Many European artists used the graphic print as their medium at the time. Norwegian artist Edvard Munch (1863–1944) may be the most famous, and Hatt's use of swirling lines in horizons and skies have much in common with his work. Her prints are also strongly reminiscent of those made by the Norwegian Sámi artist John Savio (1902–38), especially in their depiction of humans in motion and at work and in their shared creation of a Sápmi iconography.

Going Modernist

Though Demant Hatt's prints demonstrate a more modernist style than her early works, her decisive turn to modernism in painting came, by her own account, when she visited a Copenhagen gallery in 1924. There she happened to glance at paintings by Harald Giersing (1881–1927), one of Denmark's most important twentieth-century modernists.[53]

A few years later, in 1936, Demant Hatt painted the first of at least seventy large paintings visualizing the experiences in Sápmi that she had described in her two books. Sjoholm speculates that she may have suddenly focused on these scenes because Johan Turi died the same year.[54] His passing may have given her a feeling of freedom to make her own visual interpretations, without the risk of offending Turi or competing with his drawings and paintings.

One of Demant Hatt's first paintings from Sápmi was the 1936 *Bönemöte* (Religious ecstasy) (figure 5.6). One recognizes the scene from her description of an ecstatic religious experience in *With the Lapps in the High Mountains*: "The peaceful sun-filled tent was transformed in the space of a few minutes to a painful place, where human souls were whipped by remorse, fear and guilt. Men and women sobbed and rocked their torsos back and forth."[55] We see a group of fifteen adult men and women, two children, and three dogs inside a *lávvo* with an open fire and a wide opening at the top. All are dressed in Sámi clothes from the Karesuando district except for one man holding a book — a lay preacher. Everyone is in movement, some embracing; others standing alone with their arms upstretched. The scene is visualized both from above and from below; the adults seem to be soaring in the air while the fireplace, children, dogs, and one old woman appear to be on the ground.

In this painting Demant Hatt bears witness to the religious ecstasy experienced by adherents of Laestadianism, a Lutheran lay movement that had gained many followers among the Sámi. In her text, she recounted that the general nervous excitement had such a strong impact on her that she began to shiver and had to leave the tent.[56] The spasmodic sobbing and moaning of the people packed into the lávvo left her with a vivid impression that enabled her, more than twenty years later, to paint the scene from memory.

This painting is representative of the definitive shift in Emilie Demant Hatt's work from documentary observer to expressive modernist painter. Her work can be compared to that of younger Danish contemporaries such as Asger Jorn (1914–73) and Egil Jacobsen (1910–98), both of whom were also influenced by Harald Giersing. Although references to Munch's graphic art are already visible in her illustrations for *Ved ilden*, the powerful expressionist style of her late paintings coincides even more strongly with Munch's works.

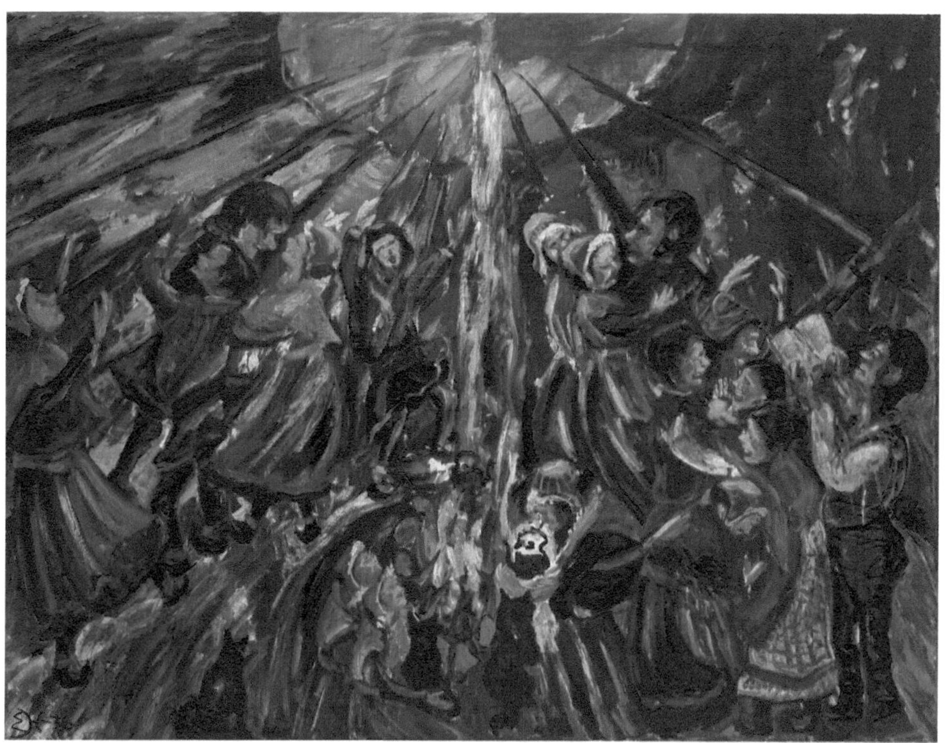

FIGURE 5.6 Emilie Demant Hatt, *Bönemöte* [Religious ecstasy], 1936. Oil on canvas, 147 cm × 115 cm. © Nordiska museet, Stockholm, NM.246065. Photo courtesy of Peter Segemark, Nordiska museet.

Asked in a 1934 interview if her travels had had any bearing on her artistic style, Hatt answered, "Basically no." The foreign places she had visited had, of course, provided her subject matter, but she claimed that the "revolution" in her painting happened independently.[57] She added that she longed to go back to Lapland. For various reasons, however, the then-sixty-one-year-old Demant Hatt continued to paint her almost exclusively Sápmi scenes in her studio, from memory.[58] As we have seen, as an artist trained in Western traditions, the tools available to Demant Hatt were very different from those of Turi, and she is thus easy to categorize in terms of the Western movements of modernism and expressionism. Ultimately, her paintings of Sápmi earned her recognition as having created "the most strange and strongest work in Danish Expressionism."[59]

Conclusion

The triangulation of Emilie Demant Hatt as the deterritorialized Western artist; Johan Turi as the colonized, dispossessed Indigenous artist; and the modernist European ideology of artistic primitivism created a dynamic interaction. Hatt's encounter with Turi enabled her to realize the dream she had had since childhood: to stay with a Sámi family throughout a year. The modest and respectful attitude with which she approached the Sámi led people to accept—or at least to tolerate—her presence among them. In her interactions with Turi, however, there was a clearer relationship of reciprocity that would profoundly alter the artistic practices of both artists. For Hatt, learning the Sámi language, living with the people, sharing their experiences, and then working with Turi on *Muitalus* changed her view of Sámi culture, as she herself states in *With the Lapps in the High Mountains*. It also, as I have argued, transformed her practices as writer and artist from a participant observer whose goals were descriptive and documentary to those of an interpretive and expressive painter giving visual form to impressions preserved in memory.

In Sápmi, Hatt was not only physically deterritorialized from her own Scandinavian region but also mentally and spiritually deterritorialized in a Deleuzian sense.[60] Gilles Deleuze and Félix Guattari describe deterritorialization as the movement by which something escapes from a given territory in the operation of a line of flight.[61] The result of this escape can be understood as a movement producing change. By following the works of both Demant Hatt and Turi, we can see a change indeed, but along different lines of flight. For Demant Hatt, one line goes through learning the Sámi language; from its highly descriptive and conceptually distinctive terms—*varit*, the name for two-year-old male reindeer, is an example—she gained a deeper understanding of what she saw during the time she spent in Sápmi. Through her awareness of the complexity of Sámi language, she probably came to understand how much was entailed in the act of crossing a river during spring migration, as well as in the religious and political dimensions of Sámi life. In combination, this mental and spiritual deterritorialization allowed her to escape from the terms in which she had written about the Sámi in her foreword to the 1910 edition of *Muitalus*, where she contrasted a "primitive" or naïve Sámi culture to her own modern and advanced Western culture. She expressed this transformation in her thinking in a speech she delivered at the Nordiska museet in 1940 and, even more strongly, in her late paintings.

Turi also became deterritorialized. He embraced the opportunity offered to leave his given territory by his encounter with Hatt, and the mental deterritorialization that followed made it possible for him to adopt a modern subjectivity. In this sense, Turi's escape was accomplished when he claimed a position for himself as a disseminator and defender of Sámi culture and as a visual artist who could exploit the opportunities offered by modernization, including the adoption of new practices he observed in his encounters with Western art and artists. Yet when Turi's art was physically deterritorialized to Copenhagen, viewers instantly reterritorialized his art in the terms of Western modernist primitivism, as "childlike" and "unschooled."

If in the early phase of the collaboration between Demant Hatt and Turi the triangulation created a stable relationship, it became destabilized as time went on. Ultimately, their positions exceeded the triangulation. Instead, I prefer to see the two artists as following different lines of flight away from the modernist European ideology of artistic primitivism in their modes of deterritorializations and further development as artists. Their different lines of flight changed them both and opened artistic practices that neither could have foreseen.

Notes

1. She was given the name Emilie Demant Hansen at birth. She used the name Emilie Demant until she married Gudmund Hatt in 1911. Then she added Hatt to her family name.

2. Berman, *All That Is Solid*, 15.

3. Turi, *Muittalus samid birra*.

4. Kuutma, "Collaborative Ethnography," 174.

5. Adler, "'Skirting the Edges of Civilization,'" 94.

6. Magga, "Johan Turi čallin," 65.

7. Kuutma, "Encounters to Negotiate a Sámi Ethnography," 515.

8. Berman, *All That Is Solid*, 5.

9. Kuutma, "Collaborative Ethnography," 175.

10. Phillips, "The Turn of the Primitive," 48.

11. Andrén, "Konsten i Kiruna," 72ff.

12. Kuutma, "Collaborative Ethnography," 177.

13. *Muittalus* is short for the title *Muittalus Samid Birra*. The spelling follows the 1910 edition.

14. Demant, *Med lapperne i højfjeldet*. In 2013, the Swedish Irish American writer and translator Barbara Sjoholm translated the book into English (Hatt, *With the Lapps*).

15. Hatt, *Ved ilden.*

16. Hatt, "Johan Turi čallin," 108.

17. Hatt, "Johan Turi čallin," 98.

18. A collection of families sharing the same grazing lands and migration routes. Some Sámi words are impossible to translate. When Sámi words appear in the text, they are in italics with an explanation in English. All translations are taken from Thomas A. DuBois's glossary in Turi, *An Account of the Sámi.*

19. Sjoholm, introduction to Hatt, *With the Lapps*, xxi.

20. Sjoholm, introduction to Hatt, *With the Lapps*, xvi.

21. Gaski, "Johan Turi," 43.

22. Sjoholm, "How the Book 'Muittalus Samid Birra' Was Created," 313–36.

23. Exceptions here are Aamold, "Representing the Hidden and the Perceptible"; and Gaski, "More Than Meets the Eye." Barbara Sjoholm also writes about the artworks. Sjoholm, "The Art of Recalling."

24. Sjoholm, "How the Book 'Muittalus Samid Birra' Was Created," 323.

25. Demant, foreword to Turi, *Muittalus*, ix.

26. Gaski, foreword to Turi, *An Account of the Sámi*, 9.

27. Turi, *Muittalus samid birra.*

28. Turi, *An Account of the Sámi*, 92–95.

29. They had their origin in a specific district, Torne.

30. Gaski, "More Than Meets the Eye," 601.

31. Barck, *Kirunas byar*, 80.

32. Manker, *Samefolkets konst*, 130.

33. Andrén, "Konsten i Kiruna," 161.

34. Turi, *An Account of the Sámi*, 20.

35. Aamold, "Representing the Hidden and the Perceptible," 83ff. *Ulda* are underground spirits, possessed of magic skills and knowledge, sometimes helpful to Sámi, sometimes harmful. A *stállu* is an ogre-like legendary character, prone to attacking and eating the Sámi, especially associated with Christmas Eve.

36. Bramsen and Voss, *Vort eget århundrede*, 75.

37. Wood and Gaiger, *Art of the Twentieth Century*, 16.

38. Gaski, "More Than Meets the Eye," 591.

39. Marainen, *Karesuando samesläkter*, 152, 361.

40. Kuutma, "Encounters," 515.

41. Berman, *All That Is Solid*, 5.

42. The association was founded as a protest against the strict rules for admission to the established and prestigious gallery Charlottenborg in Copenhagen, where Demant Hatt exhibited in 1903.

43. Sjoholm, *Black Fox*, 264.

44. Sjoholm, "The Art of Recalling," 386.

45. Sjoholm, "The Art of Recalling," 356.

46. A retrospective exhibition of her work was mounted at the Skive Museum, close to her birthplace, in 1983. Gudmund Hatt (1884–1960) was a Danish archaeologist and cultural geographer.

47. Mesch was based in Kiruna and a well-known photographer.

48. Hansen, "Fotografier i Emilie Demant Hatts," 132.

49. Pinney, *Photography and Anthropology*, 15.

50. Eglinger, "Nomadic, Ecstatic, Magic," 193.

51. Sjoholm, "The Art of Recalling," 393.

52. Hatt, *Ved ilden*.

53. See Bramsen and Voss, *Vort eget århundrede*.

54. Sjoholm, "The Art of Recalling," 385f.

55. Hatt, *With the Lapps*, 26.

56. Hatt, *With the Lapps*, 26.

57. Lefèvre, "En del af den store verden," 13.

58. Sjoholm, "The Art of Recalling," 385.

59. Lefèvre, "En del af den store verden," 18.

60. Deleuze and Guattari, *What Is Philosophy?*, 68.

61. Deleuze and Guattari, *A Thousand Plateaus*, 508.

Bibliography

Aamold, Svein. "Representing the Hidden and the Perceptible: Johan Turi's Images of Sápmi." In *Sámi Art and Aesthetics: Contemporary Perspectives*, edited by Svein Aamold, Elin Haugdal, and Ulla Angkjær Jørgensen, 69–98. Aarhus: Aarhus University Press, 2017.

Adler, Michelle. "'Skirting the Edges of Civilization': Two Victorian Women Travellers and 'Colonial Spaces' in South Africa." In *Text, Theory, Space: Land, Literature and History in South Africa and Australia*, edited by Kate Darian-Smith, Liz Gunner, and Sara Nutthall, 83–98. London: Routledge, 1996.

Andrén, Brit-Marie. "Konsten i Kiruna: Patriarkalism och Nationalromantik 1900–1914" [Art in Kiruna: Patriarchy and national romanticism]. Fil. lic., Umeå universitet, 1989.

Barck, Åke. *Kirunas byar* [Kiruna's Sami districts]. Kiruna: Tidningsföreningen i Kiruna, 2002.

Beach, Hugh. Foreword to *With the Lapps in the High Mountains: A Woman among the Sami, 1907–1908*, by Emilie Demant Hatt, edited and translated by Barbara Sjoholm, vii–ix. Madison: University of Wisconsin Press, 2013.

Berman, Marshall. *All That Is Solid Melts into the Air: The Experience of Modernity*. New York: Penguin Books, 1988.

Bramsen, Henrik, and Knud Voss, eds. *Dansk Kunsthistorie.* Vol. 5, *Vort eget århundrede: Efter 1900* [Danish art history. Vol. 5, Our own century: After 1900], edited by Vagn Poulsen, Erik Lassen, and Jan Danielsen. København: Politiken, 1975.

Deleuze, Gilles, and Félix Guattari. *A Thousand Plateaus: Capitalism and Schizophrenia.* Translated by Brian Massumi. Minneapolis: University of Minnesota Press, 1987.

Deleuze, Gilles, and Félix Guattari. *What Is Philosophy?* New York: Columbia University Press, 1994.

Demant, Emilie. Foreword to *Muitalus Samid Birra*, by Johan Turi, v–ix. Copenhagen: Græbes bogtrykker, 1910.

Demant, Emilie. *Med lapperne i højfjeldet* [With the Lapps in the high mountains]. Stockholm: Skandinaviska bokhandelen, 1913.

DuBois, Thomas A. Afterword to *An Account of the Sámi*, by Johan Turi, translated and edited by Thomas A. DuBois, 209–17. Karasjok: CállidLágádus, 2012.

DuBois, Thomas A. "Glossary of Sámi Terms." In *An Account of the Sámi*, by Johan Turi, translated and edited by Thomas A. DuBois, 218–20. Karasjok: ČállidLágádus, 2012.

Eglinger, Hanna. "Nomadic, Ecstatic, Magic: Arctic Primitivism in Scandinavia around 1900." *Acta Borealia* 33, no. 2 (2016): 189–214.

Fett, Harry. "Finnmarksviddens kunst: John Andreas Savio." *Kunst og kultur* 26 (1940): 221–40.

Gaski, Harald. Foreword to *An Account of the Sámi*, by Johan Turi, translated and edited by Thomas A. DuBois, 6–10. Karasjok: ČálliidLágádus, 2012.

Gaski, Harald. "Johan Turi: The Songs of the Sami." In *In the Shadow of the Midnight Sun: Contemporary Sami Prose and Poetry*, edited by Harald Gaski, 43–56. Kárášjhoka: Davvi Girji, 1996.

Gaski, Harald. "More Than Meets the Eye: The Indigeneity of Johan Turi's Writing and Artwork." *Scandinavian Studies* 83 no. 4 (2011): 591–608.

Gjessing, Oda Wildhagen. "Edvard Munch og det danske spontan-abstrakte maleri" [Edvard Munch and the Danish spontaneous-abstract painting]. In *Cobra i Danmark*, edited by Nordnorsk Kunstmuseum, 41–57. Tromso: Nordnorsk Kunstmuseum, 2008. Exhibition catalog.

Gullickson, Charis. "The Artist as Noaidi." In *Sami Stories: Art and Identity of an Arctic People*, edited by Charis Gullickson and Sandra Lorentzen, 9–34. Orkana, 2014. Exhibition catalog.

Hansen, Hanna Horsberg. "Fotografier i Emilie Demant Hatts bok *Med lapperne i højfjeldet*: Fotografiske møter, biografiske inskripsjoner og 'våre' historier" [Photographs in Emilie Demant Hatt's book *With the Lapps in the High Mountains*]. *Kunst og Kultur* 105, nos. 2–3 (2022): 121–41. https://doi.org/10.18261/kk.105.2.

Hatt, Emilie Demant. "Johan Turi og hvordan bogen 'Muittalus Samid Birra' blev til" [Johan Turi and how the book "Muittalus Samid Birra" was created]. *Fataburen:*

Nordiska museets och Skansens Årsbok, edited by Sigurd Wallin, Gösta Berg, and Sigfrid Svensson, 97–108. Stockholm: Nordiska museet, 1942.

Hatt, Emilie Demant. *Ved ilden: Eventyr og Historier fra Lapland* [By the fire: Sami folktales and legends]. Copenhagen: J. H. Schultz Forlag, 1922.

Hatt, Emilie Demant. *With the Lapps in the High Mountains: A Woman among the Sami, 1907–1908*. Edited and translated by Barbara Sjoholm. Madison: University of Wisconsin Press, 2013.

Kuutma, Kristin. "Collaborative Ethnography before Its Time: Johan Turi and Emilie Demant Hatt." *Scandinavian Studies* 75, no. 2 (2003): 165–80.

Kuutma, Kristin. "Encounters to Negotiate a Sámi Ethnography: The Process of Collaborative Representations." *Scandinavian Studies* 83 no. 4 (2011): 491–518.

Lefèvre, Jens Ole. "En del af den store verden fik jeg at se" [A part of the big world I got to see]. In *Emilie Demant Hatt 1873–1958: Blade til en biografi*, 9–20. Odense: Skive Museum, 1983.

Lundbohm, Hjalmar. Preface to *Muitalus Samid Birra: En bog om lappernes liv*, by Johan Turi, translated by Emilie Demant, i–iv. Copenhagen: Græbes Bogtrykkeri, 1910.

Lundström, Jan-Erik. "What Is Contemporary Sami Art and Design?" In *Contemporary Sami Art and Design*, edited by Julie Cirelli and Esther Whang, 9–11. Stockholm: Arvinus + Orfeus, 2015.

Magga, Ole Henrik. "Johan Turi čallin." *Sámi dieđalaš áigečála* (2011–2012): 49–65.

Manker, Ernst. *Samefolkets konst* [Art of the Sami people]. Halmstad: Askild & Kärnekull, 1971.

Marainen, Johannes. *Karesuando samesläkter* [Karesuando Sami families]. Umeå: Sámiid Riikasearvi (SSR), 1997.

Phillips, Ruth B. "The Turn of the Primitive: Modernism, the Stranger, and the Indigenous Artist in Settler Art Histories." In *Exiles, Diasporas, and Strangers*, edited by Kobena Mercer, 46–71. Cambridge, MA: MIT Press, 2008.

Pinney, Christopher. *Photography and Anthropology*. London: Reaktion Books, 2011.

Sjoholm, Barbara. "The Art of Recalling: Lapland and the Sami in the Art of Emilie Demant Hatt and Johan Turi." *Feminist Studies* 40, no. 2 (2014): 356–94.

Sjoholm, Barbara. *Black Fox: A Life of Emilie Demant Hatt, Artist and Ethnographer*. Madison: University of Wisconsin Press, 2017.

Sjoholm, Barbara. "How the Book 'Muittalus Samid Birra' Was Created: Johan Turi's Classic Sámi Narrative as a Publishing Project." *Scandinavian Studies* 82, no. 3 (2010): 313–36.

Sjoholm, Barbara. Introduction to *With the Lapps in the High Mountains: A Woman among the Sami, 1907–1908*, by Emilie Demant Hatt, edited and translated by Barbara Sjoholm, xiii–xxxv. Madison: University of Wisconsin Press, 2013.

Skive Museum. *Emilie Demant Hatt 1873–1958: Blade til en biografi*. Odense: Skive Museum, 1983.

Turi, Johan. *An Account of the Sámi*. Translated by Thomas A. DuBois. Karasjok: ČállidLágádus, 2012.

Turi, Johan. *Muitalus samid birra: En bog om lappernes liv*. Translated by Emilie Demant. København: Græbes bogtrykkeri, 1910.

Turi, Johan. *Muittalus samid birra: Atlas med 14 tavler*. Atlas with 14 illustrations. Stockholm: Nordiska Bokhandeln, 1910.

Wood, Paul, and Jason Gaiger, eds. *Art of the Twentieth Century: A Reader*. London: Yale University Press, 2003.

SANDRA KLOPPER

6 THE ART OF LAUGHTER

The Interdependent Creativity of Alson Zuma and David Fox

> After six hundred and forty one years, Fort Nottingham has a new poet laureate. The winner was Alson Zuma. . . . The reading of his poem brought tears to the eyes of the village elders.
>
> —ALSON ZUMA

South African artist Alson Dumisani Zuma enjoyed a meteoric rise to fame in the late 1980s, shortly after he went to work as a stable assistant for a farmer and horse breeder who had a long-standing amateur interest in art. Encouraged by his employer, David Fox, Zuma started producing densely populated, monumental relief panels of African wildlife. This led to several large-scale commissions from corporate clients (figure 6.1), among them Oprah Winfrey, and additional sales to members of the Zulu elite and other private collectors, both locally and internationally.[1] Evidently confident that he could capitalize on his burgeoning success, by the early 1990s Zuma began carving witty low-relief tableaux. On one occasion in June 1993, he produced two fanciful scenes of aquatic dinosaurs viewed from the perspective of both a bird and a fish for an exhibition mounted by the L. B. Smith Institute of Ichthyology at the prestigious Everard Read Gallery in Johannesburg (figure 6.2). When Fox was approached for comment on these panels, which were displayed along with Zuma's detailed rendition of a coelacanth, he explained, tongue-in-cheek, that because "the only fish Alson has ever seen have been covered in tomato sauce and inside a tin," he had suggested to the artist — who was by then spending long hours browsing through books in the village library at Nottingham Road not far from Fox's farm — that he should find a way of celebrating his growing fascination with

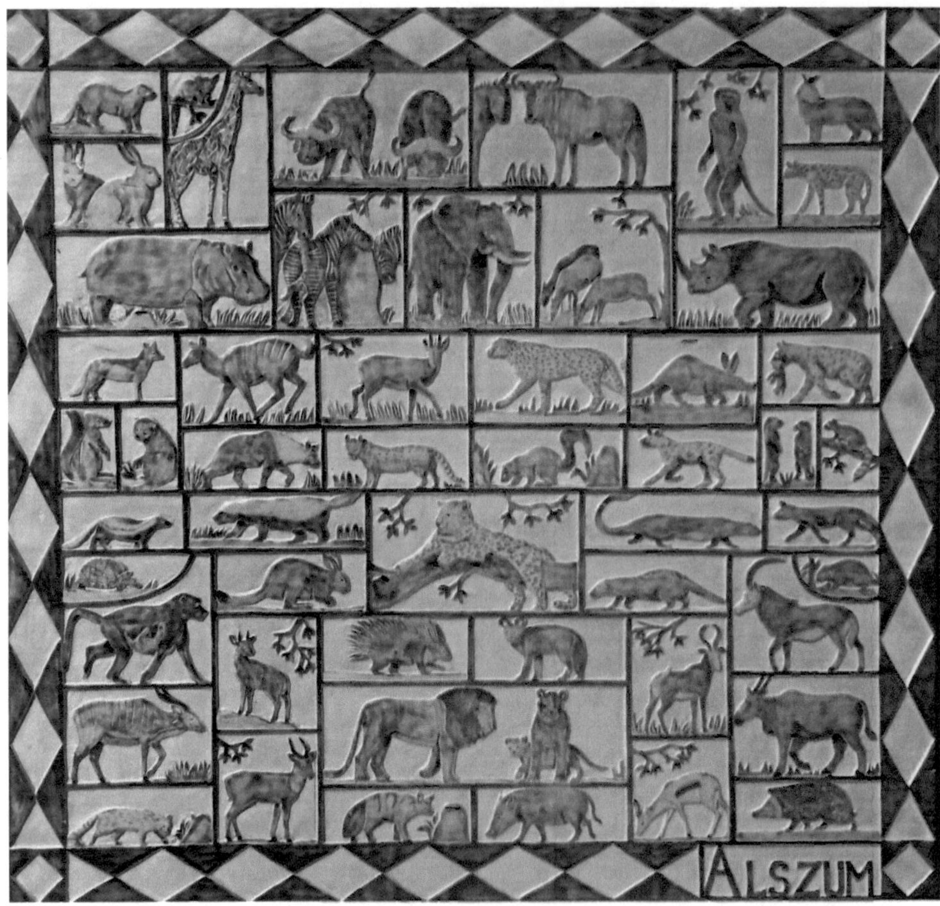

FIGURE 6.1 Wildlife relief in one of the guest lounges at the Mala Mala Game Reserve, Mpumalanga Province, South Africa, c. 1991. By Alson Zuma. Courtesy Mala Mala Game Reserve.

dinosaurs.[2] Fox added, "I know that Alson has not seen a Dinosaur either, but then neither has anyone else."[3]

Under Fox's ambitious guidance, Zuma went on to produce a series of satirical narratives on the theme of transport, relying on complex interplays between word and image to exploit the conceptual incongruities that became increasingly common in his work thereafter. Initially prompted by a 1995 exhibition titled *Moving Experience* held in Durban on the campus of the Natal Technikon, the ironic scenes Zuma produced on this theme included a tableau titled *Executive Travel*, in which a man carrying a shield and dressed in

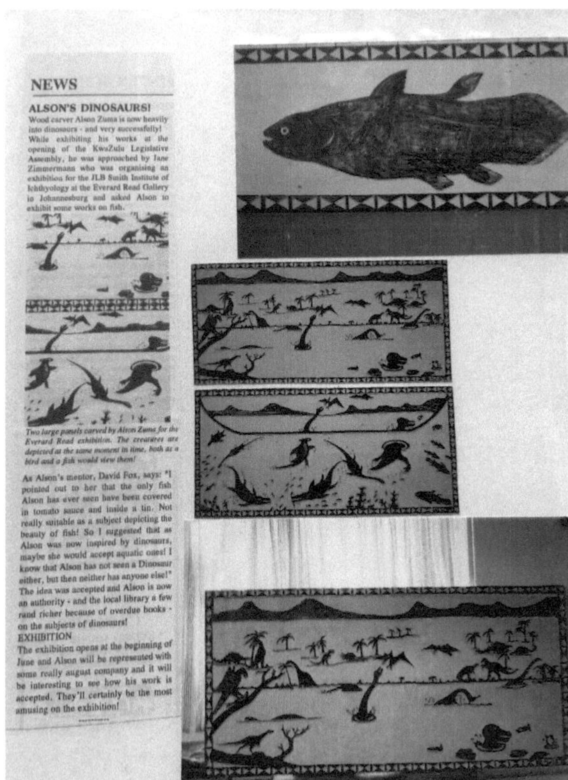

NEWS

ALSON'S DINOSAURS!

Wood carver Alson Zuma is now heavily into dinosaurs - and very successfully! While exhibiting his works at the opening of the KwaZulu Legislative Assembly, he was approached by Jane Zimmermann who was organising an exhibition for the JLB Smith Institute of Ichthyology at the Everard Read Gallery in Johannesburg and asked Alson to exhibit some works on fish.

Two large panels carved by Alson Zuma for the Everard Read exhibition. The creatures are depicted at the same moment in time, both as a bird and a fish would view them!

As Alson's mentor, David Fox, says: "I pointed out to her that the only fish Alson has ever seen have been covered in tomato sauce and inside a tin. Not really suitable as a subject depicting the beauty of fish! So I suggested that as Alson was now inspired by dinosaurs, maybe she would accept aquatic ones! I know that Alson has not seen a Dinosaur either, but then neither has anyone else!" The idea was accepted and Alson is now an authority - and the local library a few rand richer because of overdue books - on the subjects of dinosaurs!

EXHIBITION

The exhibition opens at the beginning of June and Alson will be represented with some really august company and it will be interesting to see how his work is accepted. They'll certainly be the most amusing on the exhibition!

FIGURE 6.2
Alson's dinosaurs. Press clippings from Alson Zuma's scrapbook dating to 1992.

traditionalist garments fashioned from fur and leather is followed by a long entourage of women and children, with a boy pulling a tethered goat at the rear of this procession.[4] Variations on the theme of travel continued to surface in some of Zuma's later, semi-didactic panels, many of which include narratives that openly mock Zulu traditionalists while others delight in wordplays, most obviously the use of comical puns (figure 6.3). Examples of this practice include a scene titled *Serials* in which a man appears to be watching a TV program on a box of All Bran flakes rather than paying attention to either the jug of milk or the cereal bowl and spoon on the table in front of him. Unlike folk art, which tends to "promise the romantic possibility of a simpler, more wholesomely integrated and creative way of living," works like this challenge received values and defy unambiguous expectations.[5]

Clearly impressed by Zuma's success and inspired by their collaborative engagements, Fox gradually began to revive his own early interest in producing humorous watercolors and oils. In 2004, for example, he illustrated a

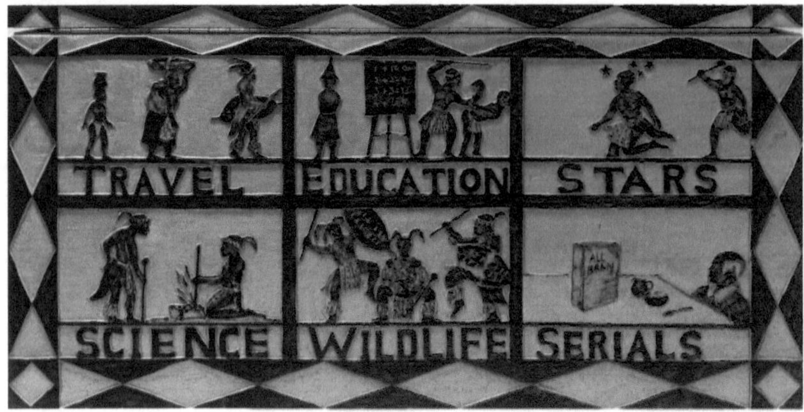

FIGURE 6.3 Side panel from *Radio Alszum*, 1999. Trunk with pokerwork panels, metal hinge, and cassette player, 30 cm × 59.5 cm × 36.5 cm. By Alson Zuma. Standard Bank Art Collection, Wits Art Galleries.

self-published children's book, titled *Some Little Known Scientific Facts about Dinosaurs*, which he dedicated to his granddaughter Ashley (figure 6.4). Fox had long been interested in expressive visual communication. He decorated Ashley's nursery walls, dressing table, and curtains after moving to the tiny hamlet of Nottingham in present-day KwaZulu-Natal's Midlands region in the 1970s. He also painted caricatures of horses on the veranda of the house he and his family lived in the 1950s and 1960s on a sugarcane farm near Gingindlovu in the coastal area north of Durban. While there, Fox began collecting local art forms, including beadwork, beaded sticks, a relief carving by the early Zulu modernist Zizwezenyanga Qwabe,[6] and two clay busts by one of Qwabe's contemporaries, Hezekiel Ntuli.[7] He later displayed items like these in a small private museum at Fort Nottingham (figure 6.5), together with a set of engraved horns documenting events related to the Anglo-Zulu War of 1879 and other memorabilia associated with various aspect of the history of present-day KwaZulu-Natal. The move to Fort Nottingham also encouraged Fox to fulfil his lifelong dream of breeding horses, and it was this new enterprise that brought him and Zuma together.

This chapter explores the gradual unfolding of Zuma and Fox's complex relationship, which became increasingly interdependent and mutually beneficial in the course of the 1990s. Their shared commitment to promoting Zuma's career eventually led them to travel together to the United Kingdom in 2001 after the artist was chosen to represent the Natal Midlands as part of an exhibition organized by the country's high commission in London. Around this

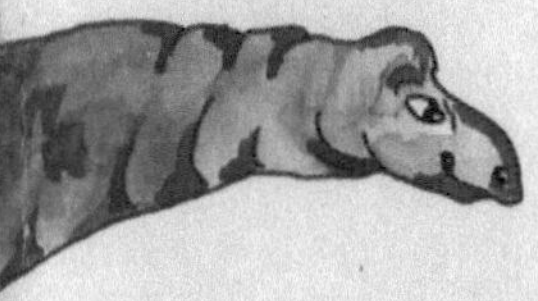

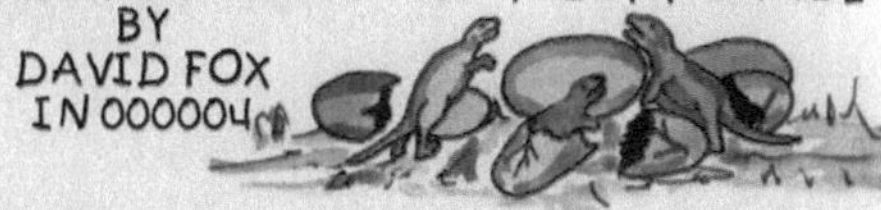

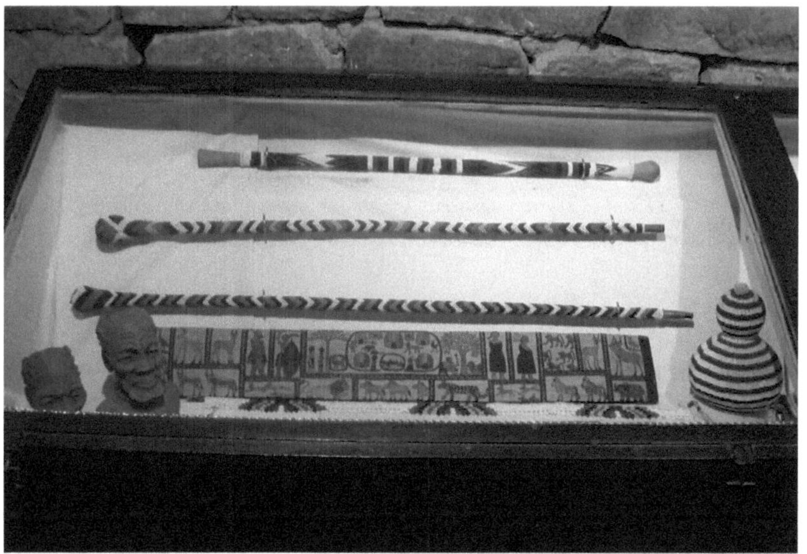

FIGURE 6.4 *top* David Fox, cover illustration for *Some Little Known Scientific Facts about Dinosaurs*, 2004.

FIGURE 6.5 *bottom* Display cabinet at David Fox's private museum at Fort Nottingham in the midlands of present-day KwaZulu-Natal, with beaded staffs, gourd, and waistband; two clay heads by Hezekiel Ntuli; and a pokerwork panel by Zizwezenyanga Qwabe. Photo courtesy of S. Klopper, March 20, 2010.

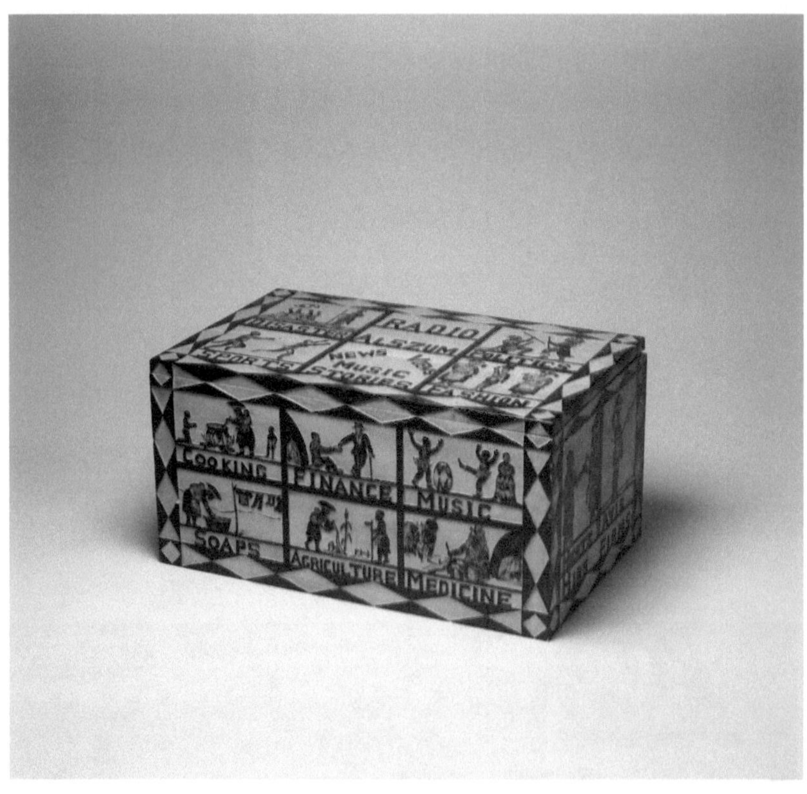

FIGURE 6.6 *Radio Alszum*, 1999. Trunk with pokerwork panels, metal hinge, and cassette player, 30 cm × 59.5 cm × 36.5 cm. Standard Bank Art Collection, Wits Art Galleries.

time, Zuma also started producing hinged trunks covered with pokerwork narrative panels (figures 6.6 and 6.7) into which he placed cassette tapes "broadcasting" absurdist accounts of the local news, weather, and traffic reports. Soon, listeners were also entertained by recordings of sometimes macabre anecdotes detailing encounters between people and wild animals. I argue that the gradual emergence of these comically disrespectful comments on the ignorance and folly of human beings were actively encouraged by Fox, and I also consider why humor appears to have played a major role in cementing their friendship. At the same time, I draw attention to the importance for Zuma's emerging vision of the political optimism that followed the release of Nelson Mandela and the unbanning in 1990 of the African National Congress. These momentous events afforded a platform for his increasingly anarchic

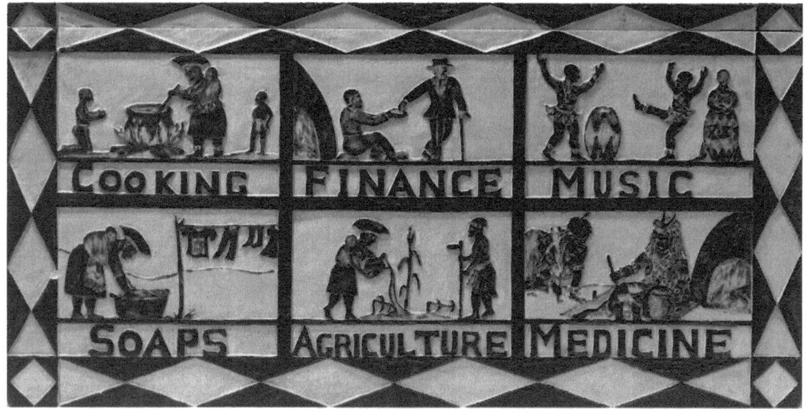

FIGURE 6.7 Front panel of *Radio Alszum*, 1999. Trunk with pokerwork panels, metal hinge, and cassette player, 30 cm × 59.5 cm × 36.5 cm. Standard Bank Art Collection, Wits Art Galleries.

irreverence, fueling his delight in producing socially disruptive images in which he poked fun at long-entrenched cultural traditions, widely accepted generational and gender hierarchies, and racial stereotypes. As Zuma readily acknowledges to this day, it was Fox, working tirelessly to promote his career both locally and abroad, who repeatedly inspired him to revise his subjects and rethink the formats in which he presented his work. The innovations generated by these interactions disappeared from Zuma's work following Fox's unexpected death in 2010, gradually giving way to the production of small-scale relief carvings and portable simulacra of Indigenous rock paintings.

"'Can't' Wasn't in His Dictionary"

David Fox came from a wealthy farming family in Lincolnshire.[8] When he was seventeen and still at school at Worksop College in Nottinghamshire, he convinced his father that he wanted to farm in Africa rather than England.[9] In 1947 the two traveled by flying boat to explore options that might appeal to Fox in east and southern Africa, but it was only when they got to Durban that David found what he was looking for, a sugarcane farm in the Gingindlovu area an hour north of this coastal city, where he settled after completing his schooling.[10] By then Durban had become an increasingly cosmopolitan shipping hub, having serviced allied fleets in the course of the Second World War. It also played an important role as a distribution center for the export of locally manufactured sugar to a rapidly expanding global market.[11] Once resident in South Africa, Fox returned annually to England and met his future wife Jean while attending the Agricultural Show at Smithfield in 1955.[12]

It was not until 1965, many years after he had immigrated to South Africa, that Fox bought his farm at Fort Nottingham where he would later meet Zuma. Here Fox established a successful stud farm and, freed from the time-consuming demands of managing sugarcane plantations, he involved himself in other activities that testify to his adventurous spirit. He founded the Natal Thoroughbred Breeders Club, and, in the early 1990s, he also contributed to the revival of Madagascar's horse racing industry. It is not clear whether Fox played a role in facilitating Madagascar's membership of the Southern African Development Corporation (SADC) in 1992, but until the coup of 2008 he served as Madagascar's self-styled consul general in South Africa. Until his death in 2010, he proudly identified himself as a "Chevalier de l'Ordre National de Madagascar" (Knight of the National Order of Madagascar) on his call cards and in some of his publications.

As an enthusiastic sportsman and amateur historian, at different stages of his life Fox participated in competitive sports and wrote credible accounts of various aspects of the history of KwaZulu-Natal. He was a keen fencer, took part in racing events at the Silverstone sports car circuit in England, and represented Natal (after 1994, KwaZulu-Natal) in show-jumping and polo.[13] In later life, he went on to establish the Fort Nottingham Highland Games, a popular celebration of Scottish traditions, which collapsed without the benefit of his driving enthusiasm four years after his death.[14] Along the way, he published *The History of Fort Nottingham 1856 to 2005* (2004), which he dedicated to "all past residents, all current residents, all future residents, and all the resident ghosts," offering the Freedom of the City of Fort Nottingham—a hamlet with five homesteads—to anyone willing to contribute a small sum for replacing the floor in the village hall. Encouraged by his interest in the history of the Anglo-Zulu War, he also wrote a polemical article on the engraved horns in his private museum, in which he challenged the scholarship of established academics.[15]

The Birth of Alszum

Born in 1968, Zuma completed his primary education near his home in the Fort Nottingham area of present-day KwaZulu-Natal. He first met Fox in 1985 when he ran away from the boarding school he attended in his early teens, later citing physical abuse at the hands of senior boys for his decision to return to the

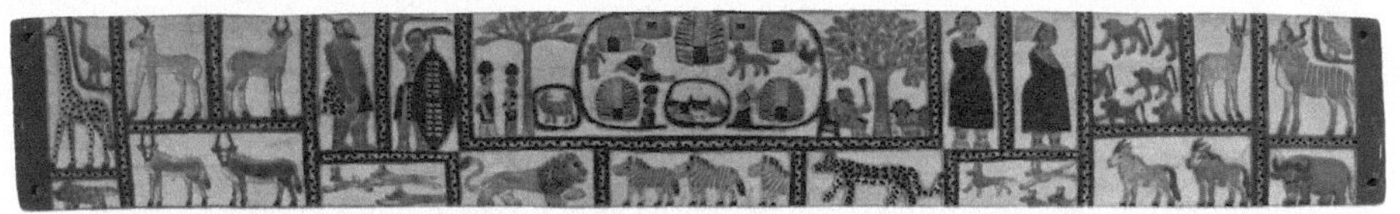

FIGURE 6.8 *top* Zizwezenyanga Qwabe pokerwork panel, late 1940s. 11 cm × 80 cm. Formerly in the collection of David Fox. Courtesy of Axis Gallery, New York and New Jersey.

FIGURE 6.9 *bottom* Copy of pokerwork panel by Zizwezenyanga Qwabe, c. 1990. 11 cm × 80 cm. By Alson Zuma. Formerly in the collection of David Fox. Courtesy of Axis Gallery, New York and New Jersey.

Midlands. While working for Fox as a stable hand, Zuma continued to pursue his childhood love of sketching whenever he had access to paper, deciding along the way to register for correspondence courses to complete his secondary school studies.[16] According to him it was by chance that his new employer saw his sketches of horses. Fox initially assumed that they had been traced from books, but after watching Zuma sketch, he told the stable hand that he had tremendous talent and the potential to be a successful artist.[17] Fox then bought Zuma some books on his favorite subject—animals—and Zuma subsequently joined the local community library. While studying illustrations to improve his skills in shading and foreshortening, in animating his figures, and in creating illusionistic depth in landscape settings, he adopted the portmanteau Alszum to sign his works, only reverting to the use A. Zuma in 2011, shortly after Fox died.

Impressed by Zuma's tenacity and growing facility, Fox intervened again. As Zuma informed a reporter in the early 1990s, "One day David brought me a carving and asked me if I could copy it. Well, I did my best and when I showed the finished product to David he told me that it was actually better than the original" (figures 6.8 and 6.9). In Fox's account of this intervention, he described his protégé's success as a fairy tale: "There are many original black artists . . . but I knew that Alszum had something that was different." He added, "Then, one day, I showed him a carving I'd bought from an old, old chap on a trip to Zululand. I asked Alson if he could do the same . . . carve something. I was thinking along the lines of the tourist market for him. He said he could."[18] When Fox saw Zuma's penknife version of the Qwabe panel housed in his private museum at Fort Nottingham, he bought his stable assistant a set of woodworking tools. Fox also discovered that carving on jelutong wood would make it easier for Zuma to complete complex narratives on an increasingly monumental scale because of its low density and uniform texture.[19] In the course of 1989, he encouraged Zuma to stop tending to horses during the day so that he could carve while looking after foaling mares at night, moving him into a makeshift studio next to their stables.

Fox initially tried to sell Zuma's burnished carvings at craft fairs, traveling to urban centers such as the Bryanston Organic and Natural Market in Johannesburg. Efforts like these met with some success, but it was only after a series of unanticipated coincidences that Zuma's career began to take off. This train of events was set in motion when the veterinarian who attended to Fox's thoroughbreds bought one of Zuma's relief panels of horses, their trainers, and riders, which he displayed at his practice in Summerveld, northwest of Durban.[20] One of his clients, Norma Rattray, was so impressed by the panel that she and her husband decided to commission Zuma to produce a series of wildlife reliefs for their exclusive Mala Mala Game Lodge in Mpumalanga province.[21] In the early 1990s, when the acclaimed designer Trish Wilson visited the lodge while overseeing the decoration of the Lost City Palace Hotel at Sun City—a major casino complex northwest of Johannesburg—she was so taken by Zuma's Mala Mala panels (figure 6.1) that she contacted David Fox. Her decision culminated in a major commission at Sun City focusing on the theme of African wildlife, which were installed at the Lost Palace Hotel in July 1992. It took Zuma four months to complete these burnished reliefs.

Qwabe's Impact on Zuma's Work

David Fox had bought the relief carving he later asked Zuma to copy while on a trip to Nongoma, two hours north of his farm near Gingindlovu, in the late 1940s. The artist Zizwezenyanga Qwabe had been carving figurative mat racks for local Zulu clients for at least three decades, eventually developing increasingly complex horizontal panels of idyllic rural scenes for a lucrative external market. Zuma has on several occasions acknowledged his debt to the Qwabe panel in Fox's collection, pointing to the importance for the development of his own relief carvings of Qwabe's practice of compartmentalizing stock narratives of rural life and various wildlife species by surrounding them with burnished frames.[22] Initially Zuma was inspired by some of the figures and scenes populating the older artist's works, including Qwabe's depiction of a Zulu king seated under a tree engaging some of his subjects and the day-to-day tasks occupying women in and around rural Zulu homesteads.[23] He has also repeatedly referenced Fox's Qwabe panel in other ways, most recently by self-consciously incorporating a copy of the Qwabe panel as a central motif in much larger compositions, although he turned motifs he found difficult to decipher, such as three quadrupeds to the bottom left of Qwabe's panel, into a scene of dogs chasing a rabbit.[24] Other departures were inspired by the specialist encyclopedias he found in the community library at Nottingham Road. His own panels include animals never found in the older artist's work, among them a rhinoceros, a bush pig, a porcupine, an aardvark, and a tortoise. Working on an increasingly monumental scale, Zuma also produced detailed illusionistic landscape settings, often animating his scenes by alluding to the social habits of lions and other animals. An early indication of his delight in indulging the playful sense of humor that eventually became a hallmark of his art was his frequent addition of an image of two baboons kissing. Whenever Zuma drew attention to this detail he always laughed indulgently at the absurdity of ascribing human agency and emotions to animals.

Ultimately, though, Zuma departed radically from Qwabe's work. Obvious differences include the fact that working on jelutong wood allowed him to produce monumental tableaux. Moreover, whereas Qwabe always burnished his comparatively small panels before carving into them, Zuma burnishes panels only after having completed his reliefs. Most importantly, unlike Qwabe, who appears to have been illiterate, Zuma has not only a sophisticated command of both English and Zulu but an abiding fascination with social media. He regales his friends with jokes and tales of the absurd antics of real and imaginary people, many of which he sources on Zulu language Facebook sites. Doing so seems, at times, to afford the artist a way of deflecting attention from challenging emotional situations, bringing to mind studies on the role of humor in fostering mental health and as a mechanism for coping with stressful situations.[25] On one occasion, shortly after Fox's death, while discussing his relationship with his former employer in the makeshift gallery at Fort Nottingham where he continued to sell his work, Zuma suddenly decided to demonstrate the ridiculous actions of a man who raised his foot to a chair to tie his shoelaces, but instead of doing so, bent down to tie the laces on

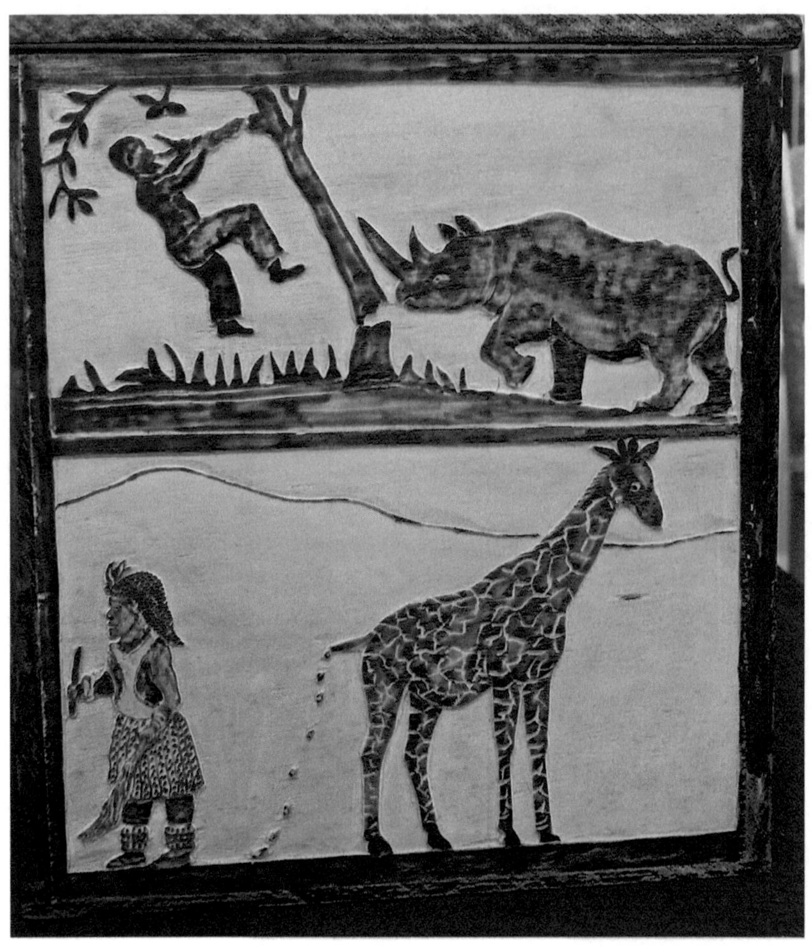

FIGURE 6.10 Side panel from *Alson Zuma's African Animals*. Trunk with poker-work panels, hinges, and printed text, 28 cm × 43 cm. By Alson Zuma. Standard Bank Art Collection, Wits Art Galleries.

his other foot. He also repeatedly interrupted our conversation to draw attention to examples of human and animal stupidity in his pokerwork reliefs — a dinosaur trapped on a precipitous ledge that, he told me, would soon be transformed into a fossil; a diviner who keeps docking the tail of a giraffe in the erroneous belief that the switches carried by members of her profession are made from the tail hairs of this animal rather than those of buffaloes (figure 6.10); and a tourist who had been duped into believing that a dog covered in a leopard skin was the real thing (figure 6.11).

New (Con)Texts

Throughout much of the twentieth century, European and American artists have repeatedly used words in conjunction with visual images. As Russell Bowman points out, the works of these modernists are "united by the fact that the words serve to increase the image's potential for meaning. Whether the words underline and reinforce the image, essentially become the image, or contradict the image to achieve a telling ambiguity, the combination of the visual image with the visual sign system we know as language always creates a compelling resonance."[26] Zuma is not familiar with these modernist traditions, possibly because of the dearth of books on art at his local village library, but he clearly shares the delight many twentieth-century artists have shown in contrasting texts and images through the addition of titles or inscriptions, sometimes forcing a reconsideration of the meaning of words or drawing attention to the potential for multivalent associations through seemingly incongruous juxtapositions.

This attraction to playful communication dates to Zuma's childhood when he started taking apart and rebuilding electrical appliances, including vacuum cleaners and irons, before turning his attention to radios. As a teenager, he discovered that he could interfere with the frequency of the radio stations people listened to at the home of his girlfriend's parents, thereby allowing him to alert her to the fact that he was waiting nearby. This later gave way to an interest in listening to the conversations of policemen traveling to crime scenes in the rural Midlands and eavesdropping on the interactions between long distance truck drivers on the highway between Durban and Johannesburg. Experiments like these eventually led to the construction of two-way radios to communicate with long-haul travelers. According to Zuma, it was this obsession with building radios that led Fox to suggest that he should think of making a series of carved wooden trunks with taped soundtracks read by the artist hidden inside them. Responding readily to this idea, Zuma produced his Radio Alszum trunks, all of which have internal speakers projecting quirky, satirical narratives related to the relief carvings on the outside surfaces. The earliest of these wooden boxes contained individually built tape recorders while later examples contained small, commercially available boom boxes.

In Alszum's radios, the voice-over texts often subvert the carved images, thereby radically reframing the seemingly bucolic, stereotypical scenes of daily life among rural Zulu traditionalists. One of the trunks now in the collection of the University of the Witwatersrand has scenes labeled "Cooking,"

"Finance," "Music," "Soaps," "Agriculture," and "Medicine," all of which depict people in rural settings that are reframed through Zuma's radio voice-overs (figure 6.3 and figure 6.6). Thus, for example, on the subject of medicine, his radio reports that "the village is very fortunate to have Mrs. Bongani as the village witch doctor. Everybody is very polite to Mrs. Bongani. Mr. Phinios Dube was not very nice to her, but we have not seen him for some time now. The frog which sits outside Mr. Dube's hut might have some connection with his disappearance." Elsewhere Zuma introduces his audience to stars, commenting that "Mr. William Jobe saw plenty of stars when he was caught with Mrs. Ngema by Mr. Ngema who returned unexpectedly from the next village. Mr. Jobe's horoscope for the day read 'avoid situations where you may get hit on the head.'"

Zuma's hinged animal trunks are similarly subversive, but by the time he decided to produce voice-overs on this subject, he had abandoned his earlier habit of adding texts to his relief carvings. Instead, these trunks rely entirely on comments emanating from the concealed speakers to contextualize his narratives. In one example, in which he draws attention to a man killed by a leopard, Zuma informs his audience that "these are about as dangerous as lions. They have an annoying habit of dropping out of trees onto peoples' heads. If they do this to you, even if you are wearing a hat, it will not save you from being chomped up. Why the Zulu people chose leopard skins many years ago as their royal national form of dress we cannot understand. Life would have been much safer for them if they had chosen to wear rabbit skins." Fascinated by baboons, always focusing on their near-human qualities, he tells the listener that "all of Mrs. Cele's bloomers were stolen off the washing line last week, although Mrs. Cele thinks that Mr. Mtetwa may have known more than he is saying about this. The women in the village are frightened to work in the fields as the Baboons creep up behind them and lift their skirts. Mr. Mtetwa also does this sometimes" (figure 6.11).

As his art developed, Zuma lost interest in the exotic touristic appeal of Africa evidenced in the large relief panels he had earlier produced for local and international clients, contemporary Zulu politicians, and the Zulu royal family. In stark contrast to these works, the radio and animal trunks are relentlessly uncompromising in their satirical vision of contemporary South Africa.[27] But their power also lies in the fact that they mask conceptual ruptures through a reliance on long-established formal techniques associated with African craft traditions. In so doing, they invariably succeed in catching

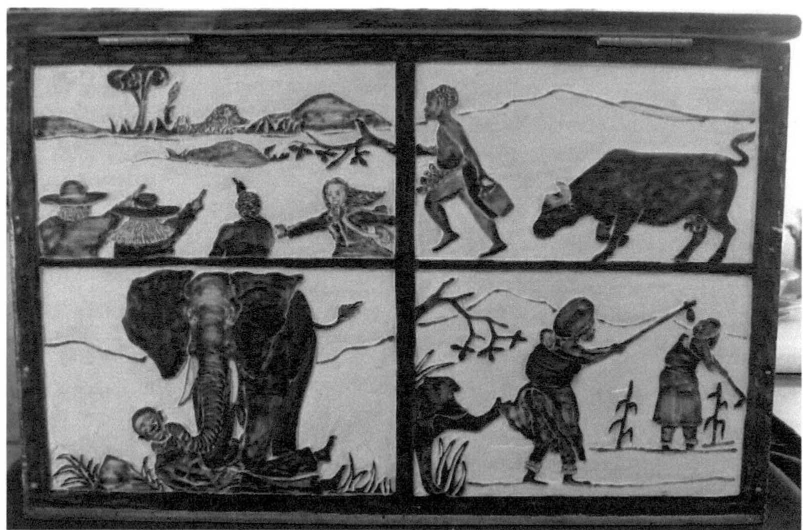

FIGURE 6.11 Side panel from *Alson Zuma's African Animals*. Trunk with poker-work panels, hinges, and printed text, 28 cm × 43 cm. By Alson Zuma. Standard Bank Art Collection, Wits Art Galleries.

the viewer off guard. Van Roebbroeck, who has described Zuma's radio trunk in the Wits Art Galleries as performative and interactive, points out that this work brings to mind Derrida's observation that "while meaning is bounded by context, context is boundless and inexhaustible."[28] David Fox, whose admiration for Zuma's capacities of invention grew over time, was clearly fascinated by this "resolute indeterminacy," which eventually encouraged him to revive his own amateur interest in art.

Bonding through Humor

It seems likely that Zuma's early interest in dinosaurs provided the springboard for *Some Little Known Scientific Facts about Dinosaurs*, the 2004 illustrated text Fox created and dedicated to his granddaughter. Obviously aimed at children, the book's sketches are accompanied by short, nonsensical statements such as: "Most dinosaurs were cross eyed. Not many people know this"; "Some diplodocus weighed 80 tonnes. Care should be taken to make sure they don't step on your toes"; and "Dinosaurs like other dinosaurs, especially at mealtimes." The book also includes a page with an unpopulated landscape, captioned "This dinosaur is very rare and has not yet been recorded." Fox concluded his book with the observation: "You now know as much about dinosaurs as I do."[29]

Zuma no longer remembers which of the ideas he helped to generate for the images and texts included in Fox's *Some Little Known Scientific Facts about Dinosaurs*, but shortly after Fox's death he reproduced some of his former friend's sketches on one of his hinged trunks. He included the dinosaur that was doomed to become extinct after getting trapped on a ledge, which Fox had described as "a young ornithosuchus who managed to get herself with her left side up against a cliff. As she is unable to turn to the right she will probably become a fossil." Two further images used for this dinosaur trunk appeared as consecutive images in the book, the first of which Fox had described as "a megalorarus at bay, being attacked by a heard of hungry hedgehogs" and the second as "a repleated [*sic*] megalosarus resting after having eaten a herd of stupid hedgehogs." After adding copies of these two images — one above the other — on his dinosaur trunk, Zuma took the liberty of including landscape details behind the sated dinosaur reclining against a tree, effectively changing Fox's two-dimensional sketch into an illusionistic three-dimensional scene.

With hindsight, it seems clear that Fox and Zuma's shared appreciation of the absurd ultimately sustained their relationship and cemented their unshakable trust in, and acceptance of, each other. Both delighted in suspending common logic and in celebrating comical situations. Doing so seems to have helped them transcend the structural inequalities of culture, race, and class that might otherwise have prevented them from working together as successfully as they did for more than twenty years. Although both were oblivious to the modernist (and postmodernist) fascination with the volatility of language, their collaborative interactions repeatedly reignited Zuma's anarchic take on life, eventually leading to the production of works that bring to mind the Bakhtinian notion of the carnivalesque in which alternative rules are constructed, thereby challenging the status quo by inverting rather than simply suspending established hierarchies.[30] For Bakhtin, the importance of carnival lay, most obviously, in the fact that it encouraged misalliances between the sacred and the profane and the already established, or high, and the still insignificant, or low. Much the same can be said for some of Zuma's later works, especially his hinged radio trunks, in which widely held assumptions about the relationship between culture and nature become so scrambled that the viewer has little choice but to abandon all preconceived notions regarding the nature of reality.

Zulu Encounters

Had it not been for Fox's inspired idea to encourage Zuma to produce hinged trunks projecting farcical news broadcasts from self-made boom boxes, it is unlikely that his career would have led to the purchase of his works by museum directors and private collectors in the mainstream art world, many of whom clearly responded to Zuma's intuitively modernist obsession with ridiculing the power of authoritative sources through absurdist humor. Like many Dadaists in the lead-up to the First World War, he has repeatedly sought to undermine established voices of authority and control by celebrating incongruity in his juxtaposition of images and texts.

Fox's important intervention went hand in hand with the impact on Zuma of the emergence of democratic governance in South Africa in the early 1990s, which afforded new opportunities for questioning the political status quo, including the far-reaching hold of patriarchy and traditionalism on the lives of both rural and urban Zulu-speaking communities. Drawing mainly on Zulu-language social media sites that challenge long-held cultural and other assumptions, Zuma was catapulted into a world that offered alternative views on negotiating identity politics in contemporary South Africa. Although not related to former South African president Jacob Zuma, he read a biography on his namesake and proudly points out that they both have prominent gaps between their two front teeth.[31] He also indicated in one of many conversations that he likes to draw Zulu people "because I know what they look like."[32] But unlike Jacob Zuma's supporters who in 2008 celebrated the future president's impending appointment as president of the African National Congress by wearing T-shirts with the slogan "100% Zuluboy," he does not support Zulu ethnic nationalism, noting on one occasion that "to be Zulu is not so important. There are other people."[33]

These views on the status of Zulu speakers and their political leaders might not have survived had Fox succeeded in realizing one of his earliest efforts to promote Zuma's works by appealing, intermittently, to members of the Zulu elite to support a large-scale burnished relief project on Zulu history. After Zuma and Fox returned from a visit to the regional legislature in Ulundi in the heartland of the former Zulu kingdom in the early 1990s, Fox received a letter from the then chief minister of KwaZulu, Mangothuthu Buthelezi, thanking him for a gift of two carved panels. Taking his cue from Fox, Buthelezi also expressed the hope that "Alson Zuma can one day use his skill for a building in which he is given the opportunity to portray Zulu history. I feel certain that this will happen."[34] In another letter addressed to Zuma in isiZulu, Buthelezi thanked the artist for the gift he had received, adding: "I wish you a long life in order that you may decorate your Zulu nation and the whole land of South Africa with your great skills."

Already in the nineteenth century, successive Zulu kings had actively supported various art forms, including music and dance. In the early twentieth century, Zulu modernists like Zizwezenyanga Qwabe and peers such as Abenigo Zulu also benefited from this long history of patronage, selling work to various members of the Zulu elite.[35] In a short article on these carvers, the American suffragist Rebecca Reyher, who visited Zululand in the mid-1920s and again in 1934 following the death of Zulu king Solomon, noted: "The Zulu Regent[36] proudly displayed one of [Abenigo Zulu's] sticks on his rondavel wall, where it attracted much admiration during the Ihlambo, the cleansing ceremonies for the late Zulu King Solomon."[37] Zuma sold numerous relief carvings to recently deceased Zulu king Goodwill Zwelethini, producing a portrait image of him along with various scenes of ritual practices and other activities at his royal homestead Enyokeni, not far from Ulundi. He also sold work on Zulu subjects at the opening of the regional parliament at Ulundi in 1992. But less than a year later, he abandoned history for humor, turning to the subject of dinosaurs. When I questioned him on this sudden shift in focus, his response was, quite simply: "I go to the library on Saturdays. I read all those books. That's where I get the ideas."[38]

Conclusion

Despite the fact that Fox and Zuma came from radically different backgrounds, they clearly respected and admired each other, on different occasions providing uncannily similar narratives of significant incidents and decisions related to Zuma's career. In conversation, Fox repeatedly marveled at Zuma's quirky energy and sense of curiosity, especially his unfailing interest in taking apart electrical appliances before reassembling them. After Fox's death in 2010, Zuma commented readily on his experience of loss and his loneliness following the unexpected passing of his friend and mentor. He also seemed uncertain about his future options and, in an effort to fill the gap left by Fox's absence, agreed to take over as custodian of the Fort Nottingham Museum, located directly opposite the building where he continues to produce and sell works to the intermittent tourists who make the effort to visit the village. Finding it difficult to access supplies of the jelutong wood that Fox had bought for him in Pinetown, a more than two hour drive from Fort Nottingham, Zuma eventually decided to emulate rock art paintings in the tradition of the San communities whose exploits as cattle raiders were commemorated in David Fox's museum.

Although a far cry from the richly resonant modernist works he had been making, these small, portable pieces are more complicated than might be apparent at first sight. Bursting into peals of laughter before picking up a book lying on the table in his gallery-cum-studio, Zuma once informed me: "I am a real Bushman painter," before showing me a photograph by a well-known South African rock art specialist. According to Zuma, the author had at some stage photographed one of his own paintings in the hills near Fort Nottingham, incorrectly ascribing it to a San rock art site in the eastern Cape.[39] Momentarily caught off guard by this claim, I remembered that Zuma, the "San" artist, had at one stage worn a kilt and adopted the pseudonym MacAlson MacZuma while actively involved in assisting Fox with the Fort Nottingham Highland Games. For a period in the early 1990s, he also became a vegetarian Rastafarian before declaring himself the poet laureate of Fort Nottingham and, in the process, bringing tears to the eyes of village elders.

Zuma will probably never abandon the mischievous joy of assuming new identities. By repeatedly reaffirming his commitment to uncertainty, he has also found a way to pay homage to Fox who in 2005 organized a ceremony to coincide with the 150th anniversary of the establishment of Fort Nottingham, at which he arranged for the British defense adviser, Brigadier David Keenan, to end the undeclared "war" between white settlers and the San by shaking hands with the last surviving member of the mountain San community Mr. Kerrick Ntusi. Fox's history of Fort Nottingham had been published to coincide with this event.

Notes

I am very grateful to Zuma for providing me with transcriptions for the texts he wrote to accompany the carved reliefs on the hinged trunks he started producing in the late 1990s. Some of these texts are quoted at various points in this chapter.

1. Oprah Winfrey commissioned several monumental panels from Zuma, now on display in the dining hall of her Leadership Academy for Girls, which she founded at Henley on Klip, south of Johannesburg, in 2007.

2. Any South African would immediately recognize this reference to Lucky Star Pilchards in Tomato Sauce, a widely valued, inexpensive source of canned protein consumed locally by at least three million people on a daily basis.

3. This is from a cutting in Alson Zuma's scrapbook. At some stage, Zuma started putting together an album of newspaper and magazine articles, together with letters and other memorabilia, including photographs of his work, which he keeps in his makeshift studio. Some of the cuttings unfortunately lack dates and other potentially useful details such as the source of the articles.

4. The Natal Technikon merged with the ML Sultan Technikon in 2002, after which it was renamed the Durban University of Technology.

5. Johnson, "A Confusing Look at Folk Art and American Modernism."

6. I first met Zuma when looking for works by the early Zulu modernist carver Zizwezenyanga Qwabe. For my research on Qwabe, see Klopper, "Reinventing Zulu Tradition."

7. For the most reliable available account of the career of Ntuli, see Miles, *Land and Lives.*

8. The obituaries that were published after Fox's death include inaccurate assumptions about his life history. One went so far as to claim that "David Fox was raised in Zululand" where "he (like many of us in KwaZulu-Natal) grew up to know and respect the Zulu people." Post to "Obituary David Glynn Fox," RDVC.com Forums, January 2, 2011, http://www.rorkesdriftvc.com/forum/viewtopic.php?p=22705&sid=98d93de5ce46e5f47af96e2590d3b503. This claim is surprising, not least because Fox's English accent was distinctly British. The quote in the subheading for this section comes from a comment by David Fox's daughter, Louise, when I interviewed her and Fox's widow, Jean, on November 6, 2016. Her exact words then were as follows: "Daddy was always in the right place at the right time. And, if it wasn't, he made it so. I don't think 'can't' was in his dictionary."

9. I regret the fact that when I first met Fox in 2008, little more than two years before he died, I didn't have the foresight to engage him on what led to his decision to settle in South Africa in the late 1940s. Because at that stage I was focused on gathering information on the early Zulu modernist Zizwezenyanga Qwabe, it never occurred to me that Fox's personal history might become relevant to my subsequent interest in making sense of Alson Zuma's meteoric rise to fame in the early 1990s. Fox and I spoke at length on three occasions before his death in December 2010. On each of these occasions, I explored his role in Zuma's success, but at that stage I had not yet formulated a clear understanding of some of the questions related to his relationship with Zuma that I now wish I might have asked him. Sadly, but understandably, neither his wife Jean nor his daughter Louise have been able to provide answers to many of these questions. Looking back, and remembering our warm connection and Fox's heartfelt appreciation of my interest in the extraordinary history of his friendship with Zuma, I can only hope that, had he survived the heart attack that led to his death, he would have taken pleasure in my efforts to make sense of this history.

10. The BOAC flying boats service to South Africa traveled via Cairo, Khartoum, and Nairobi to Durban. This service was discontinued in November 1950. Watson, "JAH," 154.

11. Lewis, "The South African Sugar Industry."

12. Originally founded in 1799, from 1949 until it was discontinued in 2004, this major livestock show was held at the Earl's Court Exhibition Centre in London.

13. "Horse Sense. David Fox," *Sunday Tribune*, January 2, 2011.

14. The Games were revived through the initiative of Fox's daughter, Louise, in 2022.

15. Fox, "Zulu Art or Sailors' Scrimshaw?"

16. Zuma ascribes his early interest in drawing to his mother, who, although not well-educated, worked at a rural school. He remembers as a young child being impressed by some of her drawings, presumably used as aids in her classroom.

17. This information comes from an interview by Gugu Marawa, "Alson, from Herdsman to Successful Artist," *Thandi*, June 1993. The article is one of many preserved in Zuma's scrapbook documenting his career but lacking publishing details, such as page numbers.

18. Mitchell, "Treasure in the Lost City."

19. This is a tree species in the oleander family that grows in Malaysia, Borneo, Sumatra, and southern Thailand.

20. Dr. Brian Baker founded the now internationally renowned Baker McVeigh Equine Clinics in present-day KwaZulu-Natal in 1963.

21. I am very grateful to the staff at Mala Mala for their gracious hospitality and assistance when I visited Mala Mala with my friend Barbara Buntman, who helped me to document the panels on November 13, 2017.

22. Partly prompted by my interest in how his own works differ from the Qwabe relief, Zuma has repeatedly discussed the Qwabe panel with me. He was interviewed on this subject by me and by Lisa Brittan, who, with her partner, Gary van Wyk, traveled with me in mid-2011 to Fort Nottingham, where they bought both the original Qwabe panel and the first copy Zuma made of this panel.

23. A gathering of this kind, historically called by a king or high-ranking traditional leader, was known as an *imbizo*. In South Africa, this meaning has since been expanded and is now often used to refer to political rallies and important meetings involving people who have no connection to the Zulu royal family or any other Zulu-speaking dignitaries.

24. Zuma's interest in quoting Qwabe seems to have been renewed through his interactions with me during my several visits to Fort Nottingham over a period of close to 10 years.

25. Samson et al., "Humorous Coping and Serious Reappraisal."

26. Bowman, "Words and Images."

27. Zuma was fascinated by the self-styled Zulu savant and traditional healer Credo Mutwa, who recorded folktales from his childhood. Mutwa, *Indaba, My Children*. This book was first published in South Africa in 1964.

28. Van Roebbroeck, "Alson Zuma," 128. Although the Wits Art Galleries bought one of Zuma's early hinged trunks, almost nothing was known about him in the

mainstream South African art world at the time of this publication. I am indebted to Yvonne Winters, former director of the Killie Campbell Library in Durban, for suggesting that I travel to Fort Nottingham to view the burnished panel by Zizwezenyanga Qwabe in David Fox's collection. As I remember, she also alerted me to the fact that Alson Zuma worked in the village. Because Winters has since died, I have not been able verify my memory of my conversation with her sometime in 2008.

29. Fox, *Some Little Known Scientific Facts about Dinosaurs*. The pages in Fox's self-published book are not numbered.

30. Docker, *Postmodernism and Popular Culture*, 284.

31. When Zuma and I visited the library at Nottingham Road in 2011, he drew my attention to the library's copy of an unflattering biography on Jacob Zuma that he said he had read soon after it was published, finding it very instructive. Gordin, *Zuma*.

32. Conversation with Zuma during the annual Highland Games at Fort Nottingham on May 21, 2010.

33. Zuma, interview with the author, 2011.

34. This letter, dating to December 10, 1992, and other related correspondence from Buthelezi to Zuma (written in isiZulu), is preserved in the scrapbook Zuma started putting together in the early 1990s on different aspects of his career.

35. Referring to a visit to Zululand in the 1950s, Katesa Schlosser mentioned in an article dating to 1975 that Qwabe was known to the "present Paramount Chief Cyprian Bhekuzulu ka Solomon and his wife." Schlosser, "Bantukunstler in Sudafrika." Working from translations I commissioned from Claudia Ringelmann, German Department, University of Pretoria, South Africa, I am unable to provide the exact page number for this quotation.

36. Following King Solomon kaDinuzulu's death in 1933, Chief Mshiyeni was appointed regent pending the coming of age of Cyprian Bkekuzulu in 1948.

37. It is not clear when or where Reyher's newspaper article on Qwabe and his circle was published. A copy was lodged in News Cuttings Book 9 at the Killie Campbell Library in Durban with the date "17.4.37" added at the top. This might be a reference either to the date of publication or the date on which the article was received by the library. The article seems to have been written following Reyher's return to the United States sometime after her second visit to South Africa in 1934.

38. Conversation with Zuma during the annual Highland Games at Fort Nottingham on May 21, 2010.

39. Woodhouse, *Bushman Art of Southern Africa*. This book includes a photograph of a rock-art site in the eastern Cape, far from Fort Nottingham, which appears to have been defaced by someone scratching the name *Alson* over part of a painting of two Eland.

Bibliography

Bowman, Russell. "Words and Images: A Persistent Paradox." *Art Journal* 45, no. 4 (1985): 335–43.

Docker, John. *Postmodernism and Popular Culture: A Cultural History*. Cambridge: Cambridge University Press, 1994.

Fox, David. *Some Little Known Scientific Facts about Dinosaurs. Observed and Recorded on Fort Nottingham Commonage by David Fox in 000004*. Self-published, n.d.

Fox, J. David. "Zulu Art or Sailors' Scrimshaw? The Decorated 'Zulu' Horns of the Anglo-Zulu War, 1879." *Military History Journal* 13, no. 4 (December 2005): 136–41.

Gordin, Jeremy. *Zuma: A Biography*. Cape Town: Jonathan Ball, 2009.

Johnson, Ken. "A Confusing Look at Folk Art and American Modernism." *New York Times*, July 30, 2015. https://www.nytimes.com/2015/07/31/arts/design/a-confusing-look-at-folk-art-and-american-modernism.html.

Klopper, Sandra. "Reinventing Zulu Tradition: The Modernism of Zizwezenyanga Qwabe's Figurative Relief Panels." In *Mapping Modernisms: Indigenous and Colonial Networks of Artistic Exchange and the Dialectics of Discourse*, edited by Elizabeth Harney and Ruth Philips, 33–62. Durham, NC: Duke University Press, 2018.

Lewis, Colin A. "The South African Sugar Industry." *Geographical Journal* 156, no. 1 (March 1990): 70–78.

Miles, Elza. *Land and Lives: A Story of Early Black Artists*. Cape Town: Human and Rousseau, 1997.

Mitchell, Colin. "Treasure in the Lost City." *Pace*, November 1992, 93–95.

Mutwa, Vusamazulu Credo. *Indaba, My Children: African Tribal History, Legends, Customs and Religious Beliefs*. Edinburgh: Canongate, 2001. First published in 1964 by Blue Crane Books.

Samson, Andrea C., Alana L. Glassco, Ihno A. Lee, and James J. Gross. "Humorous Coping and Serious Reappraisal: Short-Term and Longer-Term Effects." *Europe's Journal of Psychology* 10, no. 3 (2014): 571–81. https://doi.org/10.5964/ejop.v10i3.730.

Schlosser, Katesa. "Bantukunstler in Sudafrika." *Zeitschrift für Ethnologie* 100, nos. 1–2 (1975): 38–98.

van Roebbroeck, Lize. "Alson Zuma." In *Voice-Overs: Wits Writings Exploring African Artworks*, edited by Anitra C. Nettleton, Julia Charlton, and Fiona Rankin-Smith, 128–29. Johannesburg: University of the Witwatersrand Art Galleries, 2004.

Watson, Captain Darce. "JAH: British Overseas Airways Corporation 1940–1950 and Its Legacy." *Journal of Aeronautical History* (May 2013): 136–61.

Woodhouse, Bert. *Bushman Art of Southern Africa: 40 Significant Bushman Rock-Art Sites*. Cape Town: Art Publishers, 1993.

PETER BRUNT

7 THE PAINTER, THE PHOTOGRAPHER, AND THE TATTOOIST

Friendship and Decolonization in Aotearoa New Zealand

In an essay entitled "Together/Apart," Christina Barton compares two seemingly incommensurable art worlds in Aotearoa New Zealand in the 1970s, exemplified by two cultural events in 1976, each laying claim to different constructions of the term *Pacific*. The first was the staging of the first *Pan-Pacific Biennale* at the Auckland Art Gallery, an exhibition that featured vanguard artists from around the Pacific Rim—Auckland, Sydney, Melbourne, Tokyo, Los Angeles, and San Francisco—all experimenting with new photographic media. Intended to examine such practices in the context of conceptualism and the invention of new reproductive technologies, the exhibition marked the eclipse of painting—which had dominated New Zealand art since the 1930s—as the privileged medium of settler modernism and the attempt of emerging artists to re-imagine their place in a new "global age." Barton describes an array of symptomatic developments—social, technological, economic, and geopolitical—pointing to that globalizing shift: "Advances in communications, transport, mass media and information technologies . . . the rapid growth of capitalism and changes in the shape and direction of global geopolitics . . . the oil shocks of 1973 and 1976 . . . when Britain joined the [European] Common Market, and France and America tested nuclear weapons in the Pacific." Not least among these developments were "new internal pressures" undermining the imagined coherence of the national community: a raft of emergent social groups—women, youth, gays, left-wing radicals, alternative lifestylers, and new non-European immigrants (especially from the Pacific Islands). Above all,

Māori, due to rapid population growth, urbanization, and economic advancement, were beginning to enjoy greater visibility, develop an articulate argument for the restitution of their land, and undertake vigorous steps toward cultural revival.[1]

The second event was the second iteration of the South Pacific Festival of Arts, a week-long gathering of artists of many kinds from across the Pacific Islands, hosted by Māori in Rotorua, New Zealand's famous cultural tourism town. Initiated by the South Pacific Commission and first staged in Suva, Fiji, in 1972, the festival was designed to be hosted at a different Pacific Island location every four years for the purpose of protecting and rejuvenating "traditional" Pacific arts as a bulwark against the homogenizing effects of modernization and as a counterpart to political decolonization across the region.

Barton's essay examines the way in which both "art worlds" responded to the geopolitics of globalization in the 1970s while deploying, albeit to different cultural and political ends, the tools of mass media and communication technologies. While the biennale used photographic media and "dispassionate" conceptual strategies to deflate the expressive subject and create links with metropolitan artists around the Pacific Rim, the festival used media technologies, marketing savvy, and artistic revivals "to 'stage authenticity' as a political act" of cultural decolonization within the vast Pacific Basin.[2] But their pairing also contrasts different institutional formations within different histories of art.

The Auckland Art Gallery was established in the late nineteenth century as a settler colonial institution devoted to the transplantation and local cultivation of the European fine art tradition. While its collecting and exhibiting activities over time variously focused on the local and the international, the historical and current, it operated within a broad narrative assumption, prevalent since the nineteenth century, that art is intrinsically historical. The *Pan Pacific Biennale* was undertaken in response to that imperative within the practice and discourse of contemporary art in the 1970s, embracing new media and modes of art-making and new geographies of a globalizing art world. The festival, on the other hand, while also born of historical imperatives, was a postcolonial (rather than postmodernist) institution, drawing together an array of art traditions whose histories in modernity, with only recent exceptions, lay in contexts categorically apart from art galleries, such as tribal lands and villages, churches, craft industries, hotels, tourist enterprises, and ethnographic museums.[3] Were these events indicative of incommensurable art worlds in the 1970s, or were artists from both sides already bridging the differences between them? From a contemporary perspective, their seeming incommensurability is perplexing — at best, a moment of transition. For nothing characterizes the recent history of art in Aotearoa New Zealand more than the formal and conceptual energies of Māori and Pacific art *within* the contemporary art world — not only nationally but also regionally and globally. As a moment, however, the juxtaposition reveals a last blind spot, not only of a dying modernism but of its institutional counterparts in the art galleries, magazines, curators, and critics that constituted New Zealand's professionalized art world. Referring to a different context at the ideological beginnings of modernism in the early twentieth century, Simon Gikandi describes this blind spot as modernism's failure or inability, with rare exceptions, to engage seriously with the bodies and cultural practices of those it deemed "other" or "primitive."[4] It was this lingering blind spot that still occluded the contemporary New Zealand art world in the 1970s. This chapter aims to reexamine the conjunction of these two art worlds in the 1970s but at a different, more intimate, scale. Not through the institutional politics of biennales and festivals but as exemplified in a friendship — and *as* friendship — between three artists who attempted to cross the divide that separated them, to "jump the fence," as one of them put it in describing the origins of their relationship.[5]

One Sunday in May 1978, two Pākehā New Zealanders, photographer Mark Adams and painter Tony Fomison, drove from central Auckland to the south Auckland suburb of Māngere to meet for the first time the Sāmoan tattooist, or *tufuga tatatau*, Sulu'ape Paulo II. Adams wanted to ask the tufuga if he could photograph his practice. The impetus for this bold request came from the powerful effect of a photograph Adams had recently taken of a tattooed Sāmoan man, Mister Fiu Salati, standing matter-of-factly in his bedroom in an Auckland villa (figure 7.1). What struck Adams about the portrait was its unsettling ability to disturb and interrogate his own sense of place, time, and identity. The dissonance between the ordinariness of the room with its wallpaper of wreaths and crowns, and the presence of the man with his *pe'a* (a traditional male body tattoo from the waist to the bottom of the knees), elicited unsettling questions for Adams, as if the photograph had turned its gaze on him. "Is the man out of place in the room or is the room, with its banal wallpaper and imperial symbols, out of place here . . . in Polynesia? Where am I? Whose place is this?" he remembers asking himself. Similarly, the juxtaposition of the mundane modernity of the room and the connotations of the tattoo — "traditional," "ancient," "premodern" — seemed to unsettle the temporal and ideological assumptions on which such stereotypical oppositions rested. Adams knew next to nothing about Sāmoan tattooing at the

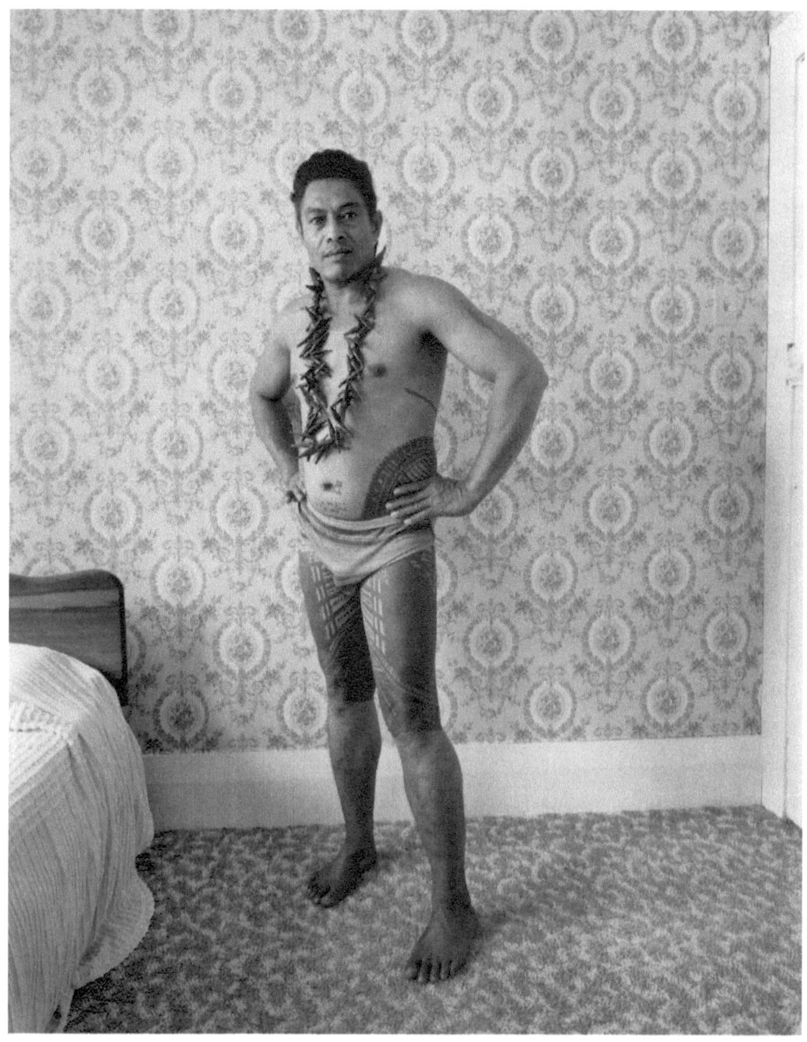

FIGURE 7.1 Mr. Salati Fiu, tufuga tatatau: Fa‘alavelave Petelo, Grey Lynn, Auckland, April 2, 1978. Photo by Mark Adams. Goldtone silver bromide print. Image courtesy of Mark Adams.

time. The opportunity to make the portrait came from the chance request by a friend to provide photographic illustrations of Sāmoan tattooing for an article the friend was writing for a craft magazine. The commission completed as required (a set of conventional ethnographic photographs of cropped sections of the man's tattooed body), Adams made the portrait for his own purposes. Its unsettling, self-questioning effect, which would come to define his aesthetic sensibility as a photographer, motivated him to learn more of the practice in Auckland and to track down the tufuga, Sulu'ape Paulo.

Fomison was an older artist who hailed from the same region as Adams: South Canterbury on New Zealand's South Island. In 1973 he had relocated to central Auckland, eager to escape the ethnic homogeneity of Christchurch, and settled in the (then) largely Māori and migrant Polynesian suburbs of Ponsonby and Grey Lynn. The painter had long had a serious interest in Māori and Polynesian art. Indeed, he began his youthful career as a trainee ethnographer and archaeologist for the Canterbury Museum, working on the documentation of Māori pictographs in regional rock shelters, but he switched to painting and the autonomous path of an artist in the early 1960s. Like Adams, Fomison was profoundly conscious of the violence, misrule, injustices, and dispossessions of Māori that marked the colonial history of the South Island, as it had the country as a whole. Their work, channeled through different mediums and aesthetic sensibilities, was an evolving language for coming to terms personally with the ethical and existential burden of that history in the context of the ramping-up of the politics of decolonization in both the nation and across the region. Both artists were drawn north to Auckland and Northland in that decade, in part from an activist commitment to the political struggles concentrated in those regions; in part from a nebulous but no less driven desire to engage with the social and embodied reality of Pacific peoples. They joined their protest marches, advocated their causes, lived in their neighborhoods, made friends with them. Fomison *got* the power of Adams's photographs of Mister Fiu and was interested in meeting the tattooist as well.

For his part, Paulo had immigrated to South Auckland in 1973 as part of successive waves of migrants from what was then called Western Sāmoa, an ex-colonial territory administered by New Zealand since 1914, which had celebrated its independence in 1962. He settled with his young family in the suburb of Māngere, working factory jobs by day and tattooing migrant Sāmoan clients at night and on the weekends. Preceded by another tufuga tatatau, Su'a Tavui Pasina Sefo Ah Ken, a cousin who shared the same title (Su'a), both had taken the unprecedented step of taking *tatau*, a customary art form with an ancient and complex modern history, from the Sāmoan Islands to a new country. Paulo was not exactly surprised after returning from church that Sunday afternoon to see two skinny Europeans sitting in his living room wanting to meet him to ask if they could observe and photograph his practice. Europeans interested in Sāmoan tattooing were not unknown to the tufuga. He had tattooed American Peace Corps workers in Apia with souvenir armbands called *taulima*; he was familiar with the ethnographic and photographic archive on tatau compiled by Europeans; there were even Europeans who had been tattooed with a full pe'a. What must have intrigued Paulo, however, was the fact that Adams and Fomison were artists.

Their meeting inaugurated a friendship characterized by a shared respect for each other's roles as artists in their respective cultures. However, those cultures were not separate spheres; they were entangled with each other as a matter of colonial history and by the nature of their work and friendship. Each man sought to involve the others in his artistic practice as part of his effort to act upon (not merely reflect) the culture he was seeking to change. For Adams, Paulo provided entrée to the practice of several Sāmoan tattooists, their clients, and their clients' families and friends, inaugurating a forty-year project documenting that milieu in portraits and "genre" scenes of the tattooing operation, set in domestic or otherwise personalized interiors. It enabled him repeatedly to return to the trope of the tattooed man in a room with its interrogative power to question the viewer's place and situation in a decolonizing world. For Fomison, association with Paulo also immersed him in the lives of Sāmoans and led to the remarkable event of his own tattooing by Paulo with a traditional Sāmoan pe'a. Begun about six months after that first meeting, the months-long ordeal was not only a life-changing experience for the painter, effectively remaking his cultural identity in Sāmoan terms, but also assumed symbolic significance in the public culture of New Zealand at a time of important political and ideological transformation. For Paulo, their association brought his work to public attention, making him a well-known tattooist in New Zealand and catapulting the practice of Sāmoan tatau — until then largely unknown beyond the migrant Sāmoan community — into public visibility. Adams's photographs showcased his work and that of other tufuga in publications and exhibitions in art galleries around the world. And Fomison became his client, a white "canvas" for a cross-cultural pe'a in an early instance of Paulo's seminal role in the globalization of Sāmoan tatau.

But their friendship also embodied the conjunction of variously fraying narratives of modernism. In what follows, I want to consider these narratives somewhat separately before returning to their intersection in the artists' friendship and work. In the case of Fomison, modernism had been the vehicle of a quest among settler artists since the 1930s for a distinctive national culture, one that "did not exist" in the comfortable, materialistic, still-colonial world of the dominant society, and "had to be created."[6] Fundamental to their consciousness was a sense of cultural rootlessness in a new land; thus their turn to the distinctiveness of the landscape, their unique locality in the Pacific, and their appropriations of Māori artistic motifs as signifiers of national uniqueness.[7] Born in 1939, Fomison was a second generation contemporary of the modernist movement who came into his own as an artist in the 1960s and 1970s. By then however, globalizing forces both external and internal were roiling and fragmenting the nationalist imaginary. Fomison was a transitional figure in this context, an artist who shared his predecessors' investment in a national community, often addressing it directly in his work. *What Shall We Tell Them?*, for example, is the title of a painting featuring a surrogate self consulting his enigmatic muse with precisely this question—recognizing, as Simon During puts it, that "older stereotypes for, and ideologies of, white New Zealandness seemed to have lost their persuasiveness."[8] During identifies Fomison as one of "a tiny minority" of young, passionate, and rebellious souls of his generation (During among them) whose utopian but also confused, excessive, and often self-destructive lives played out the structural and ideological changes of those tumultuous and ultimately transformative decades. For During, Fomison best represents that moment, "the strange, almost dreamlike last years of New Zealand welfarism and protectionism, which are also the last years of white world hegemony—and, then, the effort to find new ways of negotiating and forming lives in, to use a hack phrase, a 'new world order.'"[9] Hack phrase or not, it captures the heroic, almost mythic self-conception of the artist in those decolonizing decades that motivated Fomison to distil their meaning in his paintings, to remake his life in Polynesian Auckland, and, when the possibility presented itself after meeting Paulo, to change his identity and become other to himself by taking on the pe'a. That is what the ritual of tattooing the pe'a means in Sāmoan terms; one emerges from it "reborn," a *soga'imiti*, a "Sāmoan" man.

At the same time there is something paradoxical about Fomison's project in the context of a fraying modernism. On the one hand, his tattooing recalls both early modernist investments in the radical alterity of "primitive" cultures and stereotypes of "going native" in the desire to transcend an all-pervasive modernity: Gauguin's dream of becoming "savage" in colonial Tahiti and the Marquesas; the modernist ethnographer Leo Frobenius's desire to enter into the ritual life of the Basonge in the Congo (that Gikandi writes about) in order to truly experience African difference; D. H. Lawrence's fictional works based on his travels in Mexico, New Mexico, and the Australian outback (compared to Fomison by Mariana Torgovnik).[10] As noted, Fomison's vocational origins began in ethnography, that essential counterpart to modernism's interest in the art of non-Western cultures, and he pursued that interest in Māori and Polynesian art throughout his life. Yet Fomison was ambivalent toward modernism. A New Zealand critic called him "a modern artist but not a modernist."[11] For his work in many ways was a rejection of modernism's formal languages, from cubism and expressionism to abstraction and the vanguard experiments of the 1960s. Unlike his predecessors, Gordon Walters and Theo Schoon, who had also visited those Canterbury Māori rock art shelters twelve years earlier, Fomison never took his experience of them in formalist or abstract directions.[12] Instead, he developed an idiosyncratic and deliberately anachronistic style of figurative and allegorical paintings, meticulously crafted using old-fashioned oil painting techniques, whose social commentary and visionary independence recall the works of nineteenth-century Romantics like Goya, Blake, and Redon. Even more atavistic are his dark and strangely melancholic studies of Christ figures after old masters like Holbein, Morales, and Piero della Francesca. Such works suggest an artist willfully ensconced on the far side of the modernist turn, as if refusing the "exits" and "breakthroughs" to the "new" that defined modernism's epistemic difference from the past. And yet, Fomison's paintings were not in denial about his time. As During argues, that is what they are about. They address global decolonization in images, often appropriated from news media, of subjects such as the Vietnam War, South African apartheid, and the American civil rights movement. They construct probing allegories of the late welfare state in images of confinement and paranoia. They depict forgotten episodes of colonial violence and Pākehā expropriations of land in the context of contemporary Māori struggles to reassert land and Treaty rights. He painted weirdly empathetic images of imprisonment, torture, illness, disfigurement, and isolation as the subjective counterpart to the social order.[13] But he did not paint like a modernist. In his desire to mediate a transition to a postcolonial world for the "primarily Pakeha consumers" of his work (the "them" in *What Shall We Tell Them?*), Fomison needed to confront what modernism generally repressed: the realities of the colonial past.[14] The latter was recalled in various ways: his anachronistic, premodernist aesthetic; the mise-en-scène of his domestic dwellings, filled with colonial-era paintings, ethnographic artefacts, op-shop knickknacks, and quirky collections (egg cups and rolling pins); and his "performances" of colonial identities for various photographers. In 1990 he suggested to a newspaper reporter that his tattooing was an act of "compensation" for the shooting of Sāmoan independence leader Lealofi Tupua Tamasese by New Zealand soldiers during a peaceful demonstration in Apia in 1929.[15]

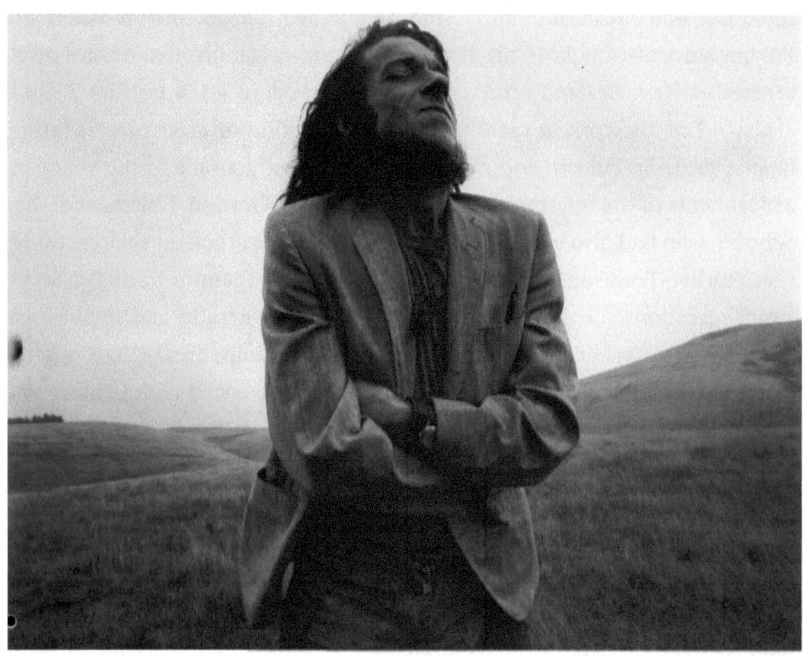

FIGURE 7.2 Portrait of Tony Fomison at Tai Tapu, Banks Peninsula, 1972. Photo by Mark Adams. Courtesy of Mark Adams.

Adams, to turn here to the photographer, had already begun photographing Fomison before their meeting with Paulo. He photographed him at work in his Christchurch studio; inhaling the wind at Banks Peninsula on the east coast of the South Island (figure 7.2); he photographed his new dwellings after his move to Auckland and, of course, his tattooing. Adams was drawn to the painter's unique persona and the strange, uncanny character of his work. He also sensed the ambitious nature of his confrontation with questions of settler identity and colonial memory, a confrontation not dissimilar to the photographer's own, albeit mediated through a different medium and sensibility. Moreover, there existed a cross-media dialectic in their work. As Wedde notes, Fomison had been a "fanatical teen photographer" with a serious passion for photo journalism, while During characterizes his paintings as fundamentally camera-like.[16] Not only are many of them appropriated from the image world of photographic reproduction — newspaper and magazine illustrations, film stills, horror movies, commercial advertising, and even photographs by Adams — their very look and feel suggest images by "a frozen movie camera."

"Yet he uses the freedom that painters have to move beyond the mechanical reproduction of light in order to exaggerate the effects of a movie-camera and show how paintings can hint at meanings, cause flesh to creep, in ways that cameras can't."[17] Adams's work, conversely, could be described as aiming to achieve the traditional nuance and complexity of European genre painting, group portraiture, and historical landscape using the capabilities of an actual camera. What for Fomison photographic reproduction could not do, was for Adams the possibility he sought to realize.

A decade younger than Fomison, Adams saw his work as already outside, and critical of, the modernist paradigm. At the same time, he was conscious of the extent to which photography — invented in the era of colonial expansion, witness to the "progress" of "History" and the "civilizing mission" of the West, accessory to travelers and ethnographers — was twinned with modernism as its inescapable counterpart. The chosen genres of his work bear the legacy of that history, even as he attempts to rework them. The origins of his photo file on Sāmoan tatau began with an ethnographic assignment, and the paradigm of otherness and objectification was always just a misstep away. What unsettles that paradigm in his photograph of Mister Salati was the modern setting of the room and the gaze thrown back on the viewing subject. But what he could not have anticipated when the project began, even if it has a certain logic in his trajectory, was the merging of his photo portrait of Fomison with his expanding photo file of Sāmoan tatau. Who knew when he started photographing tattooed Sāmoans that they would find themselves *in the picture*, so to speak, of what they initially sought only to observe and photograph?[18]

If we shift our focus to Paulo, we confront an Indigenous form of artistic practice in different but overlapping contexts of decolonization and globalization. Sāmoa was a colonial territory of New Zealand, along with the Cook Islands, Niue, Tokelau, Tuvalu, and the sparsely inhabited Kermadecs, though Sāmoa alone became fully independent. (Most of the others became independent "in free association" with New Zealand.) These islands, along with Tonga and Fiji, former British colonies, were the main sources of postwar urban migration to New Zealand, particularly in the 1970s, with the vast majority originating from Sāmoa. Paulo's presence in this milieu, along with his cousin Pasina Sefo, marked the beginnings of a major historical shift in the practice of tatau as it was taken beyond the confines of the Sāmoan archipelago. Paulo was a radical modernizer of his tradition. But was he also a "modernist"? My argument is not to claim Paulo or his fellow tufuga tatatau for the discourse of Western modernism, but it is worth asking ourselves in this context what we mean by the notion of "Indigenous modernisms"? As other scholars in this book have argued, they can refer not only to the influences of Western modernism but to Indigenous artistic responses to modernity arising from within their own cultures and artistic traditions. Such responses have produced new and unique forms with characteristics at least comparable to those associated with modernism in the West: novelty and formal reinvention, entanglement in commercial markets, transformations in the nature of artistic institutions, changes in the role and status of the "artist."[19] The modernity of tatau is the overriding subject of Sean Mallon's and Sébastien Galliot's *Tatau: A History of Sāmoan Tattooing*, in which they combine a history of its practice from the colonial period to the present, with an account of its basis in Sāmoan mythology, ritual practice, language, and social structure.[20] Both aspects are shown to be adaptive to the shifting conditions of modernity. And both cast light on Paulo's position in New Zealand in the 1970s and 1980s and his interactions with Fomison and Adams. The history they trace, however, is fragmentary and elusive. Tattooing was denigrated and banned by Christian missionaries in the nineteenth century, and although it survives as a cultural practice in outer villages, the archival evidence of it is sparse—some eyewitness accounts, a few ethnographies, a surprisingly small photographic record. Moreover, it played no evident role in the colonial politics of Sāmoa. Few, if any, Sāmoan political or religious leaders were tattooed. And it had no symbolic significance for the independence movement in the 1920s and 1930s known as the Mau. Interestingly, one place where it appears in the historical record is in contexts associated with foreign entertainments: Sāmoans in fairs, expositions, and Hollywood films. Robert Flaherty's famous *Moana of the South Seas* (1927) makes the point, for few men and women in the film are tattooed and the production had to scour the archipelago to find people suitable to stage its famous tattooing sequence as a timeless, ancient ritual.[21] After World War II, the beginnings of a marked shift appear, spurred in part by the interest of non-Sāmoans—American Marines, Peace Corps workers, and travelers—in acquiring "souvenirs" of their time in the islands (typically taulima or armbands) and the willingness of tufuga to oblige them. But the big change came in the decades surrounding national independence and with the advent of large-scale migration, which is to say, the period corresponding to Paulo's father's generation and his own.

Alongside their archival history, however, Mallon and Galliot have a second purpose, which is to show the continuity of the institution of tufuga, guild-like familial entities localized to historic villages of persons specialized in the arts of tattooing (tufuga tatatau), house-building (*tufuga fau fale*), and canoe-making (*tufuga fau va'a*). And often, as in the case of Paulo's father, all three. The services of tufuga tatatau may have been marginal, provided as and where they were asked for, but the point is they *persisted*, their marginality in fact a sign of cultural resistance to colonial domination.[22]

Paulo was from the village of Lefaga in Upolu and part of a titled tattooing family known as the Sa Su'a, one of two main tattooing families, the other being the Tulou'ena.[23] Their status was founded in their genealogy and specific mythological narratives about the origins of the art form. However sporadic, their work retained a place of high regard in specific village polities, where tattooing initiated young men to particular roles in village ceremony and marked young women with a certain status. Paulo remembers accompanying his father as a child on long visits to villages to provide tattooing services, and receiving traditional payments of fine mats and food. He also remembers 1963 to 1964 as the precise moment when the resurgence of tatau began.[24] But none of this meant he felt locked into a closed tradition. Paulo was not a traditionalist in the face of this new demand. His acquaintance with the rapidly evolving nature of the practice made him open-eyed about the new conditions of trade. In following his cousin Pasina to New Zealand, he was anticipating increased demand for tatau from that country's growing migrant population and the need to manage the demand for what was, after all, the family business.

Paulo's willingness to accommodate Adams's request and befriend the two New Zealanders attests to his openness to taking tatau into new terrain. They introduced him to the Auckland art scene as an Indigenous Pacific artist, took him to exhibition openings, invited artist friends and gallerists to watch him work. The public interest surrounding their association, and Fomison's tattooing in particular, made Paulo a renowned figure, written about in newspapers, appearing on television newscasts, and featured in documentaries. And Paulo embraced these opportunities. Like Courbet fraternizing with newspapermen in the cafés of Paris to make a name for himself when old routes to patronage and reputation were disintegrating, Paulo was publicizing his practice in a historically new context, far from the village system, for a rural-to-urban, migrant working-class clientele. Like an avant-gardist of his own tradition, he re-coded the meanings of the pe'a and *malu* to make them relevant to contemporary Sāmoans; he aestheticized their traditional forms with new and more intricate patterns; he disaggregated their composite sections to create new, stand-alone forms placed on other parts of the body; he challenged the ethnic boundaries of the tradition by tattooing non-Sāmoans like Tony Fomison.[25] We will return to the radical character of Paulo's practice, but here it is time to braid the work of the three artists together.

If Fomison's tattooing constituted a logical outcome of his project, it also arose from the contingencies and chance opportunities of his life. Getting a pe'a was something he probably wanted soon after meeting Paulo, though he kept it to himself. What brought the possibility into the open was his friendship with a Sāmoan neighbor, a young New Zealand-born law student at the University of Auckland, Fuimaono Norman Tuiasau, whom he introduced to Paulo. Fuimaono was a political activist, president of the Sāmoan Students Association at the university, and a member of the Polynesian Panthers, an activist organization modelled after the American civil rights group, that challenged anti-migrant racism and advocated improvements to the conditions of life for Polynesians in the inner city. When he expressed his desire to be tattooed with a pe'a to assert his cultural identity as a Sāmoan — "So there would be no doubt about who I was and to have the recognition of one's family and community"[26] — it triggered Fomison's decision to be tattooed as well: "If it hadn't been for Norman living nearby, I probably wouldn't've thought of getting tattooed — not so soon anyhow. But there it was in front of me. It's the custom to be tattooed with others, so when Norman was being done, me being done with him was natural."[27] The two shared occasional sessions together as "tattoo brothers" in different parts of the city: the garage of Fuimaono's parents' home in Onehunga; the living room of the tufuga's home in Māngere; the painter's studio home in central Auckland (figure 7.3). These are not irrelevant details. For Paulo, they speak of the reinvention of his practice for a new kind of clientele in a migrant metropolis. And for Adams, who began to photograph that clientele in the intimacy of their homes, the subject of "home" and "place" — of "where am I and whose place is this?" — began to unfold itself in his efforts to capture the social, cultural, and geographical complexity of the tufuga's practice. Adams photographed Fomison's tattooing in its various settings, merging his portrait of the artist with his file on Sāmoan tatau.

In one of those photographs the painter is captured lying face down on the studio floor while Paulo prepares to tattoo the back of his right thigh, shaven for the purpose. His assistant, Pio Taofinu'u, who will stretch the skin and wipe away the blood, waits smoking a cigarette. Surrounding them is the painter's studio with various works hanging on the wall. One of them, entitled *Up Up and Away* (1978–79) (figure 7.4), depicts a small, naked, white-skinned figure, strikingly unmarked given the scene in the photograph, rising from the

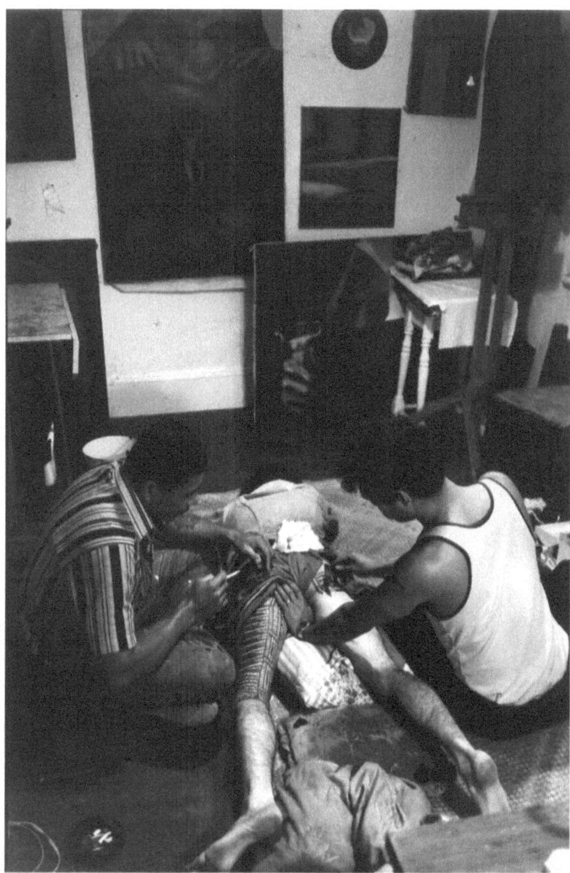

FIGURE 7.3
Tattooing Tony Fomison, Pio Taofinu'u (solo), tufuga tatatau: Su'a Sulu'ape Paulo II. The studio, Gunson Street, Freemans Bay, Auckland, 1979. Photo by Mark Adams. Goldtone silver bromide print. Image courtesy of Mark Adams.

mouth of a corpse while a ghoulish woman with blue eyes pulls back a shroud held in her mouth, as if both the enabler of his ascent toward the light and one who might envelop him again in darkness. Meanwhile, leaning against the wall, another painting called *Hand of Fate* (1979) shows a little man flexing his might while held in the grip of "Fate," not unlike the way Paulo grips Fomison from behind in preparing to tattoo him. The paintings belong to a series of works created before, during, and after his tattooing that allegorize his reflection on that ambiguous modernist figure, the self. Self-portraits and alter egos abound in Fomison's work, appearing as envoys, seers, circus hands, clowns, Christ figures, Christian saints, and Pinocchios. Sometimes they are anxious, vulnerable loners. In *The Fugitive* (1980–82) a man flees naked through an open landscape, though from what exactly is not immediately obvious. In *Not Just a Picnic* (1980–82), another sits apart from a family group in the dark

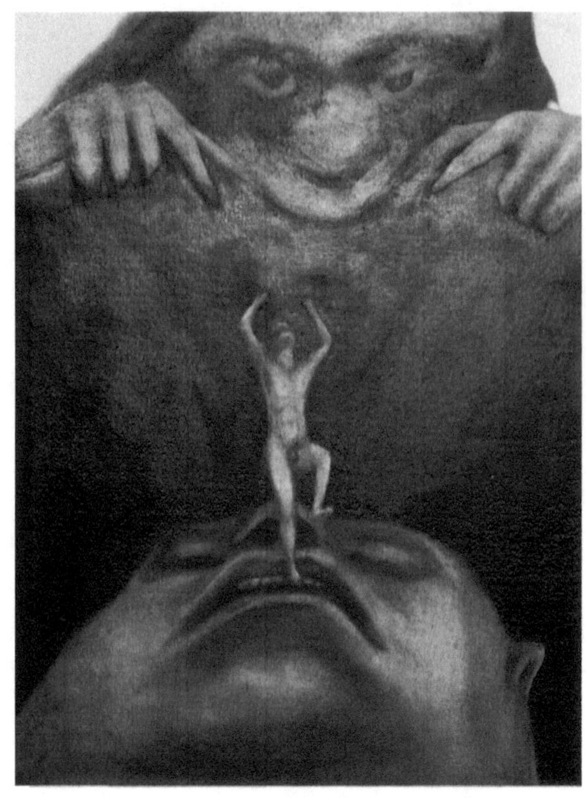

FIGURE 7.4 Tony Fomison, *Up Up and Away*, c. 1978. Oil on canvas on board, 120 cm × 90 cm. Private collection. Courtesy of the Tony Fomison Estate.

interior of a cave (figure 7.5). In *Self Portrait* (1977), Fomison depicts himself peering through a colonial window sash attempting to see what or who is on the inside while a shadow of black paint threatens to eclipse his face (figure 7.6). In his book *Sources of the Self*, Charles Taylor identifies modernism by its paradoxical turn toward both the inward subject and the decentered subject—decentered by new ideas about language, the unconscious, or the sense of some amoral primal force.[28] I read Fomison's paintings as interrogations not so much of the modernist self but of the white colonial self in the face of its historical unravelling. His paintings contemplate the eclipse of that self in the painter's desire to become other to himself in postcolonial terms: "I go to extremes about this sometimes, but I really do think we need to develop the Polynesian aspects of our life down here at the bottom of the Pacific. Getting tattooed was, for me, my vote of confidence in the important values of Polynesian culture."[29] In his desire to remake the world, Fomison's contemplation of self-eclipse finds its counterpart in the ritual of the pe'a, which is also like a

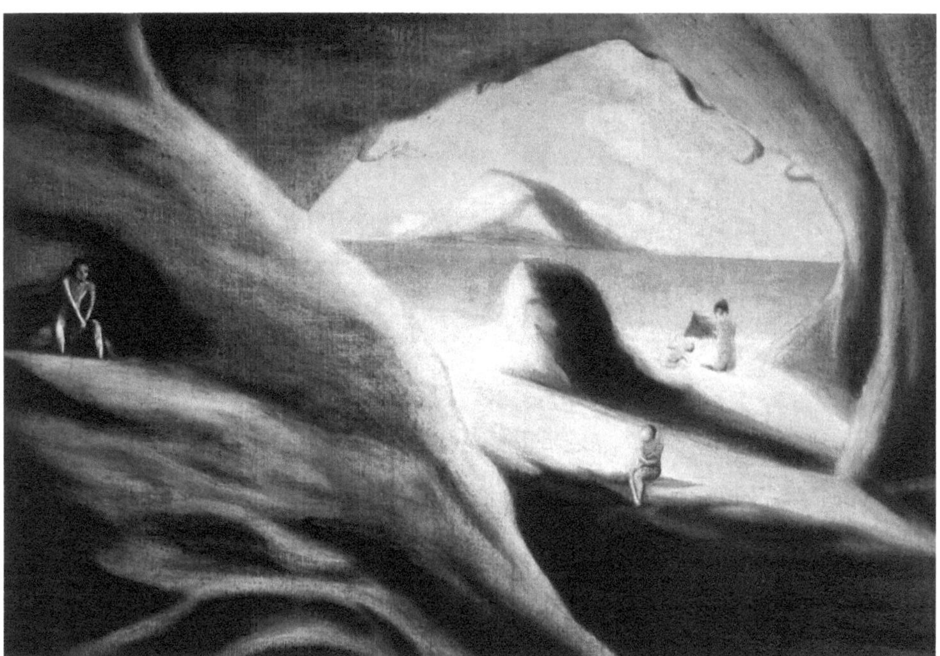

FIGURE 7.5 Tony Fomison, *Not Just a Picnic*, 1980–82. Epoxy on hessian on pinex board, 121 cm × 180 cm. Auckland Art Gallery, Toi ō Tamaki. Gift of the Friends of the Auckland Art Gallery. Courtesy of Anna Fomison and the Tony Fomison Estate.

death and rebirth. There is a common analogy for the pe'a among Sāmoans in which it is said that men endure the pain of receiving it in the way that women endure the pain of childbirth. While the analogy balances the genders, Alfred Gell thinks it is not quite accurate. Getting tattooed with a pe'a, he argues, is less like giving birth than *being born*.[30] For one emerges from it as if dying to an old self in becoming a new one, a properly Sāmoan man, a soga'imiti, ready to contribute to the ritual life and vitality of the culture. As Paulo once put it, "You are no longer a mother's boy."[31] Indeed, the last marks completing a pe'a is the *pute*, tattooed across the navel. Fomison took the implications of his pe'a seriously, learning what he could of the language, encouraging young Pacific artists in their budding careers, visiting Sāmoan villages in 1983 (where he says he used his status as a soga'imiti to criticize exploitive chiefs and priests), advocating for Pacific art in New Zealand, and continuing his relationships with Sāmoan friends and neighbors.[32] But his identity remained ambiguous, "very hard to describe," as Fuimaono put it: "The key to it in terms of him being accepted by my friends, was the tattoo. It was like a key to a big door.

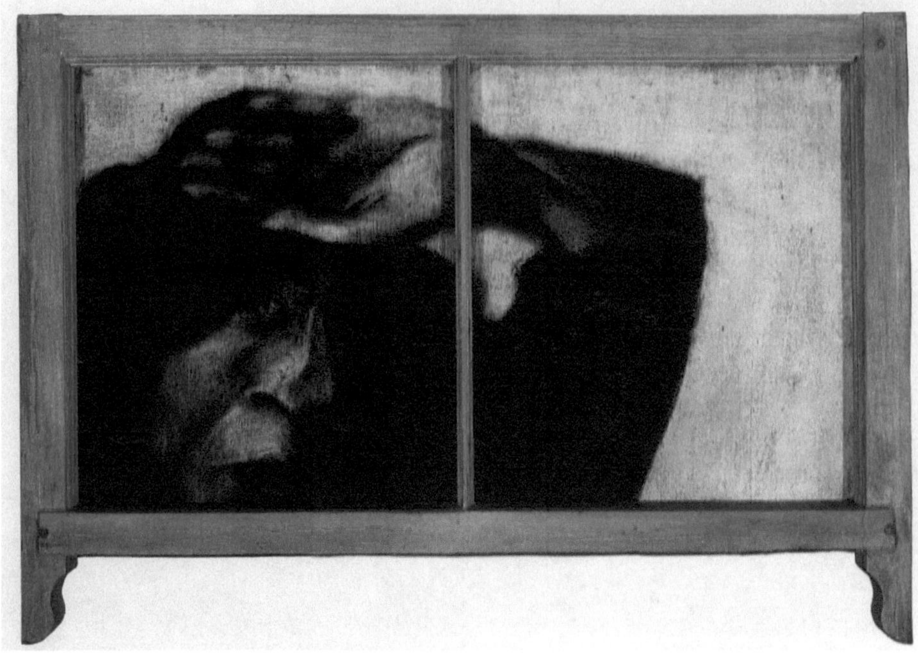

FIGURE 7.6 Tony Fomison, *Self Portrait*, 1977. Oil on board in a sash window frame, 58 cm × 85 cm. Auckland Art Gallery, Toi ō Tamaki. Courtesy of Anna Fomison and the Tony Fomison Estate.

Once my friends and family saw that he had this tattoo, it was like they considered him . . . *not quite* Samoan, it's very hard to describe. It was *almost* like part of the community — our community."[33]

For Paulo, Fomison was the first non-Sāmoan he had tattooed with a full pe'a outside Samoa (and possibly the first ever). As such, the painter was a watershed client for the tufuga, foreshadowing the geographically expansive and boundary-crossing character of his future practice. For in the 1980s and 1990s, Paulo and other tufuga tatatau of the Sulu'ape family revolutionized the tradition in global terms. They not only took tatau into the Sāmoan diaspora (Los Angeles, Sydney, Brisbane, etc.), but into European circles of tattooists and tattoo enthusiasts. There Paulo continued to tattoo non-Sāmoans, clients who, like Fomison, became friends of the tufuga by entering into his social circle or he into theirs. These initiatives were of a centrifugal and secularizing nature, unmooring tatau from its village and ritual contexts in the homeland and "freeing" the tufuga to experiment and innovate with the traditional forms of the pe'a and malu in the manner simply of a "creative artist." On a different front, however, Paulo also used his ancestral status as a traditional tufuga tatatau to legitimate the postcolonial revival of other Polynesian tattooing traditions lost under colonialism by formally gifting the tools of his practice — tools associated with its mythological origins in narratives particular to the Sa Suʻa title — to Hawaiian, Tahitian, Cook Islander, and Māori tattooists.[34] Such reinventions of tradition are also echoed among Sāmoans in migrant contexts, where, as in the case of Fuimaono, the rituals of support, celebration, and gift exchange associated with tatau are adapted to garages, living rooms, church halls, and cash economies while the meaning of tatau is resignified as "identity."

As Mallon argues, the globalization of tatau was not the loss or engulfing of the tradition within the assimilative powers of the "global age" but the opposite: the assertion of the Sa Suʻa Suluʻape as an autonomous family of tattooists within the broader dynamics of Sāmoan culture as it modernized and expanded into the wider world.[35] When asked by Mallon about being challenged by other tufuga tatatau for tattooing non-Sāmoans, referring to Tony Fomison, Paulo responded by insisting on his customary right as a senior tufuga to tattoo whomever he chooses: "This particular piece of culture does not actually belong to the Samoans, it has become a mark of a Samoan overseas and elsewhere, but it actually belongs to me and my family. We gave it to the Samoan people and we decide who does the job and how. They don't tell us."[36] The implication in this remark is not a tattooing free-for-all; rather, it reflected the tattooist's deliberate intent to take tatau into the world under the control of tufuga tatatau of the Suluʻape family as makers of the embodied signs and symbols of Samoan culture. While genealogical identity is fundamental to the meaningfulness of tatau, so too is friendship and reciprocity in relations with others, incorporating them into the culture. Indicative of that is an event Mallon describes in which Paulo intended (like a centripetal counterforce) for the Suluʻape title to be honorarily bestowed on a group of tattooist associates, close friends — a Māori, a Hawaiian, an American, a Dutchman, and another Sāmoan — in a formal ceremony at Lefaga, conducted posthumously by Paulo's brother, Alaivaʻa Petelo, in 2008.[37]

Adams's project documents the extraordinary unfolding of Paulo's practice, and that of other tufuga, through the dual framework of portraits-in-rooms and genre scenes of the tattooing operation. The project is consistent with the photographer's overall oeuvre, which has focused — in various projects — on colonial history and its postcolonizing reconciliations through attention to the particularities of place, time, and person as they are given in the spaces he observes through his camera.[38] The tatau series is grounded in an ethos of

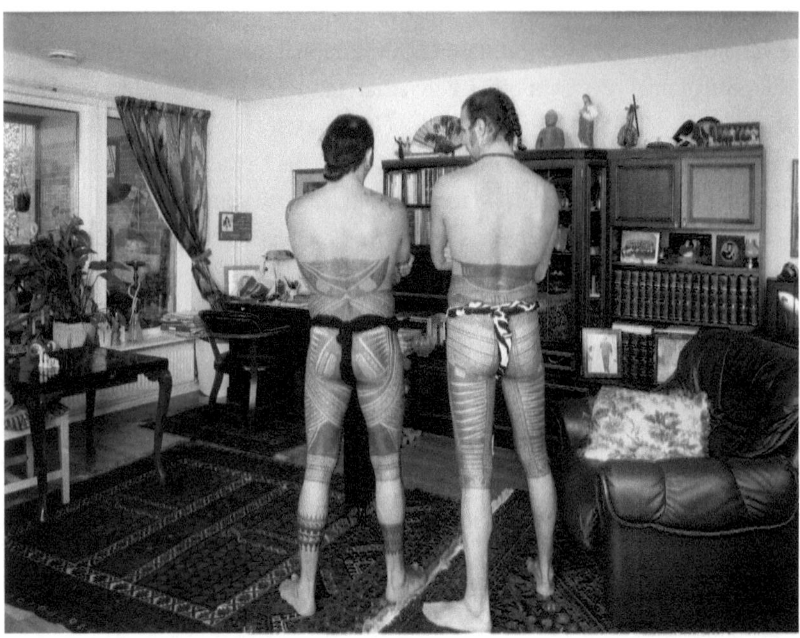

FIGURE 7.7 John and Marwan Atme, tufuga tatatau: Su'a Sulu'ape Paulo II. Gustav Hollersg, Malmo, Sweden, July 3, 2004. Photo by Mark Adams. Color photograph. Image courtesy of Mark Adams.

observation but not objectification. It tracks the shifts and cultural complexity of tatau as a globalizing practice by remaining scrupulously respectful of persons and places as who and what they are: a Sāmoan man and his European wife, dressed in a purple island dress, posing with the tufuga and his assistant in front of the television set; a Māori Catholic priest in his church, striking a challenging pose in front of the altar, decorated with Pacific tapacloth, fine mats, and a Māori cloak; two Lebanese brothers standing on Turkish carpets in their mother's home in Malmö, Sweden (figure 7.7)—all tattooed by Sāmoan tufuga tatatau.[39] They convey a contemporary ethnography via the curious metonymies of an object or gesture, a stance or prop, a rivulet of blood, or a view through a window or doorway. The series is also, as it was from the beginning, intensely personal, a self-interrogation of the photographer's own place and identity.

The Evening of the Umusaga for Fuimaono Norman Tuiasau is a photograph Adams took on May 10, 1980, after the formal ceremony marking the completion of the young student's pe'a. It depicts a gathering of family and friends in the living room of Fuimaono's parents' home in Onehunga (figure 7.8). His navel

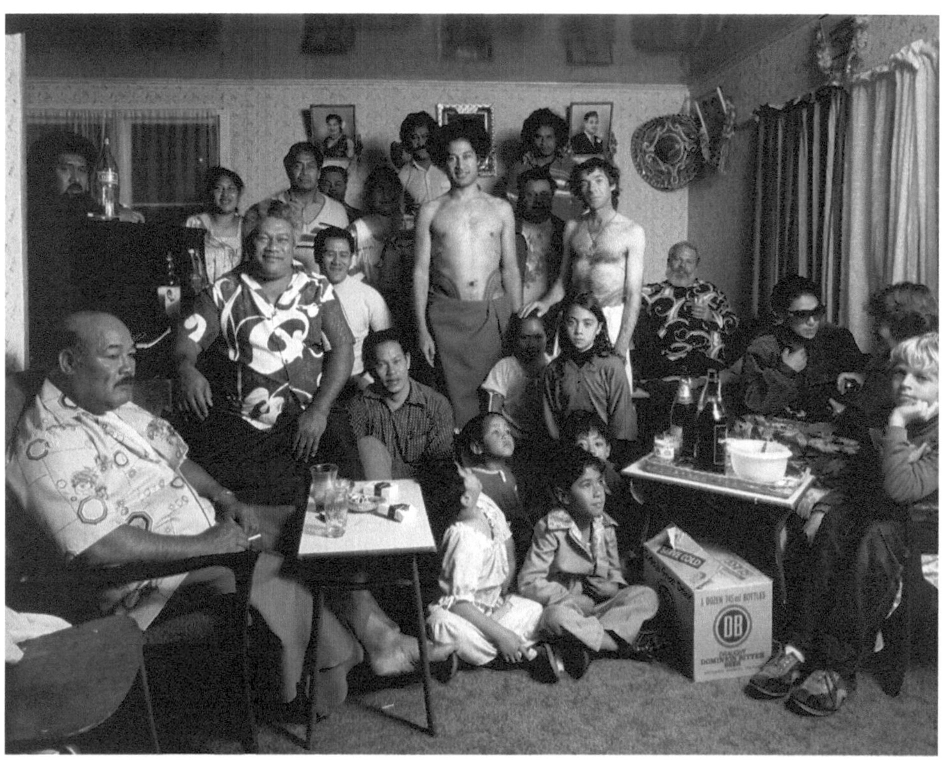

FIGURE 7.8 Grotto Road, Onehunga, Auckland. The evening of the umusaga for Fuimaono Norman Tuiasau. Tufuga tatatau: Su'a Sulu'ape Paulo II. May 10, 1980. Color photograph. Image courtesy of Mark Adams.

still swollen from earlier that day, the soga'imiti stands proudly, dressed in a lime-green lavalava, the same color as his father's, seated stoically in an armchair, holding a cigarette. Fomison stands next to Fuimaono, his right hand resting somewhat awkwardly on a young girl's head. Behind Fuimaono, in his shadow, is his mother. Most of the people are members of the Tuiasau family with New Zealand–born children and grandchildren. To the right, in dark glasses, is Donna Awatere, member of the urban Māori activist group Ngā Tamatoa and author of the book *Māori Sovereignty*, in animated conversation with an academic ally from the University of Auckland. The boy in front of her is a son of leading feminist and editor of the influential feminist magazine *Broadsheet*, Sandra Coney, who was also at the gathering. Behind Fomison is Noel McGrevy, an anthropologist who had written a master's thesis on Sāmoan tattooing. Turned toward the photographer — and us — the gathering represents a microcosm of the heterogeneous forces transforming New Zealand society in the 1970s and early 1980s, on the one hand, ushering in a national era of "biculturalism" and "multiculturalism," and on the other, an age of free markets, corporate capitalism, new communications technologies, mobile populations, and global art worlds. Whether the former is congruent with the latter is a debatable question. Indeed, it is the question posed by Adams's, Fomison's, and Paulo's work.

Notes

1. Barton, "Together/Apart," 71–72.

2. Barton, "Together/Apart," 77.

3. Māori artists influenced by modernism were active since the 1950s but remained marginal to the major civic galleries until the 1980s and 1990s. On Māori modernism, see Skinner, *The Carver and the Artist*, especially 79–125.

4. Gikandi, "Africa and the Epiphany of Modernism," 40–42, 46.

5. Mark Adams interviewed by Peter Brunt, "Photographing Tatau and the Politics of Friendship," in Adams et al., *Tatau: Pe'a*, 10.

6. Curnow and Marsh, "A Dialogue by Way of Introduction," 2; and McCahon, "Beginnings," 364. On the nationalist project in New Zealand art, see Pound, *The Invention of New Zealand*; and Thomas, *Possessions*.

7. Pound, *The Space Between*.

8. During, "Here's Trouble," 43.

9. During, "Here's Trouble," 42.

10. Torgovnick, "'The Blood Is One Blood.'"

11. Cartwright, "Recent Work by Tony Fomison," 66.

12. See Pound, *The Invention of New Zealand*, 282–97; and Pound, *The Space Between*, 75–86. For recent work on Gordon Walters and Theo Schoon, see Hammonds et al., *Gordon Walters*; and Skinner, *Theo Schoon*.

13. During, "Here's Trouble," 43–46.

14. Wedde, "Tracing Tony Fomison," 35.

15. As reported by Fenwick, "Put Art First," 121.

16. Wedde, "Tracing Tony Fomison," 15.

17. During, "Here's Trouble," 45.

18. Mark Adams in conversation with author, September 30, 2018.

19. See McLean, "Aboriginal Modernism in Central Australia"; and Phillips, "Aboriginal Modernities."

20. Mallon and Galliot, *Tatau*, especially chaps. 3 and 4.

21. See Mallon and Galliot, *Tatau*, 109; and Nordström, "Photography of Samoa," 31–35.

22. Mallon and Galliot, *Tatau*, 110–15.

23. Mallon, "Samoan Tatau as Global Practice," 147.

24. Mallon, "'A Living Art,'" 51.

25. Mallon, "Samoan Tatau as Global Practice"; and Mallon and Galliot, *Tatau*, 127–30, 134–51.

26. Fuimaono Norman Tuiasau interviewed by Peter Brunt, December 20, 2004, unpublished manuscript.

27. Tony Fomison interviewed by Noel McGrevy, March 1981, unpublished manuscript.

28. Taylor, *Sources of the Self*, 456–66.

29. Tony Fomison interviewed by Noel McGrevy.

30. Gell, *Wrapping in Images*, 91–95.

31. This statement was made in a talk given by Sulu'ape Paulo at Victoria University of Wellington in 1998, as recollected by the author.

32. From an interview with Tony Fomison by Garth Cartwright, June 1986, unpublished typescript.

33. Tuiasau, "Interview with Fuimaono Tuiasau."

34. See Awekotuku with Waimarie Nikora, *Mau Moko*, 144–46; Ellis, *Tattooing the World*, 194–95; and Mallon and Galliot, *Tatau*, 148.

35. Mallon, "Samoan Tatau as Global Practice," 163–69.

36. Mallon, "'A Living Art,'" 55.

37. Mallon, "Samoan Tatau as Global Practice," 163–67.

38. Several of Adams's photographic projects have appeared in book versions. See Adams and Evison, *Land of Memories*; Adams and Thomas, *Cook's Sites*; Adams et al., *Rauru*; and Adams et al., *Hinemihi*.

39. Mallon, Brunt, and Thomas, *Tatau*, plates 38–39, 75–77, and 72–74.

Bibliography

Adams, Mark, Peter Brunt, Lisa Taouma, and Tusiata Avia. *Tatau: Pe'a: Photographs, by Mark Adams; Measina Samoa: Stories of the Malu, by Lisa Taouma*. Wellington: Adam Art Gallery Te Pātaka Toi, Victoria University of Wellington, 2003. Exhibition catalog.

Adams, Mark, Hamish Coney, Keri-Anne Wikitera, Lyonel Grant, and Jim Schuster. *Hinemihi: Te Hokinga — The Return*. Auckland: Rim, 2021.

Adams, Mark, and Harry Evison. *Land of Memories: A Contemporary View of Places of Historical Significance in the South Island of New Zealand*. Auckland: Tandem, 1993.

Adams, Mark, and Nicholas Thomas. *Cook's Sites: Revisiting History*. Dunedin: University of Otago Press, 1999.

Adams, Mark, Nicholas Thomas, James Schuster, and Lyonel Grant. *Rauru: Tene Waitere, Māori Carving, Colonial History*. Dunedin: Otago University Press, 2018.

Barton, Christina. "Together/Apart: Regional Networks in a Global Age: Imagining the Pacific in New Zealand, 1976." *Reading Room: A Journal of Art and Culture*, no. 6 (2013): 70–85.

Cartwright, Garth. "Recent Work by Tony Fomison." *Art New Zealand*, no. 52 (Spring 1989): 66–69.

Curnow, Allen, and Ngaio Marsh. "A Dialogue by Way of Introduction." *First Yearbook of the Arts of New Zealand*, no. 1 (1945): 1–8.

During, Simon. "Here's Trouble: Some Comments on Tony Fomison and His Work." In Wedde, *Fomison: What Shall We Tell Them?*, 41–51.

Ellis, Juniper. *Tattooing the World*. New York: Columbia University Press, 2008.

Fenwick, Anne. "Put Art First." *Listener and TV Times* (1990): 118–21.

Gell, Alfred. *Wrapping in Images: Tattooing in Polynesia*. Oxford: Clarendon, 1993.

Gikandi, Simon. "Africa and the Epiphany of Modernism." In *Geomodernisms: Race, Modernism, Modernity*, edited by Laura Doyle and Laura Winkiel, 31–50. Bloomington: Indiana University Press, 2005.

Hammonds, Lucy, Julia Waite, and Laurence Simmons. *Gordon Walters: New Vision*. Auckland: Auckland Art Gallery Toi o Tāmaki, 2017. Exhibition catalog.

Mallon, Sean. "'A Living Art': An Interview with Su'a Sulu'ape Paulo II." In *Tatau: Photographs by Mark Adams; Samoan Tattoo, New Zealand Art, Global Culture*, edited by Sean Mallon, Peter Brunt, and Nicholas Thomas, 51–61. Wellington: Te Papa, 2010.

Mallon, Sean. "Samoan Tatau as Global Practice." In *Tattoo: Bodies, Art and Exchange in the Pacific and the West*, edited by Nicholas Thomas, Anna Cole, and Bronwen Douglas, 145–69. London: Reaktion, 2005.

Mallon, Sean, Peter Brunt, and Nicholas Thomas, eds. *Tatau: Photographs by Mark Adams*. Wellington: Te Papa, 2010.

Mallon, Sean, and Sébastien Galliot. *Tatau: A History of Sāmoan Tattooing*. Wellington: Te Papa, 2018.

McCahon, Colin. "Beginnings." *Landfall* 20, no. 4 (December 1966): 364.

McLean, Ian. "Aboriginal Modernism in Central Australia." In *Exiles, Diasporas, and Strangers*, edited by Kobena Mercer, 72–95. Cambridge, MA: MIT Press, 2008.

Nordström, Alison Divine. "Photography of Samoa: Production, Dissemination, and Use." In *Picturing Paradise: Colonial Photography in Samoa, 1875–1925*, edited by Casey Blanton, 11–40. Daytona Beach, FL: Southeast Museum of Photography, 1995.

Phillips, Ruth B. "Aboriginal Modernities: First Nations Art, 1880–1970." In *The Visual Arts in Canada: The Twentieth Century*, edited by Anne Whitelaw, Brian Foss, and Sandra Paikowsky, 349–69. Oxford: Oxford University Press, 2010.

Pound, Francis. *The Invention of New Zealand: Art and National Identity, 1930–1970*. Auckland: Auckland University Press, 2009.

Pound, Francis. *The Space Between: Pakeha Use of Maori Motifs in Modernist New Zealand Art*. Auckland: Workshop, 1994.

Skinner, Damian. *Theo Schoon: A Biography*. Auckland: Massey University Press, 2018.

Smith, Vanessa. *Intimate Strangers: Friendship, Exchange and Pacific Encounters*. Cambridge: Cambridge University Press, 2010.

Taylor, Charles. *Sources of the Self: The Making of the Modern Identity*. Cambridge, MA: Harvard University Press, 1989.

Te Awekotuku, Ngahuia, with Linda Waimarie Nikora. *Mau Moko: The World of Māori Tattoo*. Auckland: Penguin, 2007.

Thomas, Nicholas. *Possessions: Indigenous Art/Colonial Culture*. London: Thames and Hudson, 1999.

Thomas, Nicholas, Anna Cole, and Bronwen Douglas, eds. *Tattoo: Bodies, Art and Exchange in the Pacific and the West*. London: Reaktion, 2005.

Torgovnick, Marianna. "'The Blood Is One Blood': D. H. Lawrence and Tony Fomison." In Wedde, *Fomison: What Shall We Tell Them?*, 53–61.

Tuiasau, Fuimaono. "Interview with Fuimaono Tuiasau." In Wedde, *Fomison: What Shall We Tell Them?*, 81–86.

Wedde, Ian, ed. *Fomison: What Shall We Tell Them?* Wellington: City Gallery Wellington, 1996.

Wedde, Ian. "Tracing Tony Fomison." In Wedde, *Fomison: What Shall We Tell Them?*, 9–39.

IAN MCLEAN

8 DJON MUNDINE AND *THE ABORIGINAL MEMORIAL*

Man is by nature a political animal.

—ARISTOTLE | *The Politics*

Being highly social animals, humans tend toward the middle ground where mediation (from Latin *mediare*, "to be in the middle"), or what Jürgen Habermas called "communicative action," is most concentrated. He compared it to "a switching station for the energies of social solidarity."[1] This impulse for communication partly explains why meetings between Western anthropologists and Indigenous informants could be surprisingly successful given their colonial context, not to mention the cultural and language barriers.

Another reason for their success, argued anthropologist Peter Sutton, was that they "were typically mediated by elite pairs of individuals who felt they could trust each other" and, I would add, who could not resist the impulse to communicate with the other.[2] One example Sutton gave was the American anthropologist W. Lloyd Warner (1898–1970) and the Yolngu headman Harry Makarrwala (c. 1895–1951). Given their very different backgrounds, their relationship is a test case for Habermas's claims. "Constantly together" throughout Warner's research in northeast Arnhem Land between 1926 and 1929, they developed a deep trust in each other. Warner recalled in 1958: "I have lived most of my life in modern industrial America, yet during his life our friendship was as strong and enduring as any I have experienced with my own people. I think I knew him as well as I ever knew anyone."[3] More than an anthropological project, this was a mission between two sovereign nations in which Makarrwala and Warner were ambassadors exchanging letters of introduction. Warner's classic *Black Civilization* (1937), which, under the mentorship or supervision of Makarrwala, documents Yolngu kinship laws and ancestral stories and is also Makarrwala's epistle to *balanda* (non-Yolngu, Westerners). From their friendship Warner got his book and degree and Makarrwala got to know how balanda think, but most of all, the book is a declaration of Yolngu sovereignty.

Makarrwala and Warner's achievement as ambassadors confirms that it takes two to mediate and that the most successful mediators are those who are most open to being mediated or mentored. The real limit to mediation—the limit it cannot transcend—is not language or cultural differences but the politics in which communicative action occurs. Within the politics of mixed sovereignties (international relations), it can quickly become fraught, as is evident in the collisions of Indigenous and Western jurisdictions in settler colonialism. While settler colonies moved quickly to legally establish their sovereignty and so the indivisibility of their territories, colonial frontiers were zones of plural and contested sovereignties.[4] This has remained the case in Arnhem Land, a tract of land a little larger than Austria in northern Australia. Mainly occupied by several Indigenous language groups, settler colonialism here was never complete. While first contact with British colonists occurred in the nineteenth century, the area proved too remote and difficult for the colonists until the 1920s, when missions began to be established in the area on a permanent basis. Since then a truce has reigned in which neither party has surrendered its claims of sovereignty. War was averted, but peace has not been fully achieved. This makes a rich environment for creative mediators and mediations.

The adeptness of language to "mediate interactions," argued Habermas, is what makes it the prime "medium of . . . socialization," as is evident in the contiguity of discrete languages and social groups.[5] However, a strange language does not halt mediation. Languages can be translated, and strangers discovered long ago that a picture can speak a thousand words. In first contact situations body language (signing, gestures) and pictures are generally prime sites of mediation. The Yolngu quickly discovered that their art was a very useful site of mediation with the balanda.[6] This stimulated the development of an art movement and is still a factor in the making of art.

A recent example is *The Aboriginal Memorial* (figure 8.1). Made for the 1988 Biennale of Sydney during the Australian bicentenary, when tensions between Indigenous and official accounts of the colonial legacy were stretched to their limits, it directly addressed issues of sovereignty. Developed through a process of brokering in which the community art adviser Djon Mundine (b. 1951) was the pivotal mediator, *The Aboriginal Memorial* has been extensively examined

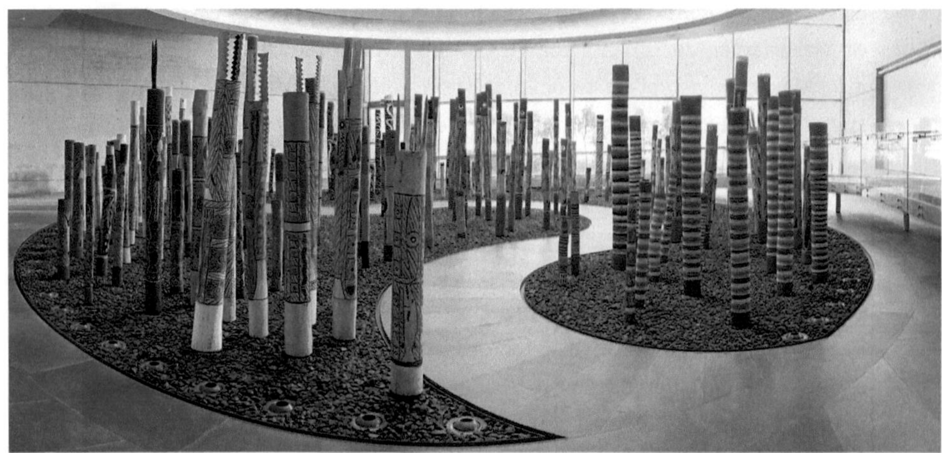

FIGURE 8.1 Ramingining artists, *The Aboriginal Memorial*, 1987–88. Installation of two hundred hollow log-bone coffins, natural earth pigments, and binder on eucalyptus wood, 327 cm H. National Gallery of Australia, Canberra. Purchased with the assistance of funds from the National Gallery admission charges and commissioned in 1987, 1987.2240.1-200. © Ramingining Artists / Copyright Agency, 2024.

but mainly in ways that skirt its processes of mediation and collective production, even when Mundine's role is discussed.[7] An exception is the conceptual artist Nigel Lendon's forensic account that focuses on the creative mediation of Mundine in the production and exhibition of *The Aboriginal Memorial*, which he compares to the relational art movement that would develop in Western contemporary art a decade later.[8] Taking Lendon's argument as my starting point, this essay positions Mundine's brokerage within a wider Yolngu history of post-contact mediation and politics.

Mundine, Milingimbi: Mediating Balanda

There are few if any who can match Mundine's forty-year career in the number and formats of exhibitions and projects curated and the number of essays written across the full cross-section of Australian Indigenous art. He first gained expertise in Indigenous art while working for Aboriginal Arts and Crafts (AAC) in the late 1970s, having previously studied but not completed an undergraduate degree at Macquarie University (Sydney), taking units in accounting, political science, anthropology, and film.[9] While working at the AAC he became acquainted with the contemporary art world and its practices, mainly through his dealings with two leading curators of contemporary art, Bernice Murphy (b. 1944) and Leon Paroissien (b. 1937). Each mentored the other in her and his respective areas of expertise.

When, in 1979, the twenty-eight-year-old Mundine left the AAC to take up the position of "art and craft adviser" at Milingimbi in Arnhem Land (northern Australia), he stepped into a well-established tradition of balanda facilitators/mediators who had worked there as part of the Methodist mission since the 1920s. However, Mundine was very different from these previous mediators. First, his recent experience in Sydney had given him a strategy to change the terms of trade from tourist artifact to contemporary art. Understanding the cultural capital of contemporary art, he saw in it a pathway for an effective Indigenous politics.

Second, Mundine was an Aboriginal Australian, a Bundjalung man from the northern territory of New South Wales who had been raised in Sydney at a time of heightened urban activism. In the rapidly colonized areas of southeast Australia into which Mundine was born and raised, Indigenous sovereignty had been quickly lost to the British colonizers through brutal conquest. Coming from a well-connected family with a history of involvement in twentieth-century Indigenous politics of Black nationalism, Mundine had a highly developed political consciousness.[10] Helping his cause was the Australian art-world's growing interest in Aboriginal art and activism and also his Aboriginality, which gave him what then was a rare kudos. He was the right person, in the right place, at the right time. It is doubtful that a non-Indigenous art adviser could have undertaken the level of intervention Mundine achieved in *The Aboriginal Memorial*, especially in his dealings with the Australian art-world. However, Mundine told me, "Being an urban Aboriginal activist in Milingimbi didn't help much." Instead of making him the ideal middleman for this job — simultaneously Aboriginal, Western, and committed — the legacy of colonialism left him, a southerner, suspect from all sides. However, there were a few well-traveled Yolngu who understood that he wasn't a typical balanda. They created a new category for Mundine: "Southern Yolngu."[11]

Mundine came to Milingimbi as a mediator but immediately found himself being mediated. As if he had slipped into a swiftly flowing stream, he was happily swept into the thick of Yolngu life and its ways of thinking. As a young urban Indigenous activist from Sydney, it felt like "Mecca: . . . a place of Aboriginal spiritual continuity and active religious practice; a place where Aboriginal people still spoke their own language and owned their own land."[12] Mundine recalled with evident delight: "My house was a large place on a small beach in Ngarrawundhu, or 'bottom camp,' near [Albert] Djiwada's home. The people who lived directly across the road, who I came to know almost like family members, were from the Gupapuyngu group. Among them was the artist Joe Djembangu, 'Big Joe,' with whom I became very close friends."[13] Mundine was placed between the song masters of two of the leading Milingimbi clans, the Liyagalawumirr and Gupapuyngu, and the two Yolngu moieties, Dhuwa and Yirritja, respectively, into which the world was divided.

Several of the artists "visited often to 'teach me' so I could perform my role as art adviser more competently," and "I was 'adopted' into a family . . . as a son by the [senior] artist Manuwa [1917–79] in order to incorporate me into the kinship structure which governs all Yolngu life." In other words, Mundine was treated like previous balanda mediators: he was mentored. The real test was the extent to which he allowed himself to be mediated. His willingness to be drawn into the region's rich ceremonial life was rewarded by being taken under the wings of Paddy Dhathangu (1915–93) and the most famous Yolngu artist David Malangi (1927–99): "Two men who, with their families, have probably had more impact on my life than anyone except my parents" (figure 8.2).[14] Placed into a grandfather/grandson classificatory relationship with Mundine, Malangi and Dhathangu were his chief Yolngu consultants or mediators in the making of *The Aboriginal Memorial*.

The Aboriginal Memorial is a seminal work in Indigenous and Australian contemporary art, and it is also a crowning achievement of modern Yolngu art. Yolngu initiation into Western society was typical of Indigenous experience. In 1885 balanda pastoralists invaded prime Yolngu resources in the Glyde River area. Then, in 1906, the new Australian nation state asserted its sovereignty by outlawing the Macassan fisherman who had been trading with the Yolngu for centuries, thus severing an enduring social contract.[15] The Yolngu beat off the pastoralist invaders, but they lost the Macassan trade and the deep cultural exchange that came with it, in which the Macassans had been incorporated into ancestral stories and ceremonial life.

Yet, not long afterward, in 1923, they welcomed a few balanda when they appeared at the former Macassan camp on Milingimbi — a small low-lying island at the mouth of the Glyde River. They had not come as visitors; they wanted to establish a new camp — a Methodist mission. Within a few decades the mission had successfully introduced modernity — a settled life, agriculture, schooling, Protestantism, and the rudiments of a capitalist economy — to the Yolngu. While they came bearing gifts and not, like the pastoralists, guns,

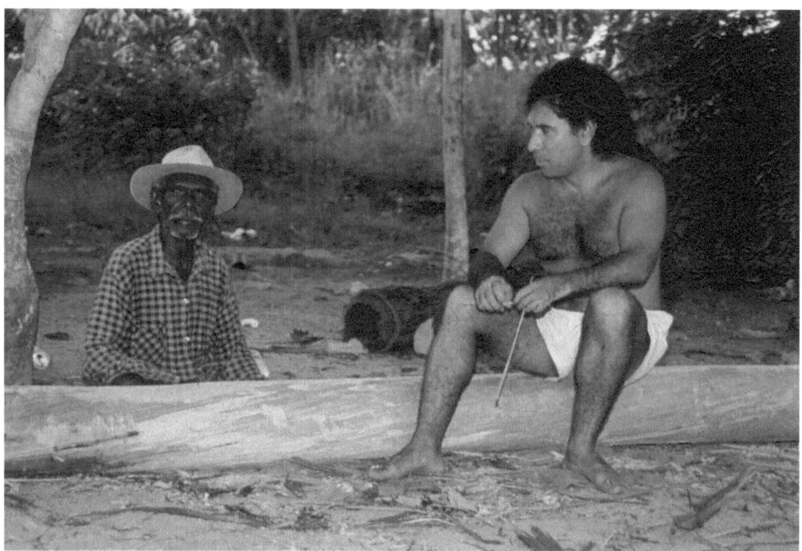

FIGURE 8.2 David Malangi and Djon Mundine, at Ramingining, 1987. Photo by John Lewis.

it was part of the Australian nation's attempts to cement its sovereignty in these remote northern regions.

As in all such exchanges, individuals on both sides had different propensities for mediation and different views on the appropriate way forward. It was never easy. Why, we might wonder, did the Yolngu welcome the balanda in the first place and persist with their engagement, especially since a pitiless frontier war, which had lasted twenty-three years and wiped out whole clans, had ended only thirteen years earlier? Were the missionaries seen as a new type of Macassan because of where and also how they arrived—as brokers not usurpers? Was the lure of modernity too great to resist or was it a ploy to mediate a peace settlement with these strange strangers? After all, the Yolngu were confident mediators, as Warner discovered when he arrived at the mission in 1926: "A number of the older men came to see me. Among them was a man who, I discovered, could speak a fair amount of English . . . and [who] was looked upon, as a person of consequence and authority among the people."[16] The person of consequence was the aforementioned Makarrwala. Well traveled and experienced in transcultural relations, he was the first modern Yolngu. It was his wit, will, and skill as a mediator that kept the experiment alive in the early years. Sutton suggests that Makarrwala was "selected by a group of senior men to act as primary mentor to . . . Warner," meaning that Makarrwala made himself available for Warner to discover him.[17] Sutton also suggests that it is likely Makarrwala put himself forward for this assignment: in Indigenous communities there was generally fierce competition for the privilege of being the chief broker with outsiders: "In some cases there has even been overt conflict between local people of prominence, who have competed . . . to control the role of so-called 'main informant' to a [Western] researcher. On one occasion I recall personally, spears were brought out."[18] Makarrwala, whose name is resonant with the sounds of Macassar, was very open to being mediated: he was curious about the other and had the intelligence to match. His outward-looking personality was evident from childhood. He remembered being drawn to stories of the Macassans from a very early age, and the highlights of his early childhood were a long journey with his father across many Yolngu clan territories and meeting Macassans. Captivated by the stories of his older brothers and old Yolngu men who had "been back to those [Macassan] countries and [how] a few of these men, while they were there, had Macassar women for wives," he dreamt of working on their boats and traveling to other places.[19] True to his dreams, at about age twelve he ran away to sea, working as cabin boy with Malay fishermen and an English captain. Over the next several years he traveled to Darwin and other parts of northern Australia. He learned English and Malay as well as the Iwaidja language from a young teenage Arrarrkbi girl, his first lover, while sojourning on Cobourg Peninsula on the western edge of Arnhem Land. He probably acquired his go-between name "Harry" in these early teenage years.

Makarrwala developed a close relationship with Warner and also T. T. Webb (1885–1948), the missionary superintendent between 1926 and 1939. Makarrwala and his off-sider were even the central protagonists in a miracle, when Jesus showed himself during a moment of extreme bravery on their part, after which Webb dubbed them "heroes of the faith."[20] Makarrwala was the first Yolngu head churchman and "the Nurudawalangu, the headman of the whole area."[21] The two went hand in hand for Makarrwala. Even his burial was transcultural, mixing traditional Yolngu and Christian rituals.[22] So powerful was Makarrwala that his dialect, Gupapuyngu, became the lingua franca of the mission even though it was not the local Milingimbi dialect. In the 1980s, Mundine reported, Makarrwala's son Bannguli was still called "master."[23]

Painting was not a site of mediation between Makarrwala, Warner, and Webb.[24] Most painting on bark traditionally consisted of roughly painted figures on the inside of wet-season shelters, while the finest painting was reserved for sacred narratives on the bodies of initiates and ceremonial objects. Warner and Webb amassed many artefacts, but the few bark paintings they collected during this period were likely from bark shelters.[25] In grasping the potential of bark painting as a vehicle for anthropological research, Donald Thomson—who worked over two periods in Milingimbi between 1935 and 1943—initiated the production of bark paintings of substantial quality and number.[26] This is because he commissioned ritual leaders to paint their sacred narratives on large pieces of bark and recorded extensive exegeses of each work. Both sides may have understood the terms of the exchange differently, but something was brokered. Aesthetics in the form of fine art bark painting became a site of mediation, which Lendon suggests brought a new authority to this modern practice: "Significantly, the person who assumes the role of ceremonial leader, who may have previously been known more for their prowess as a singer, dancer or painter or maker of objects, now also acquires the added responsibility of painting [on bark] the full count of the primary narratives to which their country refers. This creates the circumstances in which an artist's distinctive style, and the various factors which constitute their individual way of representing a narrative, contribute to each painter's performance of their authority."[27] Thus was initiated a modern Yolngu painting movement that had the backing of the ritual leaders. Makarrwala was an early painter, as were other ritual leaders such as (Sam) Yilkari Kitani (c. 1890–1956), who led the Liyagalawumirr clan. Their descendants became the main artists at Milingimbi in the 1950s and '60s and into Mundine's time. Like a few missionaries before him, Mundine was adopted into this lineage as a key mediator.

After Makarrwala's death in 1951, Tom Djawa (c. 1905–80) became "the most senior of the inner circle of elders" at Milingimbi. Closely related, they had been raised by the same man, Djawa's father Narritnarritj, who had been leader of the Gupapuyngu clan.[28] After Kitani's death in 1956, Djawa's elder brother Dhawadanygulili (c. 1900–76), who was the *dyunggayi* (cultural manager) of the Liyagalawumirr clan, stood in as ritual leader of the clan until the early 1960s, when Dawidi (c. 1921–70), Kitani's brother's son and in line for the job, was considered ready. Dhawadanygulili taught Dawidi and Malangi to paint. Dhathangu, who became leader of the Liyagalawumirr clan after Dawidi's death, was Kitani's son.

This lineage of interrelated artists that Malangi and Dhathangu inherited and into which Mundine was drawn may have been seeded by Thomson, but it took root after the Second World War with the arrival of Reverend Edgar Wells as the new mission superintendent in 1949. Wells had a passion for the art and used it as the means to learn more about Yolngu life and beliefs. After Makarrwala died in October 1951, Djawa became Wells's closest confidant.

"They seemed," said Ann Wells, "to have an ease of understanding between them that was quite remarkable, especially after Miyangala had died and Jawa was undisputed head of our *yulnu*."[29] Djawa, Wells, and Makarrwala's son, Baralja, would often talk about the art into the night.[30]

Djawa remained deeply involved in the art movement when, after Wells left in 1959, Alan Fidock became the mission's art mediator. Fidock, said Mundine, "greatly expanded on the work of Edgar Wells," increasing sales and developing a substantial overseas market. A few Yolngu — most notably Malangi — became professional artists and increasingly savvy and knowledgeable about the market and the art world.[31] Mundine called the 1950s, when Wells "worked closely with Harry Makarrwala and Tom Djawa," "the formative years," and the following two decades — the 1960s and '70s — the "golden years."[32] Government pressure to professionalize art being made on missions led to Milingimbi being the first mission to, in 1972, acquire an "art and craft adviser."

In 1979 Mundine stepped into a well-established operation at Milingimbi at a time when Indigenous art was on the cusp of radical change. Western desert acrylic painting on canvas would quickly steal the thunder, but Ramingining, twenty-five kilometers (15.5 miles) south of Milingimbi, was first off the block, with Nick Waterlow selecting three Yolngu artists from there for the 1979 Sydney Biennale. This was a coup because it was the first time that Indigenous art had appeared in a substantial exhibition as contemporary art.

Ramingining was a new post-missionary government township built to accommodate the expanding population of Milingimbi. Its newness, and perhaps its sense of competition with Milingimbi, seemed to give it an edge in this new game of contemporary art. Before his eyes Mundine saw the dynamics shift to Ramingining. When he arrived in Milingimbi he said, "The majority of the work produced was still destined for the tourist market via a series of church aid and tourist shops in southern cities." He was "told to encourage the production of suitcase art — cheap art and craft work that could fit into tourist's suitcases" — and art that looked "authentic."[33] "On the mainland opposite, however, things were moving in another direction."[34]

Ramingining

When, in 1977, Ramingining also appointed an "art and craft adviser," no doubt the aim was to capitalize on the success of Milingimbi. While an offshoot of the mission, Ramingining was also an alternative to it. On transferring permanently there in 1983, Mundine made what he called the "ideological step" of shortening his title to "art adviser," thus signaling his intent to play in this new game of Indigenous contemporary art.[35] Thinking in terms of contemporary art thematic projects, he quickly capitalized on the 1979 Sydney Biennale coup and also his relationship with Murphy and Paroissien. In 1979 Murphy was appointed curator of contemporary art at the Art Gallery of New South Wales (AGNSW), and from 1984, both were cocurators of Sydney University's Power Gallery of Contemporary Art (PGCA).[36] In 1983 Ramingining artists were included in *Australian Perspecta*—a biennale of Australian contemporary art at the AGNSW—and the 16th Bienal de São Paulo. Also that year the AGNSW acquired work by Malangi, and PGCA began building a large collection of some two hundred works from Ramingining, exhibiting it in 1984. *The Aboriginal Memorial* was the culmination of these eventful years of Mundine romancing the contemporary art scene.

Having its own rich history, Ramingining was a good place to play this new game of contemporary art. Able to draw on the experience of Milingimbi, located in one of the most abundant food sources in Arnhem Land, the Arafura Swamp, and overlooking the battlefields of a vicious frontier war, Ramingining was rich with Ancestral power and colonial history. The frontier conflict, typical of the ruthless dispossession that occurred at this time, had become part of the place's ancestral history—stories of spears, bullets, and poisoned meat passed down the generations. It was also a rare example of colonial incursion failing. This place thick with Ancestral Serpents had turned the empire back. Thus, Mundine's idea—to make a political statement during the Australian bicentenary about Indigenous sovereignty in the context of the frontier wars—struck a chord with Ramingining artists.

Mediating The Aboriginal Memorial

> Over 1986–88 I created the concept of *The Aboriginal Memorial*, a forest of *dupun*, hollow log bone coffins, and talked the artists at Ramingining through the idea. An endless set of discussions took place with most of the senior artists in the community and all took on board the concept of using what are sacred forms for a wide metaphorical honouring of all those Aboriginal people who died as a result of colonization.
>
> —DJON MUNDINE | "Is It Sacred? The Collarenebri Files"

Mundine approached part of his art adviser's role as if he were the leading architect of the interventionist-type projects that have become synonymous with

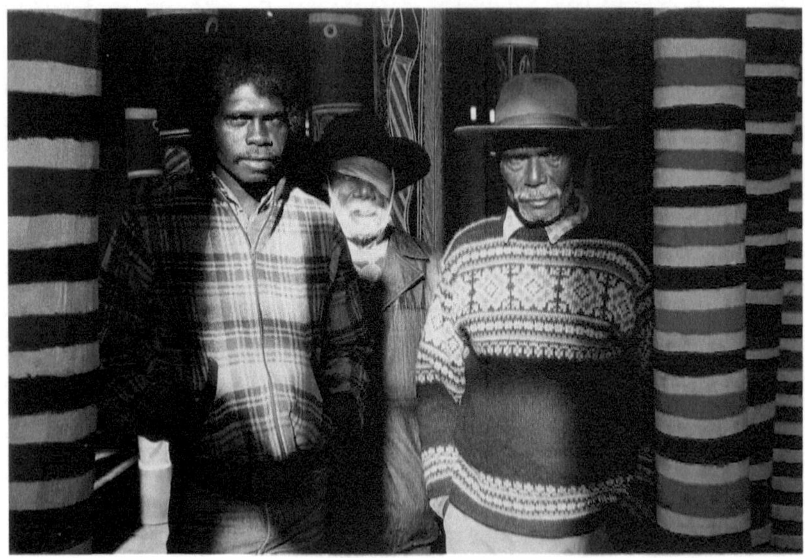

FIGURE 8.3 Johnny Dhurrikayu, Paddy Dhathangu, and David Malangi, *The Aboriginal Memorial*, 1988. Biennale of Sydney. Photo by Jon Lewis.

the contemporary art world since the 1980s. Terry Smith aptly called it the "artist-curator exchange," the origins of which he traced in the hybrid mixing (or mediation) of art and curatorial practices evident since the 1960s.[37] Its strategy, of which *The Aboriginal Memorial* is a classic example, is to create "a specific context that can make a certain form or thing look other, new, and interesting — even if this form has already been collected."[38]

Lendon established the extent of Mundine's conceptual input into *The Aboriginal Memorial*, whereas the focus of this chapter is his role in the larger mediatory process of its collective production, which went well beyond the artist-curator exchange of the contemporary art world.[39] The ambition of the project required Mundine to coordinate a number of more powerful mediators who could do things he could not. Making it happen within a contemporary art context were two senior art world commissars, Nick Waterlow and James Mollison — each a powerful broker in the art world's highest realms. Waterlow was the artistic director of the Sydney Biennale in 1988; Mollison was the inaugural director of the National Gallery of Australia. Getting *The Aboriginal Memorial* made was the responsibility of Dhathangu and Malangi (figure 8.3). Working closely with other senior artists, such as George Milpurrurru, Jimmy Wululu, Philip Gudthaykudthay, and Paddy Fordham Wainburranga, they oversaw the making of the two hundred poles by the forty-three artists and were sounding boards for Mundine in its conception and development.

The success of the project is as much a tribute to the work of these senior mediators as it is to Mundine. As enthusiastic converts to the recent idea that Indigenous art was contemporary art, Waterlow and Mollison used their art world authority to broker a new deal for Indigenous artists. In the Biennale catalogue Waterlow declared *The Aboriginal Memorial* "the single most important statement in this Biennale."[40] When it was later installed permanently in the National Gallery of Australia, Mollison said it was "one of the most important works of art ever to be created in this country."[41] This continues to be the National Gallery's judgment: it currently is installed in a specially designed space at the entrance.

The Aboriginal Memorial gains its power from the poetic ways in which Yolngu and Western art traditions are mediated. In this respect an appropriate analogy is an orchestra — a forty-three-member ensemble playing two hundred instruments with Mundine conducting — except that they are not all playing to the same score. The forty-three players are arranged into nine sections (clans and clan groups), each with its own songs.[42] There are connections between the songs but not in any obvious way to the average gallery goer. Instead there is a complex, multilayered, and multidimensional rhythm. Orchestrated by Dhathangu, Malangi, and Mundine, it echoes how Yolngu social relations are mediated.

Not just a product of mediation, *The Aboriginal Memorial* is also about the power of mediation — a hymn to ancestral relations and the way Yolngu organize social relations. This is first of all apparent in its central motif of burial poles. Painted tree trunks that had been hollowed out by termites, they were used in the final part of the traditional mortuary ritual (figure 8.4). While no longer practiced, the burial poles were an apt motif as they recall a premodern period when Yolngu enjoyed sole sovereignty of their lands. The burial pole motif is also a somewhat ironic reference to successful mediation with other non-Yolngu. Along with other hollow log artefacts — the yirdaki (didjeridu), drum, and smoking pipe — the burial pole is arguably evidence of Macassan influence but which Yolngu had long made their own.[43] At a deeper level, the burial poles resonate with the mediatory processes of the traditional mortuary ritual. The elaborate designs of *The Aboriginal Memorial* recall the very elaborate ceremonies reserved for ritual leaders. Having passed through the various initiations, they had seen "the highest grade of totem which lies deepest in the water of the totemic well."[44] Thus it was important not to lose a ritual leader's *warro* (totemic well spirit), as safely returned to the well it is available to be

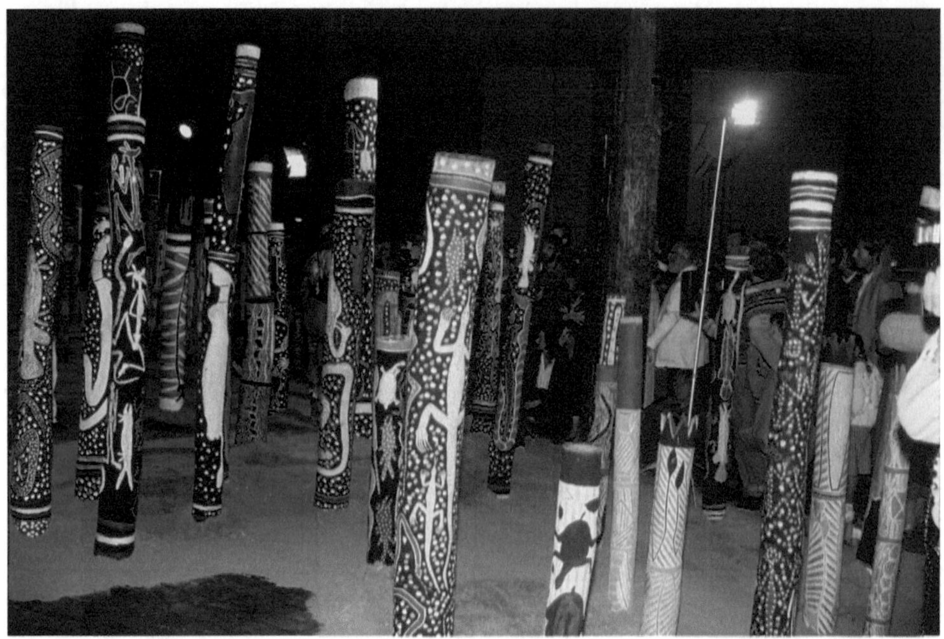

FIGURE 8.4 Opening of *The Aboriginal Memorial*, 1988. Biennale of Sydney. Photo by John Lewis.

reborn. Thus, the mortuary ritual is ultimately one of procreation and rebirth and thus resonates with the theme of *The Aboriginal Memorial*.

From the mid-twentieth century, when the traditional mortuary ceremony was replaced by Christian burial rituals, hollow logs and associated wooden sculptures had occasionally been made as art for sale, though bark paintings were the predominant commercial art. However, appropriating traditional ritual objects as modern art, in this case a contemporary art installation, had never before been attempted on such a scale or with a conceptual premise that matched the significance of the traditional ritual. Smaller groupings of poles do have traditional ceremonial precedents, but the scale of *The Aboriginal Memorial*, the number of clans involved, as well as its landscape layout and setting among several other installation artworks in a contemporary art biennale, framed it as a major work of contemporary art. In the context of the Australian bicentenary, which celebrated the birth of a British settler colony, *The Aboriginal Memorial* announced the rebirth of an Indigenous spirit and culture, its continuing claims of sovereignty and importantly, of Yolngu mediatory practices that are the deep meaning of the work.

Yolngu Mediatory Practices

One reason for the prominence of highly developed mediating practices among the Yolngu is that they comprise multiple clan sovereignties in a patchwork of clan territories in which there is no one central political authority to mediate clan relations. While people manage to travel freely across clan territories and their shared language and ritual practices indicate a well-defined cultural group, so weak was the political bond between the clans that there was no name for this cultural group. Warner adopted the name Murgin, but in the 1960s, for linguistic reasons, linguists opted for Yolngu, which means "person" in a set of related dialects that can be classed as a language the linguists called Yolngu Matha (Yolngu tongue).

While each clan enjoys sovereignty over its territory, it is not self-sufficient. There is also a web of kin and ancestral relations between the clans, but without a central authority to police these relations the clans need robust mechanisms of mediation. In 1930 there were sixty clans (according to Warner's estimate), each averaging about fifty people comprising several closely related family groups. Despite the "eternal feud with certain others," the clans are not fiefdoms of warlords.[45] The clan is a religious not a political order, though as in all religious orders it is thick with politicking. Run by a council of ceremonial leaders who inherit their authority over particular ancestral stories from their fathers and ultimately their totemic ancestor, clans are structured hierarchically according to an "age grading" measured by one's level of initiation.[46] That is, the clan is a male meritocracy.

Being patrifilial war-making units, with a hierarchical structure and territorial claims (thus closely echoing Western systems of governance and sovereignty), it is little wonder that Warner judged the clan to be, like a nation, the most "fundamental basis of the society."[47] However, more fundamental than the clan is the moiety system, which is a cosmological structure that divides the world, including the clans and its totemic sites, into two basic groups, Dhuwa and Yirritja. For all the importance of the clans, Warner also admitted their fragility. Unlike the two moieties, clans come and go; they can be absorbed into other clans, divide into two clans, die out or be wiped out. Only the moiety system is everlasting. It has no sovereign or headman, but it, not the clans, is where a cosmological (rather than political) sovereignty lies. It establishes what Warner called "horizontal lines" of relations between the strong "vertical lines" of authority in the clan structure, for the simple reason that Yolngu can only marry from an opposite moiety. Thus, mothers and wives are always of the other moiety and so have kinship allegiances to another clan. This means that individuals are not entirely beholden to one clan or nation. Warner judged these "lateral or horizontal lines" as weak compared to the vertical authority of the clans but each was sacrosanct.[48] "Open conflict never occurs within" clans, but neither, Warner admits, does it occur "between a man's clan and his wife's and mother's clan."[49]

The importance of the moiety system permeates all aspects of Yolngu life, including the clan's religious and aesthetic expressions. For example, the ritual leader is the song master but the ceremony is managed by the *djunggayi*, who is one of his wife's relations. Thus, authority in ceremonial matters is divided and by necessity mediated between clans and moieties. As well, many Ancestral Beings left several incarnations in different parts of the country during their travels, creating links (*bapurru*) between clans, especially those of the same moiety. At every turn there is a space of indeterminate possibility that necessitates mediation.

In their everyday life individual Yolngu must negotiate a web of responsibilities and obligations to ancestors, sites, kin, and moiety affiliations. This web of relations sets in play a fluid matrix of communicative action. There are rules but they are open to creative interpretation when new situations arise. This pressure to maintain a social contract in such a fluid environment means that the rhetorical skill and knowledge of the mediator holds the fort. Drawn from the council of ritual leaders, the chief mediators are the political leaders, the Nurudawalangu who mediate relations between clans and outsiders. Not just ritual headmen or leaders of their clan but with authority in other clans, they can become, like Makarrwala and Djawa, Nurudawalangu or quasi-sovereigns.

Conclusion

Modern Yolngu society is fully connected to the institutions and sovereign laws of the Australian nation-state but retains traditional lines of authority established by the clan and moeity systems that underpin it. This is particularly evident in the rich mediatory practices of its cultural expressions that permeate everyday life in ceremony and fine art production. Because both ceremonial performances and fine art are made by individual incarnations of ancestors, they have collective as well as variable meanings depending on the experiences of the song masters and artists and the histories they live through (figure 8.5). Thus, writes Howard Morphy, despite depicting or re-creating ancestral histories, "paintings [also] acquire connotative meanings that would seem at first to

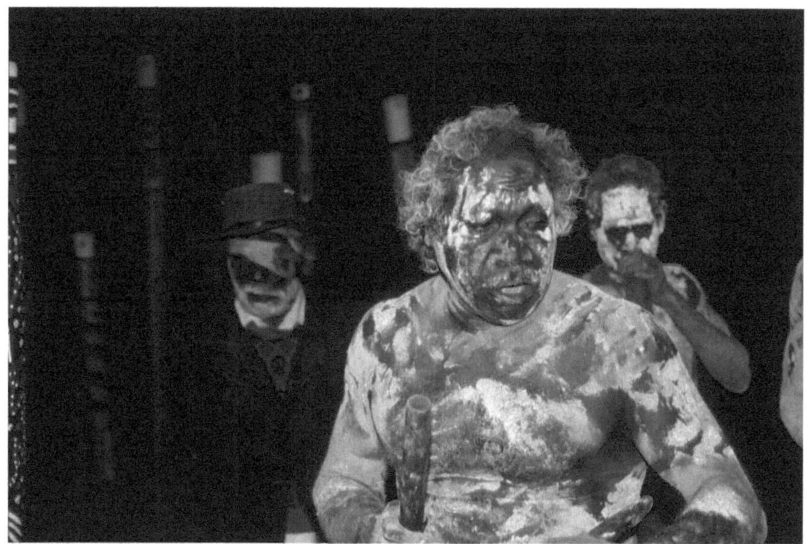

FIGURE 8.5 Paddy Dhathangu, Paddy Fordham (*foreground*), and Johnny Dhurrikayu performing the opening of *The Aboriginal Memorial*, 1988. Biennale of Sydney. Photo by Jon Lewis.

be primarily of significance to individuals participating in the ceremony."[50] This ritual reenactment of ancestral stories in paintings (and songs and dance) is constantly being mediated at multiple levels, as Wally Caruana and Nigel Lendon traced in the different renditions of the Wagilag sisters story over several generations and across several locations.[51] Listen, for example, to one of the artists in their exhibition, the plumber at Ramingining, Albert Djiwada (b. 1938), renowned songman, Yilkarri's youngest son and ritual leader of the Liyagalawumirr clan following Dhathangu's death in 1993. He is explaining some of these inter- and intraclan relations in the telling of the Wagilag Mirarrmina story, in which Wititj the ancestral python swallows the ancestral Wagilag Sisters:

> Outside, we're Liyagalawumirr, but underneath, we're Wititj. . . .
>
> . . . We are Liyagalawumirr, here at Mirarrmina, we got all the same songs, same *mardayin*.
>
> But this, David Malangi, he got a little bit different . . . he's fully Manyarrngu, and Garrawurra. His *mokoy* [the spirit figure, Gurrmirringu], comes from Mulanga first, that's right, but now comes from Manyarrnga, he was singing at Mulanga, other side [of Glyde Rover], that country. That's Malangi, he's two clans, firstly Liyagalawumirr and

then Manyarrnga. Bottom story is Wagilag, but then they turned into Liyagalawumirr. He is Liyagalawumirr, Manyarrnga, and then's he's joined into the Garrawurra mob, because two Garrawurra Sisters (Djan'kuwa Sisters), they had a waterhole in here at Dhamala. . . .

> We all have to sing, people from Mirarrmina, all the people, Lilypiyana mob, Durrurrnga mob, Manyarrngu mob, we all have to sing, Mandhalpuy, Balawuy, one Wititj, one song, *manikay*. And we are all Liyagalawumirr, but I'm Lilypiyana, Malangi's Manyarrngu, Yambal's Durrurnga, Minygululu's Balawuy.

This profusion of relations partly reflects the different names, manifestations, and doings of Ancestral Beings on their journeys from place to place: "These two Wagilag Sisters, I haven't heard what were the first names of these two Wagilag Sisters, when they travel from east, before they reach Mirarrmina. Then they called themselves Garangarr and Buwaliri, but I don't know what are the real names before they reached Mirarrmina. But before they reached other side of Mirarrmina, maybe in other places they have other names. . . . But when they came from Ngilipidji, they had other names, which I haven't been told." This in turn creates a web of relations between people and places. Impossible to fathom, it can only be mediated: "That [is] why, as Durndiwuy [said], that's Liyagalawumirr country there at Gurka'wuy, but maybe we not all own it, maybe someone else, maybe a Galpu mob, or maybe other Liyagalawumirr people, but we don't own him, right? We got Liyagalawumirr country, as Durndiwuy [said]. But we can say that there's a lot of Liyagalawumirr country owned by Durrurnga mob, Manyarrngu mob, only all based on Wititj, you know."[52] If the modern Western artist is conceived as a relatively autonomous sovereign subject, modern Yolngu live in a matrix of relations that is deeply intersubjective. *The Aboriginal Memorial* is a compendium of such relations among sixteen clans grouped into nine sections and as such is a model of—to quote Habermas—"how communicative action mediates between the ritually preserved fund of social solidarity and existing norms and personal identities."[53]

The Aboriginal Memorial represents this play of relations in Yolngu life through the arrangements of the poles—which are clustered into clan groups as a landscape or cartography of their actual geopolitical juxtapositions on the ground. The arabesque trail snaking through the middle of *The Aboriginal Memorial* symbolizes the Glyde River slithering north through the Arafura Swamp to the sea (and Milingimbi), but it also acts like an ancestral song line threading the clans together and activating their moiety and ancestral (including *bapurru*) connections. In walking along its track, the audience enacts these various connections in a quite literal performative sense, but it feels more like an undercurrent than something you can put your finger on. The effect is not revelatory but immersive. Thrown into a cacophony of songs, you are made to feel the pressure of mediation as a force in its own right. Its landscape and installation art format, which is the conceptual means of mediating or holding the various elements of *The Aboriginal Memorial* in relation, was largely Mundine's doing, but it was also arrived at through consultation with Waterlow, Dhathangu, and Malangi. From this warp and weft of Indigenous and Western art traditions, these men, with the help of their artist collaborators, wove a new cloth that is primarily about its own mediation. In this respect *The Aboriginal Memorial* is presented as a contemporary Yolngu model for social and political relations. In the context of its making—the bicentenary and contemporary art—this frontier war memorial was not a gesture of reconciliation, as it has sometimes been interpreted, but a peace plan.

Notes

1. Habermas, *The Theory of Communicative Action*, 57.
2. Sutton, *The Politics of Suffering*, 175.
3. Warner, *Black Civilization*, 467.
4. Ford, *Settler Sovereignty*.
5. Habermas, *Theory of Communicative Action*, 5.
6. Morphy, *Becoming Art*.
7. The most extensive is Jenkins, "It's a Power."
8. Lendon, "Relational Agency."
9. Aboriginal Arts and Crafts (AAC) was established by the Australian government in 1971 to regulate the marketing of Aboriginal art and operated throughout the 1970s and '80s.
10. Maynard, *Fight for Liberty and Freedom*; Attwood, *Rights for Aborigines*.
11. Conversation with Mundine, February 14, 2017. At Ramingining, Mundine replaced a local Aboriginal man, Brian Yambal—a short-lived art and craft adviser who quit to become a schoolteacher.
12. Mundine, "The Native Born," 78.
13. Mundine, "Meetings with Remarkable Men and Women," 88.
14. Mundine, "Meetings with Remarkable Men and Women," 88–90.
15. Macknight, *The Voyage to Marege*.
16. Warner, *Black Civilization*, 468.
17. Sutton, *Politics of Suffering*, 167.

18. Sutton, “Unusual Couples,” 5.

19. Warner, *Black Civilization*, 468.

20. McKenzie, *Mission to Arnhem Land.*

21. Wells, *Milingimbi*, 45.

22. McKenzie, *Mission to Arnhem Land*, 174; Wells, *Milingimbi*, 46–48.

23. Mundine, “The Native Born,” 50.

24. Hamby and Gumbula, “Development of Collecting,” 193–95.

25. They were of “modest size . . . somewhat roughly executed without the names of the artists recorded . . . [and] in stark contrast to those produced in the following decades.” Allen and Hamby, “A History of the Art of Milingimbi,” 26.

26. Allen and Hamby, “A History of the Art of Milingimbi,” 29.

27. Lendon, “A Narrative in Paint,” 23.

28. Makarrwala was a Wangurri man but after his father was killed when he was still young he was raised by two of his märi (grandmother’s brothers), the Gupapuyngu leaders Narritjnarritj and Waltjamirr (Hamby and Gumbula, “Development of Collecting,” 200).

29. Wells, *Milingimbi*, 208.

30. Wells, *Milingimbi*, 208–14. For the kin relations of these men, see Hamby and Gumbula, “Development of Collecting,” 200.

31. Mundine, “The Native Born,” 65–66.

32. Mundine, “The Native Born,” 63.

33. Mundine, “The Land Is Full of Signs,” 94.

34. Mundine, “The Land Is Full of Signs,” 95.

35. Mundine, “The Land Is Full of Signs,” 95.

36. Mundine, “Meetings with Remarkable Men and Women,” 93.

37. Smith, *Thinking Contemporary Curating*, 138.

38. Smith, *Thinking Contemporary Curating*, 71, quoted in Groys, Art Power, 40.

39. Lendon, “Relational Agency.”

40. Waterlow, “A View of World Art c. 1940–88,” 10–11.

41. Mollison, speech notes for the director, 1988. The Aboriginal Memorial opening, Australian National Gallery File 87/463: Aboriginal Hollow Log / Bone Coffin Memorial, Canberra.

42. Jenkins, “It’s a Power,” 124–86.

43. Warner, *Black Civilization*, 460–61.

44. Warner, *Black Civilization*, 402.

45. Warner, *Black Civilization*, 17.

46. Warner, *Black Civilization*, 120.

47. Warner, *Black Civilization*, 4.

48. Warner, *Black Civilization*, 8.

49. Warner, *Black Civilization*, 5.

50. Morphy, *Ancestral Connections*, 131.

51. Caruana and Lendon, *The Painters of the Wagilag Sisters Story*.

52. Excerpts of interviews by Nigel Lendon, with Albert Djiwada, in 1994, 1996, and 1997. Djiwada, "The Mirarrmina Story," 74, 76; Lendon, "A Narrative in Paint," 20.

53. Habermas, *Theory of Communicative Action*, 77.

Bibliography

Allen, Lindy, and Louise Hamby. "A History of the Art of Milingimbi." In *Art from Milingimbi: Taking Memories Back*, edited by Cara Pinchbeck, 20–35. Sydney: Art Gallery of New South Wales, 2016. Exhibition catalog.

Aristotle. *The Politics*. Translated by T. A. Sinclair. Harmondsworth: Penguin, 1962.

Attwood, Bain. *Rights for Aborigines*. Crows Nest: Allen and Unwin, 2003.

Caruana, Wally, and Nigel Lendon, eds. *The Painters of the Wagilag Sisters Story: 1937–1997*. Canberra: National Gallery of Australia, 1997.

Djiwada, Albert. "The Mirarrmina Story." In Caruana and Lendon, *The Painters of the Wagilag Sisters Story*, 72–87.

Ford, Lisa. *Settler Sovereignty: Jurisdiction and Indigenous People in America and Australia, 1788–1836*. Cambridge, MA: Harvard University Press, 2011.

Habermas, Jürgen. *The Theory of Communicative Action: The Critique of Functionalist Reason*. Vol. 2, *Lifeworld and System: A Critique of Functionalist Reason*. Translated by Thomas McCarthy. Boston: Beacon, 1984.

Hamby, Louise, and Dr. Gumbula. "Development of Collecting at the Milingimbi Mission." In *Strings of Connectedness: Essays in Honour of Ian Keen*, edited by Peter Toner, 187–214. Canberra: ANU Press, 2015.

Jenkins, Susan. "It's a Power: An Interpretation of the Aboriginal Memorial in Its Ethnographic, Museological, Art Historical and Political Contexts." Master's thesis, Australian National University, 2003.

Lendon, Nigel. "A Narrative in Paint." In Caruana and Lendon, *The Painters of the Wagilag Sisters Story*, 20–48.

Lendon, Nigel. "Relational Agency: Rethinking *The Aboriginal Memorial*." *emaj* 9 (May 2016): 1–28.

Macknight, C. C. *The Voyage to Marege: Macassan Trepangers in Northern Australia*. Carlton: Melbourne University Press, 1976.

Maynard, John. *Fight for Liberty and Freedom: The Origins of Australian Aboriginal Activism*. Canberra: Aboriginal Studies Press, 2007.

McKenzie, Maisie. *Mission to Arnhem Land*. Adelaide: Rigby, 1976.

Mollison, James. Speech notes for the director, 1988. The Aboriginal Memorial opening, file 87/463: Aboriginal Hollow Log / Bone Coffin Memorial, Australian National Gallery, Canberra.

Morphy, Howard. *Ancestral Connections: Art and an Aboriginal System of Knowledge*. Chicago: University of Chicago Press, 1991.

Morphy, Howard. *Becoming Art: Exploring Cross-Cultural Categories*. Sydney: University of New South Wales Press, 2008.

Mundine, Djon. "Aboriginal Landscape 1941." In *Margaret Preston*, edited by Deborah Edwards and Rose Peel, 20. Fisherman's Bend, Victoria: Thames and Hudson Australia, 1995. Exhibition catalog.

Mundine, Djon. "Is It Sacred? The Collarenebri Files." *Artlink* 30, no. 4 (2010): 54–56.

Mundine, Djon. "The Land Is Full of Signs: Central North East Arnhem Land Art." In *Art from the Land: Dialogues with the Kluge-Ruhe Collection of Australian Aboriginal Art*, edited by Howard Morphy and Margo Smith Boles, 85–120. Charlottesville: University of Virginia, 1999.

Mundine, Djon. "Meetings with Remarkable Men and Women." In Caruana and Lendon, *The Painters of the Wagilag Sisters Story*, 88–124.

Mundine, Djon. "The Native Born." In *The Native Born: Objects and Representations from Ramingining, Arnhem Land*, edited by Bernice Murphy, 29–112. Sydney: Museum of Contemporary Art, 2000. Exhibition catalog.

Smith, Terry. *Thinking Contemporary Curating*. New York: Independent Curators International, 2012.

Sutton, Peter. *The Politics of Suffering: Indigenous Australia and the End of the Liberal Consensus*. Carlton: Melbourne University Press, 2009.

Sutton, Peter. "Unusual Couples: Relationships and Research on the Knowledge Frontier." 2002 Wentworth Lecture, Australian Institute of Aboriginal and Torres Strait Islander Studies, Canberra, Australia, May 2002.

Warner, W. Lloyd. *Black Civilization: A Social Study of an Australian Tribe*. Rev. ed. New York: Harper Torchbooks, 1964.

Waterlow, Nick. "A View of World Art c. 1940–88." In *1988 Biennale of Sydney: From the Southern Cross: A View of World Art c. 1940–1988*, edited by Byrony Cosgrove and Nick Waterlow, 9–12. Sydney: Biennale of Sydney / ABC Enterprises, 1988. Exhibition catalog.

Wells, Anne E. *Milingimbi: Ten Years in the Crocodile Islands of Arnhem Land*. Sydney: Angus and Robertson, 1963.

RUTH B. PHILLIPS

ARCHIVAL EXPLORATION 3 NORVAL MORRISSEAU AND SELWYN DEWDNEY

Inventing Modern Anishinaabe Painting

Anishinaabe artist Norval Morrisseau had a gift for friendship. Throughout his life, his personality — intense, warm, and compelling — drew people to engage with and support him. Three men, all professionally trained artists, arrived in the Red Lake district of northwestern Ontario in the 1950s and early '60s, when Morrisseau was working at the Cochenour-Willans Mine and striving to establish himself as an artist. The aspiring young artist offered friendship and solicited their help, and each in turn provided advice that introduced him to the techniques and codes of fine art production and the art worlds of Europe and southern Canada.

The first was Joseph Weinstein, who arrived in Cochenour in 1955 as the new mining company doctor. A graduate of McGill University and the School of the Montreal Museum of Fine Arts, he had done his medical training in Paris. Through the art classes he also took at the Academie de la Chaumiére and his wife Esther's close friendship with Picasso's daughter-in-law, the Weinsteins had frequented modernist art circles where admiration for "primitive art" was well established.[1] On their return to Montreal for Joseph's medical residency, they discovered a Canadian iteration of this taste in the new productions of Inuit sculpture that the Canadian Guild of Handicrafts began to market in 1949.

Selwyn Dewdney (1909–79) and Morrisseau met five years later. Dewdney had graduated from Toronto's Ontario College of Art (OCAD) in the middle of the Depression; taught art in the London, Ontario, school system; carried out mural commissions for public and corporate buildings; and, with his wife Irene, founded Canada's first occupational art therapy program. He visited Red Lake in connection with two research projects he undertook in retirement under the auspices of Toronto's Royal Ontario Museum. One was the first systematic study of the Indigenous rock paintings found across the Canadian Shield; the second was a study of the related pictographic tradition incised on the birchbark scrolls used by shamans of the Anishinaabe Midewiwin Society.[2]

Jack Pollock (1930–92), a Toronto artist and gallerist trained at OCAD and London's Slade School of Fine Art, came to northwestern Ontario in the summer of 1962 to teach a summer course for art teachers. When Morrisseau sought him out and showed him his paintings, Pollock quickly organized the artist's first, now legendary, show at his Toronto gallery. The enthusiasm of the buyers and the positive reviews of the journalists catapulted Morrisseau to national fame (Document 6) and inspired a new movement, known as "Legend Painting," "Woodland School Painting," or, more accurately, Anishinaabe art.[3]

In most respects Morrisseau's early life had unfolded according to patterns widespread across Canada during the first half of the twentieth century. He was born in 1931 on the Sand Point reserve near Lake Nipigon and raised by his grandparents.[4] During his childhood and youth in the 1930s and '40s, the lives of Indigenous people in Canada continued to be governed by the notorious federal Indian Act, a piece of Victorian legislation that defined "Indians" as wards of the state and subjected them to projects of directed assimilation whose ultimate aim was the erasure of Indigenous languages and cultural traditions and absorption into settler society.[5] Its primary mechanism was the removal of children to underfunded, church-run residential schools that taught only industrial school curricula. Children not only suffered the loss of parental care and affection but also hard agricultural work, forms of physical and sexual abuse, and — too often — death from malnourishment and disease. They were taught to regard Indigenous languages, spirituality, and ritual arts with a sense of shame and inferiority and to fear the public exposure of shamanistic practices that continued in private. Such formal instruction as Morrisseau received was acquired during the two years he spent at one of these schools, the St. Michael's Residential School in Thunder Bay, Ontario, and three further years in a local public school.

In another respect, however, Morrisseau's young life was atypical, for although his grandmother was a practicing Catholic, his grandfather, Moses

"Potan" Nanakonagos, was a shaman and a member of the Midewiwin Society. He transmitted to his grandson ancient Anishinaabe oral traditions, beliefs, and aspects of the mnemonic pictographic system used to record Midewiwin rituals. Morrisseau later recalled tracing the outlines of the supernatural beings in wet sand with a stick and his grandfather's guidance on his first vision quest around the age of twelve.[6] In Anishinaabe tradition ritually induced visionary experience invites the pity of a *manito* — an other-than-human being — to bless a human with power. The visual representation of such an experience honors the gift and works to retain its power. The further visions Morrisseau received during bouts of serious illness in his early twenties revealed to him his life's mission and gave him confidence in his ability to fulfill it. He would record and preserve Anishinaabe heritage through public acts of writing and art making and, in so doing, both command the respect of non-Indigenous people and restore his people's pride in their unique heritage. He began to write down his grandfather's stories with ballpoint pen in ruled notebooks and to depict the great thunderbirds of the upperworld, the serpents and long-tailed beings that roil the waters, and the animals that share the Earth's surface on sheets and baskets of birch bark with the crayons and paints he could purchase in local shops.

Soon after her arrival in the Red Lake area, Esther Weinstein noticed some of these paintings leaning against a wall in the local general store, purchased them, and left an invitation for Morrisseau to drop by. During the next few years the young artist was a regular visitor to the Weinsteins' home. Browsing through the large library of art books and magazines and the African, ancient Egyptian, and modern Inuit sculptures they had brought from Paris and Montreal, he became familiar not only with modern Western art but also with other Indigenous and world arts. Dr. Weinstein offered technical advice, provided professional art materials, and — perhaps more importantly — educated him to the tastes and aesthetic values of modern art cognoscenti. By the time Selwyn Dewdney arrived in Red Lake in the summer of 1960 Morrisseau was fully aware that the visual expressions of "paganism" so despised by the white authority figures of his youth were precisely those admired as "primitive art" by cosmopolitans like the Weinsteins.

Bob Sheppard, a local Ontario Provincial Police (OPP) officer who had bought some of Morrisseau's work, introduced Morrisseau and Dewdney by letter as two people with mutual interests (Documents 1 and 2). Following that first meeting, the two conducted a lively correspondence and exchanged drawings, books, ideas, and visits in London, Ontario, and Cochenour, the small town outside Red Lake where the Weinsteins and Morrisseau lived. Preserved today in the federal government's Indigenous Art Centre, these letters offer an unusually fine-grained documentation of a fruitful, two-way episode of mediation.[7] Morrisseau shared his knowledge of Anishinaabe oral traditions and sent Dewdney his manuscript and accompanying illustrations (Documents 3 and 5). Dewdney had it typed up, did light editing, and arranged to have it published. *Legends of My People: The Great Ojibway*, which came out in 1962, was a pioneering Indigenous-authored narrative and remains a classic. The critical feedback Dewdney provided to Morrisseau after receiving his letters, drawings, and paintings constituted a kind of mail-order art course whose aim was to bring their facture up to professional standards and maximize their marketability (Document 4 and figure AE3.1). He also shared his own drawings and book on rock art, a tradition until then unknown to Morrisseau. Arguably, exposure to this tradition was the catalyst that enabled Morrisseau to formulate his signature style; he quickly assimilated the simplified outlines his ancestors had used to paint sacred images on vertical rock surfaces to his grandfather's lessons in pictography. The result was his signature use of bold form lines to delineate figures and organize his compositions.

Yet Morrisseau, always his own man, accepted advice selectively. Dewdney had, for example, recommended he stick to the earth-colored pigments used in an imagined premodern past — leaping over the nearly three centuries during which Anishinaabe artists had been glorying in the bright hues of trade cloth and glass beads. Although Morrisseau tried this out, he soon developed the superb colorism that marks his mature art. The letters also suggest the barriers that discouraged an Indigenous artist from being accepted as a contemporary fine artist rather than as a maker of ethnographic artifacts or crafts (figure AE3.2). When Dewdney consulted James Houston on Morrisseau's behalf, for example, the highly successful mediator of modern Inuit art (see Vorano, this volume) suggested that Morrisseau paint on hide "like the Plains Indians."[8] It would take Jack Pollock's modernist focus to break Morrisseau out of this categorical straitjacket.

The documents reproduced here focus on the two-way mediation evidenced in the Dewdney–Morrisseau correspondence, but the more complex mediatory processes I have briefly reviewed were equally important even if less well documented. The conceptual power of the art Morrisseau exhibited in 1962 was, in the first instance, the product of his grandfather's legacy and his own vision and sense of mission. Its aesthetic appeal to the modern art lovers who flocked to the Pollock Gallery was, however, a product of the in-

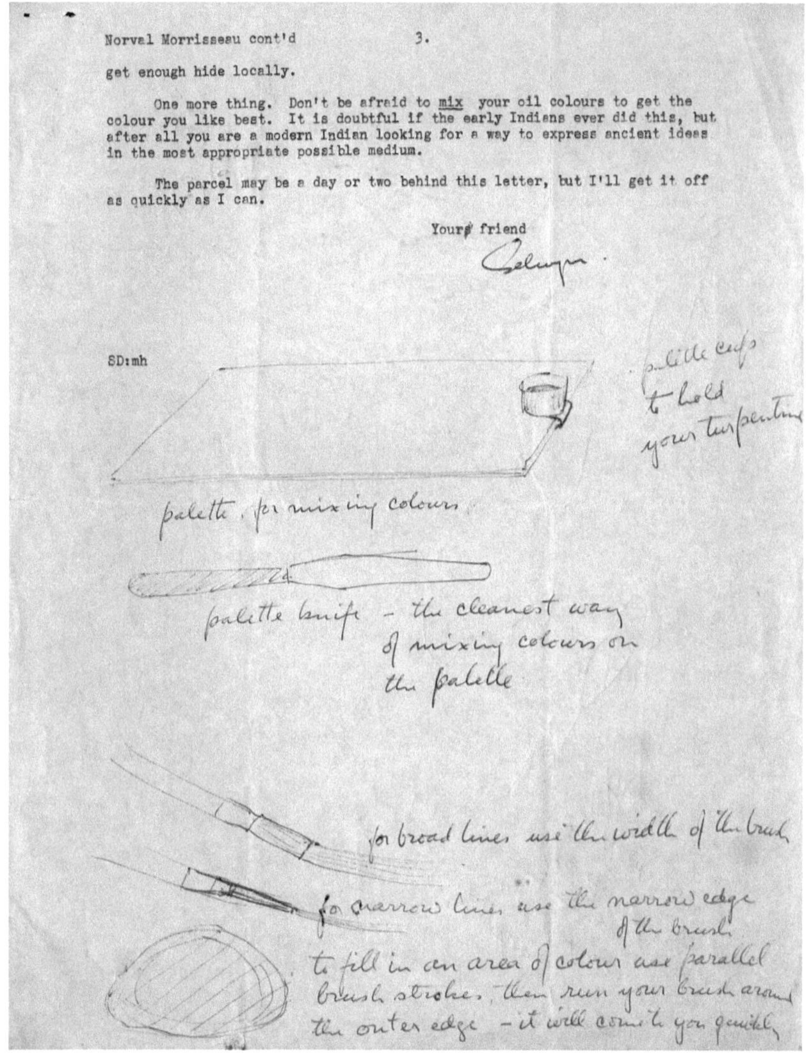

Norval Morrisseau cont'd 3.

get enough hide locally.

One more thing. Don't be afraid to mix your oil colours to get the colour you like best. It is doubtful if the early Indians ever did this, but after all you are a modern Indian looking for a way to express ancient ideas in the most appropriate possible medium.

The parcel may be a day or two behind this letter, but I'll get it off as quickly as I can.

Yours friend

Selwyn.

SD:mh

palette cups to hold your turpentin

palette, for mixing colours

palette knife – the cleanest way of mixing colours on the palette

for broad lines use the width of the brush

for narrow lines use the narrow edge of the brush

to fill in an area of colour use parallel brush strokes, then run your brush arou the outer edge – it will come to you quickl

FIGURE AE3.1 Letter from Selwyn Dewdney to Norval Morrisseau, p. 3, March 9, 1961. Dewdney Papers, CIRNAC, 306065-16.

tellectual and artistic exchanges the artist had initiated with the Weinsteins and Dewdney, the presentation deftly organized by Pollock, and the practical assistance and encouragement of a host of other people whose patronage and friendship were mobilized by the young Morrisseau's magnetic personality and irresistible drive.

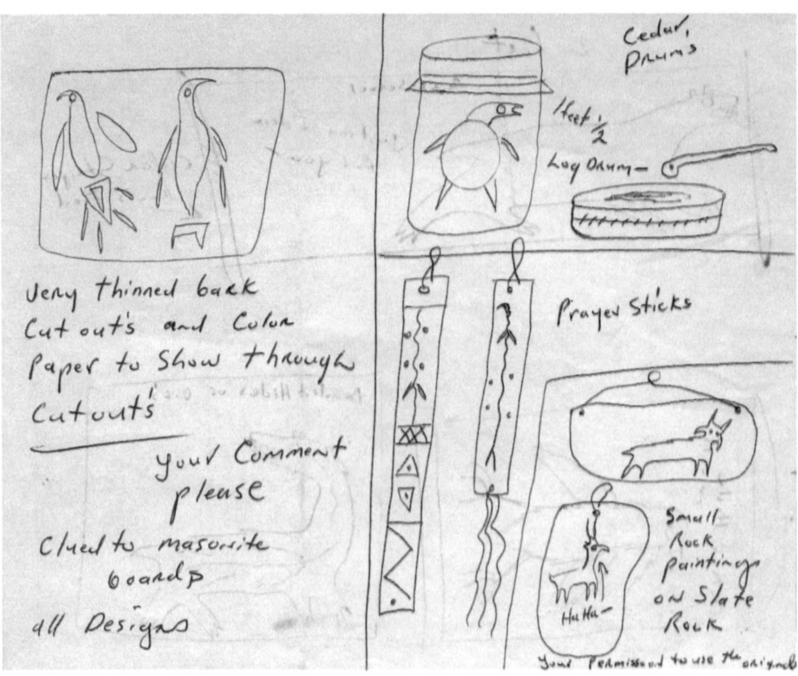

FIGURE AE3.2 One of three pages of drawings accompanying Morrisseau's letter to Dewdney of April 4, 1962. Dewdney Collection, CIRNAC, 306065-38.

THE DOCUMENTS

Document 1

Bob Sheppard's letter introducing Selwyn Dewdney to Morrisseau was written from McKenzie Island in Red Lake, where the Weinsteins and Morrisseau lived in the village of Cochenour. It was typed with a red ribbon on OPP letterhead, but it is not clear whether Sheppard or Dewdney underlined several passages in black ballpoint pen.

BOB SHEPPARD TO SELWYN DEWDNEY, HEADED "MCKENZIE ISLAND, ONTARIO/JUNE 7TH, 1960" [EXTRACT]

Dear Selwyn & Family:

Enclosed are some crayon drawings of a young Indian I have met from around Beardmore way, His crayon drawings are good and his water colours are even better. I have some of his water co~~u~~lours inside birch baskets and they are really beautiful. His name is Norval Morriseau, and he has had grade school and has done plenty of reading since leaving school, and he himself studies and collects Indian lore as well as being by way of an artist. He has plenty of access to his material being an Indian himself.

He is looking for work, married, and no children, and it seems a shame he doesn't get a chance to sell his work or find many interested people. It is not the sort of thing to sell tourists as it would go unnoticed except for the novelty. To bad the M~~e~~useum couldn't use a series of Indian paintings, or could they?

Enclosed with the picture stories you will also find the stories written out. One is about Nimkybinayshik (thunderbird) and the Devil Fish story is the second one. I also have some of his painted birch baskets but I would hesitate to send them by mail due to damage hazard.

Let me know if you are interested in meeting him and I'll get in touch with him even if he moves. Above all, send me back the drawings and stories when you have seen and read them as he wants to keep them. . . .

Please let me know if there is any way Norval Morrison [*sic*] can do his paintings where they would be most appreciated. He appears to know what he's doing and could work on birch bark, parchment, canvas, or the wall of the Museum if neccessary [*sic*].

Answer me back PDQ though if you can as Norval will be in a tizzy till I get everything back and hear from you. . . .

What do you think this boy's chances are?? He can draw and paint, grew up with the people and knows the stories by heart. I seems a shame that his talents can't be made useful and available.

Pick up the pen and drop us an RSVP right away quick.

All the best,

[handwritten] Bob,
Peg & Kids (3 now)

Document 2

In a letter to his wife written three days after his meeting with Morrisseau, Dewdney gave her his first impressions of both Morrisseau and the Weinsteins. This passage occurs between reports of his rock art investigations, daily activities, and those of his sons Donner and Peter.

SELWYN DEWDNEY TO IRENE DEWDNEY, HEADED "ON THE WAY BACK TO SIOUX LOOKOUT/WEDNESDAY, JULY 13TH/ 60" [EXTRACT]

Sunday morning [July 10] we took a L&F kicker over to Mackenzie Island, and spent most of the day with Bob taking notes on his description of Indian dance routines, eating lunch, interviewing the amazing Norval Morrisseau, recording a small site on Red Lake, with Donner along — a beautiful day — and eating supper out of cans (2 kinds of Ravioli, a big can of beef stew, and a tin of Tuna). . . .

In the morning [July 12] we broke camp, picked up our laundry, and drove over to Cochinour to view more paintings of Norval that had been bought by a Dr. Weinstein. I wanted to meet the latter, who had become a sort of patron of Norvals [*sic*]. A Montreal Jew, who lived outside of the Jewish community there, he studied medicine — and painting — in Paris. There he met his wife, a sixth generation Sabri [sic] from Israel. Both speak French exclusively with each other. We stayed for lunch, and Peter & I lingered on to converse with his wife, who is starved for the kind of conversation that you can imagine would take place.

What to do about Norval filled most of the hour and a half I had with Weinstein. It was a really weird experience the day before meeting an Indian who (a) was filled with a deep pride of race, origin, and identity (b) was almost a stereotype of everything you expect to find in an artist: sensitivity, a sureness about what he wanted to paint, didn't want to paint, liked and rejected, a craving for recognition, complete disinterest in money and material rewards. He is 29, married (to a woman he met in the San[atorium] at Ft. William, who is now pregnant), tall, unmistakeably [*sic*] Indian in feature. Maybe I'm a bit rosy-eyed about him; but there was a quiet dignity and gentleness with strength that tempt me to use the word nobility.

Weinstein, who has exhibited in Paris (whether in a well-known salon or on a street corner I don't know), paints very competent and individual abstracts — slightly reminiscent of Herb Ariss' work — and has an impressive collection of objects d'art from all over the world, is even more impressed by Norval than I am.

But what to do? Weinstein hopes to get him a surface job at Cochinour Mine (he can't work underground on account of his T.B. bout), so he can paint in his spare time and support his family. We agree that it would be fatal to get him down to Toronto for a few months of lionization and exposure to all sorts of pressures. Norval wants an exhibition. Bob Sheppard imagined they would hire him as an assistant at the Museum, and led him to hope this. I promised to use him next summer if he learns to handle a kicker and drive a car — but anything else would be impossible. He had a Grade 4 education.

That's our Norval!

Document 3

In this first letter to Dewdney, Morrisseau's understanding of the terminological and conceptual shoals he would have to navigate is clear. He states his reasons for preferring birchbark and brown-colored analogues such as plywood and his desire to exploit prospective buyers' "positive" value for the "primitive." He also outlines his entrepreneurial intention to tap government support for Indian craft production, his desire to market his work, the book manuscript he wants to publish, and implies the degree to which he was cut off from his own heritage of "Indian Designs." Morrisseau's eccentric spelling and punctuation are reproduced from the original handwritten letters.

NORVAL MORRISSEAU TO SELWYN DEWDNEY, NOV. 7, 1960

Cochenour ont.
Nove 7 1960

Dear Sir

I am writing this Letter to you No Doubt you will be Superised to get my Letter. And I will Appreciate your Reply first of all I am fine also my wife Harriet as well as my Daughter Victoria. I often Remember the Visit we all Had at McKenzie Island Last Summer and I Remember what you told me that we will see one anther again I trust this will be soon. As I Look forward to that Time. I did not Make any more Picture's Since you Left but I made about Nine pictures for the Doctor [Weinstein, written in another hand] and one Medicine Snake picture for a Doctor Head Surgeon at Winnipeg. this was Based on a Ply Board. also I made about four Pictures of the Same Manner for both Doctor's at Balmertown and here Local now I wish to ask you if you would want to Exibit Ply Board Pictures Size's are four By three feet instead of Birch Bark these are down on Ply Board and the grain

Puts a Primitive Effect on the pictures But the bark Cannot be Beat, in August or Sept I took some picture's I had as well as the Doctor's I took my Best one's and put them up for Exibit in a Handicraft Desplay and there was a Lady who work's for Toronto Some Government Project on Handicraft's as well as a man from Fort William who know's you. As both where Very pleased on my work [p 2] And theye told me to keep up the Good work, and told me Theye meet you at Whitefish Bay and you told them about Some of my Work but as I Said there wont be any Birch Bark Pictures until May and if you Still are Interest in my work I will Make some at that time but if you wish Some ply Board Pictures for an Exibit you may Have Some about Ten. but if you wish to wait until Summer then it Could be Settled until Next Summer around June meanwhile I will get Ready on ply Board and in June the Bark pictures which will be Based on ply Board. [the following passage is enclosed by NM in a square outline to emphasize it] I wish to ask you I am Sure you know a lot of people. and I Have wrote a Book on Ojibwa beliefs of all Nature This will bring some Light on the Ojibwa Indians and if this Book Could be Puplished and I to get Royaltys from this I will be glad for you to Arrange or to give me an Address of a publishing firm who would Except these Story's beliefs and Legends of the Ojibwa of Lake Nipigon and District. [end of square enclosure] I have a good steady job Now at the mine at the Cochenour mine. Also what I wish to ask you Can you Send me Some Indian Designs as well as Rock painting Picture's the ones that Could Be Put on Art. [page 3] if you Should meet or if you have time again to come into the Lake Nipigon Area Next Summer I would take you to Some places that you might have not been at the time of your trip into that Area — there is a place at Lake Superior where the Ojibwa used to put offering in a Sacred Gave to Demi-God and I Believe a lot of these Stuff Could be Recovered for the mesuem. Also if you wish to See where the Ojibwa used to get a blue and white colored Liquid that ozzed out of the Rock's and that was used for medicine I could Arrange for you to see this Place as well as a Place the Ojibwa used to Place there Dead on tree's, and other Stone medicines the Ojibwa used to get for medicine's also a place where the Ojibwa of Lake Nipigon used to get Copper for there pain's etc. this has to be very Secret as Copper is Consider Sacred among the ojibwa — and to other

Rock painting you have not Seen about 3 in all. I will Have a Holiday next Summer Perhaps then we Could Arrange this. So please Reply I will await

Yours Very truly

Norval Morriseau [*sic*]
Cochenour
Ont[9]

Document 4

In several previous letters Dewdney had reported his efforts to promote Morrisseau's work to ethnology curators at the Royal Ontario Museum, his success in interesting a publisher in Morrisseau's book, and James Houston's advice that Morrisseau try painting on hide. Here Dewdney expands on the advice he had given in his first letter (November 15, 1960): "An artist owes it to himself to experiment with many effects in order to reach the highest possible quality. And, for you particularly, who wants the world to respect your people, their beliefs and legends, it would be of value to learn all you can about the many techniques of painting, so as to earn the respect of your fellow artists in the white world." In words and drawings he provides specific instructions for working in oils in order to achieve professional quality (figure AE3.1).

SELWYN DEWDNEY TO NORVAL MORRISSEAU AT COCHENOUR, ONTARIO, MARCH 9TH, 1961

Dear Norval:

In a separate parcel I am sending you several tubes of oil paint, two oil brushes, and two pieces of moose-hide tanned by a local leather company.

The oil colours I have chosen because they are all "earth colours," that is, they occur naturally. All but the terre vert (green earth) are similar to the pigments used by the prehistoric Indians. I added the terre vert because I thought you might want to use at least one cool colour. Any of these oil colours thinned out with turpentine will apply to hide, will never change colour, and will not flake off.

The oil brushes are in two sizes. With a little practice you can get any kind of detail you wish. For instance, if you use the corner of the small brush (like this:

[empty space where a drawing would have been made on the original sent to NM]

you'll find you can show even the fisher's claws in the painting I have copied from one of your drawings. But these brushes must be cleaned thoroughly after each use. Rinse them out in turpentine, wipe them dry, then work soap or detergent into the bristles till it lathers. Rinse with water, soap again, and again, until the brush is clean. Treated like this the brushes will last for ten years or more.

The reason I could not follow your wishes about the plywood paintings was that they would not be acceptable to the Canadian Handicraft Guild. The reason has nothing to do with their artistic quality—it's a matter of craftsmanship, about which the Guild is very fussy. On your painting of Misshipeshoo, for instance, you used too much shellac in one area, so that it is noticeably thicker. In time this would be distinctly yellower than the rest. In the thunderbird painting only the medicine balls are varnished. The tempera colour elsewhere in the painting is unprotected and would flake or run under damp conditions. Also, shellac or varnish over tempera gives a "cheap" appearance that is unworthy of the quality of thought and feeling that go into your paintings. Another point, that will seem very unimportant to you, is that whoever crated your paintings for shipping, put nails through the middle of two of the paintings.

(p. 2) Perhaps I could put it this way. Your work is to show to non-Indians the richness and variety of Ojibway beliefs and legends through your paintings. Those paintings should be "dressed" as carefully as a great Meedayweninny would have dressed himself in the old days before going to a Meeday ceremony.

To put it in other words you are not only an artist but a representative of your people. To gain respect among the non-Indians your paintings must show more than the thought and feeling, forms and colours that make them works of art. They must also show craftsmanship, a concern for the way the painting is prepared for display or sale—the finish of the surface. This will help to explain to you why I am going so slowly in encouraging you. Before we make a serious attempt to sell or exhibit your work we must be sure that you have found a way of rendering it that will (a) satisfy you as an artist (b) satisfy the non-Indian viewer.

If your painting ideas are to be compared with those of other Canadian painters, and taken seriously as works of art they must be "dressed" to the best advantage.

To satisfy you, the form, design and colour must be up to your standards. This will command the viewer's respect and admiration. But if it is rendered in cheap materials, or carelessly finished, the viewer will feel that you set very little value on your own work, and the viewer will have second thoughts about taking it seriously himself.

A word, now, about oil-painting. To use oil colour on hide put a small dab of oil paint on a flat board (palette) that has been varnished and sanded smooth. Work a little colour into the brush, then dip it into turpentine and work it on the board until the paint is thinned, but still full in colour. Then apply it to the hide, which can be laid flat on a table, with stones at the edges to keep it from wrinkling.

The materials, by the way, are sent to you by the Hughes Art Galleries, at 330A Dundas Street, here in London, with the idea that they will have the first chance to sell your work. I have also left with them the painting of the white buffalo. This they feel, they cannot sell (nail holes and poor varnishing) but they hope to use it to arouse interest in your work. They have the local agency for Eskimo sculpture and prints and I thought we could first try selling your work locally — then go to Montreal. The Canadian Handicraft Guild has connections with Montreal, Toronto, and New York — when we do approach them it must be with the very best Morrisseaus in their very best "clothes."

I only wish I had more time to spend in your interests, and I know you must feel impatient at times, but among us a young artist may make hundreds of paintings over a period of ten or fifteen years before he begins to sell his work, and you are doing much better than that. I like your idea, too, of interesting other Indians in painting. Encourage them to draw or paint on birchbark and paper and send me examples of their work. But if you are to be their teacher and leader it is what you learn that matters most. I have said nothing about how the hide would be framed or stretched. If you have any ideas pass them on, but don't worry about it. Bob Hughes has a number of ideas about this, which he'll try out when he gets your painting back. I'm sending you twelve dollars (in the parcel) for your painting of Misshipeshoo which I want for myself. Perhaps you can buy some more hide with this. Turpentine you can get at a hardware or drugstore in Red Lake. Make sure it is spirits of turpentine and not Varsol or another substitute. Bo[b] hopes to get tanned deer hide very cheaply from Mexico (tanned by Indians there) if you can't. (p.3) get enough hide locally.

One more thing, Don't be afraid to mix your oil colours to get the colour you like best. It is doubtful if the early Indians ever did this, but after all you are a modern Indian looking for a way to express ancient ideas in the most appropriate possible medium.

The parcel may be a day or two behind this letter, but I'll get it off as quickly as I can.

Your friend,

[unsigned; this is a carbon copy]

Document 5

By the following winter Morrisseau was being promised support from other individuals and government agencies. He was particularly excited about the studio space provided by the mine and restates his goal of inspiring other Anishinaabe to join him in a collective project that would generate non-Indigenous respect for Indigenous people and their cultural traditions. The letter also evidences his voracious appetite for books and knowledge and the eclectic range of media and genres he saw as potential vehicles for Anishinaabe artistic expression—a sample of which is shown in figure AE3.2.

NORVAL MORRISSEAU TO SELWYN DEWDNEY, HEADED "COCHENOUR ONT" AND MARKED BY DEWDNEY "REC'D JAN 12 / 62."

Dear friend Selwyn,

I got your letter and I Excuse your Long Silence, I knewed you where up to Something good on my behalf, thank you Selwyn, We are all fine My wife Harriet my Daughter Victoria, and my son Alfred, today I Accepted the offer of being given Artist Shop, or Studio, I Expect to move [and] work in it in middle of feb/62 but mean time I am going to do art if I get the loan but if I am not given by the Indian Affairs the mine through Mr. Flagren will supply me of full my needs I am Indeed Very Pleased one Cannot Explain How I feel, I am not after any Personell Gain but for my people the Ojibwa, this is the Chance I Long awaited and this is the Chance that will see <u>our</u> (2) Dreams Come true, I was told to Stay on this Project and if Some time in future this work Demands me more then my work I was told I may take my Art work with me, even if I go away to other places my studio which will be mine will allways be there for my people, and if Someday other Branches of this Start Else where in which it will I am Sure I will be invited anyplace those Spring up—anyway I want to Built that Solid foundation here at this Studio—I want to break the Barrier Between the white worald and mine's I am Sure and firmbly believe alot of my people will take this Example I will make (3) I am very Respected and my Name has been Heard in all the Indian Homes throughout This Area, for I have all Ready planted that Seed, all it Needs Now is a Studio and many worth-while Krafts and Arts will Come, of Course there are those who are Bull headed and Ignorant Excuse the word But I know them I have no use for those who do not Respect any of thes Ancestorail Beliefs or Rights but there are those and many who, are to willing and whom I Respect and who Respect our Ancestorail Beliefs of Course this is in every people Good and Bad, we are no Different we are all Same anyway (4) I wont force any-one and I wont take those who want to take this up for money or Kicks but as I said I know plenty of the Right people. Who are Skillfull and good in Krafts SomeHow I know what is Expected by the white worald What is wanted and will be Apprecaited, I might See you this winter not sure yet any way I will Notify you—if I come, but meantime Let us get in touch with one another one Letter every 2 weeks this way you will get an Idea what is being done I want you to send me that book on Rock paint-ings. Sign your Name (5) so I will Keep it with my collection of Books' I have, Send Bob Huge's 18 Blk and Reddish Drawing if he has a Hard time Selling them at ten dollars each. Tell him to Lower them to $6.50 or $7.00 Each. With the money ask him to get me Some books about

---

Fish of North America.
Animals of North America.
Birds of the worald or N. America–

Books on Indians of North America
Different Title's—of beliefs—Lore–
BC. Sculptering—totem poles' Art—Indian Art etc,

I have a Pravate Collections of Books So far I have about 7 Books' I Never pick up no Ideas from these but I Appreciate Book of this type and I Like to Read at times (6) I have one Book Called (the Seven Rites of the OGLala Sioux, (Brown's the Sacred pipe, Blk Elk

---

Next one the Mask Gods by Waters Navaho and pueblo ceremonialish

---

This Books are very Interesting Can you get me a book on the Long House Religion of the Iroquise, or what is there belief on this,

---

anyway ask bob first if he got my Art from that Source get me Some Books as Requested

---

I am giving you Some of my work. If you do not Like None Put them into the Stove to make heat Like piccaso does, Ha Ha, aldo these are not of the best please Excuse but I will give you Some good ones Next time I Promise you my friend (7) Return take a picture of Nanabajou and Send Snap as a future use I Collect Snaps, But keep the drawing even if original. Send only SnapShot there is one More favour I wish to ask you as a keepsake from you to me, the Snake picture I want you to sign nor Name besides Mine. And get it glassed and a Narrow blk framed about ½ inch fram or 1 inch Something not to Value, Cheap frame, if I am asking to much please tell me. also I will make it up to you — Reall Soon in future, there is a piece of Cloth I am Sending along a lot of Indians know about Emproidery how would it look to have these framed — as pairs for wall panels Return cloth

---

also if Canvas textured Kraft paper is used on earth Color oils what Value would these Be for a Start

---

Well my friend I will Sign off for now I Hope to See you Not before to Long in person but Meantime Let us Thank my or our Ancestorail Gods For Leading us to that first foundation

Your Friend

Norval.
Excuse my many Mistakes and Scrippling

Document 6

The confusion reviewers of Morrisseau's first Toronto exhibition experienced about how to categorize his work is represented by Paul Duval's notice of the show in *Accent on Art*, a roundup of exhibitions in Toronto galleries.[10] While positioning the paintings both as a surviving "pocket of authentic tribal art" and as "juiced up folk art," he also signaled the modernity of its "growing personal expression."

PAUL DUVAL, "PRIMITIVE ART," *TORONTO TELEGRAM*, SEPTEMBER 22, 1962

Primitive Art

Another direction toward which the attention of our high-pressured era has been turned is primitivism. The symbols of primitive art offer a refreshing finality to the modern mind, forced as it is by a complex of decisions and concerns unknown to the aboriginal imagination

Here and there, pockets of authentic primitive art still remain. Though these are rapidly being emptied into commercial channels, the best of today's Eskimo, bushman, and American Indian art retains some evidence of tribal conviction.

A broad interpretation of primitive art would probably include the work of 22-year old Ojibway painter Norval Morrisseau. Morrisseau hails from Beardmore on Lake Nipigon and is currently having his first one-man show at the Pollock Gallery.

Morrisseau paints the legends and myths of the Ojibway on sheets of building paper and birch bark. His designs follow the patterns found in early Ontario Indian rock paintings, with the addition of brilliant red, blue, and yellow accents.

Morrisseau's designs are broad and appealing at present. They are a kind of juiced up folk art based on tribal traditions.

It will be interesting now to see how this educated Indian merges traditional folklore with a growing personal expression. If he continues to repeat the designs of his tribal past he will be in danger of disappearing into our growing host of native souvenir makers.

Notes

1. Weinstein, *The White Ojibway Medicine Man and Other Stories*, x.
2. Dewdney and Kidd, *Indian Rock Paintings of the Great Lakes.*

3. "Anishinaabe," meaning, literally, "the people," is the name used today by speakers of Anishinabemowin who live in the lands surrounding North America's Great Lakes. They are also known as Ojibwe (alternate orthographies are Ojibwa or Chippewa), Odawa (or Ottawa), Potawatomi, and Algonquin. Their northern and western neighbors, the Cree, speak a closely related language, also belonging to the Algonkian language family.

4. Biographical details are based on the chronology in Hill, *Norval Morrisseau*, 174–80.

5. The Indian Act remains in force to the present, pending agreement on measures that compensate First Nations and Metis for the services it guarantees and the losses to which they have been subjected. Its powers have been diminished by a series of court decisions and negotiated settlements.

6. Morrisseau, "My Name Is Norval Morrisseau," 45.

7. The Indigenous Art Centre is part of Crown-Indigenous Relations and Northern Affairs Canada (CIRNAC). Dewdney sold his archive of letters and ephemera to the department together with a collection of artworks from the 1960s.

8. Letter from Selwyn Dewdney to Norval Morrisseau, Dewdney Collection, binder 1-306065, Indigenous Art Centre, CIRNAC.

9. Letter from Norval Morrisseau to Selwyn Dewdney, November 7, 1960, Dewdney Collection, binder 1-306065, Indigenous Art Centre, CIRNAC.

10. For a comprehensive analysis of press reviews see Robertson, *Mythologizing Norval Morrisseau*, 59–81.

Bibliography

Dewdney, Selwyn, and Kenneth E. Kidd. *Indian Rock Paintings of the Great Lakes*. Toronto: University of Toronto Press, 1962.

Dewdney Collection, binder 1-306065, Indigenous Art Centre, Crown-Indigenous Relations and Northern Affairs, Canada.

Hill, Greg A., ed. *Norval Morrisseau: Shaman Artist*. Ottawa: National Gallery of Canada, 2006. Exhibition catalog.

Morrisseau, Norval. "My Name Is Norval Morrisseau." In *The Art of Norval Morrisseau*, by Lister Sinclair and Jack Pollock. Toronto: Methuen, 1979.

Robertson, Carmen. *Mythologizing Norval Morrisseau: Art and the Colonial Narrative in the Canadian Media*. Winnipeg: University of Manitoba Press, 2016.

Weinstein, Joseph. *The White Ojibway Medicine Man and Other Stories*. New York: iUniverse, 2009.

PART III

PATRONS/MARKETERS

"The politics of value," Arjun Appadurai asserts, "is in many contexts the politics of knowledge."[1] This statement is particularly apposite to most of the case studies in this volume, since an overwhelming majority of Indigenous modern arts produced during the mid-twentieth century were circulated as autonomous and commoditized objects and subject to the varied forces that shape perceptions of value in the marketplace. Value, however, is not inherent to the object but is subject to perennial slippages in the art market and open to new interpretations in radically different cultural contexts. It is the role of the intermediary, as Fred Myers pointed out in the context of Aboriginal Australian painting, to balance the at-times conflicting concepts of Western value, seen as an economic or business mediation, with Indigenous ideas of value, in which art was tied to cultural knowledge, intrinsically linked to the artist's sense of place and land.[2] Such mediatory figures are, in Howard Morphy's phrase, "agents of persuasion" who, through their evocative writing, social networks, and personal magnetism help to modify or create anew the existing contexts through which Indigenous modern arts circulated previously.[3]

In the context of colonial power relations and the (often engineered) segregation and distance imposed between Indigenous communities and the urban art centers of settler and imperial nations, mediators necessarily played an inordinately large role in shaping the social and institutional conditions through which the artwork's value was ascribed.

Mediators are typically situated at key junctures in broad networks, which link artists with galleries, critics, and audiences and as such they are invested with a great deal of power to regulate the back-and-forth flow of artworks and information.

Christopher Steiner's analysis of the traffic in contemporary African art posits three ways in which cultural intermediaries shape value: (1) by altering the presentation and framing of the work, both figuratively and literally, including its placement in the gallery or the museum; (2) by shaping the description of objects, writing evocative and enticing promotional texts that may reinforce or challenge well-worn and often romantic assumptions; and (3) by altering the artworks themselves, directly or indirectly, through the provision of new tools and techniques, advice, models, and working methods.

During the middle decades of the twentieth century, such mediations intervened in attitudes toward Indigenous art forms that were already being destabilized by the post–World War II postcolonial activism of both internally and externally colonized peoples. During the late nineteenth and early twentieth centuries, missionaries had redoubled their attempts to suppress Indigenous ritual practices and related arts while the rapacity of ethnographic collecting had the dual impact of imposing Western typologies of value upon Indigenous material culture and emptying Indigenous communities of much of their traditional art. Artistic creativity had been channeled into marketable souvenir productions, and even benevolent colonial officials usually saw this as the only viable artistic production of peoples as they progressed toward cultural Westernization and economic modernization. In this context, the categorical shift from "artifact" to "art" initiated by the modernist interest in non-Western arts during in the early twentieth century provided, as we have argued, a unique opening into the realm of Western fine art. The marketing of modern Indigenous arts thus responded to preexisting commodity contexts for Indigenous material culture produced by imperialism, settler colonization, and the disciplinary tension between art history and anthropology. In their marketing of Indigenous modernisms, many mediators sought to exploit the conceptual slippages between these categories to invent new modes of appreciating, consuming, and sharing Indigenous modern art.

As is shown in Roberto Conduru's chapter, which examines the interactions of the Brazilian sculptor Agnaldo Manuel dos Santos with numerous art world insiders during his short career, effective mediators tend to have an almost uncanny ability to bring together agents who are active in different spheres—museums, publishing, private collecting, the art market—all of whom contribute toward the production of value by leveraging their collective influence. Notably, Conduru demonstrates that artists like dos Santos can and did play a proactive role in self-consciously selecting or clustering certain mediators around them to further their own artistic and economic needs. This sentiment is echoed in the epigraph that opens Una Rey's chapter in which Tim Leura Tjapaltjarri, one of the founders of the Western desert Aboriginal art movement, described the well-known artistic mediator Geoffrey Bardon as "belong[ing] to us . . . you are our white man and we wish you to know who you really are." Like mediators in other contexts, Bardon wrote influential promotional texts that willfully combined different disciplinary conventions and literary genres, a bricolage-like approach described by Rey as "journalism, amateur anthropology, memoir, documentary, and creative storytelling."

Other mediators served as patrons, in the first instance, providing financial support and stability at critical moments in the artist's development. In the late 1950s, Joseph Weinstein, a local doctor who had trained in Montreal and Paris as a professional artist, and his wife Esther had collected Norval Morrisseau's early paintings, providing the financial means by which the artist could develop as an artist. In their role as patrons, they also became mentors, introducing Morrisseau to books on international modernism and providing advice on techniques and materials. In this section, the chapter by Jyotindra Jain explores the way Ganga Devi's career took a dramatic turn after meeting the modernist French filmmaker and intellectual, Yves Véquaud, who provided her with large size paper that allowed her to realize more thematically ambitious works that resonated with an elite clientele in the global art world. Because many Indigenous modern artists had little or no access to formal art education, such patrons often made it possible for artists to conceptualize and narrate their own practice or career arc and to develop a coherent oeuvre. Patronage could provide shelter from the more crass demands of the marketplace and the temptation to compromise standards to make quick sales.

There are also, however, exceptions to the centrality of marketing strategies in the emergence of Indigenous modernisms. Young Māori modernists recruited for Gordon Tovey's Northern Maori Arts and Crafts Project (described in one of our opening anecdotes) became the first generation of Māori modernist artists. Because they were trained to *teach* in the New Zealand school system, Fred Graham, Ralph Hotare, Para Matchitt, Muru Walters, Cliff Whiting, and others were relieved of the need to support themselves through their own artistic production and freed to use modern Māori art forms as a site for linguistic and cultural revival. In this instance modern Indigenous arts were premised if not on an outright *critique* of the idea of art-as-commodity, at least ambivalence toward the commodity status of their art. The ambivalence and in some cases outright hostility toward commoditization expressed by such artists is, however, the exception that proves the rule, for most mediators of modernism—and most artists—assumed that success in the marketplace was the primary means through which larger cultural or political ambitions could be realized.

Notes

1. Appadurai, "Introduction," 6.
2. Myers, "The Wizards of OZ," 183.
3. Morphy, "Aboriginal Art in a Global Context," 218.

Bibliography

Appadurai, Arjun. "Introduction: Commodities and the Politics of Value." In *The Social Life of Things: Commodities in Cultural Perspectives*, 3–63. Cambridge: Cambridge University Press, 1986.

Morphy, Howard. "Aboriginal Art in a Global Context." In *Worlds Apart: Modernity through the Prism of the Local*, edited by Daniel Miller, 211–37. London: Routledge, 1995.

Myers, Fred R. "The Wizards of OZ: Nation, State, and the Production of Aboriginal Fine Art." In *Empire of Things: Regimes of Value and Material Culture*, 165–204. Santa Fe, NM: School of American Research Press, 2001.

JYOTINDRA JAIN

9 FROM THE ICONIC TO THE NARRATIVE

Mediatory Processes in the Work of Ganga Devi

In India, as elsewhere, rural-agrarian art traditions conventionally categorized as "folk" or "vernacular" have entered into modernism through mediations motivated by the same aesthetic sensibilities as those engaged by Indigenous peoples.[1] In this chapter I interrogate the role of outside interventions into one such operative and comparatively well-anchored folk art tradition. Through a micro-study of a largely tradition-bound society in eastern India, I examine how it responded to the new while continuously revaluing and reinventing itself. I trace how an age-old practice of women's ritual wall paintings underwent a decisive transformation and how this external mediation expanded the boundaries of individual self-expression from within the fixed and founded collective tradition. In Boris Groys's words, the artists created a modern iteration of their art "not on the basis of its conformity to the cultural tradition, but with respect to its relationship to extra-cultural realities."[2] The case history presents the life and work of an exceptional and highly individual folk artist, Ganga Devi, and it affirms once again that "cultures do not impose uniform cognitive and reflective equipment on individuals."[3]

Ganga Devi consciously stepped out of the ritual wall and floor painting traditions she inherited to enter the world of imagination and expression of personal feeling and memory. At the core of her development were a range of outsider interventions to which she remained open and with which she intentionally engaged. The first crucial mediation that propelled her work into the space of the modern was the government's introduction of paper to her region. The new, profane white space of paper fired her imagination to no end and prompted her to narrativize her own life story. A second mediation resulted

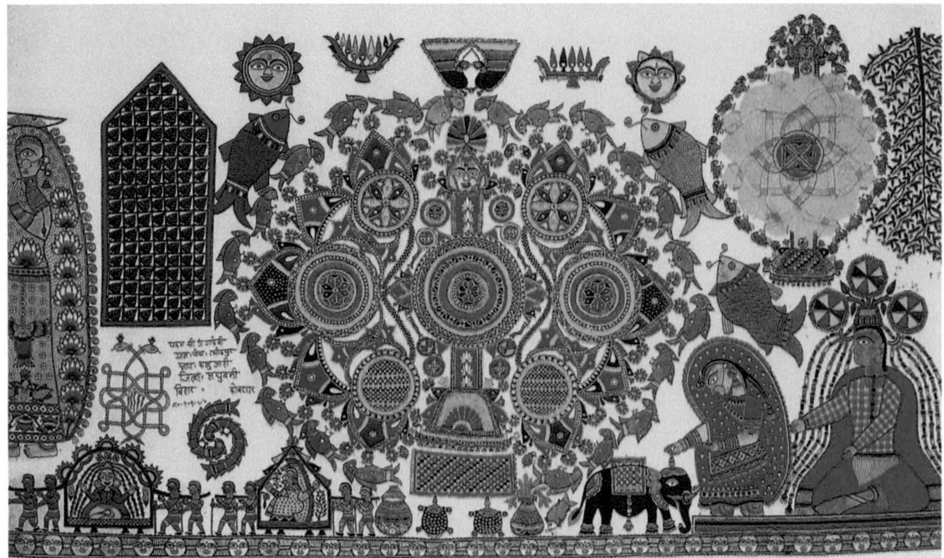

FIGURE 9.1 Sacred imagery to be depicted on the central wall of an ideal Kayasth *kohbar-ghar*, painted by Ganga Devi at the Crafts Museum, New Delhi, 1989. A *kohbar* or the lotus plant motif is depicted in the center. On its left, *naina jogin*, *pan ke ghar* (betel-leaf house), *latpatia suga* (entwined parrots), and *nag-nagin* (male and female cobras) are seen. On the right is the depiction of *bans* (bamboo groves), the branch of a *bel* tree, and the bride, accompanied by the bridegroom, performing *gauri-puja*.

from her providential meeting during the 1970s with Yves Véquaud, a modernist French filmmaker and intellectual, who provided her with much larger sheets of paper and launched her into the contemporary art world of India at a national level. The third and most pivotal mediation arose out of her own subjective drive for self-expression and modernist reflexivity, initially through her identification of herself with classic figures of the Indian epics and culminating with her remarkable cancer series. Ganga Devi, in other words, became a mediator of her inherited tradition, transforming it in light of modern conditions.

In Madhubani, situated in the ancient Mithila region of Bihar in eastern India, an old tradition required the women of a locality to collectively paint polychrome ritual paintings that incorporated iconic symbols of fertility on the walls of *kohbar-ghar*, the bride's nuptial chamber, where a marriage is solemnized and consummated. Though the women artists could individualize the rendering of each image, they had to adhere to overall ritual conventions and specifications (figure 9.1). During the 1960s and '70s a drought hit

Bihar. The government tackled the problem of providing work for the affected people of Mithila by encouraging them to paint on paper supplied to them for the purpose. The distribution of paper to the women artists allowed them to produce portable paintings that could be marketed in urban areas to augment their income.[4]

This government-authorized social welfare intervention not only brought the desired economic benefit to the community but also prompted an unanticipated explosion of visual expression, enabling the artists to break out of the confines of religious iconography and symbolism. The rise of Madhubani painting on paper in the 1970s brought about a move from traditional, ritual-bound, and collectively executed wall paintings to individual artistic creations and led to the emergence of several talented women artists. They began to explore not only possibilities for visually narrativizing their inherited mythology but also for reflecting on their personal and contemporary social and political conditions in their work. The positive critical responses to these momentous mediations fostered processes of individual artistic formation and border-crossing for the women artists of Mithila — who thereby self-consciously entered the space of the contemporary.

Ganga Devi

Ganga Devi was among the first generation of women artists in Mithila to explore paper as a new medium that could support not only the illustration of her inherited myths and legends but also the enunciation of a highly individual subjectivity, expressive of the torments of her personal life. The mediatory processes in Ganga Devi's work may be construed as two interwoven streams: the first was increasing access to sheets of paper as a new medium for painting, which determined its formal narrative structure. For Ganga Devi, rejected by her husband after his second marriage, painting appeared to be the only means of earning a livelihood, and she responded spontaneously and sensitively to the unprecedented potentiality offered by the new surface for painting. The much larger sheets of paper French collector Yves Véquaud supplied to Ganga Devi after he met her in the early 1970s fired her imagination to paint large-scale narratives. Equally important as a mediation that would enable her work to be identified with the modern, however, was Ganga Devi's invention of a visual language that enabled her to articulate the internal fabric of subjectivities.

Ganga Devi was born around 1928 to a Kayastha caste family in Chatara village, in the Madhubani district of Bihar. Her father was a well-to-do *zamindar*, a landowner, and her mother was a deeply religious woman endowed with a fine talent for painting, from whom Ganga Devi inherited the art. A few years after her marriage, and in the face of utter poverty and childlessness, Ganga Devi's husband married another woman. In order to earn her livelihood and divert her attention from this personal tragedy, she began to paint, only to be exploited by Shakti Devi, a fellow painter and childhood friend who marketed her paintings under her own name and paid Ganga Devi a pittance.[5] Yet the sheer quality of her work allowed Ganga Devi to carve a niche for herself and, with time, to earn some fame and money.

In a series of major works — *The Story of Rama*, her representation of the great Hindu epic the *Ramayana*: *The Cycle of Life*, depicting twenty-four scenes of the rites of passage practiced in her community; *Ride in a Roller Coaster*, part of the *America Series* painted after her return from a trip to the United States; and her *Cancer Series*, four paintings in which she represented the entire sequence of events of her illness and treatment from the outside, an artist seeing herself as the central character in the slowly unfolding drama of her own life — Ganga Devi invented pictorial narrative devices that translated time into space and created an unprecedented new world of images. The imagery she created largely emanated from her reflections on the personal tragedies she had experienced — her childlessness, her husband's second marriage, her exploitation by the fellow artist who made her do ghost paintings for a pittance, and finally her battle with cancer, which took her life at the peak of her artistic career — before she could fully savor the benefits of her artistic prominence.

As in the case of most women of the Kayastha caste of Madhubani, Ganga Devi's early artistic expressions were confined to joining other women in two kinds of activities: painting the walls of the *kohbar-ghar*, or the bride's wedding chamber, embellishing them with iconic symbols of fertility, and making *aripan*, or ornate floor paintings, with rice paste on a cow-dung-plastered floor in preparation for ritual installations. Ganga Devi's first encounter with paper had taken place when she was between thirteen and fifteen years old. A sketchbook, in the form of an aide-mémoire comprised of exercises set by her mother for learning to draw, shows images of regional Hindu deities. The notebook was made by stitching together loose sheets of printed registers of land records and petitions received and discarded during the British Raj. She used the narrow, marginal blank spaces beneath the printed column headings for drawing. This space constraint determined the fine miniature quality of her work, which persisted even in the later narrative paintings she made on much larger sheets, although the spontaneity of her stroke evident in these teenage exercises was later replaced by the more stylized figuration required for the shift from the drawing of individual motifs to the construction of larger autobiographical narratives.

The circumstances of Ganga Devi's second encounter with paper were crucial and fateful. She recalls:

> (One day) my husband and his new wife entered my room and ordered me to get up from near my trunk and sit elsewhere. It was like a dacoity [armed robbery]. They opened my trunk. There was nothing much in it. There were two rupees for buying paper and pigments for painting a *kohbar* diagram for my brother's son's wedding. My co-wife took away the money. I cried, I prayed, I requested her not to take the money kept for painting this particular *kohbar*, but she did not listen. . . . After initial resistance, I gave up. She also took away my sari, my blouse, soap, two bottles of hair-oil, bed-sheets . . .
>
> I was very unhappy. I thought, I will not survive. I closed my eyes. There was darkness all around me. When I woke up, I felt peaceful. A thought came to my mind: "I can paint, I can construct figures of *sikki* grass." I went to Shakti Devi, my childhood friend who, too, was from my father's village and was a renowned painter. I told her: "You are like my mother, like my sister, give me some work. I am lost in life, put me back on the track. I will work and earn my livelihood." Shakti Devi gave me some paper and I started painting. Shakti Devi, herself a painter, used to pay me one rupee, three rupees, or five rupees for my paintings. I never earned a hundred rupees from her. Along with her own work, Shakti Devi supplied buyers with paintings bought from other artists. She sold them in Delhi and Patna and retained the whole amount for herself. One day I went to Shakti Devi and requested her to lend me half a rupee to buy some soap to wash my dirty clothes. She refused to lend the money with the words: "There is no balance in your account."[6]

"I Am Ganga Devi": A Providential Meeting with the French Collector Yves Véquaud

Ganga Devi's life took a momentous turn with the "opening of the Madhubani office" in 1973, which distributed sheets of paper to women artists.[7] She was among the first recipients. Around the same time, Yves Véquaud, a French collector of Madhubani painting (also known by the name Bihko Fransi in

Madhubani), happened to see a couple of Ganga Devi's works with an agent in the city of Patna and tracked her down in her village.[8] Ganga Devi recalled:

> When the Madhubani Office came into existence, funds were released from the Patna Office.[9] Each artist was given Rs. 1,500. . . . All of us painted with material bought from the grant. The paintings were sent to Patna. Bihko Fransi, who used to buy paintings from Shakti Devi, saw some of my paintings with her and asked her about the identity of the artist. Shakti Devi said: "It is by one of my relatives," but did not give my name. From the Rs. 1,500 that I had received, I bought paper and inks and made a painting. This painting was sent to Patna. Bihko Fransi saw it there and on enquiries found out that it was my work. He learnt that I lived in Madhubani and thus came to the Madhubani Office in search of me. In those days I often did not sign my works because Shakti Devi did not allow me to sign. . . . She would say: "If you write your name, your painting will not be sold."
>
> Misra Sahib of the Madhubani Office arranged for a car to bring Bihko Fransi to my village.[10] When he reached our locality, he asked: "Where is Ganga Devi's house?" Some people showed him the house. I saw the car and said to myself: "Where is the car from? Those who come looking for my husband come on a bicycle." From the car alighted Bihko, a white man. I wondered: "Where does this white man come from?" I was watching the scene through the slits in the thatched wall. He asked: "Is there anyone called Ganga Devi here?" A voice said: "Yes, she is here."
>
> At that moment, giving up all sense of modesty, I came out and said: "Yes, I am Ganga Devi." He enquired about my work. I showed him three or four of my paintings and told him that I was working on another one. . . . Bihko gave me a sheet of paper and asked me to paint on it and send the painting to him. As arranged, I sent the painting to Bihko, and he bought it. He gave me three more sheets of paper. I painted on these. He bought them. He went on supplying paper to me and I went on painting. Once he gave me a paper roll of 5 × 7 feet. I painted on this. He took this painting to Delhi. He also made a film on me.[11] This was seen by Pupul Jayakar and Indira Gandhi.[12]

Véquaud, who was among the first collectors of Madhubani paintings, was a patron, connoisseur, collector, and photographer — one of numerous Westerners attracted to the arts and spirituality of India during the 1960s and '70s, including popular musicians like the Beatles, American poets like Allen Ginsberg and Robert Creeley, and Italian arte povera artists Alighiero Boetti and Francesco Clemente. Véquaud was an associate of Henri Cartier-Bresson and a close friend of another eminent photographer, Edouard Boubat. He first traveled to Bihar in 1970 in his quest for traditional folk painting and, in 1973, made a film on women painters and their arts with Boubat and George Luneau. His book *Women Painters of Mithila*, published in 1977, reliably documented the artists' work but did not attribute the works to individual women artists — consistent with the convention of anonymity associated with folk, "primitive," and ethnographic arts that was only just beginning to be challenged.[13] Véquaud was, however, the first to recognize Ganga Devi's exceptional talent and to introduce her work to the art world.

Ganga Devi's encounters with Véquaud, first in 1970 and then multiple times in 1973, proved fortuitous. His offer of enormous sheets of paper to paint on was, perhaps, motivated by his recognition in Ganga Devi of a creative force waiting to erupt. They opened up new horizons for the creation of her works on a grand scale and ushered in the period in which she created her master works, beginning with *The Story of Rama* (1973–83). Ganga Devi based her two-part work on the *Ramayana*, seeing in this ancient Indian epic metaphors of her own tragedy. A decade later she created her large-scale work *Cycle of Life*, depicting the rites of passage as performed in her caste. The seeds for her subsequent autobiographical paintings charged with still deeper subjectivities, most notably the *America Series* and *The Cancer Series*, were also sown in this new beginning.

As Ganga Devi recounted, Véquaud and the members of his film unit introduced her work to the powers in Delhi, after which "a thought was given to consider me for a National Award":[14]

> Misra Sahib of the Madhubani Office obtained a large sheet of paper and asked me to paint on it. I told him that I had no place to sit and paint. There was no peace at home. Misra Sahib invited me to stay in his house and paint there. On this, my husband's brother said: "You have got our nose and ears chopped," ["down-graded the family's honour by staying in another man's house"]. My husband said: "I will tear the paper to pieces." They said they would not allow me to go to Madhubani and live with Misra Sahib's family. Badridas, my sister's relative, intervened and I just left for Madhubani. Misra Sahib and his wife were very kind to me. . . . I painted day and night. My husband knew this much that I was not a woman of bad character. My co-wife was also quiet, after she learnt that I had a grant of Rs. 1,500.

I was selected for the National Award. As soon as I came to know about the award, I went to Shakti Devi to touch her feet in gratitude. Shakti Devi did not look at me and went away in anger. She stopped talking to me.

The Emergence of a New Image World in The Story of Rama*: From the Iconic to the Narrative and from Word to Image*

It is remarkable that whenever paper for painting has been introduced to any folk or tribal society in India in which a prior tradition of ritual wall painting existed, the artists have responded to it by exploring the possibilities of pictorially narrativizing their inherited myths and legends, even if there was hardly any precedent for narrative painting in their painting traditions themselves.[15] Ganga Devi responded directly to the unanticipated and unforeseen "ocean of white space," which immediately prompted her to imagine civilizational narratives of her community's culture and its legends on an equally grand scale. She evolved a new language of pictorial form, filtered through a fine sense of image-making, and she developed visual strategies for translating time into space, composing a framework within which the characters and the paraphernalia around them could operate.

Besides the ancient Sanskrit *Ramayana* of Valmiki and the medieval Hindi one by Tulsidasa, innumerable stories of Rama have survived in living folklore as well as in the theatrical performances of Ramlila, especially popular in northern India. The nucleus of the story revolves around the Hindu god Rama, whose wife Sita is abducted by the demon king Ravana, leading to a battle between the two that ends with Rama's victory and the annihilation of Ravana, the liberation of Sita from the latter's captivity, and the coronation of Rama as supreme deity. A whole gamut of stories and narratives revolve around this central story as the hero wanders across forests, rivers, and mountains during the banishment from his kingdom, hunts far and wide for Sita, and engages in the battle itself—similar, perhaps, to other epics.

Ganga Devi's pictorializing of the *Ramayana*, which comprises two panels of 290 centimeters by 155 centimeters each, is emotionally intertwined with the events of her own life. For example, she compares her situation of working on a large painting while staying in another person's house—despite her estranged husband's objection to the "blasphemy" represented by a married woman living in another person's home—to Sita's captivity. Rama fought battles to liberate Sita from the demon Ravana but ultimately banished her on the grounds that the long time she spent in Ravana's realm had compromised her chastity.

Ganga Devi's *Ramayana* series marks the beginning of her large-scale narrative paintings. Once she had envisaged the space required for each episode in general terms, she earmarked a rectangular enclosure bound by ornate borders on all four sides to illustrate the episode. The first characters she drew in each enclosure were those related to the climactic part of the episode, followed by renderings of the secondary characters. The remaining spaces are filled with sprawling vegetation — sometimes used as scene dividers, sometimes to define locations such as a forest or a garden, and quite often as space fillers. (As Ganga Devi pointed out in another context, emptiness of space is "tantamount to infecundity.")

The faces of the characters in Ganga Devi's *Ramayana* are almost invariably shown in profile — two figures in profile directly face and address each other, deeply engaged in the action of the scene. As succinctly pointed out by Meyer Schapiro: "[Profile] is broadly speaking like the grammatical form of the third person, the impersonal 'he' or 'she' with its concordantly inflected verb; while the face turned outward is credited with intentness, a latent or potential glance directed to the observer, and corresponds to the role of 'I' in speech, with its complementary 'you.'"[16]

The only consciously intended use of the frontal perspective in Ganga Devi's bipartite *Ramayana* occurs in the last scene, which depicts the coronation of Rama after he kills the demon king Ravana. Here, his coronation is also tantamount to the consecration of his image through a divine presence (figure 9.2). Now Rama and Sita are no longer characters participating in the scene-by-scene unfolding of a story but are presented as a sacred tableau, the most popular image of worship for Hindus. The transition in this dual strategy of painting from profile as third-person narrative to frontal view in which the viewer is addressed in the second-person singular marks a parallel transformation of Rama from a mere mortal king into a divinity. In this culminating scene the viewer is also transformed from spectator to devotee, directly facing the object of his veneration. Sita, seated next to him, is now shown with a halo around her head for the first time.

Illustrating the epic on such a grand scale was Ganga Devi's first project after encountering large sheets of paper, and it caused her to dive deep into her memory of watching various traveling folk theater performances of Ramlila. A few days before her husband's second marriage, she went on a pilgrimage to nearby Janakpur, Sita's birthplace, where she said she witnessed Ramlila performances continuously for fifteen days in fifteen different villages. It was about fifteen years after this major exposure to Ramlila theater that she

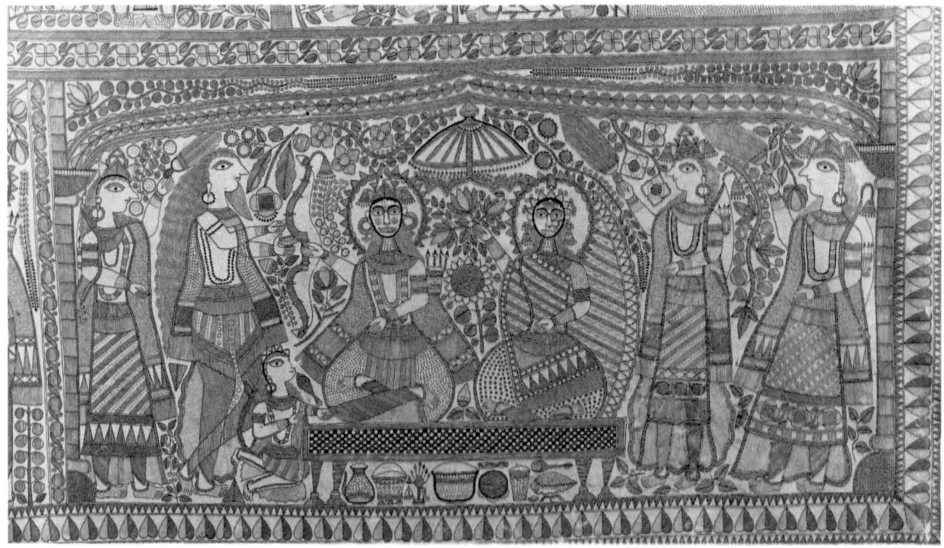

FIGURE 9.2 Ganga Devi, *The Story of Rama*, 2, detail: Coronation of Rama, 1975–77. Ink on paper, 290 cm × 155 cm (full painting). Image courtesy of the National Crafts Museum, New Delhi, acc. no. 7/54/18.

undertook the project of illustrating the entire *Ramayana*. In so doing, she evolved an effective strategy to depict the more complex narrative situations by borrowing elements from popular theater. The concluding scene depicting Rama and Sita in Ganga Devi's painting is directly based on the climactic tableau of the Ramlila theater, where it is customary on the last day of the nine day performances for Rama and Sita to be crowned and to appear seated frontally while being venerated by the audience with ritual offerings.

This theatrical tradition was also a source of inspiration in Ganga Devi's translation of time into space. A standard practice in Ramlila theater is to enact simultaneously on the stage two different episodes taking place in two different locations or at two different moments in time. Although the audience can witness both, the scenes are separated by a divider so that the characters cannot see each other. Ganga Devi frequently used this device in her *Ramayana* painting as, for example, in the scene of Sita's abduction by Ravana. Here the scenes of Ravana arriving to abduct Sita (indicated by the presence of his chariot tucked away in a corner and demarcated by a diagonally growing tree serving as a spatial and temporal divider), of Ravana approaching Sita in the garb of a mendicant, and of Rama and his brother Lakshmana leaving to hunt the golden deer are all shown within a common enclosure as one continuous scene, though the characters of each scene are unaware of the events taking place in the adjacent one. Ganga Devi brilliantly and innovatively mediates the devices from the contemporary Ramlila theater into the pictorial narrative of the story of Rama.

The Cycle of Life

Between 1983 and 1985 Ganga Devi worked on a large painting (328 centimeters by 152 centimeters) entitled *Manav Jivan*, *The Cycle of Life*, depicting the story of the human life cycle as marked by the rites of passage observed by Ganga Devi's Kayastha caste. The temporal sequence of the events of *The Cycle of Life* unfolds through four horizontal bands, one below the other, each with a series of scenes progressing from left to right and encompassing a multitude of images in a two-fold interaction of time and space. This magnificent work comprises approximately twenty-four scenes depicting rites of puberty, pregnancy, birth, severance of the umbilical cord, the worship of deities associated with childbirth, the first breastfeeding, warding off evil spirits, purification after childbirth, the worship of family deities, physical training of the child, the tonsure ceremony, schooling, participation in the rain-making ceremony, farming and irrigation, temple rituals and worship, the betrothal ceremony, wedding ceremony, and the newlywed bride in pregnancy—this last one indicating that the cycle of life continues.

The most striking feature of this painting is its fluid, continuous narrative. In her *Ramayana* paintings she used clear borders between scenes, each of which was virtually a complete episode only loosely forming a part of the ongoing narrative. In *The Cycle of Life*, however, the objective was to portray a sequential series of rites of passage, making a continuous progression of the narrative necessary. As the eye moves from the scene of childbirth inside the house, to that of an open landscape with a farmer drawing a plough, to the underwater world of fish, crabs, snakes, and tortoises, to a wedding ceremony, it moves through the space, from one scene to the next. Simultaneously, however, the beholder perceives a temporal movement of the central character from birth to adolescence and marriage. By building up a definite sequence of events in this way, the artist achieves a narrative on canvas, merging time with space.

When Ganga Devi began work on *The Cycle of Life* she had very little in her own tradition to fall back on in terms of references to pictorial narrative devices.

She appears fascinated with entangling figures in a maze of branches and creepers growing from nowhere, using these for multiple purposes in her long narrative. They have a tremendous cultural significance in the context in which they occur. The very first scene of the narrative, depicting the ritual bath of a girl who has just attained puberty and is to be united with her husband, is surrounded by creepers loaded with blossoms and bees, as if illustrating the highly popular, medieval Mithila poet Vidyapati: bees float on the air, inhaling pollen, sucking honey. The God of Love is secretly setting flower-arrows to his bow.[17]

One of the most powerful images of the painting is that of a pregnant woman reclining on the ground while the child inside the womb prays with folded hands: "Oh God, liberate me from this hell."[18] The woman is depicted holding a bunch of mangoes in her left hand (figure 9.3). Ganga Devi consciously saves the image from becoming a formalized icon of a mother goddess of similar description by letting birds pick at the mangoes and thus keeps the image rooted in the earthly world of Mithila.[19] Similarly, the auspiciousness of the tonsure ceremony is heightened by a looming branch that almost forms a halo around the mother and on which a bird perches, a fish in its beak for good luck. In the same scene, Ganga Devi places a banana tree between two women jocularly singing abusive songs to a barber. The banana tree — considered auspicious for the occasion — does not occur anywhere else in the entire painting. The roof of the house in which the mother and child venerate family deities is covered with the customary pumpkin creeper. The grove in which children play has mango trees studded with fruit being picked by squirrels and monkeys, an environment proverbially considered fascinating for Indian children. In the scene showing little girls going to school, spaces are filled with the branches of the tamarind tree, because school-going children in Mithila are reputed to be very fond of eating the tamarind fruit. Since *bilipatra* is sacred to Shiva, a *bili* tree (wood-apple tree) is shown behind the Shiva temple.

It is common to find a *pipal* tree around village shrines in India, and Ganga Devi has thus carefully placed a large *pipal* in front of the temple. A part of the wedding ceremony being conducted under a banyan tree and a blooming creeper that forms an arch over the young bride and her mother are further examples of her use of a conventional form to represent the subjective. Ganga Devi's recycling of isolated symbolic images from the traditional *kohbar* wall paintings is evident but completely different in the contexts *The Cycle of Life* is telling. The old symbols now reappear in different roles in her modern works, often acting as new metaphors appropriate to the new contexts in

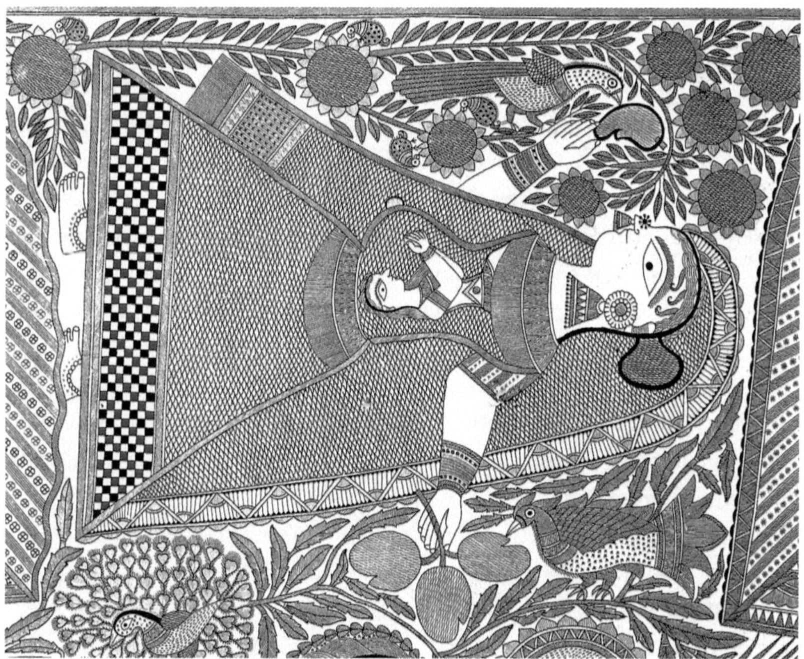

FIGURE 9.3 Ganga Devi, *The Cycle of Life*, detail: The pregnant woman reclining on the ground, 1983–85. Ink on paper, 328 cm × 152 cm (full painting). National Crafts Museum, New Delhi, acc. no. 84/704.

which they occur. *Bidh-bidhata*, a pair of birds with conjoined beaks from the *kohbar* wall paintings with erotic connotations, now appear between two pregnant women as an auspicious image that symbolizes the safeguarding of children in their embryonic stage. Similarly, another *kohbar* motif, *latpatia suga*, an erotically entwined pair of parrots, is carefully transplanted amid branches in the new context of a woman giving birth to a child, signifying creation. In the scene depicting the sixth-day ritual of the female child, two stylized geometric images of a bamboo grove painted as they would appear in *kohbar* are placed in the corners; the bamboo grove represents the male and is customarily worshipped by the female at the time of the wedding. The images of birds, bees, tortoises, fish, pairs of snakes, and lotus flowers, which appeared as symbolic images of plenty in the *kohbar*, are placed in new contexts by Ganga Devi in *The Cycle of Life* to reassert her ability to infuse her earlier images with new content.

Ride in a Roller Coaster and *The Cancer Series: The Autobiographical Works*

Such self-conscious, individual artistic innovations in the work of folk artists constitute mediations of inherited traditions. The resulting transformations constitute acts of entering the space of the modern. In the case of Ganga Devi, these acts of artistic self-formation are not merely aesthetic or stylistic but deeply personal and autobiographical—a facet that was absent in her earlier works, which adhered more closely to the inherited collective artistic tradition. As in other examples of Indigenous arts discussed in this volume, Ganga Devi's *The Cycle of Life* negotiates the forces of modernist secularism in relation to inherited ritual and spiritual practices, creating a transition to the more explicitly autobiographical works that followed, *Ride in a Roller Coaster* and *The Cancer Series*.

In 1985, Ganga Devi returned to India from the United States, where she had been sent under the auspices of that year's Festival of India to exhibit her work (and to serve as an exhibit herself!). Until that time she had rarely done any painting directly relating to her own life or personal experiences. While most of her coparticipants returned home laden with American wristwatches, cameras, radios, tape recorders, and thermos flasks bartered for their "Oriental Ware," Ganga Devi came back almost empty-handed. Rather, she was recharged by the experience of this "completely different world" that would lead to the remarkable paintings that make up her *America Series*. This series was a complete departure from traditional thematic and formal configurations and marks her entry into contemporary and experimental spaces of art.

The subject of one of these paintings, *Ride in a Roller Coaster* (figure 9.4), was based on the artist's recollection of her thrilling experience when she rode on a roller coaster during a trip to Disneyland organized for her and other participants in the Festival of India. The gravity railroad, a train with open cars that moves along a high, sharply winding trestle built with steep inclines producing sudden plunges, must have been a unique experience for Ganga Devi. Her minute observation of detail and her deft pictorialization are seen in the neat, minimalist drawing of the trestle, the way the heads of the passengers rise above the open cars, the two passengers trying to balance themselves as they clutch the moving open carriages, and the contrast between the wide-open eyes of the riders on the train as it starts and the closed eyes of those on the other train as it climbs and swiftly plunges down a steep slope. This work is unique in its treatment of space, its composition, and its conspicuous use of

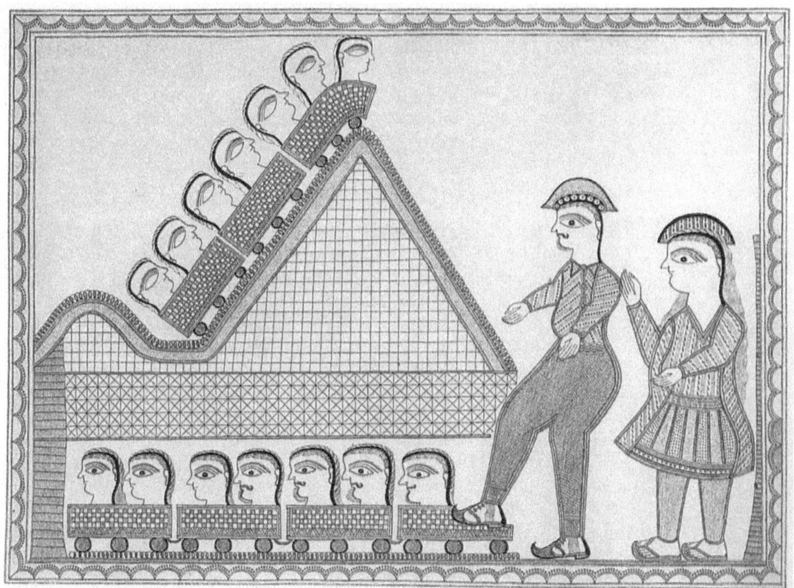

FIGURE 9.4 Ganga Devi, *The America Series: Ride in a Roller Coaster*, 1986. Ink on paper, 55 cm × 76 cm. National Crafts Museum, New Delhi, acc. no. 87/7193.

large, simplified geometric forms. For the first time the artist did not fill all the empty spaces around the key imagery—no doubt to accentuate the sense of the train soaring high in the empty sky on a steep trestle. Had the triangular trestle been surrounded by trees or anything else, the sense of sky-piercing height would not have been achieved.

Ganga Devi charmingly bends the front carriage at the peak of the triangular trestle—as though it were a centipede or a snake. Indeed, it is interesting to compare this painting to one of her traditional snake drawings used for the annual cobra worship. In this drawing the snake has been rendered in such a way that the entire drawing assumes the form of an austere, magical diagram. The exacting pattern of the diagram stems from the symmetrical movement of the convolutions of the snake along the regular grid of squares. The head and tail of the reptile (the beginning and the ends of the labyrinthine diagram) spring up in the open space, tilting in opposite directions much in the same way as the head of the first joyrider sticks out of the complex grid of the trestles in *Ride in a Roller Coaster*. Undoubtedly, in these two thematically unrelated works, Ganga Devi has recalled the past experience of neat graphic drawing of the ritual diagram of cobra worship to give form to her new experience of a ride in a roller coaster.

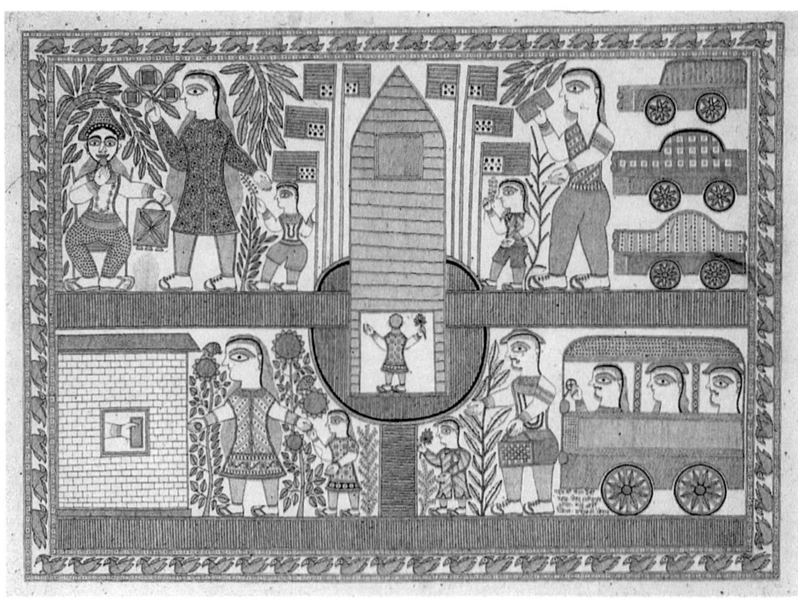

FIGURE 9.5 Ganga Devi, *The America Series: Festival of American Folk Life*, 1986. Ink on paper, 55 cm × 76 cm. National Crafts Museum, New Delhi, acc. no. 87/7194.

Another painting in her *America Series* depicts the Festival of American Folk Life, celebrated annually by the Smithsonian Institution on the mall in Washington, DC, during the first week of July (figure 9.5). At the center of the painting is the Washington Monument surrounded by American flags. The obelisk and the crossing paths leading up to it naturally divide the painting into four rectangles. The imagery includes multistoried motor cars with lotus-shaped wheels (directly recalling the chariots of her *Ramayana* series); a disembodied hand emerging from a window with a ticket to enable a visitor to climb up the monument; visitors arriving by a celestial chariot-like bus; and pedestrians carrying flowers and conspicuous shopping bags, dressed in half-American, half-Indian clothes. All are painted in Ganga Devi's characteristic Mithila style, lending the painting a fantastic quality, as though an American dream had been painted on a transparent celluloid sheet and superimposed upon a distant Mithila landscape. The dreamer, Ganga Devi herself, is shown in the elevator at the bottom of the monument. She stands there, faceless and with open arms, holding a lotus, as if poised to ascend to the sky.

Four years after her return from the United States Ganga Devi described the painting and explained the image of the hand emerging from a lone window: "In America often you do not have direct contact with people. Mostly, a hand comes out of a counter or a window, takes away your money and after a while comes out again to hand over your ticket. You do not see the person; you deal with the hand." The artist had never before depicted day-to-day images of contemporary life—motorcars, flags, ticket booths, roller coasters, elevators, or people carrying shopping bags. While the other folk artists who had participated in the festival confined themselves to demonstrating their ethnic art traditions in line with the promotion of the Indian government's cultural nationalism, Ganga Devi deviated from this agenda, charting an individual path whose mediatory process gave her a distinct and reflexive voice as an artist.

The Cancer Series

Sometime in 1987 Ganga Devi was afflicted with breast cancer. For many months the disease went undiagnosed until it had spread all over her body while the local quacks in her village made money off her illness by giving her fake ointments. Later, Ganga Devi narrated at length how she escaped a breast operation urged by a quack in Madhubani and her painful journey to Delhi to get treatment. These agonizing experiences led to the creation of four autobiographical works in which she herself appears as the protagonist watching the unfolding narrative of her own life from outside.

A doctor in the nearby town of Darbhanga advised her to go to Delhi for the treatment of cancer. On arrival at the Delhi railway station, Ganga Devi went to the Crafts Museum straight away, where she had stayed nearly two years working on her large work, *The Cycle of Life*, between 1983 and 1985.

The Crafts Museum official brought her to the All India Institute of Medical Sciences for treatment. After the initial period of about a month of chemotherapy, and after she had responded well to the treatment, the doctors discharged Ganga Devi from hospital but advised her to stay in Delhi for at least a year for periodic checkups and further treatment. A green room attached to one of the theaters at the Crafts Museum was vacated to provide accommodation for her.

Toward the end of her stay at the Crafts Museum (1988–89), Ganga Devi painted the four works (each 56 centimeters by 78 centimeters), now titled *The Cancer Series*, in which she graphically depicts her treatment by the village quacks, her brother's death, the related rituals that prevented her from proceeding to Delhi, the arduous journey to Delhi (figure 9.6), and her experiences at the cancer ward of the All India Institute of Medical Sciences.

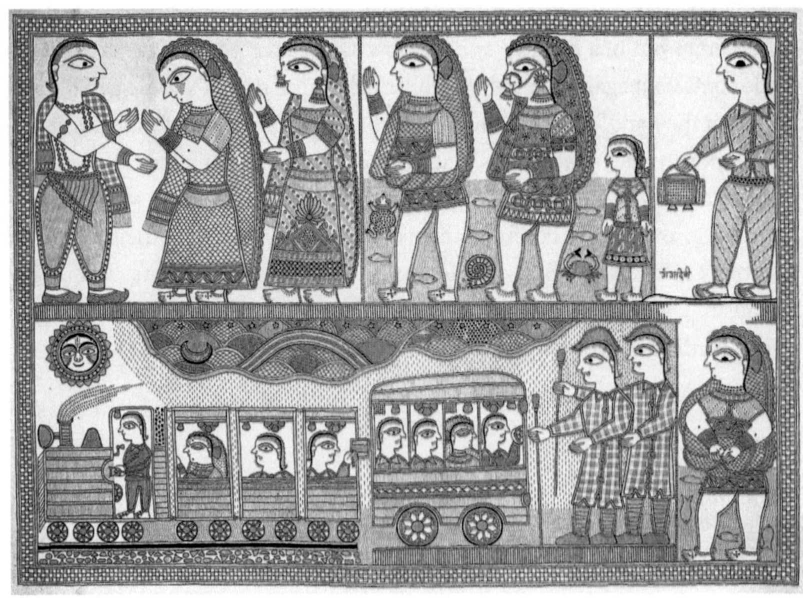

FIGURE 9.6 Ganga Devi, *The Cancer Series: Journey to Delhi*, 1988–89. Ink on paper, 56 cm × 78 cm. National Crafts Museum, New Delhi, acc. no. 89/7760 (1). Upper half (*from left*): Ganga Devi bidding farewell to a brother; accompanied by relatives proceeds to Dhagjari village; Sajjan, her younger brother's son, carries her luggage. Lower half (*from left*): Ganga Devi traveling by train from Goraul to Hajipur on a rainy and stormy night as the bus carrying her was stopped by the police on account of floods; walking through floods.

During her prolonged illness the artist often had to lie flat on her back, either when she went for medical checkups or when periodically hospitalized. Such situations conditioned her to stare at the ceiling of the hospital room for hours on end (figure 9.7). In these moments of utter loneliness, she saw ceiling fans and the typical hospital lights. These two objects — her constant companions at the time of prolonged pain — finally became the symbols of her boundless agony and unending boredom. They are prominently depicted in several registers of her *Cancer Series* paintings. The doctor's attaché case, spittoons placed under the patients' beds, temperature charts hanging on walls, and the painful moments of being given injections, blood transfusions, or measuring blood pressure had become a part of Ganga Devi's life during these years and found obvious expression in this series of paintings.

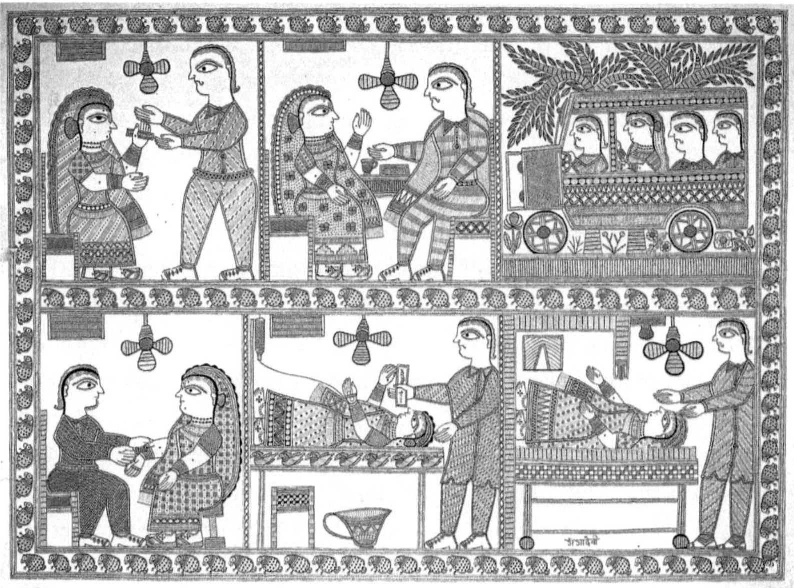

FIGURE 9.7 Ganga Devi, *The Cancer Series: The Cancer Ward*, 1988–89. Ink on paper, 56 cm × 78 cm. National Crafts Museum, New Delhi, acc. no. 89/7760 (2). Upper half (*from left*): Ganga Devi handing over her medical papers; talking to the author; proceeding to the All India Institute of Medical Sciences. Lower half (*from left*): Ganga Devi being examined by a doctor; receiving monetary help from a well-wisher; undergoing an X-ray test.

These paintings mark the climax of her departure from Indigenous ritual wall paintings, which had begun around 1970 when Véquaud's large sheets of paper led her to enter the new space of contemporary "secular" narratives and, ultimately, to an absolutely personal imagery charged by deep subjectivities. Ganga Devi died on January 21, 1991, at the All India Institute of Medical Sciences, not due to cancer but on account of a serious head injury. Her body was brought to the Crafts Museum where, coincidentally, about twenty women artists from Mithila were present. Her last rites were performed by Sajjan, her brother's son, and Gopal Madhav, her only disciple.

This highly layered case study of an Indian folk artist deeply rooted in her inherited cultural and artistic tradition as well as in a set of distinctive personal circumstances shows us an artist who responded to modernity in her art with a self-generated mediation of the modern experience. Ganga Devi was one of a small number of other tradition-bound Indian folk and tribal artists who began more consciously to engage with the conceptual transformation that the demands of the new white paper and pigments opened up for them. The features of her painterly language that attracted outside mediators like Véquaud to promote her art should not, however, be confused with Western modernism's stylizations or flattening of space. Prior to the arrival of the colonial art schools, which introduced lessons in perspective and realism, the entire spectrum of traditions of South Asian painting through the centuries was without much indication of depth dimensions, except for occasional signs of vestigial shading and chiaroscuro. Ganga Devi's use of space should thus be understood not as an example of explicit modernist intentions in a non-Western artist but as a coincidence of artistic strategies with Western modernism. The modern intentionality in Ganga Devi's work resides, rather, in her creation of a space for self-conscious and reflexive representations of her own subjectivity and experiences in the modern world. Ganga Devi fully grasped the potentialities of individual expression, both in terms of locution and personal subjectivity. Her shift from the collective rendering of ritual-bound and static iconographic symbols to fluid narrative as a more effective medium of self-expression emerged from this sentient encounter with the new.

Notes

1. The term *Indigenous* is reserved for tribal groups in India who are known collectively by the Hindi term *Adivasi*, meaning "original inhabitant." They are listed as Scheduled Tribes under the Constitution of India.

2. Groys, *On the New*, 14.

3. Baxandall, *Patterns of Intention*, 107.

4. Before the implementation of this scheme, the local administration used to make the men and women break stones to justify the payment of a daily wage as part of drought-relief measures.

5. Shakti Devi is a name that has been changed by the author.

6. Unless otherwise indicated, autobiographical passages quoted in this chapter are transcribed from interviews recorded on audio cassettes by the author who housed the artist during her recuperation from an eye operation. See also the lengthier account published in Jain, *Ganga Devi*, 11–22, and other relevant portions elsewhere in the book.

7. The Marketing and Service Extension Centre, Madhubani, functioning under the Office of the Development Commissioner (Handicrafts), Government of India, Ministry of Textiles, is popularly known among the women artists of Mithila as the "Madhubani Office."

8. Yves Véquaud was among the first collectors of Madhubani paintings. He traveled to Bihar in his quest for this genre of painting as early as in 1970. He wrote the book *Women Painters of Mithila*. He was the first to recognize Ganga Devi's exceptional talent, provide her with sheets of paper for painting, and introduce her work to the art world.

9. Here "Patna Office" stands for the Upendra Maharathi Institute of Industrial Design, Patna, Bihar.

10. Misra Sahib refers to Hari Prasad Misra, then assistant director of the Marketing and Service Extension Centre, Madhubani.

11. When the author met Yves Véquaud in Delhi in 1987, he confirmed that he and his colleague Edouard Boubat, along with a five-member team, had shot a film on the women painters of Mithila between 1973 and 1974, of which Ganga Devi had been a part.

12. Pupul Jayakar was adviser for culture to the then prime minister of India, Indira Gandhi. Indira Gandhi is known for her support for the development of Madhubani painting.

13. The author met Véquaud during his term as senior director of the Crafts Museum in Delhi, when the French collector visited the museum in 1987. He was able to verify the account Ganga Devi had given him of her interactions with Véquaud.

14. The government of India had established National Awards for Excellence in Craftsmanship in 1965. Ironically, the vague term *crafts* denoted not only professional crafts such as gold smithing but also women's domestic and ritual arts, such as Mithila painting. Ever since then the folk arts of India have remained in a single category with commercial production at policy level under the various government schemes for development and marketing. Ganga Devi was given the National Award for Craftsmanship in 1976.

15. Interestingly, when the tribal population of India, such as the Warlis, Pardhans, and Saoras, who had age-old traditions of ritual wall paintings, encountered paper, they too began to pictorially narrate the legends of their community.

16. Schapiro, *Words and Pictures*, 38–39.

17. All works by Ganga Devi discussed in this essay are in the collection of the Crafts Museum, New Delhi.

18. Ganga Devi's explanation of the scene.

19. Ambika, a prominent goddess of the Hindu and Jain pantheon, is associated with children. In her iconography, she is often shown surrounded by children and holding a bunch of mangoes.

Bibliography

Baxandall, Michael. *Patterns of Intention: On the Historical Explanation of Pictures.* New Haven, CT: Yale University Press, 1989.

Groys, Boris. *On the New*. Translated by G. M. Goshgarian. London: Verso, 2014.

Jain, Jyotindra. *Ganga Devi: Tradition and Expression in Mithila Painting*. Middletown, NJ: Mapin, 1997.

Schapiro, Meyer. *Words and Pictures: On the Literal and the Symbolic in the Illustration of a Text*. The Hague, Netherlands: Mouton, 1973.

Véquaud, Yves. *Women Painters of Mithila*. London: Thames and Hudson, 1977.

ROBERTO CONDURU

10 CARVING PRIMITIVISM

Agnaldo Manuel dos Santos and the Brazilian Art World in the Mid-Twentieth Century

In 1966, at the first Festival Mondial des Arts Nègres (FESMAN) held in Dakar, Senegal, Agnaldo Manuel dos Santos's *Animal Head* was posthumously awarded the Grand International Prize in Sculpture (figure 10.1).[1] The artist, born in 1936 on the island of Itaparica in northeastern Brazil of African and Native ancestry, had no formal art training and had worked as a sculptor in Salvador, in Bahia, from the early 1950s until his premature death in 1962.

According to Clarival do Prado Valladares, who curated the Brazilian works shown at Dakar, the judges recognized dos Santos as a symbol of "the universality of Africanism, preserved through the aesthetic expressions of new cultures."[2] In a biographical and critical text published the year after dos Santos's death, Valladares continued to present dos Santos as a "primitive artist" and his work as exceptional "both about the environment and the time in which it was done."[3] That the winning piece can more accurately be seen as an African-style interpretation of a well-known genre of Brazilian folk art, the *carranca* (figureheads used on the prows of ferryboats that sailed the São Francisco River in northeastern Brazil), dos Santos was also acknowledged by Valladares for the ancestry he expressed: "On the one hand inheriting African mythological archetypes. . . . On the other hand, drawing on canons and models from the Catholic imaginary after a gap of almost three centuries."[4]

According to this critic, dos Santos's work emerges from the amalgamation of artistic values imported to Brazil by Portuguese colonists and enslaved

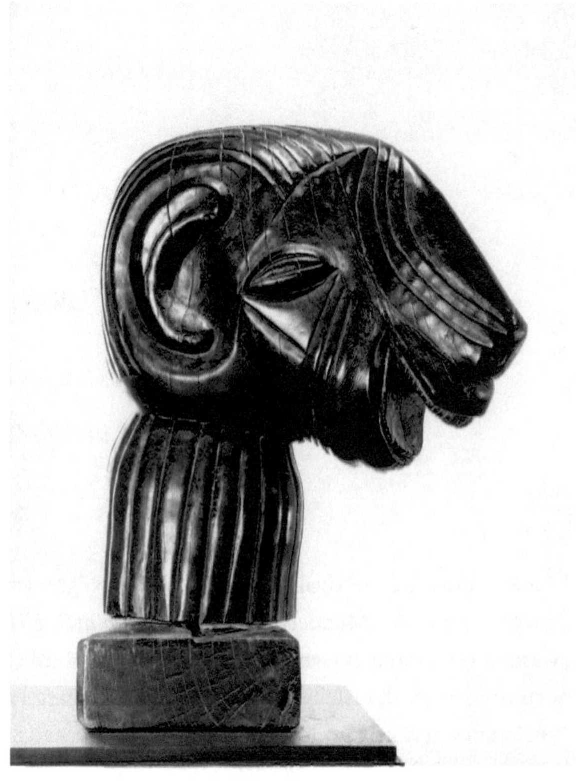

FIGURE 10.1 Agnaldo Manuel dos Santos, *Animal Head*, before 1962. Polished and bituminous wood, dimensions unregistered. Photographer unregistered.

Africans and developed into a full syncretism paralleling the prodigious ethnic mixing that generated the Brazilian people themselves. The sculpture dos Santos produced was thus genuinely Brazilian, representative of the mystified fusions that form the authenticity of the Brazilian people and their culture.[5]

Valladares was not the only critic to present dos Santos as a primitive artist. As the art historian Juliana Ribeiro da Silva Bevilacqua affirmed, "Most art critics, curators and scholars from the 1950s until recently . . . attribute dos Santos' production to his ancestral heritage, an 'atavistic feeling,' or even a 'revelation of the unconscious.'"[6] In this chapter, I assess dos Santos's formation and significance differently. In contrast to the idea of the unconscious rebirth of African and Brazilian atavisms, I argue that dos Santos consciously created his works from visual references and artistic ideas to which he gained access through the mediation of several agents in the Brazilian art world. I also argue that he was, in turn, a mediator who was both aware of his position and active in contributing to the primitivist trend of modernism.

Unconscious Atavism

On the occasion of dos Santos's first solo exhibition in Rio de Janeiro in 1955, the poet and art critic Wilson Rocha wrote that his art was "fortified by the humus that comes from the earth, intact in its African roots and the pure taste of an autonomous aesthetic, felt and realized with these immense human reserves always latent in everything that is born and grows in the deep and loving bosom of the people."[7] In part, dos Santos's life offered support for this view. He had little formal education and began to work at the age of ten on a farm that cultivated coconut, made lime, and raised cattle. At the age of twenty, dos Santos moved to Salvador, the capital city of Bahia State. With a population that was 80 percent of African descent or *pardo* (mixed) origin, it was the main center of Afro-Brazilian culture.[8] There, he had many temporary jobs (loader, shoeshiner, stockkeeper) before a chance meeting with the sculptor Mário Cravo Júnior in the late 1940s (figure 10.2). Hired initially as caretaker and watchman of Cravo Júnior's studio, he soon became the artist's assistant. As dos Santos participated in the atelier's activities, his woodworking knowledge became apparent, and Cravo Júnior encouraged him to sculpt. Before long, dos Santos's pieces started to find buyers, be exhibited, and be recognized. Critics, collectors, and curators selected examples for group and one-person exhibitions locally in Salvador, nationally in Rio de Janeiro and São Paulo, and internationally. The rapid rise of dos Santos's reputation was dramatically arrested when his talent, so suddenly revealed, was extinguished with equal suddenness at age thirty-six when he died as the result of inadequate medical treatment for barber bug fever and schistosomiasis.

The African forms that seem to emerge organically from the glossy darkened wood of dos Santos's autogenic and hieratic sculptures almost make one believe in atavism. As noted, he has been represented as embodying the silent and subliminal persistence of African arts in Brazil—arts that survived despite the violent ruptures caused by the slave trade and continuation of slavery in Brazil from the sixteenth through the late nineteenth century. In the critical reception of dos Santos's work, it is as if Africa had been reawakened in him, allowing him to carve "primitively."

Dos Santos was not unique, for other artists of African descent who lacked art school training were also inventing or appropriating African and Afro-Brazilian forms to express their worldviews. Boaventura da Silva Filho, or Louco ("Mad"), from Bahia; from elsewhere in Brazil, Gabriel Joaquim dos Santos, known as Seu (Mr.) Gabriel; Carlos Alberto de Oliveira; Heitor dos

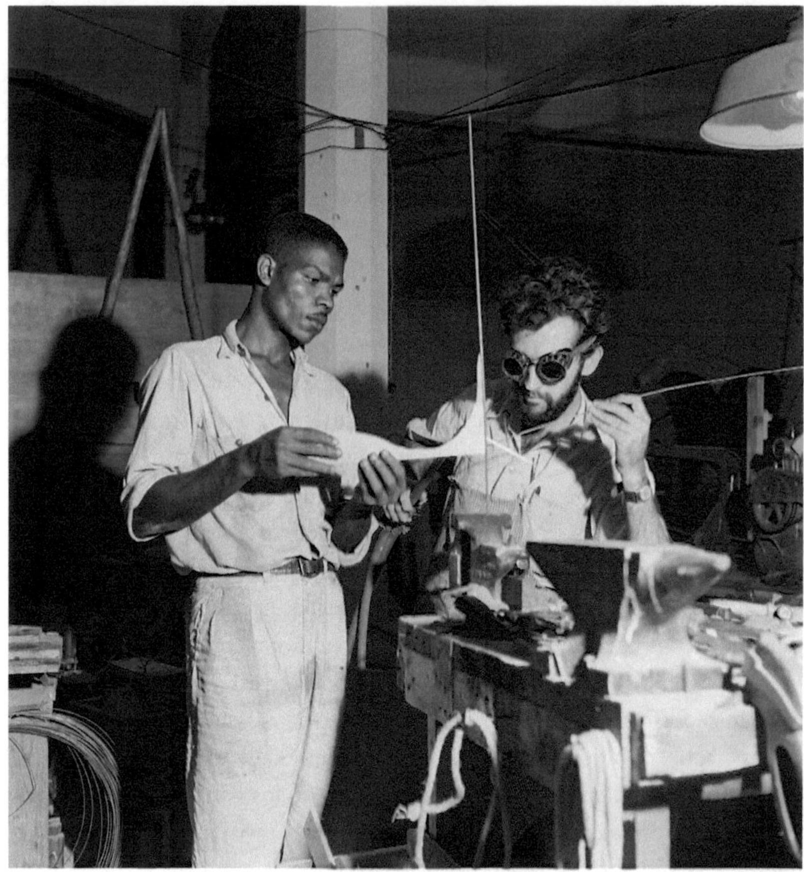

FIGURE 10.2 Agnaldo Manuel dos Santos and Mário Cravo Júnior, 1950s. Photo by Pierre Verger. © Fundação Pierre Verger, Salvador.

Prazeres; Arthur Bispo do Rosário; and Francisco Moraes da Silva (known as Chico Tabibuia) all gained degrees of renown in the twentieth century.

Despite the differences in their lives, careers, and works, these artists engaged in a slow and uneven process of reviving and building on artistic values, ideas, forms, and practices from Africa that had been hibernating during the long and oppressive years of slavery. After slavery officially ended in 1888, African and Afro-Brazilian artistic knowledge was gradually reaffirmed. It is no coincidence that many of these artists sculpted or produced unusual objects; entered the art world from apprenticeships in professions such as carpentry, jewelry, tailoring, and graphic design; and owed their artistic formations to intergenerational family relationships as well as professional practices. It is also understandable that they all encountered obstacles in defining themselves as artists and had to work in other professions to support themselves and their families. However, even if the trajectories of these artists developed independently and have seemed to outsiders to appear unexpectedly and surprisingly, when viewed together, they point toward a deeply rooted social process. The struggle of artists and other agents to achieve greater visibility for African and Afro-Brazilian artistic ideas and forms, practices, and values is, in other words, connected to both individual and collective efforts to achieve a fairer integration of Afro-descendants in Brazilian society—a pretty different context from the unconscious and spontaneous resurgences of African atavism proposed by art critics.

Discovering an Afro-Brazilian Primitive Sculptor

As noted, dos Santos has not been the only Brazilian artist considered primitive. Many critics used this label for him and other similar artists because they had little education; lacked formal artistic training; gained only a precarious mastery of the erudition, techniques, and conventions of fine art representation; and focused on themes related to popular culture. However, dos Santos's African ancestry and his preference for wood sculpture as an expressive medium gave him a special place within the group of "primitive" artists celebrated by agents and institutions of Brazilian modernism. In 1966, after the FESMAN prize, the Brazilian writer and art critic Harry Laus termed dos Santos Brazil's "most important black sculptor."[9] Similarly, a year later, the Brazilian art historian José Roberto Teixeira Leite identified his work as the "finest example of Afro-American sculpture in Brazil."[10]

From the mid-twentieth century, modernist artists, art critics, and art historians pursued the ideal of "the people" as the most authentic expression of national identity, and, in their search for Brazilian creators of folk arts, they prioritized representatives of the marginalized ethnic groups that constituted the nation. Looking to the past and present, they celebrated late eighteenth-century artist Antônio Francisco Lisboa, called Aleijadinho ("Little Cripple") and other artists of African descent without formal training as artistic symbols of Brazil as a hybrid nation. Aleijadinho was undoubtedly a significant and foundational example, but he was distant in time. They needed more recent names to demonstrate the persistence of African artistic contributions as a source of the vitality of Brazilian culture. During the mid-twentieth century, several artists emerged who could confirm the African contributions to the mythic racial mix that, it was argued, had formed Brazil as a nation. Although self-taught, their works and careers varied in styles and media and have stimulated different critical and institutional receptions. Prazeres was a painter, and Abdias Nascimento, though not, properly speaking, a maker of popular art, became a painter in the mid-1960s after graduating in economics and pursuing a career as a well-known writer, actor, and activist.[11] Taking a similarly oblique path into art, the self-taught artist Rubem Valentim had a degree in journalism and dentistry.[12] Valentim started to create objects that combined constructivist art and Afro-Brazilian religious principles and forms in the 1960s and later wrote an artistic manifesto. Deoscóredes Maximiliano dos Santos, called Mestre ("Master") Didi, occupied high positions in the Afro-Brazilian religion of *Candomblé* and transformed into artworks the artifacts he had first learned to make as a child in the *terreiros* (Afro-Brazilian religious communities).[13] When he began to exhibit his objects as art in 1964, he had already published short stories and a Yoruba Portuguese dictionary.

Among these artists, Agnaldo Manuel dos Santos occupied a unique position. Like many others, he had little instruction, yet, surprisingly, he came to be appreciated and valued by elite audiences. He was the only artist of the group to produce sculptures that resembled the African masks, statues, and objects valued by modernists in Europe and the United States — leading Leite to state that dos Santos "was not a black man who made sculpture, but a black man who made black sculpture."[14] Valentim's work, which, in contrast, derived from mixtures and was therefore judged "impure" according to the strictures of mid-century authenticity, was by no means as popular. Although the same accusation of impurity was not made of Didi's work, his objects were too closely tied to the Afro-Brazilian religions — which were only beginning to achieve greater public acceptance in the 1960s — to be as highly valued as those of dos Santos. While some of dos Santos's works also represented Afro-Brazilian religious themes, these elements were minimized in critical readings of his work, which otherwise emphasized the African references.[15] Seeing his art as almost secular in its distance from the contemporary Afro-Brazilian religious realm, the critics associated its Africanism with ancient continental Africa rather than with Brazilian history and daily life. Deemed "pure" and "ancestral," dos Santos's work was seen as remote, disengaged from slavery and its persistent effects, and therefore harmless. By carving, dos Santos enabled the rebirth of an idealized Africa in Brazil, free from past sufferings.

Besides the substantial changes becoming an artist produced in dos Santos's life, his work also provided an example of Afro-Brazilian popular sculpture that the modernist critics, collectors, and curators were looking for. Exhibiting and collecting dos Santos's work was a way of connecting to European and North American tastes for *art nègre*, as the category that unified certain types of African artifacts was then named. In light of this, it is no wonder the modernists were excited to discover dos Santos and celebrate him as an Afro-Brazilian primitive sculptor.

Being Carved

Dos Santos's professional career gave him an entry point into new and different social and cultural circles. During his time in the atelier of Cravo Júnior, he was, as noted earlier, encouraged to sculpt independently. His mentor was one of the most prominent Bahian artists of the time, a man who explored modernism's material diversity and technical multiplicity. Through him, dos Santos learned how to carve wood, cut marble, deal with metal, and handle the engraving press and other artistic techniques, and he also gained commercial knowledge and exposure for his work. Cravo Júnior presented him and his work to friends such as the artists Jenner Augusto, Lênio Braga, the Argentinian-born Julio Paridé Bernabó (known as Carybé), and Mirabeau Sampaio and writers and art critics such as Clarival do Prado Valladares, José Valladares, and Wilson Rocha. As his interactions with the art world in Bahia and beyond expanded through these encounters with other artists, art critics, and intellectuals, dos Santos's new relationships, made possible through Cravo Júnior, introduced him to a broader range of art and critical evaluation. He was enabled to move beyond the recognition of his innate abilities as a sculptor provided by the artists in his immediate circle.

While Valladares considered that dos Santos's work from 1953 to 1956 "shows the influence of the expressionist phase of Mario Cravo,"[16] he and others identified Francisco Biquiba Dy Lafuente Guarany, known as Mestre (Master) Guarany, as dos Santos's second master (figure 10.3).[17] Guarany was a renowned producer of *carrancas* — figureheads used on the prows of São Francisco River ferryboats (figure 10.4) — and had learned the technique from an older master whom the Jesuits had taught. The ferryboats went out of use in the 1940s.[18] Still, as they disappeared, the figureheads began to be valued, sold, and collected as popular art, spurring the salvaging of old pieces from boats and the production of new works for the new market. Guarany, who had stopped sculpting, began again to make figureheads, helping to reinvent the art of carrancas. Dos Santos first met him on a trip along the São Francisco River around 1953 and was greatly impressed by his work. From Guarany, dos Santos learned the figureheads'

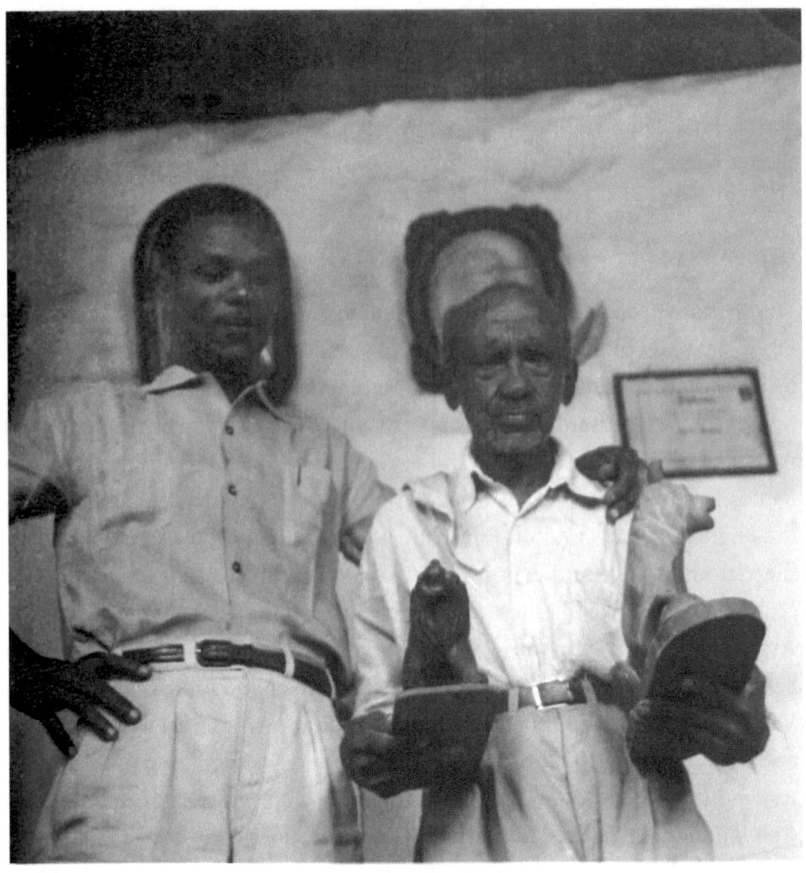

FIGURE 10.3 Agnaldo Manuel dos Santos and Francisco Biquiba Dy Lafuente Guarany, 1958. Photo by Franco Terranova. Collection Petite Galerie, 1954–2021, Rio de Janeiro.

symbolic typology and principles of artistic expression, carving methods, and three-dimensional structuring, deepening his understanding of wood as a creative material. Guarany suggested that dos Santos use cedar instead of the ipê, jaqueira, jenipapeiro, and louro woods he had thus far been using and which, some collectors complained, had a propensity to split from top to bottom.

Through fellow artists, dos Santos also had the opportunity to broaden the range of his artistic references. The painters Lênio Braga and Jenner Augusto encouraged him to carve Yoruba *Ibeji* and *Shango* statuettes, following African models that were also traditional to Bahia.[19] Pierre Verger—the French traveler, photographer, self-taught ethnographer, and Candomble *Babalawo*

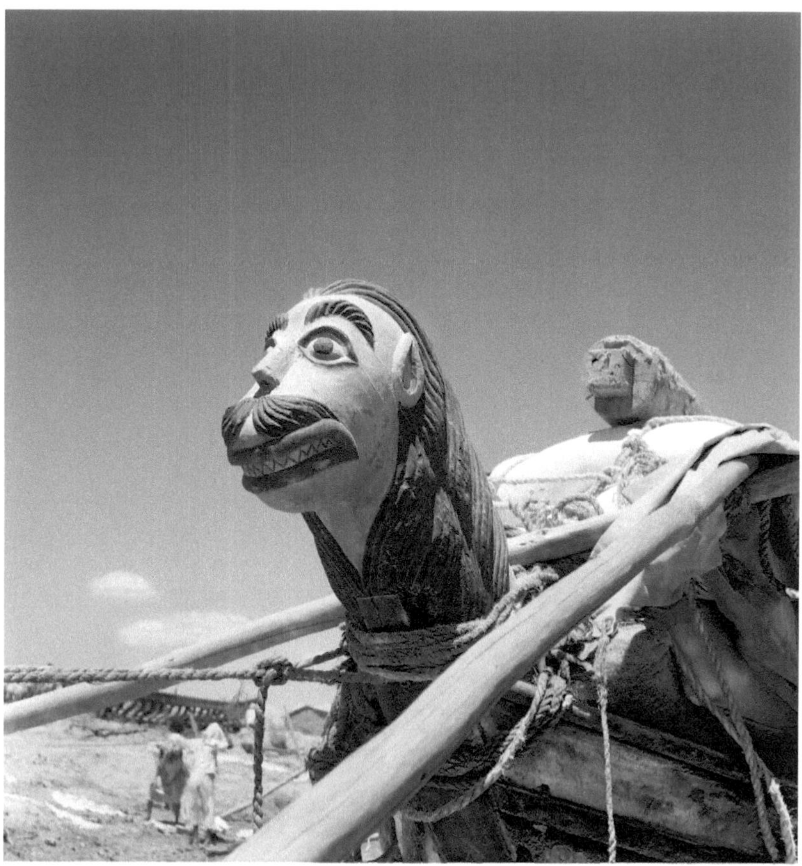

FIGURE 10.4 São Francisco River with a figurehead by Francisco Biquiba Dy Lafuente Guarany, 1946. Photo by Marcel Gautherot. Collection Instituto Moreira Salles.

(priest), who had moved to Salvador in the 1940s—showed him some photos he had taken in Africa and lent him a book with images of African sculpture. And in Sampaio's collection, the artist studied ancient Catholic imagery.

Dos Santos had the opportunity to experience African art directly in an exhibition held in Salvador in 1959, *A Arte de um Povo de Angola—Quiocos de Lunda* (The art of a people of Angola—the Tchokwe from Lunda). It included sculptures from the Museu do Dundo (Dundo Museum) of Angola, the Sociedade de Geografia de Lisboa (Geographic Society of Lisbon) in Portugal, and private collectors.[20] According to Valladares, dos Santos was extraordinarily impressed by the wood pieces he saw there.[21] Art dealers also greatly impacted dos Santos's career, notably the Brazilian poet Carlos Eduardo

FIGURE 10.5
Franco Terranova with Agnaldo Manuel dos Santos's 1958 *Seated Woman*, 1970s. Photographer unregistered. Collection Petite Galerie, 1954–2021, Rio de Janeiro.

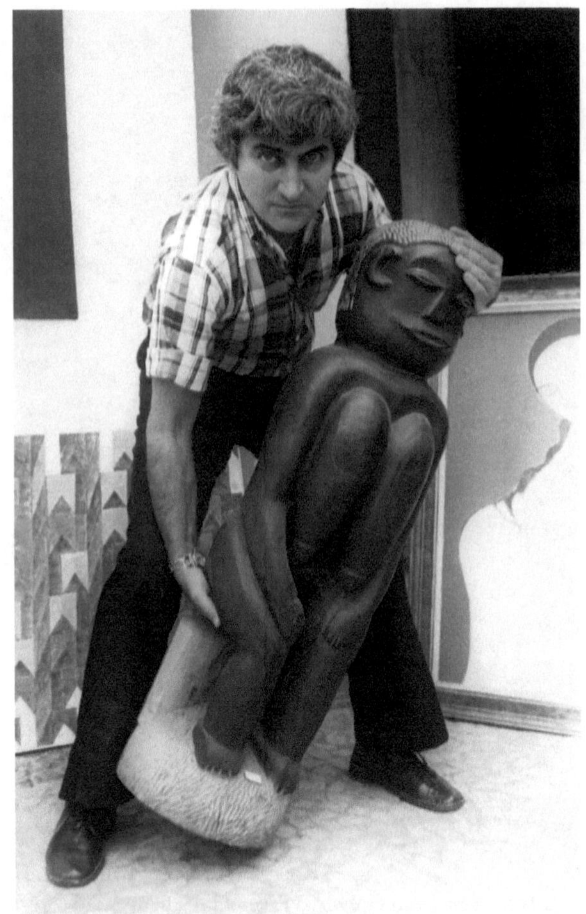

da Rocha, founder of Oxumaré Gallery in Bahia, who included dos Santos in at least two group exhibitions and one solo exhibition.[22] Terzo Lombardi, an Italian art dealer based in São Paulo in the 1950s, suggested that he should "produce heads like those of the *ex-votos* of the *sertão* (backwoods)," which the modernists then well appreciated as anonymous expressions of the mixed origins of the Brazilian people.[23] The most significant art dealer in dos Santos's career was the Italian Franco Terranova, director of the Petite Galerie, first in Rio de Janeiro and later in São Paulo. Terranova's galleries were the principal means by which dos Santos came to be represented in the cities of the southeast, then the center of the Brazilian art world — rare for Bahian artists at that time. Besides their professional relationship, the two became close friends, and dos Santos has a unique presence in Terranova's memories (figure 10.5).[24]

Although critics mention these influences, they have minimized them, highlighting dos Santos's "pure instinct" or "black ancestry."[25] Valladares, however, recognized how strongly the artist was drawn to Verger's photos of Nigerian art. He notes that his "soul was marked" by the book Verger lent him and emphasized what dos Santos said about the images published in it: "We think we have met them before."[26] The Brazilian antique dealer and critic Francisco Castro Ramos Neto recalled the surprise and strong emotion dos Santos expressed on seeing for the first time in Sampaio's collection an image of Our Lady of the Conception whose seventeenth-century maker had sculpted the image of the Virgin in a half warhead — the same solution he had himself recently adopted.[27] The same author acknowledged that dos Santos had "shown no propensity to any artistic manifestation" before experimenting in the artistic ambiance of Cravo Júnior's studio and also went further to report that according to the memory of Ernestina, dos Santos's widow, the artist's creations appeared abruptly upon awakening, when he began working as one possessed.[28] Although it is intriguing and seductive to imagine that such anecdotes signal the reemergence of collective values that have survived despite the vicissitudes of history, the evidence summarized above leads to a different understanding. They allow us to see how crucial the members of the various artistic circles dos Santos met and, more generally, the sociocultural context of Bahia at that time were to his work and professional career, providing a context that fostered connections with African traditions in Brazil and beyond. In that sense, instead of serendipitously *discovering* a sculptor, the many agents and institutions that mediated dos Santos's work *sculpted him* as a primitive artist.

Victim or Hero?

In his 1963 text, Valladares represented dos Santos as a victim of his environment, his death caused by the poor living conditions he had endured since childhood, his contraction of both Chagas disease and schistosomiasis, and the inadequate treatments prescribed by a fake doctor. Might we consider his artistic career the same way, asking whether he was also a victim of the art system? It is easier to say the opposite — that dos Santos substantially changed his living conditions out of an impoverished context through his artistic work. In the eyes of his neighbors, he was a hero, someone who was written about in the newspapers and seemed to be almost as famous as soccer players and radio singers. Although he died when his work was gaining greater international

FIGURE 10.6
Agnaldo Manuel dos Santos with a sculpture. Photographer unregistered. Collection Petite Galerie, 1954–2021, Rio de Janeiro.

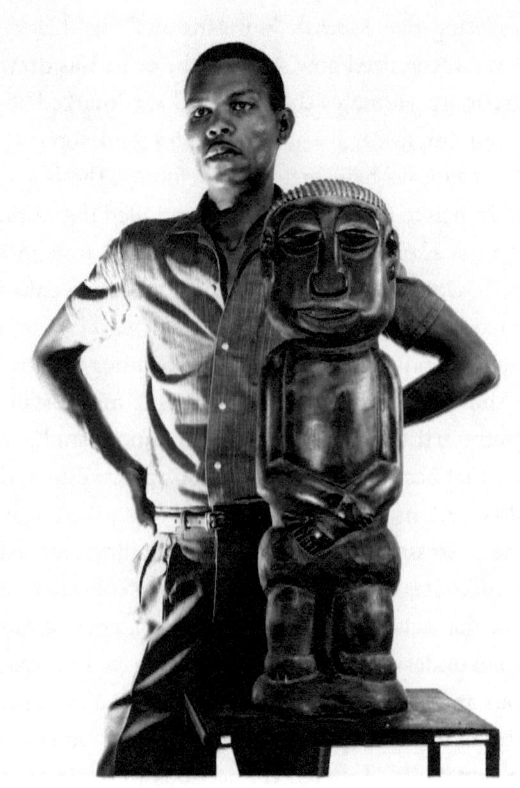

exposure, he was successful as an artist and enjoyed local and national recognition during his lifetime (figure 10.6).[29]

In 1962, the Brazilian art critic José Geraldo Vieira said that by transforming "botanic substances into telluric volumes," dos Santos "transported himself in spirit to his African origins."[30] Five years later, Leite wrote that dos Santos's art "continues, on Brazilian soil, the sculpture of Black Africa, transplanted by slaves from the vast area between the Gulf of Guinea and the Congo Valley."[31] From these botanical and migratory metaphors, we can critically expand the victim or hero polarity. Dos Santos's work can be seen as a fruit generated long after the seeds had been transposed to the Americas by the slave trade; its seeds remained more or less dormant during slavery, only to germinate and bear fruit after slavery's formal abolition. However, Africanism did not blossom purely and spontaneously in his work as in those of other Afro-descendant artists. Rather, he had the help of fertile soil—Bahia, the Brazilian region where Africanism has been most cultivated. There, as we have seen, African and Afro-Brazilian art were introduced to him; Africa was cultivated in him.

Was dos Santos an unconscious hero who enabled the spontaneous rebirth of Africa or a victim of an art system that forced him to produce a work linked to Africa because he had African ancestry? Does his work result from awakening a dormant seed by good cultivation in fertile soil or creating the desired species by manipulating rare components? Apparently opposed, these visions lead to the same problem. According to one view, dos Santos played a passive role in the rebirth of African atavism in Brazil while according to the other, his rise to fame was a product of the yearnings and agencies of his sociocultural milieu as manifested in the mid-twentieth century art world comprised of critics, galleries, and curators. Neither perspective, however, allows us to acknowledge dos Santos's own active role and agency. I argue that we can best understand his life and achievements not in terms of the hero/victim dichotomy but rather as having been shaped by his management of his artistic career through his interactions with artists, critics, art dealers, and institutions.

Dos Santos as Mediator

In addition to being an artist, dos Santos was also a mediator who initiated his interactions with dealers, critics, and collectors (figure 10.7). He met Guarany and became his disciple. After 1953, dos Santos bought eight Guarany pieces, more than 10 percent of the new figureheads the artist produced up to 1972, and old figureheads the artist found on the banks of the river and restored.[32] Furthermore, dos Santos wanted an even bigger share of Guarany's business. In an interview in 1958, during his exhibition at the gallery Gea in Rio de Janeiro, the artist was reported as saying that he would be exhibiting in Argentina soon and intended to open a small shop of Bahian artifacts in Rio de Janeiro along with a *Boate Negra* (Black nightclub) in Salvador.[33]

While none of this went forward, dos Santos did become involved in the figurehead trade from Bahia and came to dominate its values and prices. He and Terranova traveled along the São Francisco River in search of figureheads in 1958.[34] Terranova recounts that on one occasion dos Santos arrived hurriedly, shouting that a man was destroying a Guarany figurehead of a golden lion with blue eyes, which had already lost its mouth. The art dealer rushed to the boat and told the man — who said he was cutting wood to use as firewood for cooking and feeding his children — to stop destroying the piece. The art dealer then took all the money in his pockets and offered it to the man in

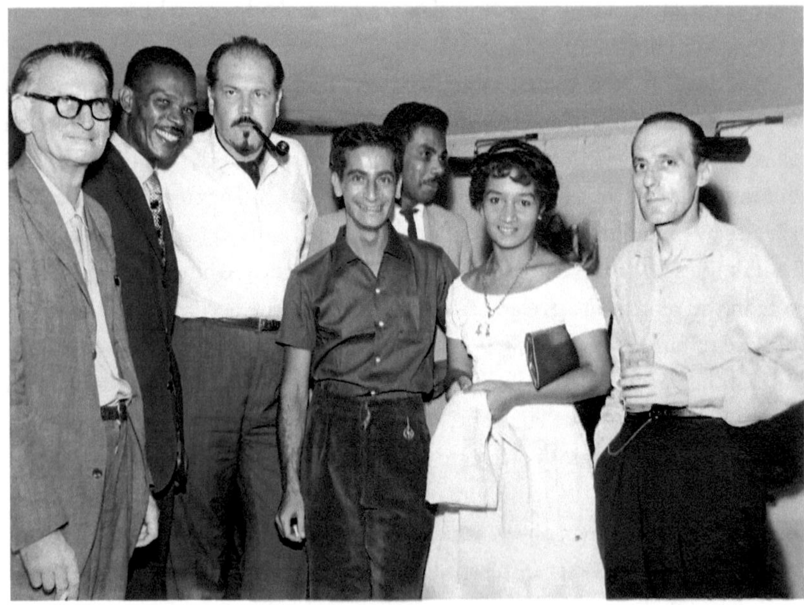

FIGURE 10.7 Exhibition opening at Petite Galerie, Rio de Janeiro, c. 1958. *From left to right:* Oswaldo Goeldi, Agnaldo Manuel dos Santos, Pedro Manuel Gismondi, Roberto de Lamonica, Octávio Araújo, nonidentified woman, and Fernando Romani. Photographer unregistered.

exchange for the figurehead, already without an eye. He also remembered that dos Santos called him a madman for having paid a sum for the carranca that would feed the man's family for a whole month—adding that he felt both corrupted and corrupting for bargaining with the human condition, which was more sacred than a simple figurehead—exchanging the hunger of children for something sacred and eternal only in his imagination. Dos Santos's laughter echoed along the river.[35]

Dos Santos's mediation was, furthermore, not solely commercial. On one of their trips, dos Santos and Terranova documented other works by Guarany and later shared the photos with Guarany himself.[36] Such anecdotes reveal dos Santos's reflexive awareness of the need to record artists' work and share the documentation process with the artists themselves. These suppositions suggest dos Santos's sense of the importance and value of the artistic work he and other members of his circle were producing. Before sending Terranova the figureheads that Guarany consigned to him, dos Santos showed them to Valladares. On these occasions, the critic noticed dos Santos's knowledge about the carrancas. According to Valladares, dos Santos identified the various artists who created the São Francisco River figureheads, highlighting those of Guarany based upon the principles he had learned from his master. He even shared his critical knowledge of the old master on one occasion, qualifying one of his pieces as a "good figurehead."[37]

Dos Santos's mediation was not restricted to trade and the domain of figureheads. At his exhibition at the Petite Galerie in Rio de Janeiro in 1957, he wanted to present his sculptures alongside paintings by João Alves. Considering Alves as "primitive too," he revealed a clear curatorial vision when he said that "painting and sculpture would result in a good ensemble."[38] His direct impact on other artists, however, varied. Although dos Santos's work does not seem to have influenced that of Cravo Júnior, Guarany began to produce colorful figureheads in response to dos Santos's demand.[39] And just as a combination of chance and mediation had led to his meeting with Cravo Júnior and his career as a sculptor, so did dos Santos play a crucial role in the early career of his neighbor Aurelino dos Santos. After learning the work of Agnaldo, Aurelino decided to express himself artistically, first carving but soon beginning to make paintings.[40] Dos Santos bought his first canvas and encouraged him to paint professionally. Thus, he played a similar role in the development of Aurelino's career to that of Cravo Júnior in his own. Just as he had previously been discovered, invented, and mentored as a primitive sculptor, so he became the discoverer, inventor, and mentor of a primitive painter.

References, Choices, Intentions

In opposition to the idea of a sculptural work that emerged independently of dos Santos's conscious will, one must conclude that dos Santos was an author who carved his work amid different artistic references: old and new, profane and sacred, Western and non-Western (figure 10.8). As we have seen, through Cravo Júnior, dos Santos first had access to modern art and subsequently had the opportunity to observe its trends in galleries, museums, and at the São Paulo Biennial. Through Guarany, he came across the old Jesuit tradition of figurehead carving. He studied Catholic art through the ex-votos Lombardi encouraged him to look at and those in Sampaio's collection. Braga and Augusto introduced him to Afro-Brazilian religious imagery while he enthusiastically responded to the photographs of African pieces Verger showed him—especially the Nigerian ones. And he experienced African art directly in the show with Tchokwe sculptures.

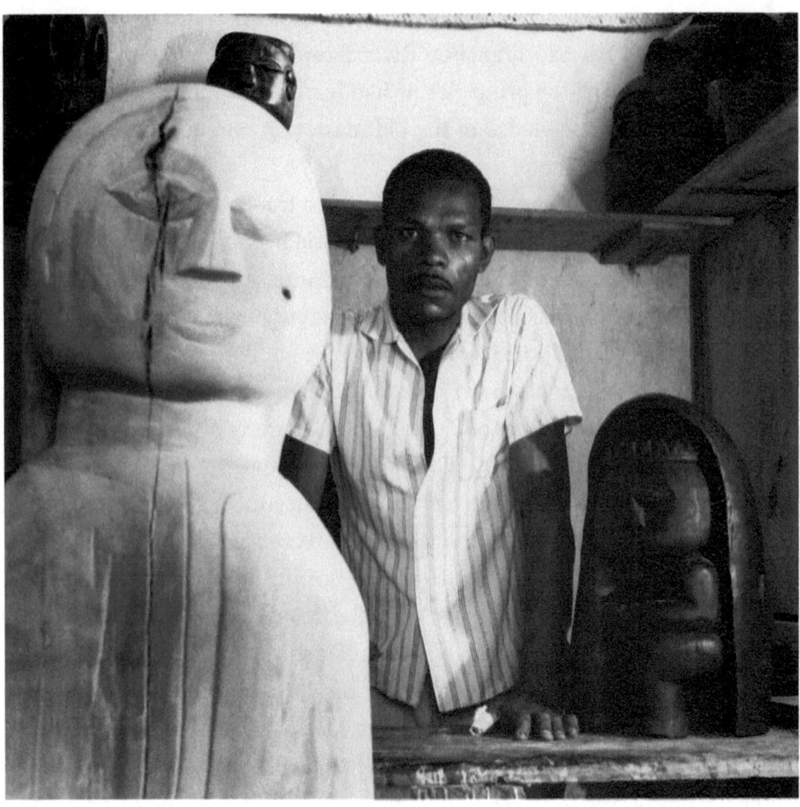

FIGURE 10.8 Agnaldo Manuel dos Santos in his studio, before 1962. Photo by Franco Terranova. Collection Petite Galerie, 1954–2021, Rio de Janeiro.

Dos Santos was aware of his artistic references and publicly acknowledged them. According to Valladares, he had only words of gratitude and friendship for Cravo Júnior.[41] As the art critic Lorenzo Mammì noted, dos Santos is the artist "who most explicitly acknowledged his debt to the art of figureheads . . . and has always mentioned the *mineiro* master as one of his main references."[42] Dos Santos was aware of what he had learned from his mentors. In the case of Guarany, according to Valladares, he kept in mind and even quoted the critical principles with which the master analyzed the works he had shown him through photographs.[43] However, although those sets of references help us to understand dos Santos's early formation, they do not fully explain the individuality of the artist's work, nor how quickly he came to outline a path of his own through his ability to interrelate materials, techniques, and themes. He not only chose which elements to develop among the many to which he was exposed but also created a body of work quite different from those of his masters and contemporaries. Although he experimented with other techniques and materials, he adopted wood as his working material, a choice that partially explains why he replaced Cravo Júnior with Guarany as his mentor.[44] Nevertheless, although, like Guarany, he devoted himself to exploring wood, he was closer to Cravo Júnior regarding his subject matter and thematic diversity. The Afro-Brazilian and Catholic themes link him to the latter while the figureheads connect him to the former.

Dos Santos also addressed subjects beyond these domains. Thematically, his work has great breadth and is not limited to Africanism or northeastern Brazilian culture. Although dos Santos committed himself to Africa, in Bahia, Africa is never an exclusive and closed domain. Instead, it permeates various social realms and is permeated by other cultural references. In addition to the African divinities, figures with mortars and pestles, oxês (Shango's double ax), and masks, dos Santos depicted a great variety of Bahian social types like the Bahian woman, but also Christ, Catholic saints, priests, kings, queens, slavers, beggars, figureheads, animals, and monsters as well as universal themes such as old age, paternity, and, especially, maternity.[45] Bevilacqua has demonstrated how the variation in dos Santos's Africanized works derives from the multiple referents he dealt with.[46] This principle could be extended to his entire oeuvre. Writing in the immediate aftermath of dos Santos's sudden death, the art critic Pedro Manuel identified qualitative differences in the thematic series he created throughout his career.[47] Despite the apparent unity of his work, it is essential to recognize that dos Santos was an artist who died while his art was still in formation. Interrupted while in a dynamic transformation process, his work is uneven, diachronically and synchronically. Dos Santos seemed himself to have been partially conscious of these disparities. Although he had a friendly relationship with his neighbors and was respected by them for the recognition he had achieved in Bahia and the art centers of Rio de Janeiro and São Paulo, his work did not please everybody. Some said it was an "Exu thing," referring to the Yoruba deity often associated with the Christian devil. This was denied by dos Santos, who argued that his work had significant variations.[48]

Valladares configures dos Santos in a contradictory way, arguing that he represented Brazil and Brazilians even if his neighbors did not understand what he was doing, what made him exceptional in comparison with his neighbors and among the idealized "Brazilian people." The dissonance the critic suggests is related to economic conditions and cultural values dos Santos was coming to accept during the 1950s and their contrast to the social spheres from which he emerged. Instead of thinking of his work as an unintentional and unconscious representation of the Brazilian people's collective values, it is better to think of dos Santos's work as a result of the choices he made to succeed as an artist within the field of possibilities available to him, in many cases in relation to the interlocutors he had. Analyzing his work soon after his death, Manuel wrote that he "achieved a high level of conscious individualization and style."[49] In this context, it is worth remembering that dos Santos discarded some of his work when he started making figureheads, just as he had done with the pieces he produced from the ex-votos. According to Valladares, the artist once called him to see his "real figurehead."[50] It was, furthermore, dos Santos's decision to differentiate some of his pieces by making their surfaces darker and lustrous by burning or tinting them with bitumen, polishing, and varnishing. These are a few examples of dos Santos's critical judgment and creative intentions.

Carving amid Modernism

Recently, Mammì defined dos Santos as an "especially self-conscious popular artist."[51] For Roger Sansi, too, dos Santos is an example of Bahia's popular artists who "joined modern cultural and artistic enterprises in curious ways."[52] In the interview given to Paulo Medeiros in 1957, dos Santos indicates that he was aware of the controversy regarding the selection of works for the Fourth São Paulo Biennial and of the prejudices existing in Rio de Janeiro and São Paulo about Bahia and its artistic production.[53]

I argue that dos Santos was also a modernist artist. Ulli Beier had a similar view, although he qualified the artist as modern by using italics and considered that his "art is not rooted in any tradition and derives little or nothing from other artists," being "highly personal."[54] Evidence of his adherence to modernity can be found in his work, career, home, and way of life. Many of the works produced by dos Santos refer to types of objects valued in modernism under the designation of folk and popular art: ex-votos, figureheads, images of Catholic saints, and orishas. Popular art, with and without attribution to specific artists, was established as an artistic trend within Brazilian modernism under the larger rubric of primitive art. For Rocha, dos Santos's style is neo-primitive.[55] Primitive or neo-primitive, this type of art was well appraised, one of the leading modernist artistic categories. Just as "the people" were the guardians of the nation's soul, primitive art was a fundamental part of Brazilian culture.

Certainly, dos Santos was impelled to do works that would give continuity to those popular art traditions. He could have tried to move between abstract and figurative art like Cravo Júnior, or he could have gone deeper into reinventing the art of figureheads like Guarany. But he preferred to deal with the manifold suggestions and configure his work from those types of objects, appropriating "foreign" references" to gain entry into the art world.[56] He even identified himself as a primitive sculptor when he applied to participate in the 1957 São Paulo Biennial.[57] However, he stressed that he did not live among artists at the *terreiros* but instead associated himself with the image of the bohemian artist, clarifying that his art was not sacred, despite its religious themes.[58]

Although artists categorized as popular were not valued as highly as were those of the modernist avant-garde, the distinction between these domains was not rigid in Brazil during the mid-twentieth century. Accordingly, dos Santos's work was not restricted to the niche of primitive art. Indeed, he participated in exhibitions focusing on popular art throughout his career, such as *Nós e a Arte Popular* (We and the folk art) at the Oxumarê Gallery in 1957, and *Brazilian Folk Art: Yesterday and Today* at the Walker Art Center, Minneapolis, in 1962. Yet, in 1956, he was also included in the exhibition *Artistas Modernos da Bahia* (Modern artists of Bahia) in the same Oxumarê Gallery and participated in the 1957 São Paulo Biennial. According to Mammì, artists categorized as popular like dos Santos "participated in Biennials not in special sections, but with the same status as artists with scholarly training, even competing for national prizes."[59] Other evidence of the fluidity and blurred boundary between popular art and avant-garde art in Brazil was the artist's inclusion in a highly varied group of artists with whom Terranova composed a memoirist poem.[60] Dos Santos's link with modernity can also be seen in his representations of Oxossi, the Yorubá orisha linked to the forest and hunting, with modern and local weapons and other props.[61] Still other links were his incorporation of some natural wood elements in the plastic configurations of his sculptures or his efforts to participate in the São Paulo Biennial, writing to the secretary of the Biennial Foundation after learning about the event when he went to help Cravo Júnior to set up his work in 1953.[62]

Aurelino's painting was not the only artwork he had in his small house in the Rio Vermelho neighborhood. On a visit to dos Santos's house, Valladares remembers having seen "an engraving by Hansen inscribed to the fellow artist, paintings by primitive painters, functional furniture and amoeboid ashtrays for intellectuals," evidence suggesting a synthetic modernist collection composed of contemporary art and design.[63] Like other emerging artists, he exchanged works with fellow friends and acquired contemporary objects and pieces made by painters who, like him at the beginning of his career, were on the margins of the Bahian art world. He configured his house according to what he knew and was able to buy as his work became more valued in the art market.

Valladares also reports that dos Santos's widow showed him a photo of the artist "on a scooter, in Copacabana, smiling with all his teeth."[64] Unfortunately lost, this image can be associated with another photo, printed in the catalog of his 1962 posthumous exhibition, which shows the artist smoking, wearing a formal shirt and a wristwatch, in an elegant pose that offers a glimpse as to why he was affectionately called Prince of the Hausa by some close friends.[65] More than signs of social ascension, these images reinforce how dos Santos was attracted to and adopted a modern way of living.

Dos Santos might have had little instruction and been ignorant of much of the art world, but he was far from being naïve or unreflexive. He dealt with different references, incentives, demands, and pressures and, like other artists working in Brazil or abroad in the mid-twentieth century, made deliberate choices from various ideals and ideas. We can thus consider dos Santos an artist who successfully negotiated between "being carved" and "sculpting himself," positioning himself as a primitive artist amid modernism.

Notes

Note: Text written in 2016.

1. Valladares, "África nova, a busca do universal."

2. Other jurors included Meyer Cotté, Michael Crowder, Max-Pol Fouchet, and Michel Troche. Valladares, "África nova, a busca do universal."

3. Valladares, "Agnaldo Manoel dos Santos," 36.

4. Valladares, "Agnaldo Manoel dos Santos," 36.

5. Valladares, "Agnaldo Manoel dos Santos," 34–36.

6. Bevilacqua, "Beyond the Revealed Unconscious," 107. On dos Santos, see also Bevilacqua, *Agnaldo Manuel dos Santos*.

7. Rocha, in Terranova, *Esculturas de Agnaldo dos Santos—Bahia*.

8. About Afro-Brazilian art in Bahia, see Polk et al., *Axé Bahia*.

9. Laus, "Escultor por vocação."

10. Leite, "Agnaldo e a escultura afroamericana."

11. Abdias Nascimento (Franca, 1914–Rio de Janeiro, 2011).

12. Rubem Valentim (Salvador, 1922–São Paulo, 1991)

13. Deoscóredes Maximiliano dos Santos (Salvador, 1917–2013).

14. Leite, "Agnaldo e a escultura afroamericana."

15. In the 1955 Petite Galerie exhibition, dos Santos presented *Assombrado de Exú* (Eshu's haunted, or Haunted by Eshu) and *Oxóssi* (Oshossi). Throughout his career,

he made many representations of Oshossi. Terranova, *Esculturas de Agnaldo dos Santos — Bahia.*

16. Valladares, "Agnaldo Manoel dos Santos," 27.

17. Valladares, "Agnaldo Manoel dos Santos," 30; Ramos Neto, "Agnaldo Manoel dos Santos: Afrobrasileiro autêntico (1926–62)."

18. The ferryboats were replaced by boats technologically more advanced and appropriate to the new economic activities.

19. Valladares, "Agnaldo Manoel dos Santos," 32.

20. Bevilacqua, "Beyond the Revealed Unconscious," 114.

21. Valladares, "Agnaldo Manoel dos Santos," 32.

22. Bevilacqua, "Beyond the Revealed Unconscious," 107–8. Oxumaré Gallery was the first commercial art gallery in Bahia. It was created by Carlos Eduardo da Rocha and ran between 1951 and 1960.

23. Valladares, "Agnaldo Manoel dos Santos," 26.

24. Terranova, *Carma Carnadura*, 4–6, 69, 86.

25. Leite, "Agnaldo e a escultura afroamericana."

26. Valladares, "Agnaldo Manoel dos Santos," 26.

27. Ramos Neto, "Agnaldo Manoel dos Santos — uma lenda viva," 205.

28. Ramos Neto, "Agnaldo Manoel dos Santos: Afrobrasileiro autêntico (1926–1962)."

29. According to Pedro Manuel, on the occasion of dos Santos's 1956 Petite Galerie exhibition, "the critics applauded him and the public bought all his works in three days." Terranova, *Esculturas — Agnaldo*. Twelve of the twenty works on display were sold at the opening. "Agnaldo dos Santos: Operário . . . e escultor," *Diário de Notícias*, 1956.

30. Jose Geraldo Vieira, "Agnaldo Manuel dos Santos," 4, quoted in Athayde, *Agnaldo dos Santos*.

31. Leite, "Agnaldo e a escultura afroamericana."

32. Benetti, "Cronologia," 192.

33. "Escultor de candomblé nunca foi a terreiros," *Tribuna da Imprensa*, November 19, 1958.

34. Caspary, "A Petite Galerie, Franco Terranova e o circuito de arte no Rio de Janeiro, 1954–1988."

35. Terranova, *Carma Carnadura*, 5–6.

36. Valladares, "São Francisco, de carrancas transfiguradas," quoted in Mammì, *A viagem das Carrancas*, 183.

37. Valladares, "São Francisco, de carrancas transfiguradas," 184.

38. Medeiros, "Agnaldo descobriu sem querer que podia tornar-se escultor."

39. Pardal, *Carrancas do São Francisco*, 98.

40. Peres, "Porque é beleza," 30; Marinho, "Aurelino," 38.

41. Valladares, "Agnaldo Manoel dos Santos," 33.

42. Mammì, "A viagem das Carrancas," 37. A *mineiro* (miner) is someone born in Minas Gerais, a southeastern Brazilian state. However, Guarany was born in Bahia.

43. Valladares, "Agnaldo Manoel dos Santos," 31.

44. In 1956, one of his drawings was published in *Diário de Notícias.* "Agnaldo dos Santos: Operário . . . e escultor," *Diário de Noticias*, 1956, Archive Petite Galerie. According to Pedro Manuel, dos Santos showed iron representations of orishas in his 1956 exhibition at Petite Galerie in Rio de Janeiro. Pedro Manuel, quoted in Terranova, *Esculturas — Agnaldo.*

45. Terranova, *Esculturas de Agnaldo dos Santos — Bahia*; Terranova, *Agnaldo dos Santos — Esculturas*; Terranova, *Esculturas — Agnaldo*; Terranova, *Agnaldo — Esculturas.*

46. Bevilacqua, "Beyond the Revealed Unconscious," 114–19.

47. Manuel, quoted in Terranova, *Esculturas — Agnaldo.*

48. Valladares, "Agnaldo Manoel dos Santos," 28–29.

49. Manuel, quoted in Terranova, *Esculturas — Agnaldo.*

50. Valladares, "São Francisco, de carrancas transfiguradas," 184.

51. Mammì, "A viagem das carrancas," 36.

52. Sansi, *Fetishes and Monuments*, 132–33.

53. Medeiros, "Agnaldo descobriu sem querer que podia tornar-se escultor."

54. Beier, "Agnaldo dos Santos, an Afro-Brazilian Artist," 32–33.

55. Rocha, "Agnaldo dos Santos na Petite Galerie."

56. Dos Santos had not had contact with candomblé before living in Salvador. Ramos Neto, "Agnaldo Manoel dos Santos — uma lenda viva," 279. He was one of the first noninhabitants of the São Francisco River Valley to produce figureheads. Valladares, *Agnaldo Manoel dos Santos*, 184.

57. Arquivo Histórico Wanda Svevo, Fundação Bienal de São Paulo.

58. "Escultor de candomblé nunca foi a terreiros," *Tribuna da Imprensa*, November 19, 1958.

59. Mammì, "A viagem das carrancas," 37.

60. Terranova, *Carma Carnadura*, 69.

61. Bevilacqua, "Beyond the Revealed Unconscious," 116–19.

62. Valladares, "Agnaldo Manoel dos Santos," 27; Ramos Neto, "Agnaldo Manoel dos Santos — uma lenda viva," 205.

63. Valladares, "Agnaldo Manoel dos Santos," 29.

64. Valladares, "Agnaldo Manoel dos Santos," 29.

65. Ramos Neto, "Agnaldo Manoel dos Santos — uma lenda viva," 279.

Bibliography

"Agnaldo dos Santos: Operário . . . e escultor." *Diário de Notícias* (Salvador), 1956. Archive of Petite Galerie, Instituto de Arte Contemporânea, São Paulo, Brazil.

Athayde, Sylvia Menezes de, ed. *Agnaldo dos Santos: Esculturas* [Agnaldo dos Santos: Sculptures]. Salvador: Núcleo de Artes do Desembanco, 1988.

Beier, Ulli. "Agnaldo dos Santos, an Afro-Brazilian Artist." *Black Orpheus* 13 (1963): 32–33.

Benetti, Liliane. "Cronologia." In *A viagem das Carrancas* [The figurehead's journey], edited by Lorenzo Mammì, 188–99. São Paulo: Editora WMF Martins Fontes; Instituto do Imaginário Brasileiro; Instituto Moreira Salles, 2015. Exhibition catalog.

Bevilacqua, Juliana Ribeiro da Silva, ed. *Agnaldo Manuel dos Santos: A conquista da modernidade* [Agnaldo Manuel dos Santos: The conquest of modernity]. São Paulo: Almeida e Dale Galeria, 2021. Exhibition catalog.

Bevilacqua, Juliana Ribeiro da Silva. "Beyond the Revealed Unconscious: Agnaldo Manoel dos Santos as the Protagonist of His Own Art." *Critical Interventions* 9, no. 2 (2015): 107–22.

Caspary, Gabriela. "A Petite Galerie, Franco Terranova e o circuito de arte no Rio de Janeiro, 1954–1988." Master's thesis, Universidade do Estado do Rio de Janeiro, 2018.

"Escultor de candomblé nunca foi a terreiros." *Tribuna da Imprensa* (Rio de Janeiro), November 19, 1958.

Laus, Harry. "Escultor por vocação." *Jornal do Brasil*, May 31, 1966.

Leite, José Roberto Teixeira. "Agnaldo e a escultura afroamericana." *GAM: Galeria de Art Moderna* 5 (1967): 16–17.

Mammì, Lorenzo. "A viagem das Carrancas." In *A Viagem das Carrancas*, edited by Lorenzo Mammì, 16–39. São Paulo: Editora WMF Martins Fontes; Instituto do Imaginário Brasileiro; Instituto Moreira Salles, 2015. Exhibition catalog.

Marinho, Justino. "Aurelino." In *Transfiguração do real: Pinturas de Aurelino dos Santos* [Transfiguration of the real: Paintings by Aurelino dos Santos], edited by Emanoel Araújo, 38–39. São Paulo: Museu Afro-Brasil, 2012.

Medeiros, Paulo. "Agnaldo descobriu sem querer que podia tornar-se escultor." *Diário de Notícias*, October 13, 1957.

Pardal, Paulo. *Carrancas do São Francisco* [Figureheads of São Francisco]. Rio de Janeiro: Serviço de Documentação Geral da Marinha, 1974.

Peres, Urania Tourinho. "Porque é beleza." In *Transfiguração do real: Pinturas de Aurelino dos Santos* [Transfiguration of the real: Paintings by Aurelino dos Santos], edited by Emanoel Araújo, 28–37. São Paulo: Museu Afro-Brasil, 2012.

Polk, Patrick, Roberto Conduru, Randall Johnson, and Sabrina Gledhill, eds. *Axé Bahia — the Power of Art in an Afro-Brazilian Metropolis*. Los Angeles: Fowler Museum UCLA, 2018.

Ramos Neto, Francisco de Castro. "Agnaldo Manoel dos Santos: Afrobrasileiro autêntico (1926–1962)." In *Agnaldo dos Santos: Esculturas*, edited by Sylvia Menezes de Athayde. Salvador: Núcleo de Artes do Desembanco, 1988.

Ramos Neto, Francisco de Castro. "Agnaldo Manoel dos Santos — uma lenda viva." In *A Mão Afro-Brasileira: Significado da contribuição artística e histórica* [The Afro-Brazilian hand: Significance of artistic and historical contribution], edited by Emanoel Araújo, 205–9. São Paulo: Tenenge, 1988.

Rocha, Wilson. "Agnaldo dos Santos na Petite Galerie." *Jornal da Bahia*, 1955. Archive Petite Galerie, Instituto de Arte Contemporânea, São Paulo, Brazil.

Sansi, Roger. *Fetishes and Monuments: Afro-Brazilian Art and Culture in the Twentieth Century*. New York: Berghahn, 2007.

Terranova, Franco, ed. *Agnaldo dos Santos—Esculturas*. Rio de Janeiro: Petite Galerie, 1957.

Terranova, Franco, ed. *Agnaldo—Esculturas*. Rio de Janeiro: Petite Galerie, 1962.

Terranova, Franco. *Carma Carnadura: Aventura de um corpo decomposto* [Flesh Karma: Adventure of a decomposed body]. Rio de Janeiro: Réptil, 2013.

Terranova, Franco, ed. *Esculturas—Agnaldo*. São Paulo: Petite Galerie, 1962.

Terranova, Franco, ed. *Esculturas de Agnaldo dos Santos—Bahia*. Rio de Janeiro: Petite Galerie, 1955.

Valladares, Clarival do Prado. "África nova, a busca do universal." *Jornal do Brasil*, April 24, 1966.

Valladares, Clarival do Prado. "Agnaldo Manoel dos Santos: Origem e revelação de um escultor primitivo." *Afro-Ásia* 14 (1983): 22–40.

Valladares, Clarival do Prado. *Agnaldo Manoel dos Santos—Origin, Revelation and Death of a Primitive Sculptor*. Salvador: Centro de Estudos Afro-Orientais, 1963.

Valladares, Clarival do Prado. "São Francisco, de carrancas transfiguradas" (1972). In *A viagem das Carrancas*, edited by Lorenzo Mammì, 182–86. São Paulo: Editora WMF Martins Fontes; Instituto do Imaginário Brasileiro; Instituto Moreira Salles, 2015. Exhibition catalog.

Vieira, José Geraldo. "Agnaldo Manuel dos Santos." *Folha de S. Paulo*, August 28, 1962, 4.

UNA REY

11 BARDON'S LEGACY

Paintings, Stories, and Indigenous Australian Art

What Tim Leura [Tjapaltjarri] was saying was simply this: you belong to us Geoffrey Bardon, not to yourself. You are our white man and we wish you to know who you really are. By your actions, it could not be any other way.

—GEOFFREY BARDON | *Mythscapes: Aboriginal Art of the Desert*

The global recognition of Australian contemporary art as Indigenous art is recognition hard-won. As the mercurial expatriate art critic Robert Hughes (1938–2012) reportedly put it, "Aboriginal art is the last great art movement of the 20th century," an assertion many Australians are eager to claim, whatever part they play in this paradoxical movement.[1] However, at closer inspection, this "last great art movement" is a cross-cultural project with a much longer history of Indigenous agents and non-Indigenous interlocutors and mediators, the latter whose supporting roles are yet to be drawn into a singular narrative.

The emergence of the white art mediator in the modern Indigenous art movement has its roots in the early twentieth century as missionaries and anthropologists engaged with Indigenous communities, commissioning artefacts for private research and interest, as well as the souvenir and primitive art markets. A formative example of such creative exchanges was the friendship between painter Rex Battarbee and Western Aranda artist Albert Namatjira, whose mastery of watercolor with Battarbee's mentorship and his management of Namatjira's career from the mid-1930s gave Australians their first Indigenous painting school at Hermannsburg and their first Indigenous art celebrity (figure 11.1). It also gave Indigenous Australians a new economic role model: the professional artist. A catalyst was Pastor Albrecht's invitation to

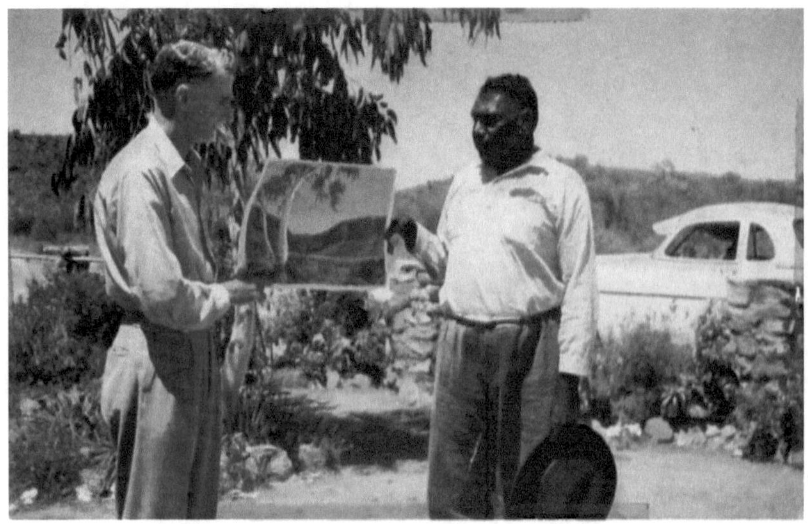

FIGURE 11.1 Rex Battarbee and Albert Namatjira (Alice Springs) with the painting presented to Queen Elizabeth II, 1954. Courtesy of Gayle Quarmby.

Battarbee and fellow painter John Gardner to exhibit their central Australian landscapes at the Lutheran mission in 1934 and 1936, which made a significant impact on Namatjira, who was already making and selling artefacts through the mission. As Battarbee later reflected in his retelling of the story, "Albrecht's action was to set a spark to one of the greatest art movements in history."[2]

While Battarbee's mediatory role is a central one, it has only recently attracted nuanced attention in cross-cultural terms, beyond the quasi-missionary teacher of amateur watercolor techniques.[3] Such relational exchanges, just one crucial link in a chain of European and Indigenous mediators connecting the art market to Indigenous traditions, remain the discreet backstories to the art movement that is now a lucrative global industry. So while "the last great art movement of the 20th century" first emerges in the 1930s out of Hermannsburg (Ntaria), it is typically understood from the 1980s when the Australian art world acknowledged and eventually championed the aesthetic, cultural, and political power of Indigenous art on its own terms.[4] For close to fifty years, the primary origin story associated with this art revolution began at Papunya in 1971, when Indigenous men started painting their designs in acrylic on board, encouraged by school teacher and artist Geoffrey Bardon (1940–2003). Situated just over 110 kilometers (roughly 70 miles) northwest of Hermannsburg, Papunya is in the heart of the continent, briefly home to Namatjira in 1959, shortly after it was established to assimilate "bush" Aborigines from neighboring clan-based groups into the modern nation-state.

This chapter examines Bardon's substantial achievements and his idiosyncratic style of mediation, as well as how the mediator's role (and its public reception) has evolved over the past half-century. It also analyzes where these mediators sit within the dynamic discourse of Indigenous contemporary art with its readily shifting politics. A challenge for this discourse in its framing of the desert art movement as an act of Indigenous agency is how to accommodate these mediators who, despite Bardon's visibility in the literature, have remained largely invisible. The Indigenous artist Richard Bell put his finger on a sore spot in this cross-cultural contract when he claimed "Aboriginal art is a white thing" in his painting *Scientia E Metaphysica (Bell's Theorem)* (2003) and its associated manifesto, in which he crudely (and humorously) deconstructed the Indigenous art industry and the white mediators in remote community art centers. However, the subtleties of cross-cultural creative exchanges, the inventiveness of the artists, and the economic and cultural dividends at stake are not so simply passed off as black or white. Over time, Bardon's polarizing mythology, much of it personally manifested, will be mediated into the *longue durée* historical account, resizing his metaphorical footprints on the global map of intercultural mediators of artistic modernisms (figure 11.2).

Born in Sydney, Bardon studied law before transferring to art teacher training, the formal qualifications that gave him license to travel to Papunya where outsiders with no business were not welcome, nor easily accommodated. Yet here, enduring the chaos of the government's policy shift from "assimilation" to Indigenous "self-determination," Bardon made a place in history as the seminal mediator of Indigenous artists. He also helped inspire a prototype for the modern Indigenous art center, which has become a central facet of life in remote Indigenous communities. A note here on the term *remote*, a common signifier for Indigenous art produced in small, centralized settlements across inland and northern Australia. To generalize, *remote* Indigenous artists have the benefit of continued occupation of their custodial lands, sustained Indigenous language, and access to ancestral estates and "Dreaming" sites. The "remote" Indigenous population also endure extreme disadvantages socially and economically, from health and education to housing and basic services. In Australian art world vernacular, "remote art" is a standard if insufficient locator for a wide range of regional styles, from figurative bark painting in the tropical north to "dot-painting" across the arid inland. These widely spread, distinct sites of remote production are located "remotely" against the equally inadequate

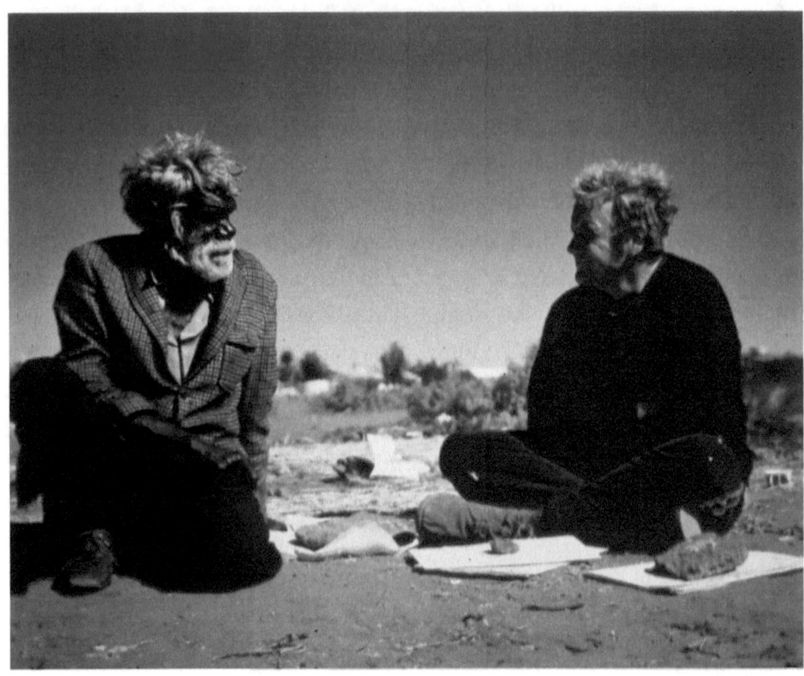

FIGURE 11.2 Old Tom Onion Tjapangati and Geoff Bardon, Papunya, 1971. Photo by Allan Scott. Courtesy of the Bardon family.

definition of "urban art" made in coastal cities and towns. These two "styles" or "movements" are frequently pitted against each other in the categorical binaries of "traditional art" and "modern (contemporary) art," especially since the 1980s.

Bardon has a double legacy within the remote categories of exchange: his catalytic role in the birth of the Western Desert painting movement, as he coined it, and his less-visible legacy as the cross-cultural mediator straddling the threshold between Indigenous and Western art worlds and temporalities, along with "remote" and "urban" social and cultural realities. Such specialist arts workers have gone by a variety of names, including the mission-based "arts and craft advisors," "art coordinators," and, more recently, "art center managers," in recognition of the professionalization of the sector. Ironically, given his stature as its archetype, Bardon's art center career ended just weeks after his formal appointment as artistic director of the Indigenous artist's collective, Papunya Tula. Though his grandiose title never caught on, the model he advocated of a federally funded transcultural cooperative, under the auspices of local government councils directed by Indigenous artists and managed by mediators on short-term contracts, is firmly lodged in the Indigenous art economy. Though frequently unstable due to conflicting power relations and contradicting world views, the art center has nevertheless become an effective small business, drawing on government subsidies and commission on art sales to support production of artwork for the market. Importantly, this "government model" art center, while not perfect, is generally recognized for its important role in cultural maintenance, social support, and ethical and transparent financial operations.

Along with earlier mission-based enterprises that had been operating since the mid-twentieth century in Arnhem Land and the Tiwi Islands, at Hermannsburg and at Ernabella in South Australia, Papunya Tula is among the earliest beneficiaries of a restructured Australia Council for the Arts and the Aboriginal Arts Board established in 1973. This federal support for art centers was emblematic of a changing of the guard: in 1967 a national referendum voted overwhelmingly to include Indigenous people in the national polity, and in 1976 the Northern Territory Land Rights Act led to significant changes across Indigenous communities such as Papunya.

This was the fragmented world that Bardon entered in January 1971, high summer in the Australian desert. The extreme climate and geographical isolation of the remote community is a central tenet of the mediator's story, and the "lone art teacher in the wilderness," as curator Judith Ryan wrote, is both literal and metaphorical.[5] A sealed bitumen road has since shortened the 240 kilometers (roughly 149 miles) between Alice Springs and Papunya, but corrugated sand was Bardon's only companion, his late night drive fueled by an earnest desire to understand Aboriginal people and their culture better than he had in his previous, brief encounters teaching Aboriginal youths in regional New South Wales and the northern capital, Darwin. Like so many cross-cultural workers in the grip of postcolonial triage, he felt he had to drink from the same cup in order to ease the suffering of the dispossessed. But what the thirty-year-old Bardon could not have foreseen as he charged into the desert seeking a cure for his creative and moral restiveness was the personal price paid by the alien in unknown territory: in the desert, as in space, no one can hear you scream. "I didn't know what I was letting myself into — but that is what I wanted to do," Bardon recalled twenty years later.[6]

Bardon's personal "genesis" narrative of the Western Desert painting movement is typically linked to five murals painted on the Papunya Special School in July and August 1971, which he judiciously documented as a cultural revival project for his young students. He and his mediator, teaching assistant and interpreter Obed Raggett (1916–89), an Aranda man from Hermannsburg, mapped out the first "practice" murals, incorporating the designs Bardon had witnessed the school children drawing in the sand. However, the gravity of the commission on the school walls where the children were being educated "white fella way" was quickly realized by senior Indigenous men who stepped in to negotiate, authorize, and execute the heraldry of the remaining murals.[7] The "hieroglyphs," as Bardon refers to the Western Desert's iconographic forms, had to be "real stories" appropriate for public display among a population of whites and Indigenous men, women, and children of all ages and ritual status, across five different language groups. The design ultimately realized in the final and eponymous *Honey Ant* mural referenced a local Dreaming site *papunya tula*, a small hill on the edge of the settlement that was a significant meeting place of honey-ant ancestors. Retrospectively claimed as an act of cultural and political agency, the murals ignited a fever of painting onto small boards numbering around fifteen hundred by thirty men between mid-1971 and August 1972 when Papunya Tula Artists Pty Ltd. was formally established to manage the innovative painting economy. Bardon's support was critical.

Until recently, missing from this story were the ambitious men's murals painted in a purpose-built Keeping Place at nearby Yuendumu, shortly before the Papunya murals were painted. However, Yuendumu had no mediator to capitalize on the murals and to help forge a contemporary art movement.[8] Also untold in the narrative was a sixth school mural at Papunya, which has slipped out of the archive. Created in April 1971 by Bardon, its figurative realism — typical of community art murals of the time — predates the famous Indigenous murals by a couple of months and, like them, was painted over by a routine government maintenance crew a few years later. Depicting an Aboriginal family group sitting in the foreground of the local landmark Haasts Bluff, Bardon's mural was conceived as an informal bid to be promoted from class teacher to art teacher. It had the desired effect on headmaster Fred Friis: from thereon until his departure, Bardon's energies were devoted to art and craft lessons with his students and encouraging and supporting the painting men, first within the school and later in the now mythologized Great (men's) Painting Room, a dedicated art studio where the men could work without interruptions (figures 11.3 and 11.4).

Contrary to the prevailing narrative, there was an existing ad-hoc souvenir art market operating at Papunya. However, Bardon's role as commissioner, mentor, and acolyte was instrumental in raising the stakes of what was possi-

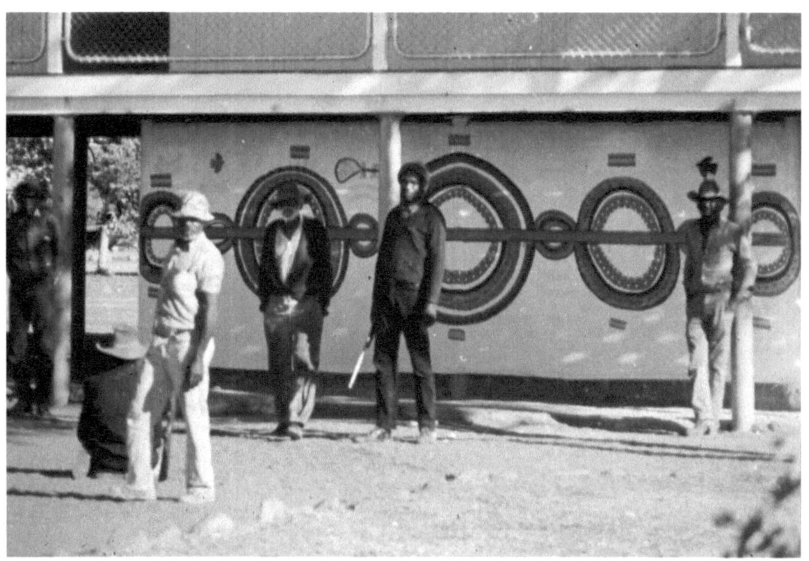

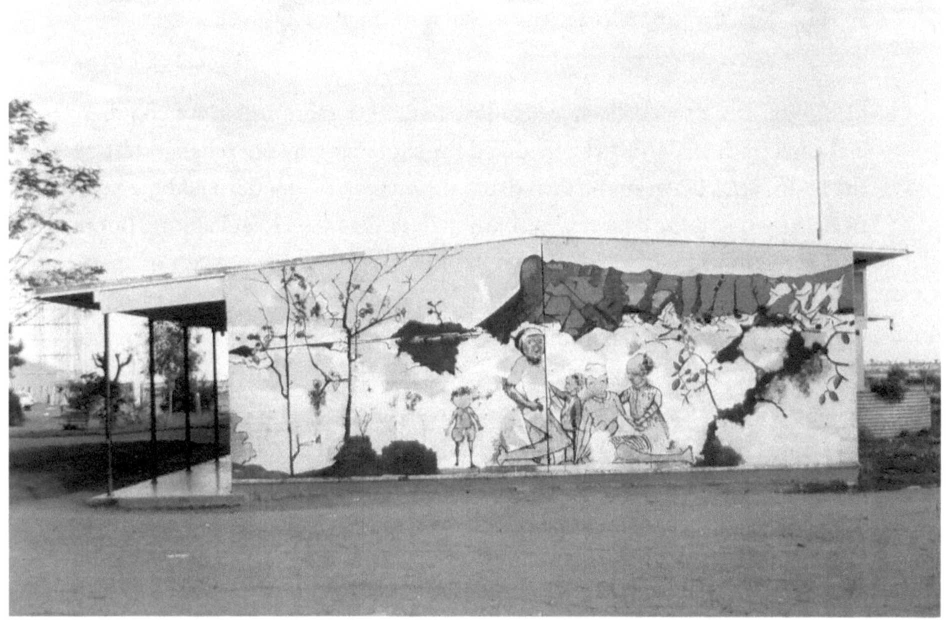

FIGURE 11.3 *top* Version 2 of the Honey Ant Mural, June–August 1971. Photo by Geoff Bardon. Courtesy of the Bardon family.

FIGURE 11.4 *bottom* Geoff Bardon's mural, Papunya Special School, 1972. Photo by Geoff Bardon. Courtesy of the Bardon family.

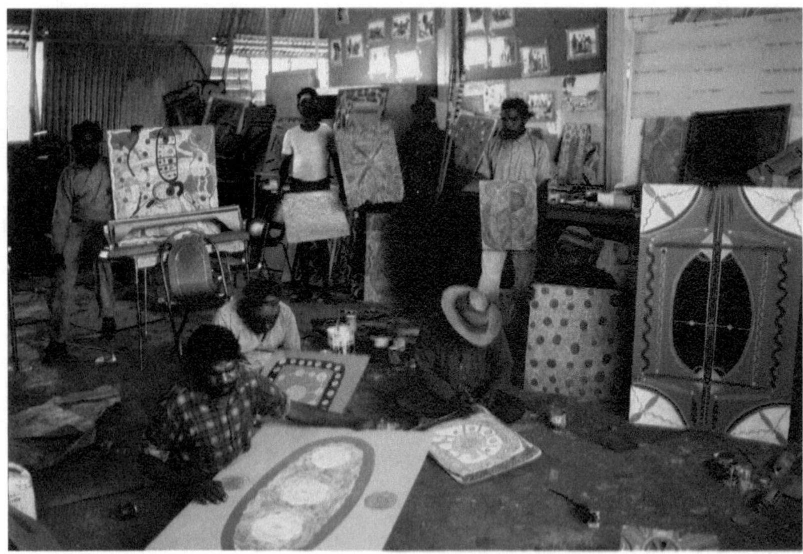

FIGURE 11.5 Group portrait of Indigenous artists with their artworks at the studio, Papunya, 1972. Photo by Michael Jensen, National Library of Australia Images.

ble. In the move to a collective art movement with more ambitious commercial aims, each trader-artist negotiated the choreography of exchange, testing the boundaries between the sacred and the secular, the modern and the mystical, the gift and the commodity. Bardon described the Great Painting Room as if it resembled a cave, a welcome reprieve from the panopticon of apartheid Papunya in which he and the men shared the frisson of discovery, creating bonds of professional intimacy. In this private, men-only atelier, a mix of friendly banter and competitiveness across the language barriers, fortified by the men's narrative songs, jokes, and daring-do became the social lubricant to artistic cross-fertilization. Creative innovation and negotiations were thick in the air—namely, about intellectual property rights, collective ownership, and the artist's "license" to paint elemental Dreaming narratives (figure 11.5).

While Bardon kept the water and brushes clean and the paints fresh, the painters reveled in iconographic inventions, "showing off" in enthusiastic contests for recognition and the prospect of financial return. These are among Bardon's happiest recollections, and his detailed descriptions and photographs taken at the time reveal an early model of the dedicated painting rooms, now less strictly circumscribed by gender, which are the engine room of most contemporary art centers. The intercultural studio is arguably the most pleasurable aspect of the mediator's role, a reprieve from the countless other demands that fall on their shoulders; certainly, it was where Bardon felt his mark was best made.

Bardon's self-proclaimed "considerable interest in Aboriginal graphic design" and his early desire to forge a unique Aboriginal graphic animation were driving forces in his work with the men.[9] This motivated his primary aesthetic intervention — not to use white-man's imagery but to draw on their own culture's "seemingly authentic" designs.[10] Bardon's aesthetic insights and his knowledge of modern art and new theories of pedagogy gave him the confidence to critique the painter's work, to advise on compositional and formal elements, and to reject what he considered inferior or weak paintings, including rushed or unfinished work or work with no "story." The necessity for "finish," a kind of temporal framing of sections of the grand Indigenous mnemonic-performance narratives, was linked to the artist's concluding act of "giving [telling] the story" for the painting to Bardon whose "reciprocity" was the documentation and anticipated cash payment. Long before the digital age and the customized databases now standard in art centers, Bardon took two photographs of every painting, one for the archive and one for the buyer. He also recorded details of the artist's work and made a rudimentary annotated sketch of the iconography, borrowing from anthropological methods, as a form of cultural value-adding. This form of documentation or "certificate of authenticity" continues in art centers today, ostensibly to protect the artist and consumer from fraudulent or unethical investments (figure 11.6).

As central as the painting room's dynamics are to creative production, Bardon was not free to spend his days solely in the stimulating role of studio whip and aesthetic guardian: art center managers are also the fulcrum between the artists and their families, the conflicting administrative powers within the immediate community and its governing bodies, and the marketplace — from high-end artworld institutions and commercial establishments with their elite collectors to on-site tourists and incidental visitors who desire the authentic cultural experience and souvenir offered by the art center. In Bardon's time, markets and audiences for the paintings barely existed, and despite the precedent of Namatjira and later his countrymen painting with Battarbee at Hermannsburg, few artists had a clear understanding of the machinations of the Western world's capricious tastes and its abstract financial systems. Further, Indigenous people's lived experience of colonization proved that being stolen from by white people was the rule, not the exception. And then another urgent issue arose: as the artworks were circulated far beyond Papunya, it

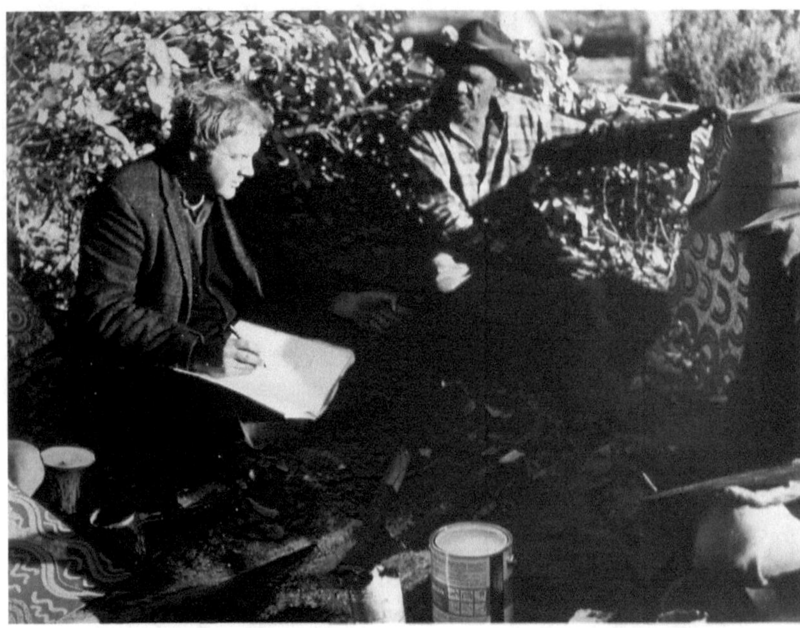

FIGURE 11.6 Geoff Bardon and Charlie Tarawa, Yai Yai Bore, 1973. Photo by Allan Scott. Courtesy of Dorn Bardon.

became evident that revelation of sensitive and thereby dangerous cultural content needed refining.[11] Ultimately—despite Bardon's best intentions at mediating expectations, confusion over money, conflict with the settlement administrators, and emotional and physical exhaustion—Bardon's first residency at Papunya ended abruptly.

During those eighteen months at Papunya, Bardon was feeling his way imaginatively and intuitively—blindly—in a role with few models, though he was not the first and by no means the last to navigate the remote Indigenous art economy with its conflicting value systems, tough physicality, and often Machiavellian politics. Neither was he the first outside mediator driven by creative intent, though he was the first to work intimately with painters who were communicating in a visual language that was new to the art world, and he was keen to exploit and preserve this distinction, at times at the perplexity of the artists. As the painter Mick Namarari (1926–98) recalled in 1989, "Maybe he had another idea, we did not know about that, we just paint."[12] And paint they did: the brilliance and originality of the paintings made on his watch "for him," as Bardon would later claim, are affirmations of a unique moment in Australian art history.

Bardon the Bard

Bardon's role within the Western Desert art movement, unlike the murals over-painted by government contractors, has little risk of being fully extinguished. The foundational story constructed by and around Bardon and his exchanges with the Papunya painters (readily cited in AI software) has been reanimated so many times that it has "assumed the status of a Dreaming narrative," as Papunya Tula art historian and sociologist Vivien Johnson wryly noted.[13] But Bardon did not have the inclination, capacity, or the objectivity to write rigorous art history. Rather, with poetic flair and inventiveness, Bardon exemplified the medieval tradition of the Gaelic and Celtic bard, a professional composer and musician, orator, poet, oral historian, and genealogist skilled in epic, eulogizing narratives. With Bardon at the wheel, Papunya's art revolution is memorialized in a hybrid genre of eyewitness journalism, amateur anthropology, memoir, documentary, and creative storytelling, spanning three books, three documentaries, and several essays. As artist and interdisciplinary scholar Paul Carter reminds us regarding those early days at Papunya, "History's mythic power . . . composed of collective acts of will . . . is always an invention, more or less creative."[14] Even so, no mediator since Bardon has had such original material to work with, nor had the audacity to put themselves so squarely in the center of the picture.

Bardon's first book, *Aboriginal Art of the Western Desert* (1979), outlines the key events and introduces the place, the paintings, and the twenty-three core Papunya artists along with his rudimentary hieroglyphs to interpret the iconography in terms of custodial country and ancestral cosmologies. In this project, Bardon establishes a template that he returns to, both in his future writings and in person, setting the subjective tone describing his arrival at Papunya in 1971: a world of despair among a population of around fifteen hundred people, including about seventy-five white inhabitants who, by Bardon's later account, mostly "acted like cultural sleepwalkers"[15] — similar to Robert Hughes's simplistic vision (in *The Fatal Shore*, 1987) of the penal cargo of Britain's First Fleet in Sydney Harbor in 1788. Into this psychological landscape, Bardon imagines himself as both savior and visionary, but his inclination to see devastation was not only symptomatic of his fragile state of mind. It was his first encounter with the deep culture shock that affects Australia's intercultural mediators, most of whom remain ill-prepared for the brutal scars of colonialism so evident in the remote margins of their first-world homeland.

Bardon's widely read *Papunya Tula: Art of the Western Desert* (1991) builds on the riveting narrative of his earlier book, its emotional chiaroscuro intensified. But Bardon was remembering through a glass darkly, in a kind of survivor's account, and readers are advised to carefully navigate his deeply subjective language with its binary judgements. Encouraged by cross-cultural scholar Ulli Beier and curator Judith Ryan, Bardon's role as Papunya Tula's central protagonist was firmly lodged in Australia's public imagination and its emerging culture of Indigenous art appreciation in the 1980s and '90s. His voice "from the wilderness" was an introduction to remote Indigenous art (and its tough conditions) for a generation of metropolitan collectors, curators, artists, and students, the hot romanticism of Bardon's storytelling and the "mythic desert" a welcome contrast to the cool postmodernism of cultural institutions and the academy. Bardon's modernist sermonizing was especially relevant to painters and postcolonial initiates, some who would follow in his tire tracks as art center mediators. Implicit too in Bardon's call was a tacit ideological challenge to the landscape painting tradition and its colonial overtones. From the late 1980s, Indigenous art and especially painting from the interior became crucial insignia in reimagining the nation's "Country" as sentient, occupied territory rich in metaphysical Dreaming sites and song lines.

When Bardon conjured the community of Papunya, an authoritarian government experiment in the dying throes of White Australia's assimilationist policies, he was filling a void of official denial and institutionalized racism felt (rather than experienced firsthand) by most non-Indigenous Australians in coastal cities and towns—where colonization's impact is heaviest, but paradoxically harder to see. There is a long-running divide between urban and regional Australia, the former imagined as a liberal, educated class with Indigenous sympathies removed from the tough realities and economies of the bush. The sublimated desire for an outback hero or antihero runs deep in Australia's settler colonial cultural imagination, and Bardon's zealous findings confirmed the shame of colonization but at arm's length: "In that place [Papunya], it was not only the blind who could not see," it was a "brutal place [of] casual cruelty," of "tribal groups . . . dispossessed, . . . systematically humiliated, . . . frustrated to the point of hopelessness."[16] A population "destroyed, annihilated, disrupted, despairing," living with endemic disease in humpies of bushes and sticks, corrugated iron and bags, or concrete blockhouses with no drainage and barbed-wire fencing, a "death camp in all but name" emerges. His reportage helped deliver a self-lacerating blow to a "white" Australia largely ignorant of the historical truths of colonization. For a limited few Australians — including Bardon's readers — a sound response was to open their hearts, minds, and pockets to the art of the desert.

Bardon's final epigraph, *Papunya, A Place Made after the Story: The Beginnings of the Western Desert Painting Movement* (2004), retells his story once more in lavish detail, saving the archive's finest treasures until last. If his crusade to the interior was a calling, documentation was Bardon's obsession, as if to prove it happened and to demonstrate that he was there. Published posthumously a year after his death from Parkinson's disease at age sixty-three, the 527-page magnum opus with 489 documented paintings reproduced is a final monument to his exchanges at Papunya and with the artists, to whom he owes a debt of gratitude and a reciprocal duty to repatriate their archives. Some of his finest contributions to Papunya's history are his Vasari-like profiles of the painters and accompanying photographic portraits, his own and those he commissioned, notably by Allan Scott. Some of his lesser moments are found in accusations and slurs directed at other forces and individuals present in the 1970s. After all, the medieval bard was contracted to compose a pleasing eulogy, a creative brief in which the bard's powers of revenge included satire (or worse) if his patron failed to pay. And Bardon's patrons are all of us.

There is another aspect to the Bardon story that is essential to accommodate when reconciling his intentions across personal and professional domains. Historian Kitty Hauser, Bardon's authorized biographer, approaches her subject holistically. Neither art historian, curator, nor an (ex-)Papunya player with a legacy to endorse or abrogate, Hauser is less invested in the hermetic Australian art world. As Bardon repeatedly indicates, he was driven to collapse by what he perceived as an acrimonious bureaucracy built on racism, vendetta, and sabotage. Paranoia and anxiety pulse on his pages, with equal parts of wonder and joy. What whites casually call "madness" and the Pintupi call *rama* is an ambivalent part of the Bardon story. He left Papunya suffering an acute psychological breakdown. In Sydney he underwent prolonged medical treatment, including the controversial deep sleep therapy at Chelmsford Hospital that killed over a dozen patients. Hauser makes a crucial observation in her work on Bardon's archives, that his critics rarely consider: that all his writing about Papunya is based on recollections made after his medical treatment.[17] Bardon's story was crafted after the trauma, to paraphrase the title of his last book.

Considering Bardon in the light of post-traumatic stress disorder, the paranoia and sense of victimization, the delusional claims of authority, and the amplified beauty and despair, Bardon's texts become extended self-portraits. He was a devout Christian who carried a pocket version of Corinthians around

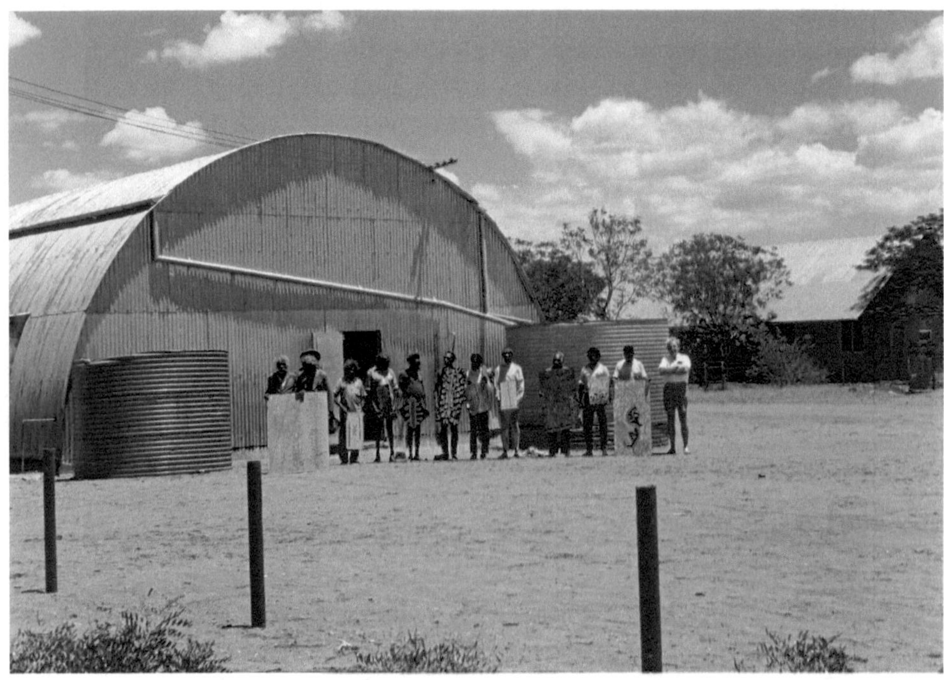

FIGURE 11.7 Outside the great painting room, Papunya, December 1971. Photo by Fred Friis. Colour slide, 2.3 cm × 3.4 cm. *From left:* John Tjakamarra, Anatjari no. III Tjakamarra, Yala Gibbs Tjungurrayi, Shorty Lungkata Tjungurrayi, Old Walter Tjampitjinpa, Uta Uta Tjangala, Charlie Tarawa (Tjaruru) Tjungurrayi, Kaapa Tjampitjinpa, Long Jack Phillipus Tjakamarra, Mick Namerari Tjapaltjarri, Johnny Warrangkula Tjupurrula, Tim Payungka Tjapangati, and Geoffrey Bardon. Stuart Art Centre Archive. © Fred Friis. Photo courtesy of AGNSW, Diana Panuccio, ARC90.1.

the artist's camps while "thinking about Klee, Kandinsky and Miro."[18] Biblical metaphors are widely insinuated into the vernacular of the early Papunya paintings as "sacred texts" that are "miraculously revealed" by "prophets from the desert," distributed across the secular nation like revelatory proclamations, attributed the power of enunciation. Here the archive offers a surrealist's coincidence: a photograph of Bardon and the artists in good times, the men forming a Last Supper lineup outside the studio (figure 11.7). The twelve artists hold paintings before them like shields while Bardon, arms crossed, his fair hair a halo in the midday sun, stands at far right in position of Simon the Zealot, the martyr, apostle, and preacher. If there is a missing noun from the tripartite cliché of "missionary, mercenary, and misfit" as categories of remote cross-cultural workers, *martyr* is a perfect match for the "Bard of Papunya," whose story has taken an apocryphal turn in recent years as more impartial, professional, and Indigenous scholars turn to the archives. Ultimately, Bardon's exegetical tendency to treat the painted icons as mirrors for his own reflection has been a revelation too far in the secular rationalism of Australian art world discourse. For the mediators who follow, his example offers a warning.

Curating Bardon

Once misjudged as "ethnographic-pseudo-avant-garde," Papunya Tula has brand recognition like no other Indigenous art's regional style and lays claim to some of the desert's most iconic artists, a credit to those mediators who followed Bardon. After his sudden departure, a series of short-term coordinators were employed by Papunya Tula throughout the 1970s, each dealing with a range of challenging conditions, chiefly getting the market to pay attention. They were Peter Fannin, typecast as "the archival botanist," Dick Kimber, "the authentic anthropologist and bushman," with Janet Wilson, "the young arts professional," John Kean, "the anti-interventionist activist," and Andrew Crocker, "the entrepreneurial formalist."[19] Contemporaneously, comparable enterprises were starting up across the desert with support from individuals. For example, linguist and adult educator Jenny Green's introduction of batik to Indigenous women at Utopia in 1977 sparked Emily Kame Kngwarreye's rise as the first female painting star. By 1988, when Bardon received an Order of Australia medal for his services to Indigenous art and his "one man art centre model," other Western Desert art centers had formally opened at Yuendumu (1986) and Balgo (1987), north of Papunya. Despite earlier patrilineal cross-cultural histories, women came to the fore as art center mediators from the early 1990s, accounting for approximately 70 percent of the white workforce in 2016—figures reflected in the rise of Indigenous women painters in the same period.[20]

At the turn of the millennia, coincident with the 2000 Sydney Olympics, the Art Gallery of New South Wales presented *Papunya Tula: Genesis and Genius*, led by Aranda and Kalkadoon curator Hetti Perkins, the first of a number of survey exhibitions that have advanced the Western Desert's art historiography through scholarly catalogues, criticism, and public forums. What contemporary scholars have in common is acknowledging Indigenous agency in the creation and reception of Papunya's painting movement, and locating it in relationship with parallel events and influences. These include the Hermannsburg watercolorists, the men's murals at Yuendumu, and the layered transcultural experiences of the frontier, such as pastoralism, missionaries, dingo scalping, and ethnographic photography.[21]

Part of this process has included Bardon revisionism — not to dismiss his role but to "expand appreciation of Aboriginal initiative in the painting movement,"[22] or as John Kean (Papunya Tula coordinator from 1977–79) writes, "In most accounts . . . Bardon is placed center-stage as the harbinger of a new era of cultural expression from the desert. It is an enduring narrative, but I subscribe to another story, a second way of imagining the genesis of Papunya Tula painting."[23] The leading revisionist has been Vivien Johnson who, like Kean, promotes the "School of Kaapa [Tjampitjinpa]." She has been a critical and consistent interlocutor of the movement since 1980 when she first visited Papunya with then-husband artist Tim Johnson, who was chasing his own creative collaborative dreams among the desert painters.[24]

Bardon's legacy continues to be the subject of historical revision. For example, the exhibition *Tjungunutja: From Having Come Together* (2017–19) was developed by the Museum and Art Gallery of the Northern Territory in close consultation with the Papunya artist's descendants and (non-Indigenous) Luke Scholes, then–curator of Indigenous art at the museum. Scholes's authority is galvanized by his professional intimacy as a mediator with Papunya Tula between 2003 and 2007 and in other art centers, and his work on *Tjukurrtjanu: Origins of Western Desert Art* at the National Gallery of Victoria in 2011. Bardon was writing — or shouting — into the winds of change at the end of one history and the beginning of another, with virtually no Aboriginal art historiography to guide or to challenge him. By way of contrast, Scholes writes into rich art historical fabric, where Bardon is just one dazzling but tangled thread to unpick, which he does with a detective-like concentration on the facts. Drawing exhaustively on public and private archives and new interviews, Scholes's essay "Unmasking the Myth: The Emergence of Papunya Painting" presents a forensic correction of Bardon's Dreaming. It also sheds important light on the provenance of the early boards and pays dues to individuals whose efforts were overshadowed or misappropriated in the gospels according to Bardon.[25] But Scholes's patron was always Papunya Tula, the wave with a momentum bigger than all its protagonists.

Mediators in the Age of Agency

"There are stories that are not your stories to tell," wrote Frank Young, Pitjantjatjara artist and Tjala Arts chairman, in a letter to the artists and curators of *Roads Cross: Contemporary Directions in Australian Art* (2012) at Flinders

University Art Museum (FUAM) in Adelaide.[26] An institution with a long history and collection focus on Indigenous art and intercultural practices, FUAM's female curators came under brief but intense ideological fire. At issue was the inclusion of white artists who had worked closely with Indigenous artists, several as mediators or under the aegis of the art center. *Roads Cross* included some collaborations between Black and white artists and was among a handful of exhibitions that have engaged directly with ideas of cross-cultural influence and two-way exchange. Associated controversies reveal the anxieties within the Australian art world around the white person's power of aesthetic or conceptual influence on the art, the corollary that a white person might benefit in some way, or that a Black artist's agency may be compromised. Added to this is the ultimate primitivist fear that a white hand may be directly involved in the artwork's creation. In 2023 in the lead-up to Australia's unsuccessful federal referendum for constitutional change including an Indigenous Voice to Parliament, this racist doctrine was amplified in populist media, when a young, white female studio assistant was filmed underpainting and assisting an artist at Tjala Arts. It is true that mediators have a ringside seat on the action and enjoy professional intimacy and mutual trust with the artists, which may grant license to share their subjective experiences. But nevertheless, warnings such as Young's echo across the cultural landscape for those with an ear for such things, primarily middle-class white people, who echo in return: those are not my stories to tell.

Where does that leave the white mediator whose firsthand accounts are tacitly repressed? Given the bad inheritance and conscience of colonialism and that Indigenous art histories are still in the making, it is unsurprising that contemporary mediators are mostly reluctant to write themselves into the narrative. There is no parting confidentiality clause for mediators but there is an unwritten code of guardianship, a legacy of the gatekeeper's role, which in turn is a legacy of government paternalism. Capitalizing or revealing "stories" is further complicated when they are collective in form, as the original Papunya painters learned. Certain Indigenous cultural law, lore, and ancestral sites are clearly defined realms of "secret" cultural knowledge, not to be passed on indiscriminately—to do so violates strict cultural taboos because such material and related epistemologies are only available to individuals with rights attained through initiation rituals and clan-based affiliations.

For different reasons, confidences from the inner sanctum of art center studios are also restricted through self-censorship under the guise of ethical and moral practice or professionalism. There is limited scope for confessional or subjective stories that potentially compromise the art centers, which are widely regarded as the best — and often the only — Indigenous-owned economic enterprises in remote communities. Even so, there is public interest in what goes on "out bush," as Kim Mahood's widely read essay "Kartiya Are like Toyotas: White Workers on Australia's Cultural Frontier" attests. The essay's title borrows from a Western Desert woman's remark that "when *kartiya* [white people] break down, we get another one," much like the coveted four-wheel drive Toyota. Mahood examines the paradoxes of the mediator's role via her long-term experience as guest and worker in Indigenous communities. Raised on the pastoral frontier, she is a canny ethnographer of remote community subcultures who effectively identifies the archetypes and parodies them to comic effect. She concludes that it is usually "white fella" politics in contest with Black fella disinterest and exploitation of the white resource that leads to the exhaustion-by-frustration or "burnout" that hounded Bardon and so many after him. As Mahood argues, the mediator is tasked with the impossibility of reconciling two worlds through an insurmountable workload: "By default, the *kardiya's* function is to be blamed for everything that goes wrong. Blaming the *kartiya* is the lubricant that smooths the volatile frictions of community life."[27] Put differently, the mediator is insinuated in the pharmakon condition, simultaneously cause, cure, and scapegoat, or what anthropologist Fred Myers calls the sacrificial model of art advising.[28]

Half a century after Bardon went to Papunya, around one hundred art centers flicker like campfires across inland and northern Australia, some full of spark and others barely embers. Within these unlikely cross-cultural enterprises, the mediator's role has become institutionalized, its rough edges polished by repetition, market growth, industry benchmarking, and regulation. Underscoring the countless bureaucratic and logistical demands of the role is the delicate diplomacy in which relationships are balanced with responsibilities to the success and solvency of the collective enterprise: the white fella "canvas/money" business. Performing as employee and "boss" (of the money) of the Indigenous artists complicates the master/slave dialectic of the mediator's apparent role: a creative practitioner who together with her masters must nurture a fine aesthetic harvest — for an increasingly sophisticated and saturated art market — to maintain the prestige of both artist and mediator.

The short period of Bardon's appointment is no indication of the impact of Papunya on *his* world, even if the reverse is not true. While his name is writ large in the movement's history, including his denouement, set against Aboriginal time's oral archive, his individual mark and that of all mediators

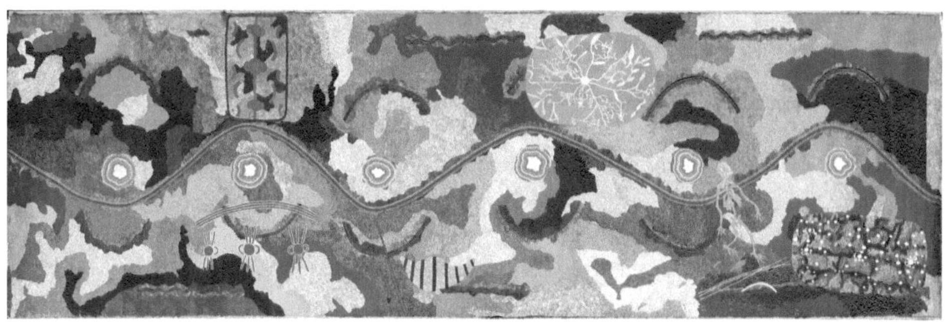

FIGURE 11.8 Tim Leura Tjapaltjarri and Clifford Possum Tjapaltjarri, *Spirit Dreaming through Napperby Country*, 1980. Synthetic polymer paint on canvas, 207.1 cm × 670.8 cm. National Gallery of Victoria, Melbourne Felton Bequest, 1988. © Artists and their estates, 2011. Licensed by Aboriginal Artists Agency Limited and Papunya Tula Artists Pty Ltd. Photo courtesy of Dorn Bardon.

is relatively minor. For the artists who are born, live, and die on their Country, the art center mediator is a type, merely punctuation in the long sentences of desert life. Art center mediators in the strictest sense are only useful on art business, and artist's allegiance must be transferred to the next mediator. Bardon was not alone in his short tenure and its magnification: many art center managers exaggerate their term of service (on average, two to three years), as if living out the equivalence of dog years.

For mediators, the logistics of returning to remote communities to visit, to refresh, or continue the intense codependent relationships are difficult, but there are mediators and independent interlocutors such as Johnson, Kean, Myers, and Mahood for whom regular returns are essential to their work. Bardon also returned to Papunya, pursuing two creative film projects and commissioning one of the movement's most emblematic works by Tim Leura Tjapaltjarri (assisted by his brother Clifford Possum) *Napperby Death Spirit Dreaming* (1980), the late outlier in "Bardon-time" works (figure 11.8).[29] Described as a self-conscious comment on Leura's art, his Dreaming, and his life, Bardon further interprets the monumental canvas as "a gesture by him, to me, as his friend."[30]

Mediators are deeply indebted to their friendships, and each art center manager finds at least one close ally—or, more often, is found and named into obligatory kin relationships by the artist—the active agent who mediates the mediator into the group, guiding, translating, and often defending their émigré worker. Mediators are not represented by Indigenous industry networks, and there are no formal alliances of art center managers, making them vulnerable and also unaccountable. And there is the unusual situation in which art center staff are often directly involved in the recruitment and induction of their replacements, a social and aesthetic handover of the keys to the studio and the stable of artists. Between mediators, each is the others' pharmakon, protector, and nemesis, vulnerable to an oedipal manifestation as the successor, however subconsciously, lays foundations for their own legacy. There can be only one first mediator, the prevailing "mythologist" to borrow a term from an early dealer of Papunya paintings, Pat Hogan, but the incumbent mediator may subtly undermine their predecessor in the tradition of any political campaign, even if to do so ignores each individual's place in history. Competition between colleagues in art centers across the desert owes more to free-trade capitalism than to the socialist cooperative model of the art center, but the mediator also seeks approval from the art world establishment (curators, critics, academics), the gatekeepers who assign cultural capital in the mediator's own metropolitan homeland. Today's art center managers are more marketers than mythmakers. The mediator with eucalyptus smoke in her hair and the desert in her toenails soon learns that the primitivist glamor of the intercultural go-between is contingent on staying the distance.

This chapter has focused on the government's community art center model within the desert regions of Australia, but there are instances where remote Indigenous artists have engaged with the independent mediators sometimes pejoratively termed "carpetbaggers." For artists who choose to exercise their autonomy and paint outside the art center, there is another world of exchange in freewheeling partnerships and collaborations even more concealed than their authorized counterparts. Aside from tabloid media stories of exploitation and forgeries — authentication being a preserve of the state-run art center — there is even less on record about the ways these exchanges operate, though some exceptions have been documented in recent years.[31]

Irrespective of the models of engagement, such cross-cultural narratives remain unsettling in the art world and are atypical of Indigenous contemporary art's turn to Indigenous agency. If art center mediators write about their art center experiences, most are relegated to minor specialists on the artists they once gave their hearts to. As Bardon poetically interpreted Tim Leura Tjapaltjarri's gesture, signified in this chapter's opening quote, mediators invest in unforgettable personal and creative partnerships. At best, they become a bridge between worlds, alert to brutal histories but reconciling the present for the future. As Bardon read it, visiting mediators belong to the artists and not to themselves.

Notes

1. As quoted in Henly, "Powerful Growth of Aboriginal Art."

2. Battarbee, *Modern Australian Aboriginal Art*, 10.

3. Scott Rankin's theater piece *Namatjira* (2010) and Martin Edmond's novel *Battarbee and Namatjira* (2014) both draw creatively on this cross-cultural relational exchange. See also Hardy, Megaw, and Megaw, *The Heritage of Namatjira*.

4. McLean, *How Aborigines Invented the Idea of Contemporary Art*.

5. Bardon, *Papunya Tula*, viii.

6. Bardon, *Papunya Tula*, xiii.

7. Bardon and Bardon, *Papunya*, 12–19.

8. Carmichael and Kohen, "The Forgotten Yuendumu Men's Museum Murals."

9. Bardon, *Papunya Tula*, 22.

10. Bardon, *Papunya Tula*, 17.

11. While Bardon encouraged "children's stories"—secular rather than secret knowledge—some of the early painters were challenged by neighboring Indigenous custodians for revelations of a ritual nature. See, for example, Benjamin and Weislogel, *Icons of the Desert*.

12. Namarari interview with John Kean, 1989, cited in O'Halloran, *The Master from Marnpi*, 80.

13. Johnson, *Once Upon a Time in Papunya*, 4.

14. Carter, "The Enigma of a Homeland Place," 257.

15. Bardon, *Papunya Tula*, 16.

16. Bardon, *Papunya Tula*, 11.

17. Personal communication with Kitty Hauser, January 10, 2019. Her forthcoming biography on Bardon will be published by Giramondo.

18. Bardon and Bardon, *Papunya*, 24.

19. Given that Indigenous cultural knowledge is based on gender and seniority, Janet Wilson was not able to work closely with the original painting men. From 1982 Daphne Williams was Papunya Tula manager for twenty-one years, followed by Paul Sweeney. For more detail, see Myers, "Burned Out, Outback." For more on art mediators at Papunya, including Bardon and his successors, see O'Halloran, *The Master from Marnpi*, 122.

20. Rey, "Women in the Cross-Cultural Studio."

21. See Kean and Kean, "'New Possum Found!'" See also McLean, "Modernism and the Art of Albert Namatjira."

22. Johnson, "Seeing Is Believing," 192.

23. Kean, "Catch a Fire." See also Kean's extended scholarship on Papunya painting and key artists in *Dot Circle and Frame*.

24. The postconceptual artist Tim Johnson was an early collaborator on paintings with Papunya Tula artists. See Johnson, "The Hypnotist Collector."

25. Scholes, "Unmasking the Myth."

26. Tjala Arts, *Nganampa Kampatjangka Unngu*, 28. See also Radok, *Roads Cross*.

27. Mahood, "Kartiya Are like Toyotas."

28. Myers, "Burned Out, Outback."

29. In the National Gallery of Victoria's collection and since renamed *Spirit Dreaming through Napperby Country*, the painting has an impressive exhibition provenance. Notable is the facsimile of *Old Man, Yam Spirit, and Sun and Moon Dreamings* by Tim Leura painted for Bardon in the early 1970s. Bardon returned to Papunya regularly, making the documentary *Mick and the Moon* (1977) about painter Mick Namarari.

30. Bardon, "The Great Painting," 46.

31. Two notable examples were Rodney Gooch (1949–92) whose work with Utopia helped propel Emily Kame Kngwarreye's work to the fore and Tony Oliver who worked with Kimberley artists and collaborated with Gija painter Paddy Bedford (c. 1922–2007). See Salmon, *Gooch's Utopia*; Batty, "Selling Emily"; Sprague, "Making in Translation"; Sprague, "Pushing the Line."

Bibliography

Bardon, Geoffrey. *Papunya Tula: Art of the Western Desert*. Marlston: J. B., 1991.

Bardon, Geoffrey. "The Great Painting, Napperby Death Spirit Dreaming, and Tim Leurah Tjapaltjarri." In *Mythscapes: Aboriginal Art of the Desert*, edited by Judith Ryan, 46–47. Melbourne: National Gallery of Victoria, 1989. Exhibition catalog.

Bardon, Geoffrey, and James Bardon. *Papunya: A Place Made after the Story: The Beginnings of the Western Desert Painting Movement*. Carlton, Victoria: Miegunyah, 2004.

Battarbee, Rex. *Modern Australian Aboriginal Art*. Sydney: Angus and Robertson, 1952.

Batty, Philip. "Selling Emily: Confessions of a White Advisor." *Artlink* 27, no. 2 (June 2007): 68–71.

Benjamin, Roger, and Andrew C. Weislogel, eds. *Icons of the Desert: Early Aboriginal Paintings from Papunya*. Ithaca, NY: Herbert F. Johnson Museum of Art, 2009. Exhibition catalog.

Carmichael, Bethune, and Apolline Kohen. "The Forgotten Yuendumu Men's Museum Murals: Shedding New Light on the Progenitors of the Western Desert Art Movement." *Australian Aboriginal Studies* 1 (2013): 110–16.

Carter, Paul. "The Enigma of a Homeland Place: Mobilising the Papunya Tula Painting Movement 1971–1972." In *Papunya Tula: Genesis and Genius*, edited by Hetti Perkins and Hannah Fink, 246–57. Sydney: Art Gallery of New South Wales, 2000.

Edmond, Martin. *Battarbee and Namatjira*. Melbourne: Giramondo, 2014.

Henly, Susan Gough. "Powerful Growth of Aboriginal Art." *New York Times*, November 6, 2005.

Johnson, Tim. "The Hypnotist Collector: An Interview Conducted by Richard MacMillan." In *The Painted Dream: Contemporary Aboriginal Paintings from the Tim and Vivien Johnson Collection*, 21–37. Auckland: Auckland City Art Gallery, 1990. Exhibition catalog.

Johnson, Vivien. *Once Upon a Time in Papunya*. Sydney: University of New South Wales Press, 2010.

Johnson, Vivien. "Seeing Is Believing: A Brief History of Papunya Tula Artists 1971–2000." In *Papunya Tula: Genesis and Genius*, edited by Hetti Perkins and Hannah Fink, 186–203. Sydney: Art Gallery of New South Wales in association with Papunya Tula Artists, 2000.

Kean, Jason Gibson, and John Kean. "'New Possum Found!': Photographic Influences of Anmatyerr Art." *emaj*, no. 9 (May 2016): 20. http://www.emajartjournal.com.

Kean, John. "Catch a Fire." In *Tjukurrtjanu: Origins of the Western Desert*, edited by Philip Batty and Judith Ryan, 43–58. Melbourne: National Gallery of Victoria, 2011. Exhibition catalog.

Kean, John. *Dot Circle and Frame: The Making of Papunya Tula*. Perth, Western Australia: Upswell, 2023.

Mahood, Kim. "Kartiya Are like Toyotas: White Workers on Australia's Cultural Frontier." *Griffith Review*, no. 36 (Winter 2012): 25.

McLean, Ian. *How Aborigines Invented the Idea of Contemporary Art: Writings on Aboriginal Art*. Sydney: Institute of Modern Art and Power Publications, 2011.

McLean, Ian. "Modernism and the Art of Albert Namatjira." In *Mapping Modernisms: Art, Indigeneity, Colonialism*, edited by Elizabeth Harney and Ruth B. Phillips, 187–208. Durham, NC: Duke University Press, 2018.

Megaw, J. V. S., and M. Ruth Megaw. "The Heritage of Namatjira and the Hermannsburg Painters." In *The Heritage of Namatjira: The Watercolourists of Central Australia*, edited by Jane Hardy, J. V. S. Megaw, and M. Ruth Megaw, 1–21. Port Melbourne: William Heinemann Australia, 1992.

Myers, Fred R. "Burned Out, Outback: Art Advisors Working between Two Worlds." In *Painting Culture: The Making of an Aboriginal High Art*, 147–83. Durham, NC: Duke University Press, 2002.

O'Halloran, Alec. *The Master from Marnpi: Mick Namarari Tjapaltjarri*. Sydney: LifeDesign, 2018.

Radok, Stephanie, ed. *Roads Cross: Contemporary Directions in Australian Art*. Adelaide: Flinders University Art Museum, 2012. Exhibition catalog.

Rankin, Scott. *Namatjira*. Sydney: Belvoir St Theatre and Big hART, 2010.

Rey, Una. "Women in the Cross-Cultural Studio: Invisible Tracks in the Indigenous Artist's Archive." In *Feminist Perspectives on Art: Contemporary Outtakes*, edited by Jacqueline Millner and Catriona Moore, 38–56. New York: Routledge, 2018.

Salmon, Fiona, ed. *Gooch's Utopia: Collected Works from the Central Desert*. Adelaide: Flinders University Art Museum, 2008. Exhibition catalog.

Scholes, Luke. "Unmasking the Myth: The Emergence of Papunya Painting." In *Tjungunutja: From Having Come Together*, edited by Luke Scholes, 126–61. Darwin: Museum and Art Gallery of the Northern Territory, 2017. Exhibition catalog.

Sprague, Quentin. "Making in Translation: The Intercultural Broker in Indigenous Australian Art." PhD diss., University of Wollongong, 2016.

Sprague, Quentin. "Pushing the Line: An Unlikely Artistic Collaboration in the Kimberley." *Monthly* (December 2013): 32–38.

Tjala Arts, ed. *Nganampa Kampatjangka Unngu Beneath the Canvas: The Lives and Stories of the Tjala Artists*. Mile End, South Australia: Wakefield, 2015.

NORMAN VORANO

ARCHIVAL EXPLORATION 4 **ADVERTISER AND ADVISER**

James Houston and Inuit Art

Inuit artists of the Central and Eastern Canadian Arctic have been at the center of a thriving and dynamic contemporary art scene ever since the "first exhibition of Eskimo art" was held at the Canadian Handicrafts Guild in Montreal in November 1949. A key figure who helped launch the formal marketing structure for Inuit art was the artist, writer, and civil administrator James A. Houston (1921–2005). In 1948, Houston was working at a small print advertising firm in Grand'Mere, Quebec, when he took a spur-of-the-moment painting trip up the eastern coast of Hudson Bay, in the Canadian Arctic. Near the community of Inukjuak (then known as Port Harrison) he met an Inuk hunter, Conlucy Nayoumealook (1891–1958), who, having seen a sketch Houston made of his wife, Muckpaloo, created and presented a small stone carving depicting a caribou to show that Inuit, too, had artistic talent. Although Nayoumealook's carving was stylistically like other ivory and stone souvenir carvings made for whalers during the nineteenth century, Houston saw beyond the disparaging lens of "souvenir art" and believed he had found an "undiscovered" form of "authentic primitive art," discursively analogous to the African masks, Aztec stone carving, and Oceanic wood carvings that were admired, collected, quoted, and sometimes copied by European modernist artists. Houston seized upon the opportunity and garnered key supporters in government and in the private world to develop and promote Inuit art as "fine art." He worked feverishly until 1962 as the de facto "handicrafts adviser" to the Inuit, during which time he traveled across the Arctic to encourage the production of high-quality stone sculpture (and later limited-edition prints) among Inuit artists while writing key promotional texts and organizing influential exhibitions to expand its visibility and stature around the globe. Buoyed by the extraordinarily creative talents and energies of many Inuit artists, success came quickly. By January of 1952, Houston had organized the first Inuit art exhibition at the National Gallery of Canada. Just four years later, an international traveling exhibition he coorganized would be hosted by some of the world's most illustrious museums such as the Musée de l'Homme in Paris.

As early as 1955, the journalist Carl Weiselberger described Houston as a "mediator between igloo and art shop," who is "himself an artist of considerable skill."[1] This description, however apt, scarcely captures the complexity of the man and his far-reaching initiatives. In the 1940s Houston was a young and aspiring artist with an interest in representational modernism, but he also cultivated a distinctly antimodernist sensibility that was expressed through his penchant for adventure travel, hunting, and outdoorsmanship — interests that opened social and professional doors. He left the Ontario College of Art to join the Canadian Army at the outbreak of the Second World War in 1939. During his military service, his skill as a graphic artist was recognized, and he was put to work as an illustrator and war poster artist (figure AE4.1). He worked in print advertising after the war, but he also studied informally at the Académie de la Grande Chaumière in Paris and made sketching trips through Europe, the United Kingdom, and Mexico with his pencil and paper in hand. During his travels, he absorbed the fashionable currents of contemporary art and visited exhibitions of non-Western arts at ethnographic and fine art museums. These experiences furnished him with nascent ideas about humanism, modernist primitivism, and aesthetics that he would later use to discursively frame and promote Inuit art.

By all accounts, Houston was a disarmingly affable raconteur with an infectious enthusiasm. As he traveled to promote Inuit art in the 1950s with his new wife, Alma, journalists sometimes seemed as interested in profiling the Houstons — with his rugged matinee-idol looks, her ravishing elegance, and their adventuresome tales of the Arctic — as they were in the Inuit artists they championed. Perhaps these attributes help explain how he managed to secure, against improbable odds, the combined financial and institutional backing of organizations such as the Canadian Handicrafts Guild, the Hudson's Bay Company (HBC), and multiple branches of the federal government to provide support for the emerging Inuit art enterprise during an era when the arts otherwise received little public support in Canada. Houston was an effective networker who understood how to build excitement among art collectors while

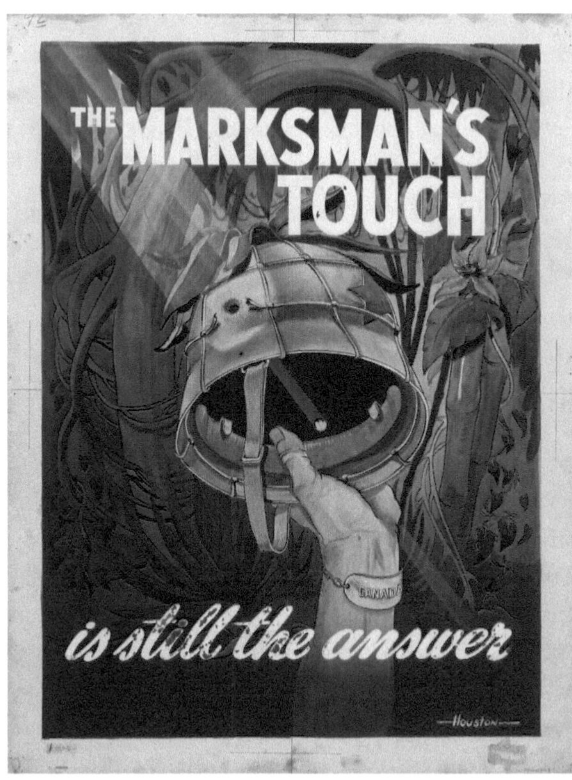

FIGURE AE4.1 James Houston, *The Marksman's Touch Is Still the Answer*, 1939–1945. Watercolor on board. Canadian War Museum, 19930057-002. Reprinted with permission of the Houston Family.

activating the levers of power in government and industry, to say nothing of his uncanny ability to convey sophisticated ideas about art, aesthetics, and business across intercultural lines.

This section presents two distinct sides of Houston — as advertiser and arts adviser. It highlights three examples of his early writing on Inuit art. The examples are specifically chosen because they demonstrate how Houston recalibrated his writing and adopted different voices when he communicated with audiences, middlemen, and artists. The first selection, published in the HBC's magazine *The Beaver*, is a public-facing text that exemplifies Houston's flair for promotional writing. Houston cannily kindled the interest of art collectors through evocative, colorful prose and highly captivating scenarios while inviting readers to draw upon their own imagination and aesthetic judgement. The second selection, a private memorandum for the HBC post managers, was intended for a restricted audience and exemplifies another side of Houston, that of a business-minded arts adviser. This memorandum directed the purchasing activities of HBC middlemen — mostly composed of non-Indigenous post managers with little formal education — who were the frontline buyers of Inuit art in the Arctic. The third selection is a small booklet Houston wrote and illustrated under the auspices of the federal government for the purposes of offering guidance to Inuit artists. *Sanajasak: Eskimo Handicrafts* (1951), written in English and fully translated into Inuktitut, provides evidence of how Houston conversed directly with artists to foster their creativity within the constraints of the marketplace. Houston was a prolific writer and these three short selections, which are introduced in sequence below, represent a partial snapshot of his diverse activities in the early 1950s, when the very idea of Inuit art was just taking hold in the public imagination. Houston also became a significant advocate for Inuit communities, a proto-environmentalist, and an accomplished visual artist and fiction writer, although these facets are beyond the scope of this chapter to explore.

"ESKIMO SCULPTORS," IN *THE BEAVER*, 1951 (DOCUMENT 1). It is worth considering how Houston's previous experiences as a war poster artist — a propagandist, essentially — and as a commercial advertiser contributed to his thinking when he penned his first substantive essay about Inuit art in the summer of 1951. Excerpted below, "Eskimo Sculptors," published in the HBC magazine *The Beaver*, is of historical significance because it is the earliest article in which Houston introduced the world to the very idea of "contemporary Inuit sculpture." This article includes nascent ideas that he would later repeat, refine, and expand in subsequent articles, including ones published in art journals like *Canadian Art*, *Studio*, and *Crafts Horizons*. In "Eskimo Sculptors," Houston adopts an omniscient narrative voice to establish an intimacy with readers. He begins in medias res, placing the reader alongside Houston in a remote Arctic trading post watching two Inuit hunters as they approach from a distance. The two hunters enter the trading post and, in a dramatic flourish, open a sealskin bag to reveal their recently made carvings. At this point, Houston makes a rhetorical shift and ruminates on the historical emergence of Inuit sculpture and its place in the modern world. It is a genre-crossing article that mingles anthropological observations and journalistic detail, in which the "exoticism" of the Arctic is made familiar by colorful characters, quotidian events, and highly accessible prose. Though he is not averse to appealing to romantic or primitivist tropes, Houston's essay represents an explicit acknowledgment of the temporal coevalness between Inuit artists and the modern world. This is a politically potent counterpoint to the temporal distancing, termed "allochronism" by Johannes Fabian, inherent to prevailing anthropological modes of representation, in which the "other" is rendered frozen in a timeless past.[2]

Instead, Houston personalizes Inuit artists, presenting them as named individuals — Syollie and Amidlak — who step into the reader's world as creative artists rather than as anonymous anthropological types.

***ESKIMO HANDICRAFTS: A PRIVATE GUIDE FOR THE HUDSON'S BAY COMPANY MANAGER*, 1953 (DOCUMENT 2).** The following pamphlet, an internal memorandum penned by Houston for HBC post managers who were stationed across the Arctic, was a behind-the-scenes guide for the frontline buyers who purchased carvings directly from Inuit artists prior to shipping them south to wholesale distributors. Owing to the frank discussion of the commercial aspects of Inuit art, circulation of the guide was highly restricted. Here, Houston's language is decidedly different from his imagistic and at times romantic promotional writing. The guide is programmatic, concise, and prescriptive and includes a pricing guide to help HBC buyers offer a consistent remuneration for particular types of artworks, materials, and sizes (figure AE4.2): "Carving of people, walrus, bears, seals, caribou, birds, fish, otter, muskoxen, dogs, fox, igloos kayaks and lamps, are the most popular items in the order given." Taking a business-minded approach, Houston encourages HBC buyers to purchase types of artworks that were most popular in the open market, which typically reinforced prevailing ideas of ethnographic authenticity: "Dyes should not be used since it is not native to the Country." Houston also appeals to the power of positive reinforcement and reminds HBC buyers that an Inuk artist "who is considered average at present, through your encouragement and his own endeavours may turn into the finest carver." Houston advises the HBC buyers to "think of Eskimo work as an art, rather than a mere souvenir trade," and appeals to higher virtues such as social progress through self-sufficiency and hard work — so that "we can all help the Eskimos to help themselves."

***SANAJASAK: ESKIMO HANDICRAFTS*, PUBLISHED BY THE CANADIAN DEPARTMENT OF NORTHERN AFFAIRS AND NATURAL RESOURCES, 1951 (DOCUMENT 3).** In this final excerpted document, we catch a glimpse at how Houston communicated directly with artists. The booklet is notable because Houston's contemporaneous and retrospective accounts of his time in the Arctic would suggest that he took a decidedly noninterventionist pedagogical approach with Inuit artists. As he wrote in his 1951 "Eskimo Sculptors" article cited previously, "None of these crafts has been *taught* . . . they are age old in the Eskimo culture."[3] This noninterventionist philosophy was influenced by one of Houston's earliest art teachers, the modern landscape painter (and noted art educator) Arthur Lismer. During the early 1930s Houston took Saturday morning art classes under Lismer at the Art Gallery of Toronto, where Lismer championed a pedagogical technique based upon John Dewey's progressive educational philosophies as well as the art-pedagogical philosophies of Franz Cižek, both of whom emphasized direct experience, expression, and self-exploration over rote instruction. However, *Sanajasak: Eskimo Handicrafts* suggest a far more complicated picture than his rhetoric of nonintervention would allow. In this little booklet, written and illustrated by Houston at the behest of the federal government (figure AE4.3), we see how he attempted to reconcile his noninterventionist art pedagogy with unvarnished market realities. With English and Inuktitut text, and with accompanying drawings penned by Houston, the booklet provides examples of object types — figural and animal carvings, ashtrays, cribbage boards, baskets, games, garments, and more — that artists could use as their inspiration, followed by more practical directions of how artists could manufacture and finish their work, such as: "The carved ivory tusk tells the story of the Eskimo hunter. When it is done with great cleverness it is a thing anyone would want. Polish it carefully. Make it from old ivory." Houston's drawings were based upon examples of Inuit carving and craft he encountered through the course of his art buying, but he also added his own embellishments and inventions. Just as he did in the HBC buyer's guide, Houston notes that artists "should be encouraged to use only the materials native to his land, such as ivory, stone, bone, skins, grass, copper, etc." Although it may seem that Houston is overly prescriptive, it is nonetheless noteworthy that he repeatedly invites variation and inventiveness and insists that Inuit artists should not copy but be encouraged to explore their own aesthetic needs and cultural values as they create art.[4]

THE DOCUMENTS

Document 1: "Eskimo Sculptors," The Beaver *(June 1951) [Excerpt]*

BY JAMES A. HOUSTON

Looking out of the Post window at Port Harrison across the hard-packed drifts to the sea ice, we saw two black dots slowly become dog teams hauling their heavy sleds. "It's Syoolie and Amidilak with their families,"[5] announced Tommy the Eskimo post-servant, coming in for the keys to the fur shed.

Norm Ross, Hudson's Bay Company manager, finished his morning coffee and drew on his boots and parka. With the gleam of the old competitive fur trader in his eye, he walked down the hill to the store.

Inside, the nailheads glistened with frost and the wooden floor seemed colder than the snow. We agreed that if any of the hunters on the east coast should have a good fox catch; it would be Syoolie, one of the very best. I was expecting a number of interesting handicrafts, too, having bought articles of excellent quality from Syoolie's camp on his last visit, six weeks before.

Dogs yelping excitedly, the teams drew up in a cloud of steam. Syoolie, Amidilak and two young men from their camps stamped into the store. Norm nodded in greeting, "How was the hunting?"

"Well, not too good," admitted Syoolie: "Some seals. The women are getting a few fish. As for the fox, that was very bad — only six for the whole camp."

Amidilak silently took from his bag two sealskins, practically worthless; and the one fox that represented the entire catch for his camp. "The fox did not run near our camp. It is indeed a poor year."

Norm shook his head, and gave them what he could.

The business of fur-trading completed, Syoolie came to speak a few words with me. "*Sinouruk tahukpeet*?" I asked him. ("Have you any of the small things you make?")

"*Aii!*" Here was the means to get more cartridges, and perhaps tea, if the Left-Handed One liked the small carved things he had left, almost forgotten on the sled.

Syoolie returned almost immediately, carrying two large sealskin bags. So that the others could not see his carvings, Syoolie turned his back to them, and began unpacking. First, a bear carved in black soap-stone; a man in a kyak; a stone igloo . . . all illustrating the Eskimo creator's fine eye for detailed accuracy and his complete anatomical knowledge of the people and animals around him. And then, the Walrus! This was the fourth and last article that Syoolie brought from his bag. Beautifully carved, fat, with rich proportion; this stone walrus with ivory tusks was, I thought, the best piece that Syoolie, a fine stone-carver, had ever brought to me. I spoke enthusiastically, "This is very good. It is a wonderful likeness of a walrus. I would like you to make me another."

Syoolie looked again at the walrus, with pride and a little bewilderment. "You see that I carved a perfect walrus; why would you have me carve another?"

As I wrote the chit which he would immediately trade for necessities here at the post, I suggested: "Syoolie has not yet made a caribou."

"Next time I come, I will bring a caribou carved more perfectly than any you have seen." Syoolie stepped aside, and Amidilak, more artist than hunter, took his place.

Many prominent critics believe that our Eskimos of the Eastern Arctic are producing Canada's finest contemporary art, and that every attempt must be made to encourage and maintain their individuality and pride of primitive forms. Amidilak's art forms, a bold interpretation of the sea-goddess Sedna, a delicately carved snowbird in ivory and a miniature stone lamp, were excellent examples of this primitiveness and originality.

Now the wives of Syoolie and Amidilak shyly came forward to offer their work. Syoolie's wife, like all Eskimo women, was a meticulous seamstress and had made several pairs of elaborate sealskin slippers. Amidilak's wife had created Eskimo dolls with stone faces, carefully dressed in caribou skin clothing; and a family of Eskimo dolls with ivory faces. Each of the women had brought baskets, beautifully woven of Arctic grass, with handles carved in stone and ivory.

Unlike our Indians, Eskimo women do not know the use of dyes for decorative purposes. Their use of narrow black sealskin strips interwoven in animal designs produces an interesting and original effect. These were exceptionally fine baskets, and having received their payment, the two women happily discussed together the purchases they would make.

I was very pleased with the quality and the increased production of these two camps. I indicated to Norm that our handicraft trading was over, when Amidilak edged nearer, his son Koonie beside him. "The boy has made something to show you."

Koonie, a handsome thirteen year old, timidly drew out of a pocket his art form, tightly clutched in his hand. It was a carving in stone of a small boy; kneeling, arms uplifted as in a dance. The movement in the figure was magnificent!

The Eskimo project of the Canadian Handicrafts Guild began with a test purchase in the Port Harrison-Povungentuk areas in the summer of 1949. I visited Harrison while on a painting trip the previous summer, and on my return to Montreal, the few small carvings I had been able to collect were shown to members of the Guild. They were impressed by the artistic importance of the articles, immediately became interested in the potentialities of the Eskimo work, and so decided upon the test purchase, requesting that I return to the arctic and carry out the project. . . .

The Guild has attempted to develop those things made by the Eskimo that are thought to be most interesting and saleable to the public. We encourage them to select better stone, to age the ivory for durability, and to clean the skins in order to remove the odour. Sinew-sewing and original designs are encouraged, and every attempt is being made to utilize the materials native to the Arctic.

None of these crafts has been *taught* by the Guild. They are age old in the Eskimo culture. The enormously strong creative urge of the Eskimos is found in children as young as Koonie. It has been the policy of the Canadian Handicrafts Guild to purchase all their works, usually at a fairly small price, to encourage children's activities in this direction, even though the work is for the most part un-saleable. They earn opportunities to contribute to the needs of the family, and their artistic improvement is rapid.

Looking towards the future of the Eskimos, with the Arctic rapidly opening up, it is his first step into industry. Government relief in these areas is being reduced, and the natives are obviously well pleased with their new earning power.

With more than seventy-five percent of their members over fourteen years of age in one area actively engaged in artistic endeavours, the Eskimos are certainly Canada's liveliest art group.

Document 2: Eskimo Handicrafts: A Private Guide for the Hudson's Bay Company Manager, *1953 [Excerpt]*

BY JAMES A. HOUSTON

This digest is especially prepared as a <u>private</u> guide to Hudson's Bay Company managers purchasing Eskimo handicrafts in the Canadian Arctic.

To the Post Manager: —

You are probably familiar with the work of the Canadian Handicrafts Guild in developing a market for various handicrafts that the Eskimos make. Perhaps you purchased crafts work on the Guilds behalf at some time. In either case this guide will be of interest to you since certain aspects of purchasing and distribution have changed since the Guild first made its test purchase in the Arctic in 1948.

The whole idea in the beginning was worked out between the Canadian Handicrafts Guild and the Hudsons' [*sic*] Bay Company at Winnipeg.

The Guild, a non profit organization, is primarily interested in aiding Canadians in finding a suitable outlet for their original works of arts and crafts, for this reason and because the Federal Government saw an opportunity to have the Eskimos directly aid their own economy, they offered the Guild a grant of money to cover salary and expenses of a Guild representative to encourage the Eskimo crafts in the field.

The Guild, the Hudsons' Bay Company and the Government are joined in a search for wider markets in Canada, the U.S. and Great Britain.

Your part will be to purchase as carefully and wisely as possible. To take great care in packing and shipping to avoid damage to goods. In this way we can <u>all help the Eskimos to help themselves</u>.

Certain handicrafts of the Eskimos have sold extremely well and others very poorly. There have been various reasons for this which generally fall into two categories in speaking of unsaleable work.

(1) Work which is undesirable and unsaleable

(2) Work which is desirable but unsaleable because of poor or careless workmanship

In work which is undesirable, such items as seal buckets, fish skin bags, beaded sealskin slippers, bead work badges, rabbit skin hats, steel clocs, bow guns, articles with wood or other materials foreign to the Arctic fall into this category.

Many of the articles which would be readily saleable are spoiled because of careless workmanship, example sealskin slippers, mitts and parkas that are not properly cleaned or poorly sewn. Ivory that has not been aged and has cracked and discoloured. Stone carving that has been carelessly done, baskets that are poorly woven.

Generally speaking, we have found that functional objects such as ash trays, pen holders, match holders and cribbage boards have been our poorest selling items.

This is because our Agents and customers are looking for primative [*sic*] work by a primitive people. This term primitive does not mean that the work is crude since many primitive people have made extremely delicate crafts, but it is true that the ash tray, pen holder and cribbage board do not represent the Eskimo culture and as a result there is little interest in buying that type of work.

Carving

When an Eskimo carves in stone, ivory or bone, the animals and people around him, he is complete master of the situation since no one understands carving in the hard materials better than he does. For this reason we hope he continues to carve in his own way instead of competing with fine china, metal and wood objects of more civilized craft workers.

We have found that our most saleable Eskimo crafts have been of stone, ivory and bone, with a fair sale of sealskin and baskets if they are not priced too high.

Stone, Ivory & Bone

Carving of people, walrus, bears, seals, caribou, birds, fish, otter, muskoxen, dogs, fox, igloos[,] kayaks and lamps, are the most popular items in the order given.

The sizes and shapes of these vary enormously. Usually we find that larger carvings are more saleable than small ones.

Pieces that are complicated such as dog teams, kayaks and igloos with many detached parts are not as popular (and are very difficult to handle by shop staffs).

Whereas the single piece (such as a bear or man) of good size and well carved is our most popular item.

Shapes

A carving with delicate protruding pieces, such as birds' wings, presents a difficult handling problem and may be easily broken — the best type is the single carving in fairly solid mass.

Skins

In purchasing skin slippers, mitts, parkas, etc., they should be scraped and washed with strong soap until they are white inside, and they should always be sewn with sinew. Great care should be taken as to sizes, since the Eskimos have a tendency to make parkas very narrow in the chest and shoulder, and slippers with a hole so small that the foot cannot be placed inside and often short and wide or too long and narrow. Slippers and parkas are much more saleable if there is some design such as a dark pattern of sealskin sewn on a light background.

In purchasing sealskin articles the best rule to follow is would you want it yourself or as a gift to a friend. A few Eskimo women in your area are probably noted as splendid sewers and these are the ones who should be doing the work on the best silver jar skins under your special care.

Basketry

The work done on the East coast of Hudson's Bay is probably best at Port Harrison and Povungnetuk where the weave is tight and regular. The habit of using a small stone or ivory handle on the lids of baskets has been well received by the public. Baskets should not be too small. 5″ across the mouth of the basket should be the smallest. They can be as large as you can conveniently ship, since they are desirably as waste paper baskets. Recently we have not seen many place mats in sets, or shallow baskets; these are both in demand (see illustration). The important thing to stress in basketry is a tight regular weave and well proportioned shapes. Such ideas as lamps, igloos, and wine glass shaped baskets in grass are unsaleable.

Dyes should not be used since it is not native to the Country, but dark strips of sealskin (well cleaned and woven into the basket to create design) is an excellent method well known to the Eskimo. NOTE. Baskets are generally thought of as purely a functional object and the public is not willing to pay too high a price for them, although they have a fair sale at a reasonable price.

Guide to Pricing

The Guild has hesitated in the past to make a price list because of the difficulty in stating a price on an unseen object of unknown size, when the quality of stone, ivory or skin plays a large part in its value, and of course, the workmanship is of even greater importance.

However, there is a definite need for such a list and we believe we can give a range of 3 prices on various articles which will act as a useful guide in purchasing.

For example: Here we have a man 5″ high carved in steatite (black or gray stone). He has two spears of ivory, stands firmly and has been carefully worked. Between the time you purchase him and he has been shipped south, stored and packed and unpacked several times, he will sell for approximately double what you pay for him. Please keep this in mind. . . .

Carvings as Art Objects

A few carvers in your area produce carvings superior to all others and these should be particularly encouraged in their work.

Try to obtain some very large carvings from these especially talented people, and if the work is excellent, you may pay up to $30.00 or $50.00 for a single piece, although this should only be done when the carving is large and very good.

These special pieces will probably find their way into exhibitions and museums and are of great importance to Eskimo Art and its future reputation.

The current trend in buying carvings of this type is to think of Eskimo work as an Art, rather than as a mere souvenir trade. So long as we are able

PAGE 6

DESCRIPTION	QUALITY	PRICE RANGE
Spearman Stone ivory spears 5" high Excellent Quality If poor, don't purchase, or pay extremely low price.	Excellent Good Fair Poor	$8.00 $5.00 $2.00 ?
NOTE: If sizes are larger than examples quoted, increase price. If smaller, decrease price.		
STONE		
Walrus stone, ivory tusks and eyes 8" long	Excellent Good Fair Poor	$8.00 $5.00 3.00 ?
Caribou stone, ivory antlers, standing, 6" long	Excellent Good Fair Poor	$6.00 4.00 2.00 ?
Caribou stone lying down, 4" long. Bone antlers	Excellent Good Fair Poor	$5.00 3.00 2.00 ?
Seal, stone 5" long, ivory eyes, head turned	Excellent Good Fair Poor	$3.00 2.00 1.00 ?
Musk ox, stone, 10" long, standing, bone horns.	Excellent Good Fair Poor	$10.00 7.00 4.00 ?
Fish, stone, 6" long, ivory eyes, markings on sides	Excellent Good Fair Poor	$3.00 2.00 1.00 ?
Fox, stone, 4" long, standing	Excellent Good Fair Poor	$3.00 2.00 1.00 ?
Woman & Child, stone, sitting 5" high	Excellent Good Fair Poor	$8.00 6.00 4.00 ?
Woman, stone, standing 8" high, Ivory details.	Excellent Good Fair Poor	$9.00 7.00 5.00 ?
Lamp Stone on Base 6" long	Excellent Good Fair Poor	$1.00 .50 .25 ?

If you consider carving of poor quality, pay much smaller price or refuse to purchase.

FIGURE AE4.2 James A. Houston, *Eskimo Handicrafts: A Private Guide for the Hudson's Bay Company Manager*, 1953. La Guilde Archives, Montreal, C10-D1-055. Reprinted with permission of the Houston Family.

to keep Eskimo carving on a basis of Art, it will continue to have a good sales demand.

Don't forget that a man who is considered average at present, through your encouragement and his own endeavours may turn into the finest carver.

In Eskimo carving, Canada has an Art form of which it may well be proud. Its future success lies not in a great quantity of carvings, or teaching on our part; but in our recognition of this special Art, and our encouragement.[6]

Document 3: Sanajasak: Eskimo Handicrafts, *1951 [Excerpt]*

WRITTEN AND ILLUSTRATED BY JAMES A. HOUSTON, THE CANADIAN HANDICRAFTS GUILD'S ARCTIC REPRESENTATIVE; TRANSLATION BY SAM FORD AND FREDERICA WOODROW

This pamphlet is published by the Canadian Handicrafts Guild with the approval of the Department of Resources and Development Northwest Territories Branch.

It is the first of a series to be published in Eskimo for the people of the Canadian Arctic, to encourage them in their native arts. It is hoped that these illustrations will suggest to them some of their objects which are useful and acceptable to the white man.

Although the articles illustrated are not produced in all regions of the Arctic they are purely Eskimo and could be made wherever materials are available.

These suggestions should in no way limit the Eskimo.

He should be encouraged to make variations and introduce new ideas into his handicrafts.

However, if the articles are to be saleable to the South, a few points are important:—

1. All articles should be as clean as possible.
2. Skins should have all smell removed. Native tanning is not acceptable.
3. All sewing must be done by hand and sinew should be used when available.
4. Ivory should be aged one year or more, or else it has a tendency to warp or crack.
5. Inlay in ivory should be of tough consistency or it will fall out in a short time.
6. Stone objects should not have delicate projecting portions which may be easily broken.

The Eskimo should be encouraged to use only the materials native to his land, such as ivory, stone, bone, skins, grass, copper, etc. The introduction of wood, cloth, and metals into his art destroys the true Eskimo quality and places him in competition with craftsmen elsewhere who have a complete mastery of the materials.

The translation of the Eskimo text beneath each illustration will be found at the end of the pamphlet.

3. The small Eskimo man and woman shown above [see figure AE4.3] are carved from ivory that is one year old or more. They could be made in any

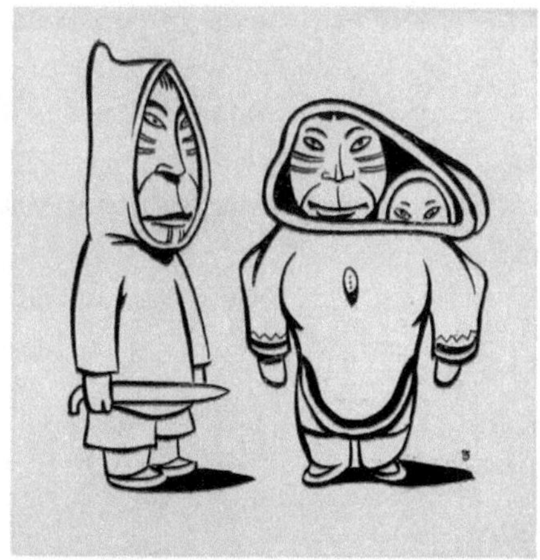

ᑕᓇ ᒥᑭᔪᒃ ᐃᓄᒍᐊᒃ ᐊᒍᑎ ᐊᓇᓗ
ᑕᑯᓴᐅᔪ ᓴᓇᓯᒪᒍ ᑐᒐᒥ ᐊᑕᓯᒥ
ᐊᒐᒍᑲᑐ ᐃᒪᑲ ᐅᒐᑕᓂ. ᓴᓇᔭᕙᓇᒍ
ᑲᓄᑐᐃᓇ. ᐃᓯᕿᒍᐊᑐ ᐅᕿᓗ
ᐱᓯᒍᐊᑐ. ᐱᓯᐊᓯᒪᒍ ᕿᑲᓯᒪᓯᐊᑐ
ᐊᑎᓗ ᑭᓂᓴᓯᒪᓯᑐ ᓴᓇᒍᓇᑭ ᐊᓯᒐᓂ?

3 The small Eskimo man and woman shown above are carved from ivory that is one year old or more. They could be made in any position, either sitting or walking. They are carefully smoothed and polished. Can you make one?

FIGURE AE4.3 *Sanajasak: Eskimo Handicrafts*, written and illustrated by James A. Houston, translated by Sam Ford and Frederica Woodrow (Montreal and Ottawa: Canadian Handicrafts Guild and the Department of Resources and Development, 1951), 3. Reprinted with permission of the Houston Family.

position, either sitting or walking. They are carefully smoothed and polished. Can you make one?

4. The carved ivory tusk tells the story of the Eskimo hunter. When it is done with great cleverness it is a thing anyone would want. Polish it carefully. Make it from old ivory.

5. The three bears show some of the ways they made be carved from ivory or stone. Often a bear and small cub are worth more — or perhaps a man with a spear hunting the bear.

6. The game board carved from the ivory tusk should have drawings of Eskimo life or animals or birds on it. The polish should be good and the inlay of strong stuff that will not fall out.

7. Above are some small things you can make in ivory. The needle case, the button, and a match holder made from the end of the tusk, and also a belt with pieces of ivory held together by a piece of seal line. . . .

14. Man throwing harpoon, or spearing through ice, dog, walrus, or seal. If they are carefully carved and polished the kaloona [white people]will buy them. . . .

16. These are other designs of grass baskets that are very useful. Make them strong and even with good grass.

17. These are baskets with designs in them. By boiling the grass with net dye the colour changes and you may then weave different patterns into the baskets.[7]

Notes

1. Weiselberger, "Inborn Strength of Hunter Nomads," 2.
2. Fabian, *Time and the Other.*
3. Houston, "Eskimo Sculptors," 39.
4. See Igloliorte, "Hooked Forever on Primitive Peoples."
5. The correct spellings are *Syollie* and *Amidlak* (John Houston, correspondence with author, February 27, 2024). Any misspellings are preserved here for historical accuracy.
6. Houston, *Eskimo Handicrafts*, 2–5, 10.
7. Houston, *Sanajasak: Eskimo Handicrafts*, 3–7, 14, 16–17.

Bibliography

Fabian, Johannes. *Time and the Other: How Anthropology Makes Its Object.* New York: Columbia University Press, 2014. Originally published 1983.

Houston, James A. *Eskimo Handicrafts: A Private Guide for the Hudson's Bay Company Manager.* Montreal: Canadian Handicrafts Guild, 1953. La Guilde Archives, Montreal. C10-D1-055.

Houston, James A. "Eskimo Sculptors." *Beaver*, no. 282 (June 1951): 34–39.

Houston, James A. *Sanajasak: Eskimo Handicrafts.* Translations by Sam Ford and Frederica Woodrow. Montreal: Canadian Handicrafts Guild and Department of Resources and Development, 1951.

Igloliorte, Heather. "Hooked Forever on Primitive Peoples: James Houston and the Transformation of 'Eskimo Handicrafts' to Inuit Art." In *Mapping Modernisms: Art, Indigeneity, Colonialism*, edited by Elizabeth Harney and Ruth B. Phillips, 62–90. Durham, NC: Duke University Press, 2018.

Weiselberger, Carl. "Inborn Strength of Hunter Nomads Key to Vigor of Eskimo Sculpture." *Ottawa Citizen*, November 26, 1955.

CONTRIBUTORS

PETER BRUNT is associate professor of art history at Te Herenga Waka Victoria University of Wellington, where he teaches and researches the visual arts of the Pacific. He received his PhD from Cornell University and is coauthor and coeditor of the books *Oceania* (2018); *Art in Oceania: A New History* (2012); and *Tatau: Photographs by Mark Adams: Samoan Tattoo, New Zealand Art, Global Culture* (2008; new edition 2023). He was cocurator with Nicholas Thomas of the 2018–19 exhibition *Oceania* at the Royal Academy of Arts, London, and the Musée du quai Branly, Paris. He is a member of the Multiple Modernisms research group.

ROBERTO CONDURU is Southern Methodist University's Endowed Distinguished Professor of Art History. His publications include *Art in Brazil in the 19th Century* (2020); *Axé Bahia—The Power of Art in an Afro-Brazilian Metropolis* (2018); *Architecture Agouda au Bénin et au Togo* (2016); *Pérolas Negras, Primeiros Fios* (2013); *Arte Afro-Brasileira* (2007); monographs on Frida Baranek, Willys de Castro, Jorge Guinle, Paulo Pasta, and Álvaro Vital Brazil; and contributions to *3rd Text Africa*, *Art in Translation*, *Arts*, *Critical Interventions*, *Juni Magazin*, *Perspective*, *Third Text*, and other journals. Among other exhibitions, he curated *Martinho Patrício—Recorte* (SESC Pompeia, São Paulo, 2023); *Quilombo do Rosário* (Museu Bispo do Rosário Arte Contemporânea, 2018); and *Incorporations—Afro-Brazilian Contemporary Art* (Centrale Electrique, 2011) and cocurated *Axé Bahia: The Power of Art in an Afro-Brazilian Metropolis* (Fowler Museum UCLA, 2017) and *Perles de Liberté—Bijoux Afro-Brésiliens* (Grand Hornu Images, 2011). He is former president of the Brazilian Committee of Art History.

HANNA HORSBERG HANSEN is a Norwegian professor emeritus of art history in the art department at the Academy of Arts at UiT, the Arctic

University of Norway. She is a pioneering scholar within the field of Sámi art. Over the last twenty-five years she has published stories about Sámi art from heterogeneous perspectives rather than as a linear, Eurocentric art history. Her publications comprise stories about contemporary as well as historic art, institution building, and the connections between Sámi art and politics.

ELIZABETH HARNEY is associate professor in the Department of Arts, Culture, Media at the University of Toronto, where she teaches histories of African modernism and anticolonialism, decolonial theory, and postwar visual cultures. Harney was the inaugural curator of modern and contemporary arts at the National Museum for African Art, the Smithsonian Institution in Washington, DC (1999–2003), where her curatorial projects included *Ethiopian Passages: Art of the Diaspora*; *Journeys and Destinations: African Artists on the Move*; *Textures: Word and Image in African Art*; *Encounters with the Contemporary*; and *Inscribing Meaning: Writing and Graphic Systems in African Art*. Her book *In Senghor's Shadow: Art, Politics, and the Avant-Garde* (Duke University Press, 2004) won the Arnold Rubin Outstanding Book Award from the Arts Council of the African Studies Association. She is coeditor, with Ruth B. Phillips, of *Mapping Modernisms: Art, Indigeneity, Colonialism* (Duke University Press, 2018). Her forthcoming book, *The Retromodern: Art, Africa, and the Time of the Contemporary*, is supported by a SSHRC Insight Grant (2020–2025).

JYOTINDRA JAIN has held the positions of director of the National Crafts Museum and professor of arts and aesthetics at Jawaharlal Nehru University in New Delhi. He has also taught as a visiting professor at Harvard University and as Rudolf-Arnheim professor at Humboldt University in Berlin. He is an eminent scholar of Indian vernacular art, popular visual culture, photography, and museum theory whose books include *Painted Myths of Creation: Art and Ritual of an Indian Tribe* (1984); *Ganga Devi: Tradition and Expression in Mithila Painting* (1997); *Picture Showmen: Insights into the Narrative Tradition in Indian Art* (1998); *Kalighat Painting: Images from a Changing World* (1999); *India's Popular Culture: Iconic Spaces and Fluid Images* (editor, 2008); *Clemente Made in India* (2011); and *Jangarh Singh Shyam: A Conjuror's Archive* (2019).

SANDRA KLOPPER is an art historian specializing in the arts of South Africa. She has served as deputy vice chancellor of the University of Cape Town and dean of the humanities faculty at the University of Pretoria. She has written extensively on the art of traditionalist communities in southern Africa;

on the expressive culture of other marginalized groups, including the urban homeless; on various aspects of South African youth culture; and on the art of several contemporary South African artists. Most recently, she has focused on the emergence of alternative modernisms, including sartorial styles, in the interface between rural and urban communities, particularly in present-day KwaZulu Natal, and on the artistic biography of Irma Stern.

IAN MCLEAN is Honorary Professorial Fellow at the University of Melbourne. For the previous twenty-five years he has written widely on Australian art and especially on the intersections between its Indigenous art and settler traditions. His books include *How Aborigines Invented the Idea of Contemporary Art* (2011); *Double Desire: Transculturation and Indigenous Art* (2014); and *Indigenous Archives: The Making and Unmaking of Aboriginal Art*, with Darren Jorgensen (2017). His recent books are *Rattling Spears: A History of Indigenous Australian Art* (2016) and *Double Nation: A History of Indigenous Australian Art* (2023).

ANITRA NETTLETON is professor emeritus at the School of the Arts at the University of Witwatersrand, where she taught from 1998 to 2011, serving as chair and director of the Mellon-funded Centre for Creative Arts of Africa at the Wits Art Museum and then professor of the history of art at the University of Johannesburg from 2012–2015. Her research encompassed historical and contemporary African arts with a focus on South African beadwork and mid-twentieth-century Black modernist arts. She explored how modernity is manifested in the arts and material cultures of peoples in southern Africa and the creation of specifically African South African modernisms by trained mid-twentieth-century Black artists such as Sidney Kumalo, Ezrom Legae, and Dumile Feni and apparently untrained artists like Jackson Hlungwani.

CHIKA OKEKE-AGULU, an artist and art historian, is Robert Schirmer Professor of Art and Archaeology and African American Studies and director of the Africa World Initiative at Princeton University. His books include *El Anatsui: The Reinvention of Sculpture* (2022); *Yusuf Grillo: Painting. Lagos. Life* (2020); *Obiora Udechukwu: Line, Image, Text* (2016); *Postcolonial Modernism: Art and Decolonization in Twentieth-Century Nigeria* (2015); and *Contemporary African Art since 1980* (2010). He is coeditor of *Nka: Journal of Contemporary African Art* and maintains the blog *Ọfọdunka*. He is a fellow of the British Academy.

RUTH B. PHILLIPS is professor of art history emerita at Carleton University, Ottawa. Trained initially as an Africanist, she published her doctoral research in *Representing Woman: Sande Society Masquerades of the Mende of Sierra Leone* (1995) before refocusing her research and teaching on Indigenous North American arts and critical museology. Her books include *Trading Identities: The Souvenir in Native North American Arts from the Northeast, 1700–1900* (1998) and *Museum Pieces: Toward the Indigenization of Canadian Museums* (2011). With Nicholas Thomas she organized the Multiple Modernisms project to address Indigenous modernisms in a global comparative framework and coedited its first publication, *Mapping Modernisms: Art, Indigeneity, Colonialism* (2018), with Elizabeth Harney. She has served as director of the University of British Columbia Museum of Anthropology and is a fellow of the Royal Society of Canada.

UNA REY is an artist, independent scholar, and curator whose writing has been published in critical anthologies, journals, news media, and exhibition catalogues. Rey has over twenty-five years of professional experience in the Australian contemporary art sector, including lecturing in art history at universities and managing Indigenous art centers in the Western Desert and at Milikapiti on the Tiwi Islands. She is currently editor of *Artlink* magazine.

MEGAN TAMATI-QUENNELL (Te Āti Awa, Ngāti Mutunga, Ngāi Tahu, and Kāti Māmoe) is curator of modern and contemporary Māori and Indigenous art at Te Papa in Te Whanganui-a-Tara Wellington and holds an additional position as an external curator at the Govett-Brewster Art Gallery in Ngā Motu, New Plymouth. Her research interests include contemporary Māori art; Māori modernism; international First Nations art; the intersection between global Indigenous contemporary, non-Western art, and the art mainstream; and First Nations art-curatorial praxis.

NICHOLAS THOMAS is a historian and anthropologist of the Pacific and author of many books, including *Islanders: The Pacific in the Age of Empire* (2010), which was awarded the Wolfson History Prize. Over 2018–19 he cocurated *Oceania* for the Royal Academy of Arts in London and the Musée du quai Branly–Jacques Chirac in Paris. He has been director of the Museum of Archaeology and Anthropology in Cambridge, United Kingdom, since 2006, and has led many projects supporting collaborative research with local and Indigenous peoples on historic museum collections. He has also written extensively about museum futures for *Apollo*, the *Art Newspaper*, and the *Financial Times*. He has coorganized the Multiple Modernisms project with Ruth Phillips.

NORMAN VORANO is an associate professor of art history at Queen's University in Kingston, Ontario, where he is also the head of the Department of Art History and Art Conservation. He is a scholar and curator of Indigenous arts of North America and a recipient of a Pierre Elliott Trudeau Foundation Fellowship. He was the curator of contemporary Inuit art and the curator of Indigenous art at the Canadian Museum of History and cocurated the 2011 traveling exhibition *Inuit Prints, Japanese Inspiration: Early Printmaking in the Canadian Arctic*, which examined the historical linkage between Japanese *sosaku-hanga* printmaking and the birth of Inuit printmaking in the late 1950s. His 2018 exhibition *Picturing Arctic Modernity: North Baffin Drawings from 1964* toured across Canada and the Arctic.

MARK ANDREW WHITE served as the executive director of the New Mexico Museum of Art and previously served as curator and director of the Fred Jones Jr. Museum of Art at the University of Oklahoma. As a researcher, curator, and writer he specializes in American and Native American art of the twentieth century with a particular focus on the Southwest.

INDEX

Note: Page references in italics indicate illustrations.